UNIVERSALS OF HUMAN LANGUAGE

VOLUME 3

Word Structure

CONTRIBUTORS

Elaine S. Andersen
Elizabeth Closs Traugott
Joseph H. Greenberg
Brian F. Head
David Ingram
Adam Makkai
Yakov Malkiel
Edith A. Moravcsik
Susan Steele
Russell Ultan

Universals of Human Language

Edited by Joseph H. Greenberg

Associate Editors:
Charles A. Ferguson & Edith A. Moravcsik

VOLUME 3

Word Structure

Stanford University Press, Stanford, California
1978

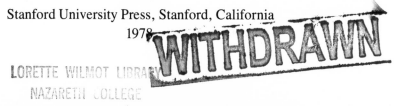

Several of the papers in this volume were published originally in _Working Papers on Language Universals,_ published for limited distribution by the Language Universals Project at Stanford University in sixteen numbers, 1970-76, as indicated in the opening footnotes to the individual papers. Most have been modified to some extent for publication here.

Preface

The mainspring of the contemporary interest in language universals is the conviction that linguistics as a science must develop broader goals than the description of the structures of the thousands of individual languages which exist in the present or of which we have records from the past. It must be broader even than a body of generalizing theory concerning how such descriptions can be carried out.

Theory of this latter type already existed by the early 1950's, although many defects have since become apparent. As compared with other human sciences of the time, it seemed to possess an evident superiority in methodological sophistication and rigor. Yet a thoughtful and alert observer could raise fundamental problems not evident to the practical purveyor who took for granted the tacit premises of his science.

It fell to the lot of one of the present writers, as a participant in the seminar on psycholinguistics sponsored by the Social Science Research Council in the summer of 1951 at Bloomington, to give an exposition of linguistics for the psychologists present. The task was undertaken with a sense of pride in the accomplishments of the linguistics of the period. One of the psychologists, Charles Osgood, was suitably impressed. He commented, however, to the effect that while linguistics had an admirable and well worked out method, it was being applied merely to the description of individual languages. Could the linguists present tell him anything about all languages? That would be of the highest interest to psychologists. To this the linguistics of the period had no real answer.

The stimulating quality of these remarks and of the other discussions that followed bore fruit in the work of the Social Science Research Council, leading ultimately to the Dobbs Ferry conference on Language Universals in 1961. This meeting played an essential part in inaugurating a period of renewed interest in this topic.

While there were several papers at that conference which stated tentative generalizations of universal scope regarding several aspects of language, it was realized that to extend such studies from these modest beginnings was an enormous task requiring relevant data regarding numerous other aspects of language to be

drawn from adequately large samples of languages. Hence arose
the notion of a research project in which scholars would undertake
concrete research of this sort on a large variety of linguistic
topics.

This took shape at Stanford where the Project on Language
Universals was organized. It began its activities in October 1967
and brought them to an end in August 1976. During its entire nine-
year period it was directed by Charles A. Ferguson and Joseph H.
Greenberg, both professors at Stanford University, as principal
investigators. Its main source of financial support was the National
Science Foundation, which, over the years, contributed slightly
below $1,000,000. In addition to the two principal investigators,
the Project staff included altogether thirty-two part-time or full-
time linguists, some of whom held short-term visiting positions
not spanning more than a few months, while others were with the
Project up to several years. The names of these linguists are as
follows: Rebecca Agheyisi, Alan Bell, D.N.S. Bhat, Jean Braine,
Richard Carter, Eve Clark, Harold Clumeck, John Crothers,
Gilles Delisle, Talmy Givón, Victor Girard, Mary Ellen Greenlee,
Helga Harries-Delisle, Laurence Horn, Charles Jennings, Joan
Kahr, Dorothea Kaschube, Ian Maddieson, James Michael Moore,
Edith Moravcsik, Chris O'Sullivan, Andrew Rindsberg, Merritt
Ruhlen, Gerald Sanders, Philip Sedlak, Susan Steele, Leonard
Talmy, Russell Ultan, Marilyn Vihman, Krystyna Wachowicz,
Werner Winter, and Karl Zimmer. The staff also included Nicholas
Zirpolo on a short-term bibliographer appointment, and Dal
Dresser, Vicky Shu, and Vicki Fahrenholz as successive secretary-
bibliographers for the Project; budgetary questions were attended
to throughout by Jean Beeson. In addition to those mentioned here,
from time to time visiting scholars with outside funding collabor-
ated with the Project for varying periods. Among these was
Hansjakob Seiler.

The original goals of the Project were stated by Greenberg in
his introductory words to the first issue of Working Papers in
Language Universals (WPLU) in November 1969. They were to
formulate cross-linguistic and, if possible, universally valid
empirical generalizations about language structure; generalizations,
that is, which hold true for some significant universe of languages
and which at the same time are capable of being refuted by actual
language data. The fact that such generalizations cannot be verified without reliable cross-linguistic data justifies the other original objective of the Project, which was to collect data from various languages of the world and store them in precise and comparable form. These two objectives were seen as not in themselves

sufficient but nonetheless necessary parts of the long-range goal
of accounting for similarities and differences among human language
in terms of increasingly general laws overarching various apparently unrelated aspects of language structure.

The particular format chosen for the realization of these two
initially conceived goals of the Project was the following. At any
one time the staff consisted of the two directors, a secretary-
bibliographer, and three or four researchers. Although the selection of staff linguists reflected adherence to the basic goals of the
Project, once on the staff, linguists were free to follow their own
philosophies and methodologies regarding research on typology
and universals. The papers in WPLU indeed reflect the resulting
theoretical and methodological diversity. The choice of topics was
similarly left up to the individual investigator, subject in principle
to the veto of the directors -- a power, however, which was never
actually exercised. Middle-range projects were encouraged,
requiring not more and possibly less than half a year to complete.
The rich linguistic resources of the Stanford University library,
as well as Ferguson's and Greenberg's private libraries, provided
most of the basic data. For some studies linguistic informants
from Stanford and the surrounding area were also utilized. Frequent biweekly or weekly meetings of the Project, attended at
times by other linguists from Stanford and from neighboring universities and by scholars visiting the area, provided opportunities for
reporting on and criticizing ongoing or completed work. The working paper series of the Project ensured informal and rapid dissem-
ination of results to wider circles.

It is in accordance with this mode of organization that the Project progressed toward the realization of its two goals. As far as
data collection is concerned, almost every one of the sixty-eight
working papers that were published in the twenty issues of WPLU
presented data from a variety of languages in comparable terms.[1]
In addition to the actual data, efforts were also made to provide
guidelines for data collection. This was done by "check lists" or
sets of parameters related to specific aspects of language data and
of use both to linguistic fieldworkers and to cross-linguistic re-

[1]This includes all full-size working papers published in the series, whether written by Project members (54) or contributed by
linguists not associated with the Project (14). The number does not
include the survey papers and shorter notes contained in WPLU.

searchers. After several years of the operation of the Project,
attempts to archive data on phonetics and phonology, an area which
seemed particularly promising in this respect, took the shape of
an independent research endeavor, the Phonology Archiving Project. This group was also Stanford-based, had the same directors
as the Language Universals Project, and received funding from the
same source. A still ongoing enterprise, the Phonology Archiving
Project has to date computer-stored the phonetic segment inventory of about two hundred languages, as well as phonological rule
information on some of them.[2] Although tentative plans for a
similar large-scale computer archiving project with respect to
grammatical information were made, their realization is still a
matter for the future.

As far as the other aim is concerned, the establishment of
cross-linguistically valid generalizations about language structures,
we believe that substantial progress has been made, as the papers
in WPLU attest, making allowances for the inevitable future revis-
ions and even the abandonment of certain generalizations in the
light of further investigation. It seems reasonable to conclude that
a substantial portion of this work will prove, in the long run, to have
contributed substantially to our understanding of human language.

As the Project's end drew nearer, it was felt that a publication
that is both more formal and also more widely available than the
WPLU series should stand as a summary of our activities.[3] Thus

---

[2]For access to this material, write to Phonology Archiving Project, Department of Linguistics, Stanford University, Stanford,
California 94305.

[3]Copies of issues 11-20 of WPLU nonetheless remain available
at $2.00 apiece. Write to Working Papers on Language Universals,
Department of Linguistics, Stanford University, Stanford, California 94305. A bibliographical list including all references cited in
WPLU papers (about 2,000) arranged according to languages (about
750) is also available from the same address (under the name
"Bibliography") for $1.00 a copy; and so are the proceedings of a
conference on nasals and nasalization held in 1974 at Stanford,
entitled Nasalfest, for $6.50 a copy. Xerox and microfiche copies
of individual papers contained in any of the twenty issues of WPLU
are also available from ERIC clearinghouse in Languages and Linguistics, Center for Applied Linguistics, 1611 North Kent Street,
Arlington, Virginia 22209.

the idea of the present book was conceived. The original intention
of simply summarizing what we have done was then complemented
by the desire to answer the very patent need in the present linguistic literature for a comprehensive statement on where exactly we
are in our knowledge about cross-linguistically recurrent structural properties of language. The "we" in the latter part of this
sentence is not confined to Project members. In the past few years
endeavors to establish and test similar generalizations have been
increasingly initiated by individual scholars and organized projects
in other countries as well as in Western Europe and the Soviet
Union. In addition, even those whose basic methodology and
approach are quite different from that employed for the most part
in the Project have taken note of its results and have felt the need
of accounting for them by incorporating them within their own
theoretical framework, or even modifying that framework to
account for them.

In accordance with these aims, we have sought to make these
volumes as comprehensive as possible, consistent with the current
stage of research and the particular interests and competences of
those scholars who were either active in or basically sympathetic
with our enterprise.

These volumes consist of forty-six papers. Roughly corresponding
to three fundamental aspects of language structure, the data-
oriented papers have been grouped into three classes: those mostly pertaining to phonology, those mostly dealing with morphological
and lexical properties of the word-unit, and those primarily involved with syntactic and related semantic problems. The second,
third, and fourth volumes of the book each contain one of these
three groups of papers. The first volume presents the general
papers which discuss questions of the theory and methodology of
typological and universals research. Each paper in the book is
preceded by an abstract and followed by its own list of references.
At the end of each volume is an author index and a language index
specific to papers in that volume.

Of the forty-six studies included in the book, thirty-five appear
here for the first time. These have been written in part by scholars
who were either members of or associated with the Stanford Project on Language Universals, in part by scholars not formally
associated with the Project who have been invited by the editors to
deal with a specific topic. Among the latter are Elaine Andersen,
Dwight Bolinger, Bruce Downing, Thomas Gamkrelidze, Brian

Head, Larry Hyman, Hans-Heinrich Lieb, Adam Makkai, Yakov
Malkiel, and Elizabeth Closs Traugott. The remaining thirteen
papers are original or revised versions of working papers that
were previously published informally. They were written by members of this group as part of their work for the Project.

In general, the arrangement is topical; it reflects the manner
in which research was actually carried out under the aegis of the
Project and of the typical product as seen in the Working Papers.
This approach has some advantages. In general, it selects areas
of research comprehensive enough not to be trivial and, on the
other hand, not so all-encompassing as to be impractical. It leads
to numerous concrete and testable generalizations. We are also
keenly aware of certain inevitable defects. Since, to begin with,
we did not provide a comprehensive a priori scheme and did not
impose particular topics on investigators, there are necessarily
major omissions. There is also the danger that a somewhat ad
hoc and piecemeal approach will lead to the neglect of topics that
do not easily fall within present classificatory rubrics, as reflected
in the overall organization of this work. For example, there is
much to be learned from the phenomenon of word accent as it
relates to morphological systems. However, this topic does not
easily fall within conventional classifications.

The other defect is more closely tied into the basically, but not
exclusively, inductive nature of this approach. Interconnections
based on the presence of similar general psychological or other principles, or of even more specific factual relevance, may be overlooked through compartmentalization. Still, as an initial strategy,
we believe it to be defensible in terms of its immediate fruitfulness.
This is, however, something for the linguistic community as a
whole to judge. Moreover, many of our investigations, it can be
claimed, have already involved at least an adumbration of more
comprehensive principles -- for example, of marking theory.

In behalf of the authors of the papers included in this work and
in our own behalf, we would like to express our deep gratitude to
all of those who made the appearance of the books possible. Thus,
we would first like to thank Vicky Shu for the competence and genuine care she brought to the editing and typing of the final camera-
ready version of the manuscript. We are furthermore grateful to
Stanford Press and to William Carver in particular for their
guidance in our endeavor to produce a book that is pleasing to the
eye. Our most sincere thanks should go to Stanford University,

especially to the Department of Linguistics and its current chair-
person, Clara Bush, for being such an understanding host to the
Language Universals Project in the past nine years, and to Deans
Halsey Royden and W. Bliss Carnochan, and Provost William
Miller for their generous financial support toward the preparation
of the manuscript in final form.   Finally, we thank the National
Science Foundation for its continuing support of the work of the
project.

J.H.G.
C.A.F.
E.A.M.

Contents

Contributors

Elaine S. Andersen is an Andrew Mellon postdoctoral fellow and a Visiting Assistant Professor of Linguistics at the University of Southern California.

Elizabeth Closs Traugott is Professor of Linguistics and English at Stanford University.

Charles A. Ferguson is Professor of Linguistics at Stanford University. He was Co-Director of the Stanford Project on Language Universals and is Associate Editor of these volumes.

Joseph H. Greenberg is Professor of Linguistics and Anthropology at Stanford University. He was Co-Director of the Stanford Project on Language Universals and is the Editor of these volumes.

Brian F. Head is Professor of Linguistics at the State University of Campinas in Brazil. In 1974 he was a visiting scholar at Stanford University.

David Ingram is Associate Professor of Linguistics at the University of British Columbia in Vancouver, Canada. From 1969 to 1971 he was associated with the Stanford Project on Language Universals as a guest member.

Adam Makkai is Professor of Linguistics at the University of Illinois at Chicago Circle.

Yakov Malkiel is Professor of Linguistics and Romance Philology at the University of California, Berkeley.

Edith A. Moravcsik is a Visiting Assistant Professor of Linguistics at the University of Wisconsin in Milwaukee. She was a member of the Stanford Project on Language Universals in 1968-72 and again in 1975-76. She is Associate Editor of these volumes and was the Editor of Working Papers on Language Universals.

Susan Steele is Assistant Professor of Linguistics at the University of Arizona. In 1975-76 she was associated with the Stanford Project on Language Universals.

Russell Ultan is an American Council of Learned Societies postdoctoral fellow conducting research in Turku, Finland. His association with the Stanford Project on Language Universals, longer than that of any other Project member, spanned the years 1968-74.

Introduction

CHARLES A. FERGUSON

Language consists of words, such is the verdict of folk linguistics everywhere. Languages generally have an expression that means something like the English term 'word.' The range of meaning of the expression varies from language to language, often extending to quite large stretches of speech, but the notion of 'words' in the sense of the units of language that are listed in a dictionary, is very widespread, quite possibly universal, in human speech communities. Many linguists have assumed that the 'word' in this sense is, in fact, a universal unit of language, definable within an accepted body of linguistic theory, and at various times in the history of linguistics serious attempts have been made to formulate such a definition. Juilland and Roceric(1972, 1977) provide a review of these attempts. During the period of American structuralism, however, the word was deemphasized as a linguistic unit in favor of the morpheme. The chief reasons for this deemphasis were two: the structural and functional diversity of the word across languages and the generally unstructured nature of the lexicon in comparison with grammar and phonology. Much attention was lavished on the morpheme, which as the minimum unit of meaning or the minimum unit of grammatical structure was by definition universal, whereas the role of the word varied so much from one language to another that it was conceivable that in some languages the word could be almost or fully identical either with the morpheme or with the sentence. Study of the word, as a 'minimal free form' (Bloomfield's definition, and the most popular one of the period) was generally in terms of its morphemic constituency. Lexicography as the study of the properties of words and relations among them came to have only a marginal position in linguistics.

The period of transformational grammar continued the deemphasis of the word. Even the 'formative,' which was the successor to the morpheme and in a rough way the same thing, got relatively little attention as such, as linguists focused on syntax and phonology. For the most part the word was examined from the phonological side (e.g. What are the phonological characteristics of lexical representations?) or from the syntactic side (e.g. At what place(s) in the grammar does lexical insertion take place?). Although new attention was paid to the semantic structure of words in connection with the elaboration of semantic theory, no attention was paid to the morphemic structure of words.

During the whole period 1940-1970 only a few linguistic articles
or books of significance appeared in the United States devoted to
universal properties of words (e.g. Greenberg 1954a, 1954b;
Householder and Saporta 1962). In the 1970's, however, there is a
renewed interest in the word, signaled by Halle's article published
in Linguistic Inquiry (Halle 1973), which rediscovered the need for
a morphological or word-formation component in the grammar of
a language. Other evidence for the interest appears in studies of
language change (e.g. Wang 1969) and child language (e.g. Ferguson
and Farwell 1975). The renewed interest has not led toward the
construction of a lexical theory comparable to phonological and
syntactic theories (Aronoff 1976 is limited to derivational rules),
and current studies of words and word-related phenomena represent
a broad spectrum of different interests and goals. Four kinds of
research on lexical universals are appearing and all are represented in this volume: word categories, constituent structure of
words, relations between words, and the processes of lexicalization.

Under the heading of word categories can be included studies
which seek universal properties or processes regarding word
classes ('parts of speech'), or the grammatical categories which
they exhibit, Lyons' primary and secondary categories, respectively (Lyons 1968: 270-333). American structuralists distrusted
the traditional system of parts of speech (nouns, verbs, adjectives,
adverbs, prepositions, conjunctions, interjections) but they continued to use the terms and modifications of them in defining the
word classes of particular languages. Thus the term 'adjective'
was used both for a Japanese word class which is morphologically
and syntactically related to verbs and for an Arabic word class
which is morphologically and syntactically related to nouns; in each
instance the word class is roughly equivalent semantically to English adjectives. This problem of identifying the defining characteristics of possible word classes and assuring the comparability
of word classes across languages was not fully faced by the structuralists, and the transformationalists have largely avoided the
issue by focusing on word classes at a deeper level. Yet it is
likely that this is one of the most fruitful areas for cross-linguistic
research leading to the characterization of human language. In much
the same way, the secondary grammatical categories such as number, case, person, tense, aspect, gender, and definiteness were
not treated cross-linguistically or universalistically by structuralists and have been treated by transformationalists at abstract
levels not readily verifiable by data from languages in accordance

with agreed-on canons of identification and comparison. Boas' classic introduction to the Handbook of American Indian Languages has been reprinted and read with interest by many (Boas 1968), but linguists have only rarely provided basic data on grammatical categories in a form that could be readily compared for universals research (e.g. Ferguson 1964 attempted to do this). Most of the contributions in this volume, however are -- in one way or another -- cross-linguistic studies of grammatical categories as exhibited by particular word classes. Ingram examines the kinds of pronoun systems to be found in the world's languages in terms of such categories as person and number, building on the typo-logical study of Forchheimer (1953). Head also examines pronoun systems, but in terms of the category degree-of-respect, which is overtly represented in many languages, especially in forms of address; his paper, which modifies and extends the classic study of Brown and Gilman (1960), includes a stronger component of social or 'pragmatic' information than most of the papers in this book. The papers of Greenberg on gender and Ultan on future tense are also of this type, and Malkiel's paper deals with deriva-tional categories in contrast to the inflectional categories of the others. Finally, Greenberg's study of numeral systems, although different in many respects from the other papers, deals with char-acteristics of word classes and grammatical categories. It is interesting to note that all these papers include some reference to diachronic processes, in several cases as a major consideration. Perhaps the willingness to include a diachronic dimension in lexi-cal studies is related to the fact that traditional philological studies of lexical phenomena are so heavily historical or etymological in orientation.

A second type of study is the analysis of the internal structure of words. Such studies may focus on the phonological, morphemic, or semantic constituents of words. In any given language the phono-logical criteria which define a word (the 'phonological word') and the morphological and syntactic criteria which define a word (the 'grammatical word') may not determine an identical set of words, but there are doubtless universal tendencies and limits of both kinds as well as universal characteristics of the relations between them (Matthews 1974). Ultan's paper deals with the internal struc-ture of words, although his principal focus is on the means expres-sion of a grammatical category. Andersen's paper is clearly con-cerned with the semantic structure of the words of one lexical domain. Many lexical studies of the Ultan and Andersen types, as well as others focused directly on phonological and grammatical structure, are needed before linguists can speak with assurance of universal characteristics of word structure.

The third kind of lexical research is the analysis of external relationships of words. By this I do not mean syntax in general, which treats words in relation to larger grammatical units such as sentences, but the whole range of phenomena which involve lexical relations rather than grammatical constructions. One prime area for this kind of research is what British linguists call 'collocations' (i.e. favored cooccurrences of words). In the United States collocations are studied chiefly by lexicographers and translators, and purely linguistic studies are rare. Another area consists of the grammatical processes which do not fall clearly into either word formation or syntax, such as repetitions, reduplications, echo words, types of word-play and 'secret languages', and the like. The Moravcsik paper deals with one set of phenomena here, attempting to characterize reduplicative constructions in human language, and Makkai's paper examines the troublesome issue of lexical units larger than the word and the problem of anomalous structures at various levels.

Finally, there are lexicalization studies: How are given semantic primes or combinations of primes expressed in different languages and what universal principles or constraints operate in such mapping of meaning onto form? Traugott has discussed elsewhere universal lexicalization processes such as that of 'segmentalization', by which lexical items are decomposed into simpler semantic units in pidginizing contexts (e.g. Traugott 1974); here she discusses the expression of spatio-temporal meanings across languages. The Andersen paper also has implications for lexicalization processes, and to some extent every paper in the volume touches on this question. Steele's contribution is directly on the topic of lexicalization, although it is not phrased in such terms: she is, in effect, examining the likelihood of a particular cluster of semantic primes (AUX) being lexicalized in certain ways across languages.

The four types of studies listed here overlap with one another and in any case do not constitute a comprehensive classification of possible lexical research, but these types and the papers which represent them in this volume give some idea of the richness of the phenomena which can be explored in order to find out about universal properties and processes of words in human language. Perhaps in another decade or so, if linguists' attention remains on semantic issues, the word will again be recognized as one of the basic

linguistic units (cf. Greenberg 1954c) and the elaboration of lexical
theory will be as hotly debated as phonological and syntactic theory
are at the present time.

BIBLIOGRAPHY

Aronoff, Mark. 1976. Word formation in generative grammar.
Cambridge, Mass.: MIT Press.

Boas, Franz. 1968. Introduction to the handbook of American
Indian languages. Repr. with introduction by C.I.J.M. Stuart.
Washington, D.C.: Georgetown University Press.

Brown, Roger and A. Gilman. 1960. The pronouns of power and
solidarity. In T.A. Sebeok (ed.), Style in language. Cambridge,
Mass.: MIT Press. 253-276.

Ferguson, Charles A. 1964. Basic grammatical categories of
Bengali. In H. Lunt (ed.), Proceedings of the IXth International
Congress of Linguists. 881-890. The Hague: Mouton.

Ferguson, Charles A. and Carol B. Farwell. 1975. Words and
sounds in early language acquisition. Language 51. 419-439.

Forchheimer, P. 1953. The category of person in language.
Berlin: W. Gruyter.

Greenberg, Joseph H. 1954a. A quantitative approach to the
morphological typology of language. In R.F. Spencer (ed.),
Methods and perspectives in anthropology: papers in honor of
Wilson D. Wallis. 192-220.

_____. 1954b. The word as a linguistic unit. In C.E. Osgood
and T.A. Sebeok (eds.), Psycholinguistics: a survey of theory
and research problems. 66-71. Baltimore: Waverly Press.

_____. 1954c. The definition of linguistic units. In Essays in
linguistics. 18-34. Chicago: University of Chicago Press.

Halle, Morris. 1973. Prolegomena to a theory of word-formation.
Linguistic Inquiry 4. 3-16.

Householder, Fred W. and Sol Saporta (eds.). Problems in lexicography. (= IJAL 38.2 Pt. IV.) Baltimore: Waverly Press.

Juilland, Alphonse G. and Alexandra Roceric. 1972. The linguistic concept of word. The Hague: Mouton.

_____. 1977. The decline of the word. (= Studia Linguistica
et Philologica 1.) Saratoga, California: Anma Libri.

Lyons, John. 1968. Introduction to theoretical linguistics. London:
Cambridge University Press.

Matthews, P. H. 1974. Morphology: an introduction to the theory
of word structure. London: Cambridge University Press.

Traugott, Elizabeth. 1974. Explorations in linguistic elaboration:
language change, language acquisition, and the genesis of
spatio-temporal terms. In J.M. Anderson and C. Jones (eds.),
Historical linguistics, Vol. I. 263-314. Amsterdam: North-
Holland.

Wang, William S-Y. 1969. Competing changes as a cause of
residue. Language 45. 9-25.

The Category AUX
as a Language Universal

SUSAN STEELE

ABSTRACT

The category AUX was hypothesized for ENGLISH originally
in Syntactic Structures. Although there has been much debate
over the analysis in terms of ENGLISH, whether other languages
have a comparable category has not been investigated. Using criteria suggested by the ENGLISH analysis, an examination of a
number of other languages argues that AUX is a universal category. Further, certain essential characteristics of the AUX are
established within this cross-linguistic study.

This paper has profited substantially from comments and criti-
cisms made by Adrian Akmajian, Peter Culicover, Richard Oehrle,
and the members of the Stanford Language Universals Project.

Susan Steele

CONTENTS

1. Introduction

1.1   Descriptions of ENGLISH grammar have traditionally
recognized that ENGLISH verbs can be accompanied, and preceded,
by certain auxiliary elements. [1] The elements include do, modals
like should, must, and might, the negative not (or n't), and auxiliary verbs like have, be, got, go, come, and perhaps a few others.
All, except the negative, occur with some non-finite form of the
verb; [2] at least do and some of the auxiliary verbs take the regular
verb inflections for tense and person. The recognition of this property of ENGLISH was formalized in Syntactic Structures where it
is claimed that certain of these elements are dominated by a category AUX. There the AUX is introduced by a phrase structure
rule.

S ⟶ NP - AUX - VP

There the AUX is analyzed as follows, where C stands for the -s
or the lack of it in the present tense or -ed in the past tense and
M stands for the modal auxiliary.

AUX ⟶ C (M) (have+en) (be+en)

This analysis excludes at least some of the elements mentioned in
the traditional descriptions. [3] The analysis departs from the traditional descriptions more substantially; most importantly, it makes

---

[1] The term "auxiliary" is not always applied to these. For example, Jespersen (1940) calls at least the modals and some of the
auxiliary verbs verbs, verbs that take another verb as their object.
However, there is uniform recognition in traditional ENGLISH
grammars of certain syntactic differences between these elements,
whatever they are called, and regular main verbs.

[2] Some modals (e.g. ought) and some auxiliary verbs (e.g. got
in some uses) can occur with an infinitive with to. There are
usually other syntactic considerations which require them to be
part of this class of auxiliary elements.

[3] The elements not mentioned in the phrase structure rule for
AUX, but traditionally part of the same set of elements, are excluded for various reasons. Do is inserted, in this analysis, by a
transformational rule; the negative is, as well, in Syntactic Structures, although later analyses generate it clause initially and move
it into the AUX. The place of go and come in relationship to the
AUX is simply not considered in this initial analysis.

a claim that the AUX is a category.[4] This claim has since been
the subject of much analysis and debate, specifically in regard to
ENGLISH. Although arguments continue over the details of the
analysis and the basic premises, I begin with the assumption that
the category is justified for ENGLISH. The subject of this paper
is whether it is justified in other languages as well.[5] That is, the
question is whether AUX is a universal category; this paper will
argue that it is.

  1.2   It is worth spending some time and space considering why
the question is important in the first place. First, the issue of
what categories are primitive in the grammar and how we decide
is basic to linguistics. One segment of the linguistic community
has faced the issue explicitly, but the arguments it has adduced in
favor of whatever categories it proposed have been based in no
small part on formal properties of the grammar. Whatever can be
said in favor of this approach, it has left a relatively large segment
of the linguistic community unconvinced — and unsatisfied. On the
other hand, the issue of universal categories has seldom been explicit in the work of those concerned with substantive language
universals. The categories have been assumed prior to investigation or the question of categories has never arisen in the first
place. Although the substantiation of particular grammatical categories has been an implicit result of some cross-linguistic studies,
it is important that we explicitly test particular theoretical constructs against the data of a number of languages. The AUX is
one of those constructs — and this paper will test it.

  A second reason that the question is important pertains exclusively to the category AUX. Although I will define AUX below,

---

  [4] The phrase structure rules for the AUX also produce a deep
structure, and the concept of deep structure is, of course, an important break with traditional analyses. Following from the fact
that phrase structure rules produce deep structures, the form of
the AUX can differ dramatically from its surface manifestation.
So too is it possible to refer to tense and subject agreement (in C)
as separate from the other elements of the AUX.

  [5] Actually, my belief that the category AUX is justified for ENG-
LISH is an outgrowth of work with other languages, languages which
exhibit a phenomenon similar in many respects to what has been
analyzed as the ENGLISH AUX. That is, the progression of this
paper — from an AUX for ENGLISH to testing the category against
other languages — reverses in certain important respects the development of my ideas on the subject.

note at this juncture that as defined by Chomsky above, the AUX contains a certain notional set, a set containing tense, aspect, and modality elements. The traditional descriptions of auxiliary elements focused on the same notional set, although the elements contained therein are a larger class. This notional set involves elements which are sentential in scope, i. e. they place the situation described in the sentence in a certain time (tense), ascribe a temporal contour to it (aspect), and assess its reality (modality). Not uncommonly, some or all of these will be realized in a form which is dependent on the verb in some fashion. But in a substantial number of languages, some or all of these will be realized in a form totally independent of the verb. As long as we concentrate on the verb and the relationship to it of the elements expressing these notions, certain cross-linguistic regularities cannot be revealed. By concentrating our attention on the AUX, a category in its own right, these regularities are no longer obscured.

1. 3   Preliminary to undertaking to discover what, if anything, corresponds to the ENGLISH AUX is the problem of recognition; how do we know an AUX in another language when we see one? To answer this question, let me consider the claims implicit in the analysis of the ENGLISH AUX referred to above.

The analysis of the AUX in Syntactic Structures makes three claims, the first two of which are intimately connected. First, there is a deep structure unit AUX. Second, the AUX and the main verb occur in the same clause; that is, the main verb is not (at any point in the derivation) subordinated to the AUX. Third, the unit AUX involves certain notional categories. I noted above that C refers to (past or present) tense[6] and M, to modality; the other members of the AUX are the auxiliary verbs for perfect and progressive aspects and the auxiliary verb for the passive.

1. Mary has drunk too much.
2. Mary is drinking too much.
3. The entire bottle of scotch was finished in one evening.

Tense (realized as the presence or absence of subject agreement in the present tense) is obligatory; all other members of the AUX

---

[6]It also subsumes agreement, what minimal agreement there is between subject and verb in ENGLISH. Subsequent analyses have assumed that agreement is accomplished by a rule which copies the features of the subject onto the verb. I will return to the place of agreement in the AUX in Section 3.

are optional. (Tense is attached to that part of the AUX which immediately follows it, or to the verb if no other part of the AUX is
present.)

The first claim has of course been questioned by those who reject a level of deep structure; disputation of the second claim follows automatically. That is, if it is assumed that the semantics of
a sentence are directly represented in the underlying representation,
rather than projected from a deep structure, at least the tense,
aspect, and modal parts of the AUX will be higher predicates,
predicates embedding the surface main verb. (See e.g. Ross 1969
and McCawley 1970.)[7] But even in that segment of the linguistic
community that accepts a phrase structure rule introducing AUX,
arguments continue over what the AUX includes. One camp argues
that the AUX includes only tense and modality; <u>have</u> and <u>be</u> are
part of the VP. (See Jackendoff 1972.)[8]

> AUX ⟶ Tense (M)

Another camp argues that the AUX includes all the elements of the
original proposal except for the passive (<u>be</u> + <u>en</u>). (See Akmajian
and Wasow 1975.)

> AUX ⟶ Tense (M) (<u>have</u> + <u>en</u>) (<u>be</u> + <u>ing</u>)

The first revision excludes aspect and the passive auxiliary from
the AUX; the second excludes only the passive auxiliary.

---

[7]Chafe (1970) is to be included among those who reject a level
of deep structure and an AUX like that proposed in <u>Syntactic Structures.</u> However, tense, aspect, and modality -- considered verb
inflections by him -- are not abstract higher predicates.

[8] Jackendoff argues for a structure like:

VP
(<u>have</u>) (<u>be</u>) V

Another proposal which distinguishes between tense and modality
on the one hand and <u>have</u> and <u>be</u> on the other is that of Gee (1975).
He argues for:

V̿
SPEC   V̄
(<u>have</u>) (<u>be</u>)   V

In the search for an equivalence to the ENGLISH AUX in other languages, I took the three claims above as roughly criterial, even though they are surrounded by debate. I looked for a surface unit separate from the main verb which contained at least modality or tense or aspect and which did not subordinate the main verb. That is, the second claim was adopted absolutely. The first claim was modified from a claim about deep structure to a claim about surface structure. We needn't argue for or against a deep structure unit; the AUX is a surface unit in ENGLISH regardless of whether it is a deep structure unit.[9]

The third claim was modified to exclude the passive notion and, although I didn't otherwise require exact notional equivalences, I assumed that an overlap on at least one point was essential. We will see that the debate over the inclusion of <u>have</u> and <u>be</u> is reflected in a cross-linguistic division between two types of elements, both of which meet the criteria here suggested.

Let me elaborate briefly on how I implemented the first two of the three criteria. To be considered a surface unit, the notional categories discussed above have to occur separate from the verb. In ENGLISH, the AUX is separate from the verb -- unless tense, alone of the potential members of the AUX, is present. In LUISEÑO, modality elements and tense/aspect clitics (and subject agreement) occur separate from the verb.[10]

4. mariya = xu = p = po xwaani ˀari
    "Mary=MODAL=agreement=TENSE/ASPECT John:object kick"
    'Mary should kick John.'   (Steele, n.d.)

To be considered a surface unit, the notional categories which are realized separate from the verb cannot be positioned in a number of positions in the sentence.[11] So, the ENGLISH auxiliary precedes

---

[9]Of course, in the theory which has argued for a deep structure AUX, it is impossible to have a surface category which is not a reflection of a deep structure category.

[10] = represents a clitic boundary.

[11]This criterion excludes adverbial elements from consideration, since adverbial elements are generally subject to less rigid positional restrictions. The exclusion was premeditated; to have to consider elements which correspond to ENGLISH <u>possibly</u>, for example, an adverb which expresses a modal notion -- obscures the particular phenomena I am trying to examine.

the verb. Similarly, the clitic complex of LUISEÑO in 4. above
has to occur after either the first word or the first constituent of
the sentence. 4. illustrates the position of the LUISEÑO clitic
complex; all of the sentences in 5. are ungrammatical.

5. a. *xuppo mariya xwaani ?ari
        "CLITIC:COMPLEX Mary John: object kick"

    b. *mariya xwaani = xuppo ?ari
        "Mary John: object = CLITIC:COMPLEX kick"

    c. *mariya xwaani ?ari = xuppo
        "Mary John: object kick = CLITIC:COMPLEX"
                                        (Steele, n.d.)

Finally, if a sequence of the elements which express these notional
categories is possible, the sequence is not interruptable by any of
the major constituents of the sentence and the relative order of the
elements within the sequence is fixed. [12] In ENGLISH modal elements occur first, aspectual elements follow, and tense is attached
to whatever member of the auxiliary is first (or to the verb if neither modality nor aspect is overtly expressed.) In LUISEÑO the
clitic elements mentioned above cannot be reordered, so 6. is ungrammatical because the sequence of clitics illustrated in 4. has
been rearranged.

6. *mariya=p=po=x xwaani ?ari
    "Mary=AGREEMENT=TENSE/ASPECT=MODAL John:obj. kick"
                                        (Steele, n.d.)

The requirement that what will be called an AUX not subordinate
a main verb is met here solely by surface phenomena, characteristics which differentiate the relationship between the two from other,
subordinate, constructions. As will be seen, a special form of the
main verb -- a participial or infinitival form -- is often required
with elements indicating tense, aspect, or modality that are also
separate from the main verb. Participial and infinitival forms are
also used as indications of subordination. So, in ENGLISH, we have
poss-ing and infinitive complements.

7. We discussed Mary's drinking to excess.
8. Mary decided to drink herself into oblivion.

---

[12]Let me stress major constituents. Various things can occur
within the ENGLISH AUX, as e.g. negatives or sentential adverbs.

Other languages exhibit similar overlaps. If a similarity was evident between the form of the main verb with separate tense, aspect and/or modality elements and the form of certain subordinate verbs, I looked for syntactic distinctions between the two constructions. Most obviously, in ENGLISH, the infinitive form of the verb with a modal doesn't take a to, unlike regular subordinate constructions. I take the lack of to to indicate the absence of a clause boundary between the modal and the main verb; it therefore indicates that the main verb is not subordinated to the modal. Where other languages exhibit similar overlaps in form, I looked for some similar indication of the absence of clause boundaries.

It should be noted that this requirement that there be no surface clause boundary between what will be called an AUX and a main verb removes from consideration certain elements which express modal or aspectual notions. For example, in LUISEÑO, the construction that indicates obligation is the verb miy- 'be' and a sentential subject complement.

11. wunaal po-naačaxan-pi miyq
     " [[she her-eat-subordinate] is] "
     'She has to eat.'   (Steele, n.d.)

miy- , because it takes a sentential complement, will not be considered an AUX.

To recapitulate, I used three criteria which follow from the analysis of the ENGLISH AUX as defining what would be considered an AUX in another language. One final comment is necessary about this definition. Two assumptions are often made about the AUX, perhaps because the term AUX is reminiscent of the term auxiliary verb. It is commonly assumed, first, that the AUX will be adjacent to the verb and, second, that the AUX will be verblike. Neither assumption is either explicit or implicit in the original proposal; as will be shown neither is necessarily characteristic of AUX. For now, though, let it simply be noted that neither of these will be criteria in the search for AUX.

1.4   Depending on your perspective, one of two objections could be raised to my definition of AUX.

It could be objected that the definition, specifically as it applies to notional categories, is too narrow. By focusing at the outset on the three notions of modality, tense, and aspect, I exclude from consideration here other types of elements which often share (certain of) their syntactic properties, elements like negatives, conjunctions, or question markers. Negatives, for instance, often occur in the same position as the set of notional categories with which I am primarily concerned. For example, the ENGLISH negative follows the first member of the surface auxiliary.

12. Mary hasn't been drinking very long.

Similarly, the LUISEÑO negative either directly precedes or directly follows the clitic complex discussed above.

13. qay=xuppo hunwuti pati
    "NEG=clitic:complex bear:object shoot"
    'He shouldn't shoot the bear.'   (Steele, n.d.)

14. xwaan = xuppo qay hunwuti pati
    "John=clitic:complex NEG bear:object shoot"
    'John shouldn't shoot the bear.'   (Steele, n.d.)

A sharp division between these elements and those with which I am primarily concerned is probably impossible to make, but I will maintain the definition as stated for two reasons. First, there are occasionally hints that what we will want to call an AUX is to be differentiated, however subtly, from elements like negatives. For example, in LUISEÑO, the clitic complex above can occur either after the first word or the first constituent of the sentence. In 15. below, the clitic complex follows the first constituent nawitmal yawaywiš 'beautiful girl;' in 16. the clitic complex follows the first word of that constituent, nawitmal 'girl.'

15. nawitmal yawaywiš = apil hunwuti ʔariquś
    "girl beautiful=CLITIC:COMPLEX bear:object was:kicking"
    'The beautiful girl was kicking the bear.' (Steele, n.d.)

16. nawitmal = apil yawaywiš hunwuti ʔ ariquś
    "girl=CLITIC:COMPLEX beautiful bear:object was:kicking"
    'The beautiful girl was kicking the bear.' (Steele, n.d.)

So can the negative.

17. nawitmal yawaywiš=apil qay hunwuti ʔariquś
    "girl beautiful =clitic:complex NEG bear:object was: kicking"
    'The beautiful girl wasn't kicking the bear.' (Steele, n.d.)

18. nawitmal=apil qay yawaywiš hunwuti ʔariquś
    "girl=clitic:complex NEG beautiful bear:object was:kicking"
    'The beautiful girl wasn't kicking the bear.' (Steele, n.d.)

But if the clitic complex follows the first word the negative need
not; it can follow the first constituent. [13]

19. nawitmal = apil yawaywiš qay hunwuti ʔariquɬ
     "girl=CLITIC:COMPLEX beautiful NEG bear:object was:
     kicking"
     'The beautiful girl wasn't kicking the bear.' (Steele, n.d.)

A second reason for maintaining the definition of AUX, and perhaps
a more important one, is that the definition gives results when it is
applied to other languages. It may be that what we will want to call
an AUX and negatives -- or other types of elements excluded here
-- are not to be distinguished in other languages. But at this
point I am concerned only with establishing the existence of the
AUX. Whether it will eventually have to be expanded to include
other than tense, aspect, and modality must await that establishment.

An objection of a different sort could be raised about my insis-
tence on establishing AUX as a surface phenomena. After all, the
original proposal was a claim about deep structure. I assume,
however, if there is a surface unit which corresponds to the (hypothesized) deep structure AUX of the analysis of ENGLISH, that this is
powerful evidence for the category. To find surface regularities
is not the trivial accomplishment it has been sometimes suggested
-- occasionally by the man who proposed the AUX in the first place; [14]
if surface regularities can be established, it is compelling evidence
for underlying similarity across languages.

---

[13]However, the negative cannot follow the first word if the clitic
complex follows the first constituent.
    *nawitmal qay yawaywiš= apil heelaquɬ
    "girl NEG beautiful=CLITIC:COMPLEX was singing"

[14]". . . it has been emphasized that the deep structures for which
universality is claimed may be quite distinct from the surface structures of sentences as they actually appear. Consequently, there is
no reason to expect uniformity of surface structures, and the findings of modern linguistics are thus not inconsistent with the hypotheses of universal grammarians. Insofar as attention is restricted
to surface structures, the most that can be expected is the discovery
of statistical tendencies, such as those presented by Greenberg
(1963)." (Chomsky 1965: 118).

1.5   The language sample is given in I.

I. CHINOOK (PENUTIAN)
    ENGLISH (INDO-EUROPEAN)
    GWARI (CONGO-KORDOFANIAN)
    CLASSICAL AZTEC (AZTECO-TANOAN)
    JACALTEC (PENUTIAN)
    KAPAMPANGAN (AUSTRONESIAN)
    KAPAU (INDO-PACIFIC)
    KAROK̃ (HOKAN-SIOUAN)
    LUISEÑO (AZTECO-TANOAN)
    JAPANESE (JAPANESE)
    MOJAVE (HOKAN-SIOUAN)
    NARINJARI (AUSTRALIAN)
    SAHAPTIN (PENUTIAN)
    SQUAMISH (ALGONKIAN-MOSAN)
    TAGALOG (AUSTRONESIAN)
    TERA (AFRO-ASIATIC)
    THAI (SINO-TIBETAN)
    SOUTHEASTERN POMO (HOKAN-SIOUAN)
    VOTIC (FINNO-UGRIC)
    WALBIRI (AUSTRALIAN)

An attempt was made to make the sample both genetically and typologically representative. The genetic affiliations are given in I.[15]
As regards typology, two factors were given consideration in selecting the language sample. [16] Languages representing each of the
three major word order types are contained in the sample. [17]

---

[15]The most comprehensive genetic groups are listed in I;
agreement on the validity of these genetic groups ranges from near
universal to chaotic disagreement. By the labels in I, I do not
indicate either commitment to or rejection of any particular genetic
group.

[16] The language sample represents other typological divisions
as well, although they were not given primary consideration nor
were they ultimately of predictive value. Most importantly, both
ergative and non-ergative languages are represented in I.

[17]The decision as to which category a language belonged in was
based on its most common word order. The third category is labelled VSO/VOS under the assumption that these two are basically
similar.

II. SOV | SVO | VSO/VOS

SOV	SVO	VSO/VOS
VOTIC	THAI	TAGALOG
S. E. POMO	GWARI	KAPAMPANGAN
JAPANESE	ENGLISH	SQUAMISH
KAROK	CLASSICAL AZTEC[18]	CHINOOK
LUISEÑO	TERA	JACALTEC
WALBIRI		SAHAPTIN[19]
MOJAVE		NARINJARI
KAPAU		

Languages with both rigid and relatively free word order are contained in the language sample.[20]

III. Rigid: | | Relatively Free:

Rigid:		Relatively Free:
SAHAPTIN	NARINJARI	CLASSICAL AZTEC
ENGLISH	SQUAMISH	KAROK
GWARI	TAGALOG	LUISEÑO
JACALTEC	TERA	CHINOOK
KAPAMPANGAN	THAI	WALBIRI
KAPAU	S. E. POMO	
JAPANESE	VOTIC	
MOJAVE		

---

[18] CLASSICAL AZTEC SVO word order is only slightly more common than VOS.

[19] SAHAPTIN also regularly has SVO word order; it is to be distinguished from many of the other languages in this category in that SAHAPTIN SVO word order doesn't necessarily involve topicalization.

[20] A better classification, but not one that is particularly revealing for my purposes, would be between languages with grammaticalized word order (as e. g. ENGLISH), languages where the order of elements reveals something about their "communicative dynamism" (i. e. languages where word order indicates focus, topic, and the like as e. g. KAPAMPANGAN), and languages with what seems to be freely scrambling word order (as e. g. LUISEÑO). The second type is classed as rigid in III., and there is a basic distinction to be made between the first two and the last. The last has fewer restrictions on the position of the verb. If a language is SOV or VOS/VSO in its most common word order and yet allows the verb to occur either initially or finally respectively, the language is of the last type. If a language is SVO and yet allows sentences with clause initial and clause final verbs, the language is of the last type.

Furthermore, there are both rigid and relatively free word order
languages within each of the three major language types.

IV.	SOV		SVO	
Rigid:	**Free:**		**Rigid:**	**Free:**
VOTIC	LUISEÑO		THAI	CLASSICAL AZTEC
S. E. POMO	KAROK		ENGLISH	
JAPANESE	WALBIRI		GWARI	
MOJAVE			TERA	
KAPAU				

VOS/VSO	
Rigid:	**Free:**
TAGALOG	CHINOOK
KAPAMPANGAN	
SAHAPTIN	
JACALTEC	
SQUAMISH	
NARINJARI	

2. The Equivalences

2.1 All the languages in the sample have some way of indicating
various tense, modal, and aspectual notions. Tense includes indication of present, past, and future time.[21] By modal, I mean elements which mark any of the following: possibility or the related
notion of permission, probability or the related notion of obligation,
certainty or the related notion of requirement. The ENGLISH sentences below illustrate these notions respectively.

    20. a. Mary may be drinking when we arrive.
       b. It's after dark. You may drink now.

    21. a. Mary should be aware of the degeneration of her liver.
       b. Someone should tell Mary about the other effects of the
          pill.

    22. a. Mary must be drinking again; look at her hands shake.
       b. Everyone must quit offering Mary cigarettes.

Excluded from the category modal by this definition are notions like
subjunctive and elements which mark questions or indicate that the

---

[21] These are simply semantic notions. Grammatically, tense
usually involves a distinction between present and past.

source of the information contained in a particular sentence is
something other than the speaker's own experience (e.g. quotatives or evidentials).[22] Aspect is left relatively undefined; it
includes (at least) such notions as perfective or imperfective and
progressive, but is not restricted to these. Within these semantic
parameters, the languages of the sample make different distinctions overt, but the categories of modality, tense, and aspect, as
defined, appear to be universal.

2.2   In almost all of the languages in the sample, at least one
of the notional categories meets the criteria established above.
That is, at least one of the notional categories of modality, tense,
and aspect will be expressed in an element which is separate from
the verb and which does not subordinate it. In CLASSICAL AZTEC,
the overt expression of modal notions meets these criteria.

    23. kwiš tokonmokwiilis
       "MODAL you:will:take:it:from:him"
       'Perhaps you will take it from him.' (Dibble and Anderson 1969:27)

In KAPAU, the expression of (certain) aspectual notions meets
these criteria.

    24. änga yamakmna qi?ya
       "house I:will:build I'M:DOING"
       'I'm gonna build a house.' (Oates and Oates 1968: 42)

In LUISEÑO, modality and tense/aspect together form a unit which
is separate from the main verb. (See 4. above.) Only in SOUTH-
EASTERN POMO are all the categories mentioned exclusively
verbal affixes.[23] 25. is the schema described in a grammar of
the language.

    25. V + Modal + Aspect

---

[22]There is probably no absolute cross-linguistic distinction to
be made between modals, as I defined them, and what has been
called the subjunctive or quotatives and evidentials. However, in
general, these last do not pattern syntactically with the modals as
defined.

[23]It is possible -- and I wouldn't be at all surprised to discover
-- that SOUTHEASTERN POMO had a construction like those discussed in 2.3; the grammar I read would simply have failed to
discuss it.

Although all the languages in the sample except SOUTHEASTERN
POMO have, therefore, some unit which could be said to resemble
the ENGLISH AUX, they are not of a uniform type. In particular,
it is important to distinguish between two basic types. In one, the
unit meeting the criteria established above is roughly equivalent
to what has traditionally been called an auxiliary verb; in the other,
such auxiliary verb constructions may exist, but there are other constructions which meet the AUX criteria as well.

2.3   MOJAVE, KAPAU, VOTIC, CHINOOK, NARINJARI, and
JAPANESE all allow their respective equivalents for the verbs be,
have, do and/or certain motion verbs to occur with a form of the
main verb.[24]   The first example below is a CHINOOK sentence;
the second, a MOJAVE sentence, and the third, a JAPANESE sentence. A KAPAU example was given in 24.

26.   λux níxux iqíčxut
      "come: out IT: DID black: bear"
      'The black bear came out.'   (Silverstein 1972: 393)

27.   ʔinʸeč ʔtapuyk ʔaʔwiim
      "I   I: kill   I: DID"
      'I killed him.'   (Munro 1975: 9)

28.   John ga hon o yonde iru
      "John subj: marker book obj: marker reading IS"
      'John is reading a book.'   (Kuno 1973: 148)

I have already referred to these as auxiliary verb constructions.
It isn't necessary to merely intuit what an auxiliary verb is; there
are two characteristics which the constructions illustrated in the
above sentences have in common, characteristics which I take to
define an auxiliary verb. First -- and pertaining primarily to the
auxiliaryness of the auxiliary verb -- the auxiliary verb takes
whatever inflectional affixes would otherwise appear on the main
verb, that is, if no auxiliary rule were present. In all the examples above, the auxiliary verb is inflected for tense; in all but
JAPANESE, a language without subject agreement, the auxiliary
verb also carries whatever subject agreement would otherwise
appear on the main verb. I will return to this second point. From
the fact that the auxiliary verb is inflected for tense it follows that

---

[24]The set of verbs which participate in this type of construction
may include as well verbs of position, e.g. like sit, or verbs like
say. The set is, however, very restricted.

the main verb will usually appear in some non-tensed and occasionally participial form. In CHINOOK, the main verb is in a totally
uninflected form in such sentences as 26. above; the NARINJARI
main verb has the same characteristic. In JAPANESE, the main
verb is in a participial form; in 28. above, -de on the verb yon
'read' corresponds roughly to ENGLISH -ing. VOTIC exhibits a
parallel construction. In MOJAVE the main verb is in a sort of
semi-subordinate form; in 27., the form ? tapuyk is to be analyzed
as follows, where -k is one of a set of suffixes indicating that a
verb has the same or different subject as another verb.[25]

29. ? -tapuy-k
     "I-kill-same: subject"   (Munro 1975: 9)

KAPAU is aberrant; the main verb is inflected for what is called
the "immediate future" -- the -na suffix on the verb yamak.

While one defining characteristic of an auxiliary verb is that it
has certain auxiliary attributes, a second characteristic pertains
to the verbness of the auxiliary verb. The auxiliary verb is actually
verblike. This is more than saying that it can be inflected like a
regular verb. The auxiliary verbs are generally verbs in their own
right, in other constructions.[26]

Auxiliary verb constructions are not exclusive to these six languages. ENGLISH has constructions like these; ENGLISH have
and be act as aspectual auxiliary verbs. (See examples 1. and 2.
above.) ENGLISH, though, appears not to be representative of the
remaining languages in the language sample. At least CLASSICAL
AZTEC and LUISEÑO do not have such constructions at all. In
LUISEÑO, motion verbs which might conceivably be like those discussed above are verb suffixes.

30. noo heelax-ngi-q
     "I sing-GO : AWAY -present"
     'I am going away singing.'   (Steele, n.d.)

---

[25]The MOJAVE construction can still be classified as an AUX;
subordination of the main verb is not at all obvious even though it
has the suffixes of a subordinate verb. See Munro 1975.

[26]They, even in these cases, are usually at least morphologically
aberrant and we might not want to call them regular main verbs.
But they nonetheless can be the only verb in a clause.

Verbs like be embed a subordinate verb.

31. wunaalum pomngeepi miyq
     "they their: leave: subordinate IS"
     'They have to leave.'   (Steele, n.d.)

SQUAMISH is closer; a number of aspectual elements have verbs
as their (diachronic?) sources. "The continuous-iterative clitic
/ṷa/ is etymologically identical with the reduplicated root /uə'?u/
'continue'." (Kuipers 1967:159). But the constructions in which
such aspectual element occur do not otherwise resemble those discussed.

The auxiliary verb constructions just considered generally indicate aspectual notions, although they may also involve indication
of such things as stativity or the lack of it and the verifiability or
non-verifiability of the situation described in the sentence. VOTIC
and NARINJARI use the equivalent for be as the auxiliary verb for
the perfect and progressive aspects respectively. CHINOOK and
KAPAU auxiliary verbs are intimately involved with the stative or
non-stative distinction between main verbs. MOJAVE and KAPAU
auxiliary verbs are as well, but the former has strong aspectual
overtones, the latter strong overtones of modality.

2.4   The languages left to be discussed -- LUISEÑO, TAGALOG,
KAPAMPANGAN, GWARI, TERA, JACALTEC, CLASSICAL AZTEC,
SAHAPTIN, WALBIRI, KAROK, SQUAMISH, THAI, and ENGLISH
-- also have some unit which meets the criteria established above.
Examples of such have been given for LUISEÑO (4.), CLASSICAL
AZTEC (23.), and ENGLISH. The unit in these and the other languages in the language sample is, however, to be distinguished
from the constructions just discussed. A different notional category is primary in this second set; the element which expresses
it -- and other notional categories as well, in some languages --
is not an auxiliary verb.

The constructions in 2.3 revolve around indicating various
aspectual notions. In this second set of languages, elements which
indicate various aspectual notions may occur separate from the
main verb as well. In JACALTEC, SQUAMISH and THAI, aspect
is indicated separate from the main verb.

32.   xc = ach wila
      "ASPECT=you I-see"
      'I saw you.'   (JACALTEC; Craig 1975: 64)

But these aspectual elements may have strong tense overtones; in LUISEÑO and TERA, some notion roughly between aspect and tense is indicated separate from the main verb. [27]

33. ʔawaal = p =il waʔiquś
    "dog=agreement=TENSE/ASPECT was:barking"
    'The dog was barking.'   (LUISEÑO; Steele, n.d.)

Furthermore, in SQUAMISH, KAROK and WALBIRI, there are tense elements which are necessarily separate from the main verb.

34. natju ka=na puḷani
    "I TENSE=agreement shout:nonpast"
    'I am shouting.'   (WALBIRI; Hale 1973: 309)

Most importantly, however, all of the languages in this set have modality elements which meet the criteria established in 1.3. The CLASSICAL AZTEC sentence in 23. above is one example; below are examples from JACALTEC, ENGLISH and SAHAPTIN:

35. tita xmunla naj
    "MODAL work he"
    'He may have worked.'   (Craig 1975: 93)

36. I should love you.

37. xtu = x̣ac iwa
    "strong=MODAL he:is"
    'He certainly must be strong.' (Jacobs 1931: 130)

V. sums up the notional categories in this set of languages expressed by some element which is separate from the main verb.[28]

27
    In LUISEÑO, it isn't clear whether we would want to call the element a tense clitic or an aspect clitic; in TERA, on the other hand, the notion indicated is a combination of both aspect and tense.

[28]Excluded from the summary of elements in V. are auxiliary verbs, if the language has such.

V. Modality alone: CLASSICAL AZTEC, TAGALOG,
                                 SAHAPTIN, GWARI

    Modality and Aspect: JACALTEC, THAI[29]

    Modality and Tense: LUISEÑO, KAROK, WALBIRI, TERA,
                         ENGLISH, KAPAMPANGAN

    Modality, Tense, and
    Aspect: SQUAMISH

The chart above lists only the elements which are (potentially) separate from the main verb. If a language has aspect and/or tense elements which are separate from the main verb, all may occur together, in a sequence which usually begins with the modal element. The following is an example from LUISEÑO of the dominant type.

38. wunaal=xu = p = po ʔawaali ʔari
     "she=MODAL=agreement=TENSE/ASPECT dog: object kick"
     'She should kick the dog. '   (Steele, n.d.)

JACALTEC is not of the dominant type. At least one of the JACALTEC modality elements follows an aspectual element. (Most don't occur in a sequence with aspect at all.)

39. xma = m to naj
     "ASPECT=MODAL go he"
     'He may have gone. '   (Craig 1975: 93)

As it was possible to characterize an auxiliary verb in the first set of languages, so in this second set the elements which are separate from the main verb, but which are not auxiliary verbs, do not exhibit these characteristics.

First, the elements which indicate the notional categories tense, aspect, or modality and which are also separate from the main verb are not otherwise main verbs. In ENGLISH, for example, modals may be descended from main verbs, but synchronically

---

[29]JACALTEC is described as marking aspect to the exclusion of tense; THAI is usually considered to do the same thing.

they are not both modals and main verbs.[30] In LUISEÑO modals
are not even descended from main verbs but rather from conjunctions. (See Steele 1976.)

Second, although elements indicating modality are basic to this
set, it is seldom the case that the aspect and/or tense elements
that can cooccur with them are regular verb inflections, and that
the verb is, thereby, left in some non-tensed or special (participial)
form. Let me first discuss the elements themselves and then the
form of the main verb as each bears on the question of inflection.

The majority of languages in the set under consideration are
of one of two types in regard to those tense/aspectual elements
which are separate from the main verb. Either the tense (or aspectual) element is always separate from the main verb. JACAL-
TEC, SQUAMISH, TERA, GWARI, and THAI seem to be of this
type.[31] In the following example from JACALTEC the verb is uninflected, the aspectual notion being indicated solely by the separate
aspectual element.

40. xc = ach wila
    "ASPECT=you I:see"   (Craig 1975: 64)
    'I saw you.'

Or tense elements which are separate from the main verb cooccur
with a verb otherwise also inflected for tense; the tense elements
which are separate from the verb agree, in some sense, with the
verb inflections. LUISEÑO, KAROK, and WALBIRI are of this
type. The following are examples from LUISEÑO. In the first, po
is a clitic indicating, roughly, 'future' and the verb is inflected
for future; in the second, il is a clitic indicating, roughly, 'past'
and the verb is inflected for past durative.

---

[30]By saying that modals are descended from main verbs, I mean
only that what are now forms that express modal meanings were
once main verbs. The process of coming to express modal meanings carries with it the necessity that the form no longer be a main
verb.

[31] GWARI does have some, minimal, verbal inflection for tense
under certain conditions.

wò kū - í ɓa gye - (i) wyé
"he ASPECT-PAST them see-(past) ? "
'He saw them.'

41. wunaal = po hunwuti ?ari-n
     "she=FUTURE bear: object kick-FUTURE"
     'She will kick the bear. '   (Steele, n.d.)

42. wunaal = p = il hunwuti ?ari-quɬ
     "she=agreement=PAST bear: object kick-PAST:DURATIVE"
     'She was kicking the bear. '   (Steele, n.d.)

Only in ENGLISH and KAPAMPANGAN is it possible to talk about
the modality element taking the tense inflection which is usually
attached to the verb. ENGLISH may and might are formally present and past respectively; KAPAMPANGAN kaylangan and kelangan
have the same relationship (but see section 4).

I noted in the discussion of auxiliary verbs that the fact that the
auxiliary verb took the regular verb inflection required that the
main verb would assume a non-tensed form; occasionally, the non-
tensed form is a special (participial) form. Following from the
discussion above is the expectation that the main verb will not, in
this second type of language, have a participial or otherwise special
form to indicate its relationship to the modality (and tense or aspect)
elements which are separate from it. Further, since the verb in
some of these languages is uninflected necessarily (e.g. JACALTEC)
and in others the tense (or aspect) elements separate from the verb
agree with the inflections on the verb (e.g. LUISEÑO), the absence
or presence of inflections on the main verb has, in general, nothing
to do with their attachment or non-attachment elsewhere in the sentence. This is not to say that there is an absolute distinction to be
made between the first set of languages and this set in this regard.
In those languages, like ENGLISH and KAPAMPANGAN, where the
modal element takes the tense inflection of the verb, the verb in a
sentence with a modal occurs (usually) in an uninflected form. [32]
More importantly, in those languages where tense is always a
verbal inflection or where tense elements separate from the verb
agree with verbal inflections, like CLASSICAL AZTEC and LUI-
SEÑO respectively, the verb is not always normally inflected or,
at best, may allow only a restricted set of inflections. In LUISEÑO
the verb in a sentence with a certain modal may be uninflected for
tense:

---

[32]There is a distinction between infinitive and uninflected; the
ENGLISH verb, for instance, in a sentence with a modal is uninflected but is not an infinitive.

43. wunaal = xu = p = po ?awaali ?ari
     "she=MODAL=agreement=TENSE dog:object kick"
     'She should kick the dog.'   (Steele, n.d.)

and in another modal context it can be inflected only with -ma 'habitual.'

44. wunaal = xu = p = po = kwa ?awaali ?ari-ma
     "she=MODAL=agreement=tense=tense dog:object kick-
     HABITUAL"
     'She should have kicked the dog.'   (Steele, n.d.)

But even though in this second set of languages the verb can take
either no inflection or a restricted set of the usual verbal inflections, the basic distinction between the two sets of languages remains. In the languages with auxiliary verbs the presence or
absence of inflection on the verb -- and the type of inflection -- is
intimately connected to the presence or absence of the auxiliary
verb; in the second set of languages, the verb and the elements
separate from the verb which express the notional categories of
modality, tense, and aspect have more independent existences.

I have defined this second type of construction which meets the
criteria suggested in Section 1 primarily in terms of its contrast
with the first type, the auxiliary verb type. Although the languages
in this set are somewhat more diverse than the first type, a general picture of the type of construction they exhibit has emerged;
it involves at least modality and, if some other notional category
may be separate from the verb as well, it is usually tense. These
elements occur in the same sentential position and can occur in a
sequence usually beginning with the modal. And, finally, the main
verb is either uninflected or inflected with regular tense inflections.

2.5   In this section I have examined the expressions of tense,
aspect, and modality which meet the criteria established by the
analysis of the ENGLISH AUX. The languages in the language
sample are to be divided into two groups, one of which has a traditional auxiliary verb, the other of which has a construction that
doesn't fit that characterization. Foreshadowing my conclusions,
I will refer in the remainder of this paper to these as AUX_V and
$AUX_{\sim V}$ respectively. One language in the language sample had neither; I will return to this fact in the final section of the paper.

3. Other Characteristics

3.1   The above can only lead to the conclusion that there is indeed some cross-linguistic reality to the category AUX. Beginning with certain criteria which follow from the ENGLISH AUX, we find comparable phenomena in other languages. It is important to note that the procedure is not circular. It is certainly possible that the criteria established with the ENGLISH AUX would have revealed absolutely nothing when other languages were examined. That similarities did appear -- without any logical necessity that they do so -- is, therefore, of real importance.

However, differences between the languages do indeed exist within the established criteria, both between AUX_v and $AUX_{\sim v}$ types and within each type. The problem is to discover some bases to predict the differences. The next section considers this problem. Regardless of these differences, though, the AUX cross-linguistically has certain characteristics, at least two of which don't necessarily follow from the ENGLISH analysis. This section is concerned with these other characteristics; it, thus, offers a refinement of the initial proposal for an AUX, a proposal which was based solely on ENGLISH data. For this discussion, I simply assume that all of those constructions discussed above -- regardless of what notional categories they include or what form they take -- are to be considered an AUX; justification of that assumption follows in section 4.

3.2   I have discussed two types of constructions which resemble the ENGLISH AUX, one of which is the traditional auxiliary verb, one of which is not. Although this paper has been concerned with the three notional categories of tense, aspect, and modality, there is another type of element which is consistently found in either type and which cannot possibly be ignored – subject agreement or subject marking.

Subject agreement or subject marking is a continuum of types ranging from the minimal agreement exemplified by ENGLISH -s to pronominal affixes like those of CLASSICAL AZTEC:

45.   ni-mic-Laso? La
      "I-YOU-love"
      'I love you. '   (Anderson 1973: 21)

to clitic pronominal elements like those of LUISEÑO.

46. wunaal = up heelaq
    "she=CLITIC: PRONOUN is: singing"
    'She is singing. '   (Steele, n.d.)

Three languages in the language sample -- JAPANESE, THAI, and
GWARI -- have no subject agreement. [33] Other languages have two
different types of agreement in the same clause. For example, in
LUISEÑO, the verb shows number agreement with the subject and
the clitic pronominals agree in both number and person with the
subject. In 46. the subject is third person singular; the verb has
the singular present tense ending -q and the clitic pronoun up is
third person singular. In 47. the subject is third person plural;
the verb has a plural present tense ending -an and the clitic pronoun is third person plural.

47. wunaalum = pum heela-an
    "they=CLITIC: PRONOUN sing-present: PLURAL"
    'They are singing. '   (Steele, n.d.)

Of those languages that have subject agreement, only in CLAS-
SICAL AZTEC, KAROK, and JACALTEC is it possible for the
notional categories which are indicated separate from the main
verb to also be separate from any of the elements indicating subject agreement. In CLASSICAL AZTEC and KAROK, subject
agreement is indicated by verbal affixation; 45. is an example
from CLASSICAL AZTEC. Modality in CLASSICAL AZTEC and
modality and tense in KAROK are separate from the main verb;
23. is an example from CLASSICAL AZTEC. In JACALTEC,
there are two types of subject agreement -- one for the subject of
intransitive sentences, the other for the subject of transitive sentences. While the first is part of the AUX, the second is a verb
prefix.

48. xc = in aẍni
    "aspect=AGREEMENT bathe"
         AUX
    'I bathe. '   (Craig 1975: 110)

49. x-w-il hamam
    "aspect-AGREEMENT-see your: father"
    'I saw your father. '   (Craig 1975: 110)

---

[33] GWARI pronouns combine in special forms with the auxiliary
verbs, but this doesn't constitute subject agreement.

In all the other languages that have subject agreement, the AUX
will include it. Below are examples for both AUX_V and $AUX_{\sim V}$
types .

50. λˀ x̌λˀ x̌ a-n-i-úx̌-a   iλaλqa
"tear: up ? -I-it-do-future his: body"
         ‿‿‿‿‿‿‿‿‿
              AUX
'I will tear up his body. ' (CHINOOK; Silverstein 1972: 393)

51. mariya=p=il heelaquʂ
"Mary=AGREEMENT=tense was:singing"
       ‿‿‿‿‿‿‿‿‿‿‿‿‿
             AUX
'Mary was singing. '   (LUISEÑO; Steele, n.d.)

The possibility noted above that a language may have subject agreement of various types at various points in the sentence is important
here, since in such a language the AUX will not exhaust the agreement possibilities. In LUISEÑO, for example, the clitic pronouns
of 46. and 47. above are part of the AUX, but the verb has agreement for number as well. This possibility does not alter the essential point, however -- agreement is still part of the AUX in
such languages.

   Whether a language will have agreement or not does not, at the
moment anyway, appear to be predictable.[34] But once it is established that a language has agreement, we can predict that it will
almost always be part of the AUX. CLASSICAL AZTEC, KAROK
and JACALTEC are the languages that make the "almost always"
stipulation necessary. All are $AUX_{\sim V}$ types; none has an auxiliary
verb to express the notional categories under examination. This
fact is another instance of the difference between the two types in
terms of inflections -- the inflection which usually occurs on the
main verb will occur in AUX_V but not in $AUX_{\sim V}$. If a language of
the first type has subject agreement or subject marking, it will
occur on the auxiliary verb, usually rather than on the main verb
(as illustrated in 50.), but occasionally in addition to on the main
verb, (as illustrated in 52.).

----

[34]There is an interesting correlation between (certain types of)
agreement and the relative freedom of word order a language will
have, but the question still is which predicts which.

52.   ?in^{y}eč ? -tapuy-k   ? -a? wii-m
      "I I-kill-same:subject I-do-tense"
      'I killed him.' $\underbrace{}_{AUX}$ (MOJAVE; Munro 1975:9)

In a language of the AUX$_{xv}$ type, subject agreement will usually,
but not necessarily, occur with the other notional categories separate from the main verb; it may rather be indicated solely on the
main verb. It is important to note, however, that this particular
difference is not nearly as regular as the difference in terms of
other types of, primarily tense, verb inflections. While the two
types of AUX are to be distinguished in terms of whether they take
certain verb inflections, subject agreement or subject marking is
more nearly a characteristic of all AUX.

   3.3   I noted above that a common assumption about the AUX is that it
will be contiguous to the main verb in the clause. The AUX may
indeed be contiguous to the main verb, but it need not. VI. divides
the languages of the language sample according to whether the AUX
is contiguous to the main verb or not.

VI. Contiguous   Not contiguous

     KAPAMPANGAN   CLASSICAL AZTEC
     SAHAPTIN   TAGALOG
     SQUAMISH   LUISEÑO
     JAPANESE   WALBIRI
     NARINJARÎ   KAROK
     THAI
     GWARI
     ENGLISH
     TERA
     VOTIC
     KAPAU
     JACALTEC
     MOJAVE
     CHINOOK

The first two sentences below illustrate an AUX which is contiguous
to the verb; the third illustrates an AUX which is not.

53.   ux níxux iqíčwut
      "come: out it: did black: bear"
      $\underbrace{}$
      V   AUX
      'The black bear came out.'

54. ho ìn ɓái si obwi
"you <u>modal future</u> buy groundnuts"
               AUX   V   (GWARI; Hyman and
    'You must buy groundnuts today.'   Magaji 1970: 75)

55. ʔom=xuppo tukmal samsa
"you = AUX basket buy "
    'You should buy a basket.'   (LUISEÑO; Steele, n.d.)

All of the languages in this language sample with AUX_V have an
AUX which is contiguous to the main verb; 53. is an example.
However, contiguity to the verb is not a necessary characteristic
of auxiliary verbs; GERMAN <u>haben</u> and <u>sein</u> are not contiguous
to the main verb, nor are the auxiliary verbs of GWARI.

56. Ich habe den Lehrer gefragt.
"I AUX the teacher   V"
    'I asked the teacher.'

Languages with $AUX_{\sim V}$ are distributed between the contiguous and
non-contiguous sorts; 54. and 55. are examples respectively. Contiguous $AUX_{\sim V}$ are slightly more common than non-contiguous
$AUX_{\sim V}$, at least in this language sample.

   To the extent that AUX's which are non-contiguous to the main
verb are of the $AUX_{\sim V}$ type and to the extent that AUX_V are usually
contiguous to the main verb, the contiguity or non-contiguity to the
main verb of the AUX is a characteristic which correlates with
which of the two types of AUX the language has. The characteristic general to all AUX is not the position relative to the verb, but
its position in the sentence. An AUX will occur in one of three
sentential positions -- first, second, and final -- but it appears to
prefer sentential second position. The chart below indicates the
position of the AUX for each language in the language sample.

VII.   <u>Initial</u>   <u>Second</u>   <u>Final</u>

       CLASSICAL AZTEC   TAGALOG   VOTIC
       KAPAMPANGAN   LUISEÑO   JAPANESE
       SQUAMISH   THAI   KAPAU
       JACALTEC   GWARI   MOJAVE
       NARINJARI   KAROK
                            ENGLISH
                            WALBIRI
                            CHINOOK
                            TERA
                            SAHAPTIN

57. is an example from CLASSICAL AZTEC of a clause initial
AUX; 58. is an example from WALBIRI of a second position AUX;
59. is an example from MOJAVE of a clause final AUX.

57. kwiš tokonmokwiilis
"AUX you:will: take:it:from:him"
'Perhaps you will take from him.' (Dibble and
Anderson 1969:27)

58. ngatju lpaṇa puḷatja
"I AUX shouted"
'I was shouting.'   (Hale 1973: 310)

59. ?in^{y}eč ?tapuyk ?a?wiim
"I I:kill   AUX"
'I killed him.'   (Munro 1975: 9)

Which of these three positions an AUX will take in a particular
language is largely predictable from the intersection of two factors
-- the basic word order of a language and its relative freedom of
word order. All the languages with sentence final AUX are rigid
SOV languages. All the languages with sentence initial AUX, with
the exception of CLASSICAL AZTEC, are rigid VSO/VOS languages; CLASSICAL AZTEC has relatively free word order, but
one of the two most common word orders is VOS. The languages
with a second position AUX are predominantly either rigid SVO
languages (ENGLISH, TERA, GWARI, THAI) or SOV languages
with relatively free word order (LUISEÑO, WALBIRI, KAROK).
TAGALOG, KAPAMPANGAN, and SAHAPTIN are relatively
rigid VSO/VOS languages; CHINOOK is a relatively free VSO
language.

I said that the position of the AUX is largely a correlate of the
intersection of two factors. The languages found with either clause
initial or clause final AUX are of uniform types; the languages
with sentential second position AUX are of much more diverse
types — although they do exclude rigid SOV languages. This suggests that sentential second position is the predominant position
cross-linguistically for an AUX.

3.4 A final general characteristic of the AUX has to do with
the form its members can take. Elements of an AUX -- especially
the aspectual and tense elements are often either cliticizable or
necessarily clitic; that is, if they are not already affixes like ENG-
LISH -ed.

It is not always obvious what element is a clitic and what element is not, nor is it easy to say when a particular element is a
clitic and when it is not; fully aware of the difficulties, I will use
the term clitic to refer to an element that is unstressed and attached to a contiguous element;[35] reduction from a stressable,
non-attached form may or may not be synchronically evident. As
an example of a clitic, ENGLISH will has a clitic form l.

    60. I'll do it.

    Given this (admittedly sketchy) definition, let's consider evi-
dence of the claim that the members of an AUX will either be
clitics or be cliticizable. In LUISEÑO both modality elements and
tense/aspectual elements are necessarily clitics, that is, they
are unstressed and necessarily follow some other element in the
sentence; examples of LUISEÑO clitics have been given above.
Likewise, in TAGALOG modality elements are enclitics.

    61. Maglakad kaya kayo doon
         "walk MODAL you there"   (Schachter and
         'Perhaps you should walk there. '   Otanes 1972: 426)

In JACALTEC and SQUAMISH the AUX appears to encliticize to
whatever precedes it, but if nothing does, it will be proclitic to the
verb. 62. is an example from SQUAMISH of a proclitic AUX.

    62. čnua=šuk?um
         "AUX=bathe"
         'I am taking a bath. '   (Kuipers 1967:159)

In ENGLISH have, has, and had can reduce, as can the various
forms of the auxiliary verb be.

    63. I've gotten tired of playing this game.

    64. I'm gonna run away.

The potential cliticizability of the MOJAVE AUX is revealed in
a comparison with WALAPAI, a closely related YUMAN language,

---

[35]Attachment may be difficult to define, since it is probably not
necessarily phonological. Consider the interaction in ENGLISH
between the position of the particle in verb particle constructions
and whether the object is a noun or a pronoun.

where what in MOJAVE is a separate auxiliary verb has become a verb suffix.[36]

It may not be that every language will have an AUX the members of which are cliticizable; I have no doubt, however, that it is a near universal characteristic. It is not always something that grammars comment on and this fact makes testing the claim of universality difficult. Compounding the difficulty are differences in cliticization potential between types of elements. Tense is most likely to be cliticized (if it is not already an affix); aspect the next likely; and modality, the least likely of the three. For example, in ENGLISH the aspectual elements have and be are cliticizable, but not all modals have clitic forms. A final problem in the claim that one characteristic of AUX is its cliticizability is the fact that a rough distinction could be made between the two types of AUX in terms of clitic status. The $AUX_{\sim v}$ type of AUX is necessarily clitic in at least half of the languages in the sample; the first four languages mentioned above, languages with clitic AUX, all are of the $AUX_{\sim v}$ type. The AUX_v type of AUX tends to be simply cliticizable; the MOJAVE AUX_v is an auxiliary verb. (ENGLISH have and be are auxiliary verbs, as well, and have clitic forms.) Not all languages with $AUX_{\sim v}$ have a necessarily clitic AUX, of course; as noted above, not all ENGLISH modals even have clitic forms. In sum, the conditions under which (the members of) an AUX will cliticize remain to be elucidated, but the data of the six languages above, languages representative of this particular language sample, leave no doubt that one characteristic of AUX is its cliticization.

In characterizing the AUX, it is enough to say that the AUX -- or at least some of its members -- will either be clitics or be cliticizable. Unless some reason for this characteristic can be suggested, we should remain unsatisfied, however. I expect that cliticization of the AUX, and the destressing that precedes or accompanies it, is intimately connected with the fact that the set of elements which express modal or aspectual notions and the like is very small. In ENGLISH 've is obviously have.[37] And where reduction produces potential ambiguity, the context will usually make the necessary distinctions clear. I also expect that the differences in cliticization potential between the categories of tense,

---

[36]This is referred to in Munro 1975.

[37]'ve has also been reanalyzed as of, so it is obviously have only in the sense that it could not be any other of the elements which are part of the AUX.

aspect, and modality is in large part a function of the number of
distinctions made overtly in each category. These comments are
admittedly speculative, but I would be very surprised if they are
wrong in their essentials.

4. The Category AUX

4.1 I have already suggested that the category AUX is a universal category. In the preceding section, I considered three
characteristics of the AUX. But in section 2. I discussed two
types of AUX. One consists entirely of auxiliary verbs; the other
does not, although it may contain them in addition to other types of
elements. The former revolves around marking aspect; attached
to the aspectual auxiliary verb are the regular verb inflections.
The latter contains primarily modality elements, elements which
may occur in a sequence with (and usually precede) other elements
indicating, most typically, tense. The question, therefore, is
whether some overarching regularity to these two types of AUX
can be discovered.

4.2 Whether a language has one type or the other finds interesting correlations in and is in large part predictable from word
order type. All but one of the languages with exclusively the auxiliary verb type of AUX are rigid word order languages; moreover,
they are predominantly rigid SOV languages. CHINOOK is an
exception on both counts, being a VSO language with relatively free
word order; NARINJARI has rigid word order but is not an SOV
language. More importantly, none of the languages with AUX_{-v}
are rigid SOV languages; they are either languages with relatively
free word order or languages with rigid SVO or VOS/VSO word
order.

There are two obvious questions in this regard, however. First,
is the question of why such a division should exist in the first place.
It's a question for which I have, at the moment, no good answer.
The languages which have auxiliary verb types of AUX also have,
usually, an AUX which is contiguous to the verb. But this particular fact isn't enough to predict the auxiliary verb nature of the
AUX. As noted, not all auxiliary verbs are necessarily contiguous
to the verb and, more importantly, not all non-auxiliary verb types
of AUX are non-contiguous.

Second is the question of why the distinction in type should correlate with word order type and the relative freedom or rigidity
of word order, that is, what is there about word order type and

freedom or rigidity of word order that allows such a correlation.
Although there are good reasons to expect that both should be factors, the reasons don't explain the division into two types. First,
word order. In an earlier paper (Steele 1975) I argued that there
is a tension in language for elements such as those found in an
AUX between attraction to the verb and attraction to the beginning
of the sentence, i.e. either sentence initial or sentential second
position, but primarily the latter. The tension is reconcilable in
SVO or VSO languages, because both tendencies can be satisfied
simultaneously; in SOV languages, on the other hand, the two
attractions are in absolute contradiction. Thus, we would expect
that word order type has a bearing on at least the position of the
AUX. The reason that the relative freedom or rigidity of word
order should play a role in the AUX typology is less transparent.
The languages with free word order all have an obligatorily second
position AUX, with the possible exception of CHINOOK. I suspect
that the AUX acts, in such languages, as the anchor for the sentence, allowing subject, object, and verb to float with freedom.
If my suspicions are right, it is to be expected that freedom of
word order would be a factor in any consideration of the AUX.
Thus, both word order type and word order freedom are important
in considerations of the AUX, but it is not obvious why they correlate with the type distinction for AUX.

4.3 AUX_V expresses primarily aspect; tense is attached to the
aspectual auxiliary verb. $AUX_{\sim V}$ expresses modality primarily;
tense (and less often aspect) may also be expressed in the AUX as
well. While it is not possible to subsume aspect and modality in
some super-category, it is possible to refine the statement of $AUX_{\sim V}$.
By so doing, the notional choices for an AUX are much clearer
and there is a much more obvious notional similarity between the
two types.

Although modal elements and tense elements can cooccur in
$AUX_{\sim V}$ (see 4., an example from LUISEÑO), there is good reason
to argue that the categories of modality and tense are disjunctive.
In those languages with modality and an element which indicates
primarily tense in a sequence, the tense elements in such a sequence don't indicate tense notions. Rather they modify the modal
notions -- and thus the reality ascribed to the situation described
in the sentence -- along a realis/irrealis parameter. Consider
ENGLISH, first, in this light. The analyses of the ENGLISH AUX
presented in Section 1 have, regardless of other disagreements,
argued that tense is obligatorily present; therefore the relationship
between the modals may and might, for example, is the difference

between present form and past form. Although <u>might</u> may be used
as the past tense of <u>may</u> in certain, very restricted, instances --
reporting indirect discourse, for one:

65. I may come.
66. Nancy said she might come.

<u>may</u> and <u>might</u> are usually related not by tense but rather by the
degree of reality which is attributed to the situation they describe.

67. I may come.
68. I might come.

That is, the additions of the past tense element <u>-ed</u> reduces the
reality which is ascribed to the situation described in the sentence.
The other languages which allow the forms indicating tense and
the forms indicating modality to cooccur operate in roughly the
same fashion. In LUISEÑO, modal clitics are almost always followed by tense/aspect clitics, but the tense/aspect clitics no longer
agree with the tense of the verb. Rather they modify the modal
notion. 41. above illustrated <u>po</u>, the future clitic; 42. above illustrated <u>il</u>, the past clitic. In the first sentence below, <u>po</u> occurs
with a verb marked for past -- and a modal clitic; in the second
sentence <u>il</u> occurs with a verb marked for future -- and the same
modal clitic.

69. wunaal=xu=po hunwuti ?ari-k
    "she=MODAL=FUTURE bear: object kick-PAST"
    'Apparently she used to kick the bear. '   (Steele, n. d.)

70. noo=n toowq xwaan mariya weh=ś=il wa?aanilax-kutum
    "I-aux see   John   Mary both=MODAL=PAST carry-GONNA"
    'I see that John and Mary are gonna carry it. ' (Steele, n. d.)

If modality and tense are disjunctive categories in the languages
with AUX_V then AUX_V and $AUX_{\sim V}$ no longer look particularly different. Aspect can occur in both; tense, although disjunctive with
modality in one, is essential to either. That is, including only the
notional categories of tense, aspect and modality and ignoring the
linear order of these, AUX_V looks like:

Aspect   Tense

and $AUX_{\sim V}$ looks like:

(Aspect) $\left\{ \begin{array}{l} \text{Modal} \\ \text{Tense} \end{array} \right\}$

If we subsume tense and modality in some category -- call it Super
Tense -- then the two collapse to:

Super Tense (Aspect)

Whether this is realized as the former or the latter above will
depend on language type, since we have seen that the type of AUX
is basically predictable from the word order of the language.

4.4   I have argued, then, that there is indeed an overarching
regularity to the differences between the two types of AUX. The
differences within any one type came down to language particular
choices within the general schema suggested. I take these to be
the idiosyncracies of a language particular grammar.

5. Conclusion

5.1   I began this paper with a definition of AUX. The question
was whether, using that definition, any cross-linguistic generalizations would be revealed. The answer is an unqualified yes. We
can posit AUX as a universal category. We know that the AUX
will have certain characteristics. It will occur in one of three
sentential positions, primarily sentential second position; it will
almost always include subject agreement; it will contain either
clitics or elements which are cliticizable. We know that there are
two types of AUX, one of which is based on aspectual auxiliary
verbs and the other of which is based on modal elements. We know
that which type a language exhibits is dependent on certain other
aspects of the language, primarily basic word order type and the
relative freedom or rigidity of word order.

Not only are we able to make these generalizations, the investigation of this paper has made abundantly clear that the original
analysis of ENGLISH AUX was an important insight into language
structure generally. I began with a restricted definition of AUX;
I mentioned that other types of elements may very well occur with
tense, aspect, modality -- and subject agreement -- although there
may be distinctions in at least some languages between these other
types and the notional categories used as definitional. Therefore,
an exhaustive definition of AUX is impossible in this paper. But
we can at least say that the category I called Super Tense is basic
to all AUX.[38] A language may build on that base, to some extent
idiosyncratically, but the base is well-founded.

---

[38] It is worth noting that in the analyses of the ENGLISH AUX
tense is the only obligatory category.

5.2   The conclusions above lead to a number of restrictions on
what is a possible language.

    a. No language of AUX_V type which has subject agreement will
    not include it in the AUX.

    b. No language of AUX_V type will exist in which the AUX does
    not take what is usually verbal inflection.

    c. No language with free word order will have a clause final
    AUX

    d. No language with SVO or VSO basic word order will have
    a clause final AUX.

    e. No language will exist where AUX does not potentially
    include tense; that is, in a sentence with tense and an AUX,
    tense will always be part of the AUX.

5.3   Although the category AUX has been established and a
number of claims have been made about the characteristic of a
language, a few questions do remain, one of which is very important.

That AUX_V includes aspect and $AUX_{\tilde{V}}$ primarily modality points
to a basic difference in syntactic form between the expressions of
aspect and modality; why there should be such a difference is a
question to which I, at the moment, can offer no response.[39] More
important is the issue raised by the existence of languages like
SOUTHEASTERN POMO. To call AUX a universal category is
not to argue that every language will choose it. But the overwhelming majority of languages in this particular language sample
do; SOUTHEASTERN POMO is the one exception. It would obviously be much nicer to be able to claim that every language has
an AUX, and I suspect that this is indeed the correct claim. The
question, then, is whether my data on SOUTHEASTERN POMO is
simply incomplete. Sally McLendon informs me (personal

---

    39 In ENGLISH, of course, both aspectual and modality elements
share certain syntactic properties, such as inversion in questions
and the like. I expect these are properties of the ENGLISH AUX
itself and the existence of such properties is, thus, not an argument against this basic cross-linguistic distinction.

communication) that in EASTERN POMO there is a construction
which I would consider of AUX_V type. If SOUTHEASTERN POMO
isn't like EASTERN POMO, we can only argue that AUX is a category available to language, but not that it is necessarily chosen.
In this case, we need to know what distinguishes between those
languages that have an AUX and the very small number that don't.

The really vital question is why such a unit as an AUX should
exist at all. The obvious answer is that languages cluster all the
grammatical information about the sentence; the fact that negatives,
question particles, and like elements often occur in the same position as the AUX is simply another instance of the same tendency.
This answer may be all that we can expect at the moment, but it
simply pushes the question back one step. We must then ask why
all grammatical information should cluster.

The importance of these questions cannot be discounted. But
the fact that I close this paper with unanswered questions doesn't
detract from the major point. The cross-linguistic reality of the
category AUX has been established and (certain of) its essential
properties have been elucidated.

BIBLIOGRAPHY

Akmajian, Adrian and Thomas Wasow. 1975. The constituent
structure of VP and AUX and the position of the verb BE.
Linguistic Analysis I. 205-46.

Anderson, Arthur J.O. (trans.) 1973. Rules of the Aztec language.
(a modified version of Francis Xavier Clavigero's Reglas de la
lengua mexicana). Salt Lake City: University of Utah Press.

Ariste, Paul. 1968. A grammar of the Votic language. Indiana
University Publications, Uralic and Altaic Series Volume 68.
Bloomington: Indiana University Press.

Bright, William. 1957. The Karok language. University of California Publications in Linguistics 13. Berkeley and Los Angeles:
University of California Press.

Chafe, Wallace. 1970. Meaning and the structure of language.
Chicago and London: The University of Chicago Press.

Chomsky, Noam. 1965. Aspects of the theory of syntax. Cambridge: M.I.T. Press.

_____. 1957. Syntactic structures. The Hague: Mouton.

Craig, Colette. 1975. Jacaltec syntax: a study of complex sentences. Doctoral dissertation, Harvard University.

Dibble, Charles E. and Arthur J.O. Anderson. 1969. Florentine codex, Book 6, rhetoric and moral philosophy. Translation of Fray Bernardino de Sahagun, General history of the things of New Spain. Monographs of the School of American Research, No. 14, Part 2. Santa Fe, New Mexico: School of American Research and University of Utah.

Emonds, Joseph. 1969. Root and structure preserving transformations. Doctoral dissertation, M.I.T.

Gee, James Paul. 1975. Perception, intentionality, and naked infinitives: a study in linguistics and philosophy. Doctoral dissertation, Stanford University.

Hale, Kenneth. 1973. Subject marking in Walbiri. A Festschrift for Morris Halle, ed. by Stephen Anderson and Paul Kiparsky, 308-44. Cambridge: M.I.T. Press.

Hyman, Larry M. and Danil J. Magaji. 1970. Essentials of Gwari grammar. Institute of African Studies, University of Ibadan, Occasional Publications no. 27. Nigeria: Ibadan University Press.

Jackendoff, Ray. 1972. Semantic representation in generative grammar. Cambridge: M.I.T. Press.

Jacobs, Melville. 1931. Northern Sahaptin grammar. University of Washington Publications in Anthropology, Volume 4, 87-291.

Jespersen, Otto. 1940. A modern English grammar on historical principles, Part V. Copenhagen: Ejnar Munksgaard.

Kuipers, Aert H. 1967. The Squamish language. Janua linguarum, series practica LXXIII. The Hague: Mouton.

Kuno, Susumu. 1973. The structure of the Japanese language. Cambridge: M.I.T. Press.

McCawley, James. 1969. English as a VSO language. Language 45. 286-99.

Mirikitani, Leatrice. 1972. Kapampangan syntax. Oceanic Linguistics Special Publication 10. Honolulu: University of Hawaii Press.

Moshinsky, Julius Barry. 1970. Southeastern Pomo grammar. Doctoral dissertation, U.C. Berkeley.

Oates, W. and L. Oates. 1968. Kapau pedagogical grammar. Pacific Linguistics, Series C, No. 10. Canberra: Australian National University.

Munro, Pamela. 1975. Subject copying, auxiliarization, and predicate raising: the Mojave evidence. MS.

_____. 1974. Topics in Mojave syntax. Doctoral dissertation, U.C. San Diego.

Newman, Paul. 1970. A grammar of Tera. University of California Publications in Linguistics 57. Berkeley and Los Angeles: University of California Press.

Ross, John R. 1969. Auxiliaries as main verbs. Studies in Philosophical Linguistics, Series 1. Great Expectations Publications.

Schachter, Paul and Fe T. Otanes. 1972. Tagalog reference grammar. Berkeley and Los Angeles: University of California Press.

Silverstein, Michael. 1972. Chinook jargon I. Language 48. 378-406.

Steele, Susan. n.d. Luiseño field notes.

_____. 1975. On some factors that affect and effect word order. Word order and word order change, ed. by Charles Li, 199-268. Austin: University of Texas Press.

_____. 1976. The auxiliary in Uto-Aztecan: comparison and reconstruction. MS.

Yallop, Colin. 1975. The Narinjari language 1864-1964. Narinjari: an outline of the language studies by George Taplin with Taplin's notes and comparative table. Oceanic Linguistics Monograph no. 17, Part 1, 1-109. University of Sydney.

How Does a Language
Acquire Gender Markers?

JOSEPH H. GREENBERG

ABSTRACT

The bulk of this paper is devoted to outlining a process by which, in a number of languages, a definite article which agrees in gender with the noun passes through a stage in which it combines the uses of a definite and indefinite article and finally becomes a gender marker on the noun. It is also shown that this process can occur even when the definite article does not agree in gender, in which case it ends up as a sign of mere nominality. The rôle of the demonstrative from which the definite article usually arises in generating agreement phenomena is also discussed. The problem of the origin of gender is then briefly reconsidered in the light of the evidence adduced in the body of the paper.

48   Joseph H. Greenberg

CONTENTS

1. Introduction

By a noun gender system will be meant a system in which the noun stems of a language are divided into a set of genders, this distinction being based on the fact that the choice of a noun belonging to a particular gender determines the choice among a set of alternative "agreeing" forms in one or more other classes of morphemes or words, e.g.: articles, demonstratives, adjectives, unbound anaphoric pronouns, pronoun incorporated in a verb complex, etc. Such systems are often called noun class systems. However, it is not usual to apply this term when sex is among the bases of classification. Structurally, such systems do not differ in any basic way from those in which sex does not figure. 'Gender' ultimately comes from LATIN genus which simply means "kind," and there is ample precedent for applying the term gender to all such systems. When sex figures among the bases of classification, we will refer to sex gender. There is a further advantage in using the term gender system rather than noun class system. There are at least two other systems of noun classification than gender systems numeral classifier systems and possessive classifier systems. We are therefore free to use noun class system as the superordinate term which includes all systems of this type.

The present study is based on a broad but by no means exhaustive sample of languages with noun gender systems. The approach is largely in terms of diachronic process. Our ultimate aim is to establish how such systems arise, their typical course of development, and the factors involved in their ultimate extinction. While such an ambitious goal is clearly not attained here, it is hoped that this study at least represents significant progress in this direction. The content of this paper falls into four main sections. The first of these (Sec. 2) poses certain basic questions relevant to the study of nominal gender systems including some fundamental definitional ones. The second one (Sec. 3) which constitutes the main body of the paper develops a processual theory as to how, in languages which already have gender systems, the nouns come to acquire gender markers, whether they were present at an earlier period or not. If the former is the case, we have a "renewal" of old markers which in some cases have been weakened by phonetic attrition. The existence of two historical layers of markers is in such cases usually evident from the existence of double markers. If, however, such did not exist previously, we have a pristine case. Many gender systems, of course, do not have overt markers on the noun, and genders are distinguished only by agreeing forms outside of the noun. For reasons of space the remaining topics are discussed

much more briefly, details being reserved for future treatment.
The third section (Sec. 4) deals with the spread of syntactic agreement which is coincident with the process by which the nouns receive
overt marking, but which also develops in its absence. The final
section (Sec. 5) is devoted to some speculations regarding the rise
of gender and the relations of the conclusions of the present study
to previous theorizing concerning gender origins. The important
topic of the classificational system as such in relation to its semantic
bases is only touched on incidentally and is also reserved for future
treatment.

2. Types of Noun Classification

Our preliminary definition of a noun gender system in the initial
paragraph is clearly in need of further specification. It will be
repeated here for convenience. By a noun gender system will be
meant a system in which the noun stems of a language are divided
into a set of genders, the distinction being based on the fact that the
choice of a noun belonging to a particular gender determines the
choice among a set of alternative "agreeing" forms in one or more
other classes of morphemes or words, e.g. articles, demonstratives, adjectives, unbound anaphoric pronouns, pronouns incorporated in a verb complex, etc.

A noun gender system may be regarded, then, as involving the
intersection of two basic factors, classification and agreement, the
two being in a relation of mutual determination, the gender being
defined by the agreements and the agreements being determined by
the genders. The mutual determination here defined as constitutive
of gender systems is not, however, a logical requirement. Agreement is possible without classification. For example, in HUNGARIAN
ebben a kertben 'in this garden' there is agreement in case between
eb-ben 'this and kert-ben 'garden,' both being in the locative. Yet
HUNGARIAN is not a gender language, since differences in agreement
patterns do not divide the noun stems of the language into classes.
In HEBREW yeled tov 'good boy,' versus hayyeled hattov 'the good
boy,' there is agreement in definiteness between yeled 'boy' and tov
'good,' but although HEBREW does have sex gender, it is not shown
in this construction because all noun bases behave similarly in regard
to it. It would be useful, then, to distinguish the wider notion of concord from agreement, the latter being a subtype in which the choice
of alternative concord elements depends on the class to which the
stem of the governing item belongs, whether marked by an affix or
not.

Noun classification can exist without concord just as concord can exist without noun classes, though whether, synchronically viewed, such a classification can be considered grammatically significant is another question. Of course any number of classifications of nouns, as of any other word class, can be carried out, which are syntactically irrelevant, though some may be relevant from some other point of view, e.g. the declensional classes of LATIN. Others might be perfectly arbitrary, e.g. a classification of bases into those with at least one stop consonant. The following, however, turns out to be a kind of classification which, while it does not involve agreement, may be of potential diachronic relevance to the origin of noun classes. In MALAY and certain other languages there is widespread and compulsory use of certain superordinate terms in lexicalized phrases parallel in formation to ENGLISH 'apple tree.' Thus, in MALAY one cannot say merely Djawi for 'Java' but rather tanah Djawi where tanah means 'land' and occurs as an independent word, and so for a number of other superordinates. One might say that this constitutes a classification in which each superordinate term defines a class and in which those nouns which do not have such a superordinate term constitute an additional class with a zero marker. In JAVANESE this type of classification has absolutely no syntactic function, and it might therefore be considered far-fetched to consider it grammatically relevant.

However, just such a system in principle exists in the Daly River subgroup of general AUSTRALIAN, spoken in the northwest of the continent. In some of these languages it seems to have absolutely no syntactic function. Yet, for example, in Tryon's grammar of MARANUNGKU, a language of this group, this type of system is called a noun class system (Tryon 1970). A noun must belong to one of four classes. The first consists of nouns preceded by awa, it itself a noun meaning 'meat' which can occur independently. These nouns all designate edible animals or insects, e.g. awa pat-pat 'grasshopper.' Similarly, class two consists of nouns always preceded by yili 'stick' and comprising tools, weapons and wooden implements, while class three nouns are preceded by miya 'vegetable food' and precedes nouns indicating kinds of vegetable foods. The fourth class which has a zero marker and is highly heterogeneous is noted as being by far the largest. As far as can be seen from Tryon's account, this classification has no syntactic relevance. However, in other subgroups of the Daly River group, there are languages which have a system of classification clearly related to that of MARANUNGKU in which it forms the basis of agreement

phenomena. For example, in MARENGAR (Tryon 1974: 122) the
same four classes are found, but we find, for example, agreement
with adjectives. Thus, corresponding to class two in MARANUNGKU
are words prefixed by yeri 'stick' = MARANUNGKU yili. With the
adjective -kati 'good' we have yeri-kunt^yikin^y yeri-kati 'good boom-
erang.' With nouns in the large class with a zero marker we find,
for example, wat^yan kati 'dog' in which neither item has a class
marker.

In this instance, for reasons discussed at the end of Sec. 3.5,
I believe we have to do with a nascent system. At the other end of
the development, diachronically, are languages like LOBI in the
VOLTAIC subgroup of NIGER-CONGO which has paired singular
and plural suffix sets, historically related to those of VOLTAIC
languages with functioning systems, but no longer having syntactic
relevance. Viewed synchronically, LOBI simply seems to have a
very elaborate system of plural formation by affix replacements,
falling into a number of different patterns.

Viewed synchronically, then, and no doubt tautologically, a noun
classification system, if it is syntactically relevant, involves some
form of agreement. But what of numeral classifier systems? These
classify nouns in accordance with the classifier they take, and the
classification is clearly a syntactically relevant one. A choice of
a particular noun determines the choice of the classifier. There
are, however, some differences between such systems and those
usually called gender systems. One important difference is that in
a full-fledged numeral classifier language, there are considerable
number of nouns which are non-countables and do not take classifiers,
whereas in gender languages, literally every noun has a gender. Secondly, in numeral classifier languages, with a few exceptions, agreement is confined to the construction with quantifiers. In spite of
these differences and others that will be mentioned later, it will be
shown in the final section that there is a possible diachronic connection between numeral classifier and gender systems. What is said
here about numeral classifier systems applies mutatis mutandis to
possessive systems, such as those found in some OCEANIC and
AMERIND languages. Agreement is confined to the possessive
construction. Corresponding to non-countables in a classifier language are inalienably possessed nouns which are not subject to classification.

One further aspect of the definition of gender system as stated
here is in need of further elucidation. What is meant by the noun
stem of a language being divided into a set of genders? Ideally,

a classification is supposed to be exhaustive and to divide the universe under consideration into mutually disjoint sets. The latter
requirement is probably not fulfilled in any of the languages which
are usually considered to have gender systems. To begin with,
there are instances of individual stems which belong to more than
one class, e.g. SPANISH hij-o 'son,' hij-a 'daughter. This is what
is traditionally called 'motion,' and insofar as there is a systematic
semantic relationship, it becomes one of the objective bases for
assigning meaning to classes. More drastically, two inflectionally
different classes may share all of their stems. This is frequently
the case with paired singular and plural classes. Such classes may
be said to be in equipollent relationship, and in a sense, to be considered a superclass. Specialists in BANTU, for example, have
differed as to whether in such pairs they are dealing with one class
or two. Since viewed as a superclass it does have a distinct membership, we may say that this does not detract from the overall
system in classifying the noun stems.

Sometimes, however, the relationship between two inflectionally
different classes is not equipollent. This is often true for diminutive, augmentative and piace gender as found, for example, in many
BANTU languages. Most, if not all, stems found in such classes
are also found in others. There may be a productive rule by which
a member of any other class becomes a number of this class by
affix replacement or even by addition. In these cases we may say
that we are dealing with a derivative gender. Where, as is sometimes the case, a gender does not have a single stem which is unique,
it will be called a minor gender. An example is the neuter gender
in NAMA HOTTENTOT. In view of these considerations, we will
mean by a gender classification one in which there are at least two
classes, including in the term 'class' also 'superclass,' as mentioned above, but excluding minor genders in our count.

3. Overt and Covert Systems

In defining agreement, nothing was said about the existence of
a gender marker on the noun itself, merely that membership in a
particular gender determined selection in agreeing forms. However,
in such paradigm cases as BANTU, the noun itself has an overt class
marker as, for example, in the SWAHILI phrase ki-ti ki-nene hi-ki
'stool large this,' and this is also generally true in INDO-EUROPEAN.
Sapir mentions the "relentless rhythm" of LATIN illōrum saevōrum
vīrōrum 'of those savage men.' Where a marker exists in the noun
itself, the system will be called overt; where it is not found, the
system will be called covert. Viewed once more diachronically,

there are two types of covert systems, those in which overt expression formerly existed, e.g. FRENCH, as compared to ITALIAN,
and those in which, as far as can be seen, it never existed. There
are many examples of this, for instance, the NORTHERN CAUCA-
SIAN languages (except the northwestern group which has no gender).[1]

This is one more point of difference between gender systems and
other systems of noun classification. In numeral classifier systems
the classifier goes syntactically and is sometimes fused with the
numeral and never seems to occur additionally with the noun itself.
Similarly, in possessive systems the classifiers go with personal
possessive affixes and do not appear on the noun. They thus fail to
give rise to phenomena such as the "alliterative concord" of BANTU
languages.

3.1 From covert to overt gender: Niger-Congo languages with simultaneous prefix and suffix marking

The NIGER-CONGO languages have an inherited system of noun
genders involving the existence of overt class markers on the noun.
In some of the major subgroups, these are generally prefixed to the
noun (as in the well known instance of BANTU), but in other branches
they are normally suffixed. The markers themselves, whether prefixed or suffixed, exhibit clear relationship in phonetic form and
semantic function. The WEST-ATLANTIC, KWA and BENUE-
CONGO branches are basically prefixing, while the VOLTAIC and
ADAMAWA-EASTERN branches are suffixing. The MANDE branch,
which is the most divergent genetically, shows no clear traces of
this system. An example of prefixing is SWAHILI ki-ti, pl. vi-ti
'chair' and suffixing, MOSSI (VOLTAIC) bi-ga, pl. bi-se 'child.'
Alongside of this, however, there are a few languages in each major
branch except, of course, MANDE which have prefixes and suffixes
simultaneously. An example is AKASELE (VOLTAIC) ke-ji-ke/
n-ji-m (< *m-ji-m) 'knife.' How is this diversity to be explained?
One of the suggestions has been that languages with both prefixes
and suffixes represent the original state of affairs and that subsequently some languages lost their suffixes and some their prefixes
(e.g. Welmers 1973: 209). However, a closer look at languages
with double affixing tells a quite different story.

We will start with GURMA, a VOLTAIC language which was often
cited in the literature as a typical example of a language with prefixes

---

[1]However, in most CAUCASIAN languages there are a few words
which have class markers. This matter is discussed later at the
end of Sec. 3.5.

and suffixes. However, the detailed grammar of Chantoux, Gontier and Prost (1968) shows that whereas the suffixes are a normal part of the noun, the prefixes are often omitted. When a prefix is present, it corresponds fairly closely to the definite article in languages like ENGLISH and FRENCH, e.g. niti-ba 'men,' ba niti-ba 'the men.' In fact the authors of this grammar write the "prefixes" as separate words. Furthermore, as we shall see, there can be no reasonable doubt that the preposed article is recent and the suffix old.

GURMA gives its name to the whole subgroup of VOLTAIC languages of which it is a member. An examination of the other languages of the subgroup shows that in regard to what corresponds historically to the preposed article of GURMA, they fall into a number of typologically distinct groups. To begin with, there is MOBA which shows no prefixes at all. It is thus similar to the great mass of VOLTAIC languages which have class suffixes only. There is GURMA itself in which, as we have seen, the preposed class marker functions as a definite article. Another language, GANGAM, has a preposed marker like GURMA, but unlike GURMA, it is not merely a definite article. It combines, roughly speaking, the uses of the ENGLISH indefinite article when it is [+specific], that is, it involves an existence assumption and can in general be replaced by 'a certain,' e.g. 'I am looking for a certain notebook.' Statistically, it occurs with the noun in the vast majority of its textual occurrences. However, there are a minority of constructions, especially generic ones, e.g. as a verb object in negative sentences, in which it does not occur. I shall call this type of "article" a non-generic article. However, as will be indicated in later discussion, by no means all instances of absence of this article involve genericness, and the name is not an entirely appropriate one. Articles of this kind are found in a number of languages in various parts of the world and, as it appears, relatively little attention has been paid to this phenomenon.

Finally, within the GURMA group are the AKASELE and TOBOTE-BASARI languages in which there are no contrasts between prefixed and non-prefixed forms. In general, with a few exceptions to be discussed, all nouns have both prefixes and suffixes, and the pair functions basically in the way as prefixes or suffixes by themselves in the NIGER-CONGO languages.

We thus have, within the same subgroup, four stages of a process leading ultimately to the development of a new set of prefixed class markers reinforcing the previously existing suffixes. These stages are: 1) no marker, 2) definite article, 3) non-generic article, 4) class prefix.

That this is the order of development is shown in a number of ways. To begin with, the suffixes are representative of a set found through the entire VOLTAIC subgroup and reconstructible for PROTO-VOLTAIC. They are often irregular phonetically and sometimes reduced to zero or tonal alternations. The prefixes, in contrast, are transparent and in fact identical with the verb subject pronouns which agree with the noun in class. Moreover, that a functional prefix detaches itself from a noun, gradually becomes a definite article, and then disappears is like running the historical camera backwards. Manessy, well-known as a VOLTAIC specialist, in an article discussing the phenomenon of double affixes in VOL-TAIC languages, comes to the following conclusion. "Thus Tamãri and Ngangam appear to mark an intermediate stage in the development of a process quite comparable to that by which the Latin demonstrative became the French article, a process whose commencement can be discovered in Gurma and of which Akasele illustrates the highest stage of development" (Manessy 1965: 175).

Manessy here mentions, in addition to NGANGAM, TAMÃRI as illustrating the same stage of a non-generic article. However, in subsequent publications he correctly assigned TAMÃRI to a different genetic subgroup of VOLTAIC.

But if suffixes can be renewed by prefixes, why cannot prefixes be renewed by suffixes? In fact this process is well attested in the languages of the WEST ATLANTIC subgroup of NIGER-CONGO which are, as noted earlier, basically prefixing. The definite article stage is represented by DYOLA which has, in addition to the usual WEST ATLANTIC prefix system, a suffixed article which duplicates the prefix, e.g. <u>fu-nak</u> 'day,' <u>fu-nak-af</u> 'the day' (Sapir 1965). In certain other WEST ATLANTIC languages the original prefixes have been reduced to initial consonant alternations and, in the case of WOLOF, even these have been reduced to the status of archaic survivals in a few words. The system has been renewed, however, by suffixed class markers which can in certain constructions still be separated from the noun and which function as a definite article. SERER-NON illustrates the stage of the non-generic article. FULA which still has functional initial consonant alternations illustrates the last stage. The class suffixes have become markers on virtually all nouns, and no contrasts exist between constructions with and without the suffix. WOLOF, SERER-NON and FULA are the three members of one subgroup of northern WEST ATLANTIC.

Similarly, in the KWA group which is prefixing, there are languages like KEBU and AVATIME in which suffixes are found. In the case of AVATIME once more they function like the definite article. In KEBU we have a language in which nouns are normally both prefixed and suffixed and in which, on internal evidence, it appears that the suffixes are more recent, though the evidence is perhaps not decisive.

Among BENUE-CONGO languages, TIV which is closely related to BANTU has both prefixes and suffixes. The suffixes are clearly recent. The suffixes essentially exhibit an advanced stage of the non-generic article. Nouns can appear without the suffix mainly in one construction, the locative. As we should see from a more detailed examination of the non-generic article, this is a typical construction in which the form without the article tends to survive.

But if suffixes can be renewed by prefixes (e.g. GURMA) and prefixes can be renewed by suffixes (e.g. DYOLA), why cannot prefixes be renewed by additional prefixes or suffixes by suffixes? Regarding the former of these possibilities, there are examples in NIGER-CONGO, but I do not know of any instances of the latter.

In almost all dialects of TEMNE, a language of the Southern branch of WEST ATLANTIC (the other languages already mentioned belong to the Northern branch), the prefixed class marker has an additional marker, usually the same as the vowel of the prefix which functions as a definite article. Wilson (1961:13) notes that in one dialect, that of KONIKE, "the nouns in all contexts are in what looks like the definite form." This dialect, then, has probably entered into the final stage in which the former definite article has become part of the class marker on the noun.

The most important example of prefixes being renewed by prefixes is that of the BANTU languages, for so, I believe, the well-known pre-prefix vowel found in many BANTU languages should be interpreted.

In the majority of instances the pre-prefix functions as a typical non-generic article and indeed provides the most abundant evidence we have anywhere of the characteristics of this stage. Examples include LUGANDA, KIRUNDI, BEMBA, KONDE, LAMBA, ZULU, XHOSA and SOUTHERN KIKONGO. Thus far I have noted only one example of a BANTU language with a pre-prefix which functions as a definite article, namely DZAMBA. The south-western group of

BANTU including such languages as HERERO, OVAMBO and OCHIN-
DONGA illustrates the last stage in which the pre-prefixes have
become part of the class marker on nouns in general.[2]

3.2 The development of class markers outside of Niger-Congo

A priori, there is no reason to expect the process by which a
definite article becomes a marker on the noun to be confined to
NIGER-CONGO languages. Secondly, there is no reason why it
should only occur in gender systems which do not include sex as
a semantic basis for gender. Thirdly, there is evidently no necessity for the process to be one of renewal confined to languages which
already have overt markers, as is true with NIGER-CONGO languages outside of the MENDE group. Fourthly, as we shall see,
there is no reason even for this process to be confined to languages
with gender classification at all.

All of these possibilities can be illustrated from languages in
Africa. The languages of the EASTERN NILOTIC subbranch of
the NILOTIC languages, which in turn belong to the EASTERN SU-
DANIC substock within CHARI-NILE, the major branch of NILO-
SAHARAN, all have sex gender. These languages fall into two
subgroups, one consisting of BARI and other languages very
closely related to it. The other consists of a set of internally
more divergent languages including MAASAI, LOTUKO and TESO.
BARI has a sex gender classification without any marker on the
noun or a definite article. The gender elements appear in certain
constructions, e.g. in the demonstratives, pronominal possessives
and relatives. In the other group of languages, there are genetically related prefix markers for sex gender (TESO, in addition,
has a neuter) which are typical non-generic articles. As against
the NIGER-CONGO case, these are from all evidently pristine
markers, and none of the languages has reached the stage at which
the prefix has become a mere classificatory mark on the noun.

A further possibility is exemplified by the SOUTHERN NILOTIC
(KALENJIN) languages which constitute another subbranch of
NILOTIC. The NANDI-KIPSIGIS and POKOT (SUK) groups have
genetically cognate suffixes for singular and plural, without gender
classification. In POKOT these function like a definite article,
while in NANDI-KIPSIGIS they are in the stage of the non-generic
article.

---

[2]However, these languages do have the unarticulated form for
the vocative of common nouns so that, strictly speaking, they are
still in the stage of the non-generic article, albeit an advanced stage.

Another example of a pristine marker, in this instance without connotations of either gender or number, is provided by the South-western MANDE languages. We have here a suffixed -i which func-tions as an ordinary definite article in KPELLE, but is a non-generic article in the remaining languages: MENDE, LOKO, GBANDI and LOMA.

As a final African example, we may cite a main subgroup of lan-guages of the Central group of Southern KHOISAN languages including here the various dialects of HOTTENTOT and the closely related languages of the Naron Bushman. These languages have a system of three genders, masculine, feminine and neuter. They all, with the possible exceptions to be noted, have a pristine non-generic suffixed article as gender-number markers. However, the extinct HOTTENTOT dialects of Griqualand East and West are known from word lists in which the gender-number suffixes do not occur. In languages with the non-generic article, it is usually employed in citation forms. Hence, in these dialects the affixes were probably either definite articles or not used at all (cf. Planert 1905).

The phenomenon under discussion is not confined to Africa, al-though it seems to be more frequently encountered there than in any other major region. I will not, here, cite either the numerous cases of languages with definite articles of the usual sort or languages with gender classification in which the noun has an overt marker, but rather those instances in which the tell-tale and hitherto neg-lected stage of the non-generic article is known to occur. A par-ticularly interesting case is ARAMAIC which, in a recorded history of almost 3000 years, has gone through the three stages mentioned here. An -ā̱ (< *hā̱) suffixed to nouns in the masculine and feminine, singular and plural, which were already provided with sex/number markers based on the inherited SEMITIC system, functions as a definite article in the earliest inscriptional language (ninth century B.C.) and as late as the ARAMAIC portions of Daniel and Nehemiah (generally dated second century B.C.). From the early Christian era onward, we have to reckon with two dialect groups, Western and Eastern, in which the former is more conservative in this mat-ter. The Eastern literary dialects (e.g. SYRIAC, BABYLONIAN TALMUDIC) have a non-generic article while the Western literary dialects still have a definite article (Christian Palestinian SYRIAC, TARGUM ONQELOS, etc.). The contemporary dialects of ARAMAIC still are distinct in this respect, but each group has advanced one further stage. WEST ARAMAIC now has a non-generic article while in EASTERN ARAMAIC, it is a general noun marker. One Eastern dialect, that of ṬŪR-ABDĪN, has developed a new prefixed article, this time distinguished for gender and number, thus renewing the process which started in prehistoric times at least 3000 years earlier.

KHASI, an AUSTROASIATIC language of Assam, has a three gender system: masculine, feminine and neuter with a prefixed non-generic article.

A number of AUSTRONESIAN languages on New Britain and New Ireland possess non-generic articles. These include MENGEN (New Britain) with a suffixed article (Müller 1907) and TOLAI (New Britain), and the only dialectically differing LABEL (New Ireland) with a prefixed article (Franklin 1962 and Peekel 1929).

Native Australia offers interesting examples. DYIRBAL in northeastern Australia, a member of the PAMA-NYUNGAN group which comprises most of the continent, has a non-generic article at an advanced stage associated with a classification of nouns into four genders: masculine, feminine and two inanimate genders, with animals divided between the masculine and feminine (Dixon 1972). In the northwest of the continent there is a concentration of languages belonging to various other subgroups than PAMA-NYUN-GAN, most of which have gender classification. An interesting case is that of WORORA and the closely related UNGARINYIN. Both languages have a system of four genders much like that of DYIRBAL, with class markers that are clearly related to each other historically and more remotely to those of DYIRBAL. WORORA, however, has suffixed class markers on a large proportion of its nouns which have reached the final stage of complete amalgamation and universal use while these are lacking altogether, as far as can be made out from the rather sparse information on UNGARINYIN (Love, n.d.).

I do not know of any certain instances of the non-generic article in AMERIND languages, except possibly GOAJIRO, an ARAWAKAN language as described by Holmer (1949). This is a sex gender language in which gender marking has been renewed through a set of suffixed non-generic articles. The development, if reliably reported, must have been very rapid, since Celedón less than a century previously, although describing GOAJIRO as a sex gender language, gives no indication of the existence of the specific markers cited by Holmer. There are a number of AMERIND languages with sex gender with markers on the nouns, which indicate that they should have gone through the sequence of stages postulated here, e.g. CHI-NOOK, a PENUTIAN language, and CHIQUITA, a MACRO-GE language of Bolivia.

There are also some instances of what appears to be the last
stages of a non-generic non-classifying article, e.g. the -s of
KLAMATH and other PLATEAU PENUTIAN languages of Oregon,
which appears on most nouns and in most constructions. The "absolutive" of UTO-AZTECAN and other AMERIND languages possibly also belongs here. This requires further investigation.

The foregoing review is far from exhaustive. There are doubtless
other examples of languages in the stage of the non-generic article
or instances of closely related languages which exhibit different
stages of the development just outlined.

3.3 The cycle of the definite article: the initial stage

In the foregoing sections three stages in the process by which a
definite article ultimately may become a noun marker were briefly
indicated. It remains to consider this process in greater detail.
The three stages were: 1) definite article, 2) non-generic article,
3) noun marker. It will be convenient in subsequent discussions to
call these Stage I, Stage II, and Stage III articles, respectively.

Each of these stages is initiated by a significant change by means
of which it can be defined. However, there are instances of transitional phenomena such that certain languages are on the borderline
between two stages. In some cases it is possible to see that a language is well advanced within a particular stage, while in other
instances it is clear that it has only entered the stage recently.
Hence, the whole development is to be viewed as a single continuous process marked by certain decisive turning points.

Since the most common origin of the definite article is the demonstrative, a development of which there are numerous and well-attested
examples, we might speak of the demonstrative as stage zero. The
historical development of definite article has been studied in a number of instances in considerable detail. It develops from a purely
deictic element which has come to identify an element as previously
mentioned in discourse. Such a use is often an additional function
of an element which is also a pure deictic, but sometimes there is
a particular demonstrative which has assumed this as its basic
function. The source deictic is most often one which points to location near the third persons rather than the first or second person,
e.g. LATIN ille. The point at which a discourse deictic becomes
a definite article is where it becomes compulsory and has spread
to the point at which it means "identified" in general, thus including
typically things known from context, general knowledge, or as with

'the sun' in non-scientific discourse, identified because it is the
only member of its class. Such an article may, as with GERMAN
der, be an unstressed variant of the demonstrative, which continues
in its former use in stressed form.

An interesting case in a gender language of a nascent article
which is, so to speak, at a point between a zero stage demonstrative and a Stage I definite article is BWAMU, a language which
appears to be a genetic isolate within the VOLTAIC branch of
NIGER-CONGO. In this language the original suffixes have been
phonetically eroded to the point at which they no longer exhibit a
clear indication of membership in a gender. Moreover, all vestiges
of agreement have disappeared with the exception of two demonstrative type elements, both of which precede the noun and indicate
previous mention. Unfortunately, our only major source for the
language (Manessy 1960) is devoted to noun morphology and says
little about syntax. Manessy calls one of the two elements a determinative and the other a demonstrative pronoun. However, even the
first of these does not appear to be a definite article. He notes
that its presence is "facultative et relativement peu fréquent dans
le discours" (Manessy 1960: 93). Moreover, he does not translate
it as an article. Yet it is only these two elements which indicate
the gender membership of the noun. The determinative is a monosyllabic element, basically similar to the obsolescent class affixes.
We have, it would appear then, a case of renewal of gender by a
demonstrative element which is not yet an article and whose next
stage would presumably be comparable to that of a language like
GURMA which has a clear Stage I article.

3.4 Stage II of the definite article

Stage II was in the earlier sections of this paper referred to
as the non-generic article. We shall see that this is not really an
adequate designation. We may define Stage II as the stage in which
we have an article which includes, along with possibly other uses,
both definite determination and non-definite specific uses. Specific,
opposed here to generic, is the use of such an article in contexts
in which a specific but unidentified item is referred to, that is,
there is a presupposition of reference. Thus, ENGLISH 'I am looking for a book' is ambiguous as between specific reference, i.e.
there is a certain book for which I am looking, and a reading in
which there is no such assumption I might mean any old book, for
example, to prop up an unbalanced table leg.

Our definition is minimal. In fact, languages in Stage II generally include instances of non-referential use so that they correspond

grosso modo to the combined uses of a definite and indefinite article. Frequently, existing descriptions are simply not sufficient for us to decide. We must also include in our definition a maximal condition to distinguish Stage II from Stage III in which the former article is a mere marker. There must be at least one construction in which common nouns regularly appear in their non-articulated forms so that all common nouns have two contrasting forms, one with and one without the article. This may involve minimal contrast as when the non-articulated form of the noun is used in generic sentences like 'I don't like meat,' as against an articulated form in 'I don't like the meat,' (i.e. some particular specimen which has just been mentioned or can be identified by non-verbal context). However, in languages with Stage II articles the choice of articles is always largely grammaticalized, being determined by the syntactic construction and is thus redundant. For example, most of them have generalized either the articulated or non-articulated as negative object, and they do not express the semantic distinction which has just been noted. This is a large step in the direction of a Stage III article. Languages with Stage II articles show varying degrees of advancement towards a situation in which the distinction between the two forms is completely redundant, being dependent on the construction, e.g. negative objects are always articulated or always non-articulated, the same for nominal predicates, etc. With the attainment of complete grammaticization, the analogical tendency sets in for one or the other form to become universal. If the articulated form, which is the one which has usually spread to more contexts, predominates, we have a Stage III noun marker. If not, the articulated form disappears. I believe this is what has happened in Eastern BANTU languages without pre-prefixes.[3] In the proto-language the pre-prefix was probably a Stage II article which in some languages remained in this stage, in some moved in Stage III and in some languages disappeared. These varied developments often took place in quite closely related languages of the same subgroup.

In languages with Stage II articles the articulated form has become the normal form of the noun. It is usually the lexical citation form and it heavily predominates in text. Grammars of such languages

---

[3] There are in some instances, probably, also sociolinguistic factors. Carter (1963) in an interesting article asserts that the Tonga are quite conscious of the distinction between nouns with and without pre-prefixes and consider the excessive use of the former as "undignified." There are in this language considerable variations in frequency of these forms in texts of various styles.

habitually list not the uses of the articulated form, but rather situations in which it is <u>not</u> used. As is evident from the earlier discussion, no more than is the case with the ordinary definite article,
or for that matter individual cases in case languages, is there a
single overall semantically based definition which will completely
delineate the respective uses of the articulated and non-articulated
forms. As is usually done in the grammars, however, it is easier
to distinguish the relatively limited set of uses of the non-articulated
forms and view the articulated forms as an unspecified remainder.

As we may conclude from the earlier discussion, we cannot
expect that all languages with Stage II articles will have the same
set of uses for the non-articulated forms. However, there is a
common core of functions which recur in languages of this type.

Most of the functions of the non-articulated form can be placed
in one of two categories. Strangely enough, on a scale of degree
of determination, these two categories are at exactly opposite ends.
In some instances the article does not occur, because the noun is
inherently determined (e.g. proper names) or because it is determined by something else in the particular construction (e.g. a
demonstrative modifier). In these instances the noun which would
not usually have an article in Stage I does not acquire it in Stage II.
It is because of these uses that the name 'non-generic article' is not
really appropriate. At the other end of the determination spectrum
are the generic uses, as in negation and predication. These opposing uses of the non-articulated form bear a certain resemblance to
the use of non-articulated forms in languages with both a definite
and indefinite article. In such languages proper names do not usually have an article, but the article may also be absent in generic
uses, e.g. FRENCH <u>je n'ai pas d'eau</u> 'I don't have water;' <u>il est</u>
<u>tailleur</u> 'he is a tailor.' The generic uses of the non-articulated
forms in languages with Stage II articles, it may be noted, largely
coincide with the totality of two sets of categories enumerated by
Moravcsik in her discussion of determination, on the one hand, as
inherently definite and on the other, as generic (Moravcsik 1969:
especially p. 72).

Instances of automatic definiteness will be considered first.
These include proper names, vocatives and noun modified by demonstratives and personal possessive pronouns. Of these, proper
names, both personal and place, are the group most consistently
used in unarticulated form. No exception was found to the rule that
in languages with Stage II articles, the article is not found with
proper names. This was the reason for the specification of the

existence of contrast between articulated and non-articulated in common nouns as a part of the definition of a language with a Stage II article. For some of the languages a minimal contrast is reported when the same noun is used both as a common and proper name. For example, in BEMBA amafupa or mafupa, depending on the usual rules for the use of the articulated and non-articulated form, is a common noun meaning 'bones,' but as the name of a river it takes the form Mafupa, without the pre-prefix. In some languages an animal name, when used to designate a character in a folktale, is in the unarticulated form, but when used as a common name, is articulated or non-articulated in accordance with the general rules for the use of the two forms in the language.

Common nouns, when used in the vocative, commonly occur without the article. In one language of Stage II, LOTUKO, both articulated and non-articulated forms occur, but the latter is said to be more emphatic as well as more elegant.

In construction with demonstratives, there is some variability. The predominant tendency is to add the article to the noun redundantly, a tendency already visible in some instances in languages with ordinary Stage I articles, e.g. ARABIC and CLASSICAL GREEK. Sometimes, when the article is not on the noun, it is added to the demonstrative. There are some indications that the principle involved here is that definiteness is a property of the noun phrase as a whole. There are instances of word order variation where, in one order, the marker is on the noun and in the other, on a demonstrative or other modifier. In TESO and MAASAI, with Stage II prefix articles, almost all noun modifiers follow the noun. However, those form which precede take the article which in that case does not occur with the noun. Cases of alternative word order show clearly that what is involved is that definiteness is marked once only and always initially in the noun phrase in these languages. A MAASAI example is il-kuti tuŋana 'few people,' with its alternative il-tuŋana kuti 'people few.'

The interrogative which corresponds to the demonstrative is the specifying interrogative 'which?' Its usage as request for identification in ENGLISH is to be distinguished from its employment in the sense of 'what kind of?' 'Which wine do you want?' illustrates the potential ambiguity. In the identificational sense it is not usually accompanied by an article on the noun in Stage II languages.

The personal possessive construction, like the demonstrative construction, shows a tendency to mark definiteness redundantly on the noun, and once more, this is a tendency which is already visible occasionally in languages with class I articles, cf. ITALIAN la mia casa '(the) my house.' Kinship terms, as inalienables, however, show far less affinity for the definite article, a point that can also be illustrated from ITALIAN which has mio padre and not *il mio padre.

When, as often, there are two constructions, one for alienables and one for inalienables, it will usually only be the latter in which the possessive pronoun is directly affixed to the noun. Often, also, the kinship term can only occur with possessives so that, e.g. 'John's mother' is always John his-mother or the like. In these cases the article is, so to speak, blocked from attachment to the nouns. Whatever the factor involved, kinship terms rival proper names in their resistance to the acquisition of a Stage II article.

We turn now to the instances in which a Stage II article is not used with nouns taken in a generic sense. These may be classified as falling roughly into four main types: 1) negation, 2) predication, 3) adverbial and locative uses, 4) generic verb objects and dependent genitives in compounds. These last two items can be shown to be basically similar.

In regard to negation, two observations can be made. The first is that non-articulated forms are confined to the objects of verbs in negative sentences and to subjects in negative existential sentences. It does not ever seem to occur with definite subjects in negative sentences, e.g. with 'girl' in the sentence 'the girl did not pick the flowers.' With indefinite subjects we are evidently dealing with instances in which an existential sense is involved. The somewhat strange sentence 'a girl did not pick the flowers' is either contrastive and really predicative that is equivalent to 'it was not a girl who picked the flowers,' or equivalent to the negative existential 'no girl picked the flowers,' 'there was not a girl who picked the flowers.' Such sentences are generally expressed in these two latter ways in languages, in which case they fall under predication and existential negation, in both of which cases non-articulated forms are common in languages with Stage II articles.

The second observation is that verb objects in negative sentences can also be divided into instances with generic and with definite objects, but very few languages in Stage II make a consistent distinction. The languages which I have examined which are closest to making this distinction consistently are ZULU and XHOSA, two closely related BANTU languages. Elsewhere, the rule is generalized so that either negative objects always take the article, or they never do. The latter is more usual.

Two BANTU languages from very different areas, SOUTHERN KIKONGO and LUGANDA, show the following variation. A negative object takes the article when it precedes the verb but does not when it follows. A closer consideration of these two cases shows the following. The usual order is for the object to follow the verb. When it precedes, it is always definite in meaning, initial in the sentence, and referred to by a pronominal object on the verb. In other words, it is topicalized and the definiteness of topicalization takes precedence in the linguistic expression. An example from Tucker and Mulira's grammar of LUGANDA is the following: tog-gyawo bitanda 'don't take away the bedsteads' in which bitanda does not have the pre-prefix, but e-bitanda tobiggyawo 'the bed-steads, don't take them away' in which we find e-bitanda with the pre-prefix, and in addition, the incorporated object pronoun bi- in the verb (Ashton et al. 1954: 33).

A second major type of construction in which the articulated form usually does not occur is with nominal predicates in sentences of the type 'the man is an iron worker,' but not where the sentence is equational so that the predicate is definite, e.g. 'he is the chief.' Predicative adjectives are treated analogously and usually do not have the articulated form.

The third major type is adverbial under which may be subsumed locative and temporal constructions. These are similar to expres-sions in ENGLISH without the article such as 'by hand,' 'on foot,' 'at home,' and 'at night,' as well as words which double as adverbs and prepositions like 'behind' and 'above.' There is here, as in other instances, a strong tendency towards grammaticalization which takes the following form. All nouns governed by preposi-tions are in the non-articulated form even when their meaning is specific, but the articulated form reappears when the noun has a qualifier such as an adjective or dependent genitive, even if the meaning is generic. A rule of this sort occurs sometimes even with a Stage I article as exemplified by RUMANIAN in which, with a few minor exceptions, all these prepositions, constituting the large majority, which are not themselves articulated nouns fol-lowed by the genitive, take the noun without the postposed article. The articulated form is used, however, if the noun has qualifiers. Thus, we have în gradină 'in garden' but în gradina cea mare 'in the garden the large.'

Since body part nouns are frequently the source of adverbs and
their corresponding prepositions, we often see a contrast between
body parts as nouns which will in Stage II languages have the articulated forms in most constructions, as against their adverbial and
prepositional uses in which they are non-articulated. A grammar
of ATESO states that "many prepositions are derived from nouns
by dropping the noun prefix" (Hilders and Lawrence 1957: 66).

The last major group is that of generic noun objects and nominal
compounds based on a genitive construction. Again, we may cite
examples from languages like ENGLISH in which we have phrases
like 'take care' and even occasional object-incorporation as in 'baby-
sit.' An example of a Stage II language in which this occurs extensively is KHASI. In GUNWINGGU which is really a Stage III language, nouns in classes III and IV, the two thing-classes, may be
incorporated in the verb as objects, in which case they do not have
their class-prefixes.

Compounds based on the genitive construction, or genitive expressions in the border of lexicalization, show similar characteristics. The genitive in such cases is taken generically, just as is
the noun object of the verb. These expressions can be distinguished
from genitive expressions in which the regens is non-generic.
These are often systematically distinguished. An instance in point
is TAMĀRI, a VOLTAIC language with older noun class suffixes
which has a prefixed Stage II article. From fa nafa 'cow' and li
yini 'horn,' we have li na yini 'une corne de vache,' 'a cow-horn,'
as against fa nafa kwa li yini 'la corne de la vache' or 'une corne
de la vache.' The reason fa occurs in cow's horn without either a
prefix or suffix is that in the first round of gender suffixation, the
same phenomenon occurred so that the first member of a compound
did not acquire the suffix, as can be seen in VOLTAIC languages
which are suffixing only. In fact, because this is productive contrast, one can say that languages like TAMĀRI were still in the
final stages of a Stage II suffixed article when they began to develop
a new prefixed article.

A special case here is that of diminutive constructions which are
based, in many languages, on a compound of the form 'child of X.'
Since this is highly productive and any noun in principle can have a
diminutive, the unarticulated form of the noun sometimes survives
in this formation, even when the dependent genitive acquires the
article at a later point in the development of Stage II languages.

One further construction should be mentioned in which non-
articulated nouns sometimes appear, namely with numerals.

Numerals appear more frequently in indefinite constructions like
'five houses' than in definite constructions like 'the five houses.'
However, even the former construction is not generic. Hence,
the noun should in Stage II have the articulated form with numerals,
and this is generally the case, but there are occasional deviations.
MENDE, a language without noun-classes with a suffixed Stage II
article -i, distinguishes indefinite from definite numeral constructions along the lines to be expected in a language with a Stage I
article, e.g. maha felenga 'chief two,' as against maha feleisia
'the two chiefs.' In the latter expression, as is normal in MENDE,
it is the following modifier which takes the definite form. An even
more striking example is ARAMAIC. In modern WESTERN ARA-
MAIC, an advanced Stage II dialect, the only productive use of nouns
in the non-articulated form which has survived is with numerals.
As noted earlier, the development of the article through the stages
enumerated here was much more rapid in EASTERN than in WEST-
ERN ARAMAIC dialects.

3.5 The Stage III article

It was indicated that during the second stage there is a decreasing
set of environments in which there is direct contrast between the
articulated and non-articulated form. In general it is the articulated form which spreads until it becomes the normal form of the
noun. In the absence of significant contrast, there is an analogical
tendency for one of the forms, usually the articulated, to spread
to all the remaining environments so that, synchronically, the mass
of common nouns now only have a single form, usually the one which
is historically the reflex of the articulated form. When this happens,
we are in Stage III in which the former article is a pure marker
which no longer has any synchronic connection with definiteness or
specificity. The line between Stages II and III is somewhat arbitrary.
How restricted and non-productive must the alternating forms of the
noun be for a language to be assigned to Stage III rather than Stage
II? We will not so much be concerned here with the problems of
assignment of borderline languages in terms of our somewhat rough
and ready definition, as in considering the first stages of the process,
and the synchronically non-functional survivals which are characteristic of Stage III languages.

There are two distinct classes of cases to be considered, those
in which the original demonstratives which gave rise to the process
were classifying so that the final result is a set of gender markers
on the noun, and those in which this was not so, so that the final
result is rather the existence of an 'empty' marker, a mere sign of
nominality on the large majority of common nouns.

Where the original demonstrative was a classifying one, the essential outcome is, of course, that the nouns are now classified by markers, either pristine or renewing an older system (i.e. double affixation). There are, however, always tell-tale signs of the process by which the markers have come into existence. The first of these is that proper names, kinship terms, and frequently, borrowed nouns which entered the language at a point in the development in which there was no longer a synchronically relevant alternation between articulated and non-articulated forms, all end up without having gender markers. Involved as they normally are in a system with gender agreement, they are assigned gender on a semantic basis.

This is the presumed explanation for the existence of the class 1.a in BANTU languages, a phenomenon which is in fact found throughout NIGER-CONGO with the exception, of course, of MANDE which has no noun classes. Class 1.a typically contains personal proper names and kinship terms, lacks the class affix, and has the agreements of class 1, the singular personal class which in BANTU has the prefix *mu- .

The second consequence of this process has to do with locative and adverbial expressions in general. It will be recalled that body part terms and other nouns, e.g. 'earth' (='down') in Stage II languages, frequently contrast non-articulated forms in adverbial and prepositional uses with articulated forms in nominal uses. Such adverbs and prepositions tend to survive because of the absence of productive alternations. Prepositions and adverbs, being a restricted and fairly closed set, also often survive in the face of lexical replacements of the corresponding common noun. An examination of adverbs and prepositions will generally uncover relict forms without class markers. For example, OVAMBO, a BANTU language in Stage III, in which nouns only occur in pre-prefixed form, has posi 'under' to be analyzed as po- 'on' and -si 'earth,' the latter without the pre-prefix. The root *-si is general BANTU root for 'earth,' but in OVAMBO and related languages it has been replaced by edu.

There are also consequences for the nominal member of locational and other prepositional constructions. It was seen that the noun governed by a preposition does not usually take a Stage II article. A characteristic result in Stage III is the reinterpretation of the preposition as itself a gender marker, since the noun has none, and the development of agreements with it parallel to that of the earlier gender classes. Hence, the rise of so-called place genders as in BANTU languages. A further facilitating factor at

work here is that place demonstratives in these languages often
have two elements, one meaning 'place' and the other a deictic
element found also with the regular gender demonstratives. For
example, in SWAHILI we have ha-pa 'here, this place,' parallel
to ha-wa 'these,' referring to nouns in class 2 (plural personal
class) which have the prefix wa-. Syntactically it is plausible, as
pointed out in Givón 1976, that such agreement should start with
sentences in which place is topicalized. The final chief area of
survival of the non-articulated form is, as might be expected, in
fossilized nominal compounds and incorporated verb objects. We
might also add here that sometimes words like 'person,' 'thing,'
etc. survive in pronominal uses without the article (cf. FRENCH
personne, pas, point; ITALIAN cosa 'what?').

Instances of class 3 noun markers where the original demonstrative article was not classifying are especially intriguing,
because we do not have here the guide of gender-agreement. All
we have is that virtually every noun in the language has a particular marker which has, as it were, become a sign of nominality
as such. Such cases will illustrate in a graphic manner how the
study of generalized diachronic process extends the reach of internal reconstruction. Our evidence for the interpretation of such
a marker as a former article rests on the fact that it shows the
same characteristic survivals as where there is gender classification.

A case in point is HAUSA. With rare exceptions HAUSA nouns
end in a vowel. This vowel is almost always long. A text count
of nouns would probably show something like 99% final long vowels.
However, forms with short vowels do exist, falling into two main
and apparently unrelated types, proper names and adverbial expressions. To take the former, there are, to begin with, minimal contrasts between the same word as a common noun and proper name.
Thus, gàmbóó designates a child born after twins, but Gàmbó is a
proper name which may be given to such a child. There is a town
Dáwáákí contrasting in final vowel length with dáwáákíí 'horses,'
the source of its name. Many proper names have short vowels
without such a contrast, e.g. Kánò, Zààríyà, which are cities. In
some instances the reason may be that they are borrowed words,
for example, the personal names Béllò (from FUL), ʔAlhájì (from
ARABIC). Borrowed common nouns constitute another short vowel
category, e.g. ʔàngúlú 'vulture' borrowed from NUPE and síísì
'six pence' from ENGLISH.

With regard to adverbial expressions, there are a whole series
of terms, many of them body parts which have special forms with

short vowels when used with the preposition ?à. These forms are
called locatives in the grammar. They also exhibit tonal and other
differences. Thus, ?ídòò is 'eye,' but ?à ?ídó 'in the eye;' bààkíí
'mouth,' but ?à bákà 'in the mouth.' Examples of words that are
not body parts are wútáá 'fire,' but ?à wútá 'in the fire;' k'ásáá
'country,' but ?à k'àsà or just k'ásà 'on the ground, below.' There
are also time expressions with the preposition dà, e.g. dáréé
'night,' but dà dáré 'at night.' In addition words like jíyà 'yesterday,' (?à) bààrá 'last year,' yànzú 'now,' etc. have short vowels
without contrasting long vowel forms. Those numerals which end
in vowels have them short, e.g. bíyú 'two,' except units, which,
as generally in languages, are treated as nouns, e.g. dáríí 'hundred.'

None of the adverbial expressions can have modifiers without
being replaced by long vowel forms. At present these forms are
more and more being replaced by the corresponding long vowel
forms as alternatives even without modifiers. [4]

In light of the above account, we can explain the long vowel forms
as the resultant of former article which has reached Stage III, while
the short vowel forms are the original forms still surviving in some
of their most typical uses. Note that there is no possibility of a
unified account of HAUSA short vowel forms on a purely synchronic
base. HAUSA does have sex gender, but it appears that the demon-
strative-article which is the presumed source of the long vowel
forms, just as with ARAMAIC -ā, did not vary for gender or number.

A somewhat similar case to that of HAUSA, namely TIV, a language of the BENUE-CONGO branch of the NIGER-CONGO family,
may be mentioned in passing. The old prefix system has here been
renewed by suffixes which, however, only appear in those classes
which had consonantal affixes. Their presence in the other classes
can be detected by tonal changes which parallel those of the consonantal class. The earlier non-suffixed form of the noun, called the
prepositional by Abraham (1940), survives after prepositions, e.g.
m̀gérèm̀ 'water,' šá m̀gèr 'in the water.' This form may not be
used with a preposition if the noun has modifiers. It also survives
in diminutives and augmentatives, which are old compounds with
the noun as second members, in mostly identical form. A perusal

_____
[4] Data regarding HAUSA final vowel quantity is very inadequate
in the existing literature. I am indebted to W. Leben and Mohammed
Tairu for checking some cases of final vowel quantity in HAUSA.

of Abraham's dictionary shows that many other compounds with the non-suffixed form as second member are reflecting an older direct construction without a class marker of the <u>regens</u>. There are also adverbial uses of words like 'ground' for 'down.'

Where the article was not a gender classifier, one additional phenomenon may be noted. Since in this case virtually all nouns receive the same mark, it becomes a sign of nominality as such and is used to derive verbal nouns. The -<u>s</u> of PLATEAU PENU-TIAN functions this way.

The entire account given here has been on the basis of the category of determination. This seems natural enough, because we are dealing with developments deriving from what is a definite article in its first stage. There is, however, another way of looking at the process which at first blush seems very different, but is in fact ultimately related to the notion of determination, namely case.

If we consider the Stage II article which is the decisive turning point, we can roughly state the matter as follows. The characteristic constructions without Stage II articles include the vocative and adverbial uses corresponding to the locative and instrumental of languages which have these cases. The genitive and accusative are the cases in which real contrast between the articulated and non-articulated form occurs, particularly the latter where negative and generic, sometimes incorporated objects, are without the article which occurs in other uses. The subject case is, par excellence, the case which takes the article. Nominal and adjectival predication has to be considered separately. Here the subject is articulated, but the predicate often is not. However, as with the verb-object, there is the possibility of contrast roughly between permanent properties (articulated) and non-permanent (non-articulated).[5] Proper names do not enter here. For them an account based on determination is primary.

The case hierarchy just sketched is clearly related to definiteness. Subjects, as favorite topics, tend to be definite. In some languages

---

[5] The SLAVIC short and long form of the adjective, the latter containing a suffixed demonstrative or relative, belong here. The long form starts out as definite and tends to become like a Stage II article plus adjective, until, as for example in RUSSIAN, it only serves as a predicate adjective, and here only in certain uses.

they must be so. The accusative where the contrast is clearest
is precisely the case which in some languages, e.g. TURKISH,
PERSIAN, is the only one which formally distinguishes definiteness by a marker.

All this bears on the origin of case markers. In INDO-EURO-
PEAN it is striking that the two cases which can be reconstructed
with zero inflection are the vocative and the locative. The latter
has , in the singular, two variants: zero and -i. In the plural
it has long been noted that -sí (with a variant -su) is really -s
'plural' + -i. In fact a form with just -s is also found. In SAN-
SKRIT the plural oblique forms for instrumental, dative, ablative
and locative have sandhi forms like that at word boundary, thus
being in effect added to the pure base form. Note that the locative
and other oblique cases, being marked forms, do not usually remain in the zero form, but acquire prepositions or postpositions
as with HAUSA ?à, TIV šá and, presumably, INDO-EUROPEAN
-i. This view also strengthens the case for those who equate the
nominative singular -s with the demonstrative *so. Accusatives,
on the other hand, often derive from old prepositions marking an
indirect object. The case hierarchy just described is obviously
related to that discussed in much recent work in regard to sub-
jectivization and topicalization, including relational grammar.

The entire foregoing account of how noun classes acquire markers is subject to two important reservations. One is that sometimes only a few nouns within a class come to have markers, and
this by a mechanism which is essentially different from that just
described. In almost all such cases we have "motion," that is,
a minimal contrast of the same stem in different classes. This is
common in NORTH CAUCASIAN. The nouns here do not in general
have markers, but there are instances like AVAR v-as 'boy,' j-as
'girl.' I believe that these arise from substantivization of adjectives
which do have concord markers.

Another and more fundamental reservation is the following. While
the development of markers from the article is no doubt the usual
process, there is what at the moment is, to my knowledge, the
unique case of the DALY RIVER language in Australia described
in Sec. 2. Here, a new system has been superimposed on an older
Australian-wide formation of the usual type. In this new system,
as it appears, the source of the marker is a superordinate noun and
in which concord subsequently develops in the adjective to produce
a gender system in the sense defined here.

4. The Spread of Grammatical Agreement

From the account in foregoing sections we see that the demonstrative, as the normal source of Stage I definite article, plays the
rôle of initiator for the whole process described here. It also plays
a further rôle in that it constantly generates concordial phenomena,
sometimes producing gender agreement where the demonstrative
is classifying, and sometimes not. If we look at the impressive
tables of concord series often found in grammars of BANTU languages, we can see that for every one of them, there is abundant
synchronic and diachronic evidence of the rôle of the demonstrative.
A detailed treatment of this process is not within the scope of this
paper. We may note, however, a few principal considerations.

The term used up to now has been simply 'demonstrative,' but
this requires some further specification. If we consider once more
our initial example of the GURMA group of VOLTAIC, we note that
the new prefixes which arise match synchronically not the demonstratives of these languages, but the verb subject and object pronouns.
This does not exclude the diachronic possibility that they come from
earlier demonstratives which, on the one hand, developed into pronouns and on the other, into articles. The present demonstratives
also would have these as source with the addition of new deictic
elements. If we look at present day FRENCH, the article matches
the object pronoun. Historically, both come from the primarily
demonstrative _ille_ which also had anaphoric uses in LATIN.

In fact the synchronic boundary of these forms is a shifting
one. In most languages the demonstrative pronoun and demonstrative adjective are identical. In many languages the third person
pronoun is identical with a demonstrative, and often an article is
identical with one or the other. It is not excluded that the article
should arise from what is ultimately a demonstrative, but come
more directly from a third personal pronoun. In the NEO-ARAMAIC
of Ṭur-'Abdīn, it was noted earlier that a new prefixed article has
arisen. Nöldeke derived it from the demonstrative, while Siegel,
in a more recent treatment, argues probably correctly for a prefixed pronoun. In any event the pronoun and demonstrative are very
similar. Hence, when talking about the demonstrative in the present
connection, I will not be drawing a strict line between demonstrative
and third person pronoun.

We may distinguish in somewhat rough and heuristic fashion
three types of concordial phenomena. The first is that of a noun
with its immediate modifiers in the noun phrase, e.g. adjective,

with its immediate modifiers in the noun phrase, e. g. adjective,
demonstratives and numeral. The second is predicate agreement,
that of a subject noun with predicate adjective or demonstrative.
The third is anaphoric use. We may distinguish under these two
types. Where a deleted noun has no modifier, we have a pronominal substitute. Where the noun has modifiers, there may be a
substitute, e.g. 'one' in ENGLISH 'the good one.' Languages with
noun classes in such cases, however, usually attach the class
marker to the noun modifier. This is probably one of the sources
of modifier agreement, as soon as it is redundantly applied, when
the noun is present also. Another kind of redundant anaphora is
intraclausal, but not within the noun phrase as when the verb com-
pulsorily contains a pronominal mark of the subject or other noun
phrase head. The origin here is no doubt in topicalized sentences.

Much of this may be illustrated by the development in RUMANIAN
of two new so-called improper articles which now exist alongside
of the earlier suffixed definite articles. The first of these, cel, is
originally a demonstrative from LATIN ecce illum 'behold that,'
the last element of which by itself gave the RUMANIAN suffixed
article. Alongside of om-ul bun 'man-the good," one can have om-ul
cel bun "man-the that good." With deletion of the noun, we get cel
bun 'the good' = LATIN bonum, cei drepţi 'the just' = LATIN justi,
and with relative-like uses om-ul cel cu boi 'the man with cattle.'
The second article is al in the masculine singular. It derives
from the preposition a and same demonstrative ille, found in the
suffixed article, and in the first improper article al. Its basic use
is possessive and can be seen from such examples as the following:

        pom-ul   bun   al   vecinu-lui
        "apple-the good that-of neighbor-the"

        pom-ul   meu   şi   al   vecinu-lui
        "apple-the my and that-of neighbor-the"

        ai   noştri   sosiră
        "the our (people) have:arrived"

These parallel BANTU examples in that cel goes with the noun modifier, agreeing with the noun in gender and number, and al, as with
the BANTU genetive, agrees with the regens which is followed by
the rectum. In such a phrase as

        femeí-le   ce-le frumoase a-le   satu-lui
        "woman-the those beautiful those-of village-the"

the basic structure is similar to that of SWAHILI:

wa-kwe wa-zuri   wa   m-ti
"women beautiful those-of village"

In fact, in Tagliavini's grammar of RUMANIAN, he notes the basic resemblance in such instances to languages like SWAHILI (Tagliavini 1923: 274).

Demonstratives, then, are constantly producing concord phenomena. However, specific demonstratives, as they become bleached
of deixis by anaphoric uses, are constantly being replaced by new
demonstratives usually formed from the older ones by the addition
of new deictic elements, by reduplication, etc. These in turn lose
their deictic force to be replaced by others. In relation to gender
there are several possible courses of development. If the demonstratives themselves have gender classification, they will give rise
to further phenomena of gender agreement. If they pass through
the phases described earlier in the paper, they will end up in the
noun, all the while producing concord from diachronically successive
layers of demonstratives. The existence of such layers is shown
in languages like BANTU in which the varying concords for the same
gender exhibit a number of different forms. The persistence of the
genders provides the cement which puts together, in the same set of
concords, forms which differ phonetically.

The development of the article and that of the other concordial
phenomena may not take place at the same pace. If the former
proceeds more rapidly, we have languages in which gender is shown
with the articulated noun and usually with the anaphoric pronoun also,
but not with non-articulated nouns or on noun modifiers. Examples
of such languages include IJO, particularly the BRASS dialect, with
suffixed Stage I articles which distinguish masculine, feminine and
neuter in the singular and with the same distinction in pronominal
reference, but without agreement in the noun phrase. TUNICA, a
GULF AMERIND language, only shows gender in definite nouns
and also has pronominal elements incorporated in the verb, but no
agreement in the noun phrase.

If the demonstrative is not a classifying one, it will still produce
phenomena which are on the surface concordial, if the same demonstrative is at work, as in HEBREW <u>hay-yeled hat-tov</u> "the-boy the-
good." Where, however, there is no classification and the "concord"
elements involve varying forms of deictics of different periods, we
will have at best suspicious similarities among some forms as in
ENGLISH 'this,' 'that,' 'the,' 'they,' 'them,' whereas others, e.g.
'she,' though of demonstrative origin, will exhibit no overt connection.

Incidentally, we see from this why it is the noun par excellence
which gives rise to classificational systems of syntactic relevance.
It is not so much that the noun designates persisting entities as
against actions or temporary states of persistent entities. It is
that nouns are continuing discourse subjects and are therefore in
constant need of referential devices of identification. As soon
as we wish to talk about an action as such, we nominalize it;
classification is a help in narrowing the range of possible identification.

The theory of the special role of the demonstrative in the development of agreement advanced here is not intended necessarily to
encompass concord in case or number. It is plausible in regard
to number and is in fact almost always an incidental by-product of
gender agreement where that occurs, since gender systems, except
in a few instances in Australia, always intersect with the category
of number.

5. The Problem of Origins

It is the thesis of this paper that, given a classifying demonstrative and the constant tendency of demonstratives to generate
agreement, the result will be a gender system. Further, if the
demonstrative goes through the stages outlined, the result will be
a marker on the noun as well as on the agreeing element. Given
the existence of classifying demonstratives, the whole process will
unfold with something close to inevitability. However, it has not
been explained how classifying demonstratives arise in the first
place. This remains for further investigation. There is one possible origin which is just that. That is, it is not asserted that in
any actually reconstructible case it occurred this way, nor that
there are no other mechanisms.

This possible source is numeral classifier systems. As was
pointed out in an earlier study (Greenberg 1972), the first construction to which the numeral classifier spreads is to the demonstrative,
as has happened in CHINESE, THAI and other instances. This
gives us just what we need, a classifying demonstrative. In fact,
in KIRIWINA in the Trobriand Islands, it has spread from the demonstrative to some adjectives; in standard THAI it occurs with
adjectives in some constructions so that true agreement phenomena
begin to appear. In northern THAI languages the classifier functions
like an article, and in JACALTEC MAYA, as an anaphoric pronoun.
It may, however, not be necessary to go so far afield. The fundamental bases of contrast, animate and inanimate, human and non-

human, male and female, tend to occur in demonstratives, third
person pronouns and interrogatives as a guide to identification.

It is possible that gender systems in their initial stages are of
this type. The way in which gender arises needs not be the same as
that by which the system can expand by the development of new
genders. A mechanism by which place gender might develop was
described in the course of this paper, namely, through the reinterpretation of a preposition or postposition as a class marker.
Such prepositions frequently derive from locational nouns. Minor
genders such as diminutives, and less often augmentatives, probably
arise by a similar mechanism involving an element meaning 'small'
or 'large.' Three parallel instances may be cited in which it appears that a neuter has just developed or is in the process of developing in a system with masculine and feminine. Boas, in his grammar
of CHINOOK (1911: 602), notes that the neuter in CHINOOK can be
used with any masculine or feminine stem to give an indefinite
meaning. He notes also that the neuter is close to being what in
the initial discussion was called a minor gender. He states that
"the number of words which appear only in the neuter gender is so
small that we may almost suspect that the neuter was recently indefinite and used to indicate both singular and plural." In KHASI,
alongside of a masculine and feminine, there is a neuter which
does not distinguish number. Its meaning is diminutive. It is my
overall impression that there are no stems here which are exclusively neuter. A third case is HOTTENTOT, also with masculine
and feminine and a neuter, common gender used for words like
'child' in distinction from 'boy' and 'girl.' As with KHASI, there
appear to be no stems which are exclusively neuter. KHASI has
?i as the neuter marker and HOTTENTOT has -i for neuter singular,
the common sound symbolic vowel for diminutive. A remarkable
parallel between CHINOOK and HOTTENTOT is shown in Meinhof's
statement regarding NAMA HOTTENTOT. "The i of the genus
commune was originally an indefinite article which had nothing to
do with gender and it is still used this way at the present time. It
can be added to every substantive whether of masculine or feminine
gender to signify an instance of the appropriate class" (1909: 48).
Why common gender should arise from indefiniteness, I cannot
really say. Meinhof believes that "this indefinite meaning of i
easily led to the further result that little or no attention was paid
to sex in its use so that its use as genus commune came into existence."

It has not been possible here, for reasons of space, to treat the
relationship between the views presented here and the large and

frequently murky literature on the origin of gender.[6] Suffice it to point out that the notion of a special rôle for the demonstrative in the development of gender is far from novel, being found after a fashion even as early as Bopp, who found the origin of inflectional elements in pronoun. In most speculation about gender, it has been assumed that classification starts with the noun, and the problem is to discover how it spreads. If the thesis is valid that the usual course of events is that it starts with the demonstrative and only sometimes ends up in the noun, the statement of the problem should be reversed. There are some examples of earlier speculations which point in this direction, though none of them seem to be very clear. The closest approach encountered was in the writings of that frequently acute but generally neglected thinker Raoul de la Grasserie. After I had arrived at the notion that the NAHUATL absolutive was probably an old determiner, I found in his essay on the article the following statement: "In the Nahuatl language, the substantive ending tli is not a derivational suffix, but an indication of determination whose function has disappeared" (1896: 293).

BIBLIOGRAPHY

Abraham, R.C. 1940. The principles of Tiv. London: Crown Agents for the Colonies.

Ashton, E.O. with E.M.K. Mulira, E.G.M. Ndawula and A.N. Tucker. 1954. A Luganda grammar. London, New York, Toronto: Longmans, Green and Co.

Boas, Franz. 1911. Chinook. Handbook of American Indian Languages, Part I. 561-677. Bureau of American Ethnology, Washington, D.C.

Carter, Hazel. 1963. Coding, style and the initial vowel in north Rhodesian Tonga: a psycholinguistic study. African Language Studies 4. 1-42.

Celedón, R. 1878. Gramatica, catecismo i vocabulario de la lengua goajira, ed. by E. Uricoechea. Paris.

Chantoux, A., A. Gontier, and A. Prost. 1968. Grammaire gourmantché. Dakar: Institut Fondamentale d'Afrique Noire.

---

[6] For historical reviews of the literature on gender, see particularly Royen 1919 and Fodor 1959.

de la Grasserie, Raoul. 1896. De l'article. Mémoires de la
Société Linguistique de Paris 9. 285-322, 281-394.

Dixon, Robert W. 1972. The Dyirbal language of North Queensland.
Cambridge University Press.

Fodor, Istvan. 1959. The origin of grammatical gender. Lingua
8. 1-41, 186-214.

Franklin, Karl J. 1962. Tolai language course. Division of Extension Services, Territory of Papua and New Guinea.

Givón, Talmy. 1976. Topic, pronoun and grammatical agreement.
Subject and topic, ed. by Charles Li, 149-188. New York, San
Francisco, London: Academic Press.

Greenberg, J.H. 1972. Numeral classifiers and substantival
numbers: Problems in the genesis of a linguistic type. Working Papers on Language Universals 9. 1-40. Stanford University.

Hilders, J. and J. Lawrence. 1957. An introduction to the Ateso
language. Kampala.

Holmer, Nils M. 1949. Goajiro (Arawak) II: nouns and associated
morphemes. IJAL 15. 110-120.

Love, J.R.B. n.d. An outline of Worora grammar. Studies in
Australian linguistics, ed. by A.P. Elkin, 112-124. Sydney:
Science House.

Manessy, George. 1960. La morphologie du nom en Bwamu (bobo-
oulé), dialecte de Bondoukuy. Université Dakar.

_____. 1965. Les substantifs à prefixes et suffixes dans les
langues voltaïques. Journal of African Languages 4. 170-181.

Meinhof, Carl. 1909. Lehrbuch der Nama-Sprache. Berlin:
Georg Reiner.

Moravcsik, Edith A. 1969. Determination. WPLU 1. 64-98.

Müller, Hermann. 1907. Grammatik der Mengen-Sprache. An-
thropos 2. 80-99, 241-257.

Peekel, G.P. 1929. Grammatische Grundzüge und Wörterverzeichnis
der Label Sprache. Zeitschrift für Eingeborenen-Sprachen 20.
10-33.

Planert, W. 1905. Über die Sprachen der Hottentoten und Bushmän-
ner. Mittheilung des Seminars für orientalische Sprachen. Abt.
3, Berlin.

Royen, Gerlach. 1919. Die nominalen Klassifikations-System in
den Sprachen der Erde. Mödling bei Wien.

Sapir, J. David. 1965. A grammar of Diola-Fogny. Cambridge
University Press.

Siegel, Adolf. 1968. Laut- und Formenlehre des neuaramäischen
Dialekts des Tûr Abdîn. Hildesheim.

Tagliavini, Carlo. 1923. Grammatica della lingua Rumena.
Heidelberg: Julius Groos.

Tryon, D. T. 1970. An introduction to Maranangku, Northern
Australia. Australian National University.

_____. 1974. Daly River languages, Australia. Department
of Linguistics, Research School of Pacific Studies, Australian
National University.

Welmers, William E. 1973. African language structures. Berkeley
and Los Angeles: University of California Press.

Wilson, W. A. A. 1961. Temne: an outline of the Temne language.
London: School of Oriental and African Studies.

The Nature of Future Tenses

RUSSELL ULTAN

ABSTRACT

The general observation that future tenses often differ from
other tenses more than present or past tenses do from one another
was explored from two standpoints: structurally in terms of markedness and semantically in terms of atemporal functions of future
tenses, categories associated with the latter, their etymologies,
and atemporal categories that also may be used to mark future time.
Markedness features investigated included: relative boundness of
forms, temporal gradation, obligatoriness of occurrence, and neutralization in several environments (subjunctive, gapping, negative,
subordinate temporal and sequential clauses, participles,and others).
Markedness features were also examined for correlations with a
proposed basic tense typology: prospective (future may be neutralized with present) vs. retrospective (past may be neutralized with
present). In general, it was demonstrated that future tenses are
more marked than either past or present. Semantically, future
tenses show a greater tendency to evolve from and develop into
modal categories representative of varying degrees of uncertainty
which is in conformity with the inherent uncertainty of futurity.
While future tenses often evolve from spatial categories, they
apparently do not develop into the latter.

Reprinted from Working Papers on Language Universals 8,
August 1972, 55-100.

CONTENTS

1. Introduction

1.1 Purpose and scope

Even superficial familiarity with the forms and functions of future tense markers in a number of languages is sufficient to observe that they generally tend to be more marked than either present or past tenses. The general purpose of the present study is to examine some of the ways in which this is so in an attempt to provide at least a partial explanation of the facts as they appear in the approximately fifty languages sampled. This explanation and an investigation of the semantic characteristics of future tenses in those languages for which such information was readily available will form the basis for certain general proposals regarding formal-semantic temporal relations in language and a general hypothesis of tense-system types.

1.2 Tenses and tense types

In order to refer to time — or perhaps more properly sequence of events or states — in natural languages, one or more points of reference are required. These are of two types:

1. the moment of speech (MOS), that point or span of time in which the speaker produces an utterance;

2. relative time (R), any point or span of time that occurs before, after or contemporaneously with the MOS and functions as a surrogate MOS which serves as the basis for predications involving time (or sequence) relative to itself. Thus in ENGLISH, for example, the simple (MOS) past functions as an MOS with reference to anterior or posterior R tenses as in:

    He said (MOS) that he had seen (R) her. (anterior R)
    He said (MOS) that he would see (R) her. (posterior R)

MOS tenses are primary. They commonly mark the time of the event[1] relative to the speaker in simple sentences or independent clauses with no or neutral modal, aspectual, evidential or other

---

[1] Unless otherwise specified or obvious from the context, the term "time" will also refer to sequence and the term "event" to state, as appropriate.

implications. These form the core of any tense system and serve
to establish the formal and semantic contrasts involved. Some or
all of them may also be used to mark R time.

R tenses mark the time of the event in dependent clauses relative to the MOS time (used as R time vis-à-vis R tenses) of the
appropriate independent clauses or in independent clauses with
reference to antecedent or subsequent portions of the discourse.
These may partially or wholly coincide formally with MOS tenses
but semantically they differ.

For the purposes of the present study it early became apparent
that some sort of operational definition of tense was necessary.
Thus, for instance, the question arose as to whether purely lexical
indicators of time such as today, tomorrow and yesterday should
be included or whether systematically contrastive nominal temporal
markers, like GUARANÍ: -kwé 'past, former' as in hŏgakwé 'his
former house;' -rã 'future' as in hemi.apòrã 'his future work'
(Gregores and Suarez 1967: 127-8), should also be considered. Similarly, as regards categories generally associated with the verb,
whether an essentially modal category with occasional or clearly
peripheral temporal function such as QUILEUTE -ł basically
referring to result or eventuality but also used intentively:

he.swółli   'I am going to give it to you.'

(Andrade 1933-8: 265) or an aspectual one like RAROTONGAN e
imperfective (i.e., incompletive) which marks future after the
negative or in conjunction with temporal particles or adverbs:

| kāre au e rutu i te pa?u | 'I won't play the drum.' |
| āpōpō e rutu ei au i te pa?u | 'I'll play the drum tomorrow.' |

(Buse 1963a: 156-7) are to be included. On the other hand, elements
that function in most contexts as temporal markers also have atemporal functions in others (is this true of all languages?). Thus in
ENGLISH, KOREAN and KWARA?AE,[2] for example, the future
tense form may be used as an imperative; in LITHUANIAN, ROTU-
MAN and TAGALOG, it also serves to indicate a customary event
in the MOS past; in FRENCH, GERMAN and ROTUMAN, it may
signal a supposition on the part of the speaker. While it is sometimes

---

[2] Languages cited in this fashion throughout this paper are not
intended to be exhaustive lists either for the present sample or for
languages in general.

difficult to ascertain which of the general functions, temporal or
atemporal, is most important in terms of criteria such as inflectional versus derivational, frequency of occurrence, basic meaning,
syntactic range, and so on, in most cases it is reasonably feasible
to determine whether the temporal function is primary or secondary.
We therefore subsume under the term tense:

> any grammatical form (affix, particle, auxiliary, etc.) whose
> primary function is to mark MOS time.

1.3 Special tenses

Before going on to an exposition of our basic hypothesis of tense
systems and the role of future tense markers, we must examine
two general functions of tenses that involve temporal considerations
of a somewhat special nature: gnomic and historical.

1.3.1 Gnomic tenses Gnomic or general truth uses of tense
markers in effect neutralize all the temporal distinctions of the
system. Thus a statement like: water boils at 212° F does not
have a specific temporal referent (past, present or future); rather
the simple present tense in this case refers to an event which may
occur at any time. Gnomic "tenses" are often represented by a
simple or unmarked present but not necessarily so. In FRENCH,
CLASSICAL GREEK, TONGAN and DAKOTA, as well as in ENG-
LISH on occasion, the future tense may be used and examples of a
past tense serving the same purpose are also to be found in GREEK
and ENGLISH (see Lakoff 1970: 847-8). Since gnomic "tenses" are
not really tenses at all (in spite of the forms they take), any generalizations we can make about temporal markers cannot be expected to apply to them, at least not those involving actual temporal
contrasts.

1.3.2 Historical tenses With historical tenses, true temporal
referents exist but, through a process of actualization to achieve
"more vividness" or "greater narrative power," present and future
tense forms are substituted for the expected past tense forms.
That is, an MOS past is shifted to an MOS present or future. Compare the following example from FRENCH which includes both present and future forms representing respectively MOS past and R
posterior:

Napoléon arrive à Ste-Hélène où il mourra en 1821. (Schogt 1968:44)

Historical tenses are probably best regarded as special stylistic
uses of the basic MOS tenses. They are always identifiable in

terms of the larger narrative contexts in which they occur. As
with gnomic "tenses," any general statements on tenses either do
not apply to historical tenses or must contain provisos accounting
for the formal actualizations of temporal relations.

1.4   Prospective and retrospective tense systems

If we limit ourselves to MOS-tense systems, excluding insofar
as possible from consideration atemporal factors such as mode or
aspect, often formally bound to tense markers, and also gnomic
and historical tenses for the reasons stated above, all tense systems may be divided into two types:[3]

1) Prospective: If a present tense may ordinarily mark an MOS
future or if the latter may be unmarked, the system is prospective.
This is true of most INDO-EUROPEAN languages,[4] FINNISH and
HUNGARIAN, KOREAN, TONGAN, MANDAIC and MIWOK, to name
but a few.

2) Retrospective: If a present tense may ordinarily mark an MOS
past or if the latter may be unmarked, the system is retrospective.
Some examples are: DAKOTA, GUARANÍ, ONONDAGA, HOPI,
ROTUMAN and TAIRORA. Note that, although the number of retro-
spective languages sampled was only a little less than the number
of prospective languages, all of the former with the exception of
ROTUMAN, TAIRORA and possibly LITHUANIAN were AMERICAN
INDIAN languages.

---

[3] There is, of course, a third logical possibility: a tense system
that is neither prospective nor retrospective. HAUSA may be a case
in point but I would suspend judgment pending access to more detailed
information on the functions of the "present" tenses. I had insufficient data to decide on the status of BASSA, BERBER, COOS, CUNA,
ESKIMO, HAIDA, HUPA and TLINGIT but all others appeared to be
identifiable as either prospective or retrospective languages.

[4] LITHUANIAN may be an exception. According to Senn (1966: 451)
the present tense may be used not only to mark a customary event
in the past but also a past event described in a clause which is the
complement of a verb of perception. He further states (p. 452) that
future reference cannot be expressed with a present tense; however,
there are examples which contradict this (e.g., future result expressed by present tense, p. 487).

Furthermore, if, in addition to a clearly demarcated past-present-future system, there is a tense that overlaps in temporal range present and future reference, the system is prospective. Thus in CLASSICAL MANDAIC, the "imperfect" was commonly used to express both present and future events alongside two peri-phrastic constructions used for future reference only. If there is a tense that overlaps present and past reference, the system is retrospective. In ONONDAGA, for example, an aorist covers the past-present range alongside a specific past marker.

Thus for prospective languages, the dichotomy past-nonpast is primary; for retrospective languages, future-nonfuture. In the extreme case, the former shows no distinction between present and future. This is so in MODERN MANDAIC and has been claimed for certain SICILIAN dialects (Ebneter 1966: 33, 41), and in both FINNISH and HUNGARIAN the future auxiliary is rarely used in colloquial speech, future reference being expressed by the present tense. Similarly for retrospective languages where the distinction between present and past is lost, as in ROTUMAN, DAKOTA, FOX, et al. While it is generally true that future is more marked than other tenses, there are apparent exceptions. If the prospective-retrospective typology is a significant one, we would expect it to have certain effects on the markedness of future and past tenses. Hence retrospective languages would tend toward greater marked-ness of future time than prospective languages.

2. Markedness

Within this framework a number of general hypotheses concern-ing the markedness of future tenses in relation to present and past tenses will be tested: relative boundness of temporal markers, asymmetrical directions in tense gradation, obligatory versus op-tional occurrence of future and past tenses, and neutralization of future tenses in certain environments. [5]

---

[5] Another index of future markedness is low frequency of occur-rence vis-à-vis past and present tenses. This factor has already been pointed out by Greenberg (1966: 87-8) for VEDIC SANSKRIT, LATIN and RUSSIAN and it holds for ENGLISH as well (see espe-cially Allen 1966: 149-52). Unfortunately, the information I have on text frequencies of tenses for other languages is either too scanty or unreliable to prove or disprove the hypothesis.

2.1 Boundness

While in some languages the basic tense markers belong to the same formal class (e.g., suffixes in LITHUANIAN, preverbal particles in TONGAN), in many there is an asymmetry between future and the other tenses or more often between future and past since present is often unmarked. Thus in ENGLISH the commonest form of the simple past tense is a suffix as opposed to an auxiliary verb which marks future. The same is true of most other GERMANIC languages (e.g. DUTCH, GERMAN, SWEDISH), SOMALI, TAKELMA, RUSSIAN (imperfective), et al. This is also the case in FINNISH, HUNGARIAN and SICILIAN; however, in these languages the future auxiliary is rarely used in colloquial speech. In BASSA, the present and three past tenses are formed by the addition of postverbal particles as opposed to the common future with a preverbal particle or either of two auxiliaries ('come' or 'go'). In HAUSA, the tenses are marked by preverbal pronominal forms that indicate modal, temporal and aspectual differences by the use of different pronominal allomorphs or subsets. For the intentive future, however, a construction consisting of a future auxiliary followed by the object pronoun is used. In TAGALOG present and past are usually marked by prefixes; the noncontinuous future is formed by preposing an auxiliary ('wish') to the present stem. In MODERN GREEK the past tenses are marked by a discontinuous prefix-suffix, the future by an auxiliary (from 'wish, want') plus the present stem. In CLASSICAL MANDAIC past (perfect) and nonpast (imperfect) were formed by different vowel patterns intercalated into the root but future was also represented by auxiliary constructions (imperfect or present participle of hua 'be' plus present participle or present participle of baa 'wish, seek' plus infinitive). In CHUKCHI the nonfuture is unmarked whereas the future may be marked by a prefix-suffix or an auxiliary ('desire').

Aside from these periphrastic futures, some languages show similar kinds of asymmetries in boundness between future and nonfuture forms. Thus in retrospective languages like QUILEUTE, DAKOTA and WINNEBAGO, nonfuture is unmarked and future is marked by a suffix, while in ROTUMAN the same holds for nonfuture but future is marked by a preverbal particle. In HUPA the simple past is formed by internal root changes (length and accentual shift) as opposed to suffixes for the two future tenses. In KWAKIUTL the past tense markers may be suffixed to the stem or appear as enclitics; the future tense is enclitic only. In MANDAN, a primarily suffixing language, past and nonfuture are suffixes while future may be marked by either a suffix or a prefix. Similarly, in GEORGIAN and RUSSIAN where one of the ways in which future is commonly marked is by prefixes (determinative in GEORGIAN, perfective in RUSSIAN).

In all these instances the future tense form is less bound in some sense than either the past or the present.[6] On the other hand, I know of no case where the converse is true. Thus we may formulate our first universal:

> Future tense markers may be less bound than present or past but never more so.

and its corollary:

> A periphrastic MOS past implies a periphrastic MOS future but the converse is not true.

While most of the languages with future auxiliaries were prospective, a few were retrospective (although several of the latter showed other differences of boudness as noted above). In view of the relatively small size of the present sample and the general unlikelihood that there might be any significant correlation between tense type and a predilection for or against auxiliaires, we chalk this up to chance.

2.2 Auxiliary forms

Before leaving the subject of future auxiliaries, let us interject some observations on their form, even though they do not have any direct bearing on the general topic of markedness. Of the 16 languages in the sample that use such constructions, 12 have present tense forms for the auxiliary as in e.g., FINNISH, SOMALI and BENGALI. In HAUSA, TAGALOG and TAKELMA, the auxiliary is unmarked for tense and in CLASSICAL MANDAIC the nonpast form of the verb is used. In MENDE, the future suffix (or enclitic?)

---

[6]Another kind of a symmetry noted was in TONKAWA where the present and past suffixes occupy one position class in the verb and the future suffix a different one. Furthermore, the future suffix is much closer to the theme, presupposing a derivational class as opposed to the inflectional position of the other tense suffixes. A similar situation is found in ONONDAGA where future is marked by a prefix (only two prefix classes) and past belongs to the penultimate suffix class (one of many).

is identical in form with the present continuous auxiliary. These
considerations lead us to propose the following:

If the future is periphrastic, the auxiliary will always be a
present tense or unmarked form.

2.3 Temporal gradation

Another measure of markedness in tense systems may be found
in those languages that divide the basic temporal sectors of past,
present and future into finer degrees. Thus in GUARANÍ, for
example, the past is divided into recent, general and remote,
marked by three different postverbal particles (there is also a
customary past but this represents an essentially aspectual category overlapping the entire range of past tenses). On the other
hand, in CHUKCHI a distinction is made between general and remote future but none in the past. In such cases, one might expect
-- in terms of the neutralization of future with present or of past
with present -- prospective languages to have finer gradation in the
past and retrospective ones in the future. The evidence, while not
conclusive, seems to point to the opposite conclusion.

	Number of Languages with:		
	More P-grades	More F-grades	P-grades = F-grades
Prospective	Ø	2	22
Retrospective	8	2	9
?	1	1	2

Tense Gradation

As the table indicates, there is a fairly strong tendency for retrospective languages with tense gradation to have finer grading in the
past than in the future. The two exceptions are CHUKCHI and TON-
KAWA. In CHUKCHI the distinction between more immediate and
more remote futures appears to be fictitious. There are several
devices for marking future: a desiderative prefix or auxiliary, the
desiderative prefix with a continuative suffix, a hortative prefix
with the continuative, or simply the continuative suffix. Of these,
according to Bogoras (1922: 773, 776), hortative plus continuative
may be used as an intentive or general future but also occasionally
as a remote (i.e., nonimmediate) future. In TONKAWA the basic
temporal contrast is future-nonfuture. Remote future appears to be
formed by adding the nonfuture suffix to the proximal future suffix.
The nonfuture suffix is identical in shape with a locative auxiliary.

If these two have the same origin, the ultimate meaning would perhaps be deictic (in fact, Hoijer 1933-8: 85 refers to the nonfuture as
a "definite past, near or remote") in which case this suffix would
actually mark distance from the basic tense, i.e., unmarked nonfuture or future. However, the resulting forms do mark two different grades in the future and TONKAWA does constitute an
exception to the general pattern.

If, on the other hand, we analyze our findings in terms of that
characteristic of Greenberg's markedness theory referred to as
syncretization (1966: 73), the expression of past time as a whole is
more unmarked in relation to that of the future in retrospective
than in prospective languages. If this is a valid interpretation of
the data, we would expect the converse to be true, i.e., that the
expression of future time is more unmarked in prospective languages, but the facts do not support this view, or do so only in
meagerly fashion as shown in the above table. The explanation for
this apparent discrepancy may lie in the empirical observation that
future tenses in general are more marked than past tenses and
simply more is known about past events; hence, in the case of
prospective languages, the tendency toward greater markedness
of past tenses and corresponding unmarkedness of future tenses is
at least partially interfered with by the overall supremacy of future
markedness. Furthermore, in the two prospective languages with
finer tense gradation in the future, SOMALI and TONGAN, two
grades are involved: immediate and nonimmediate; and in both
instances, immediate future is marked by the present tense forms.
Of course, by definition this is one of the functions of the present
tense in any prospective language, but in SOMALI and TONGAN
the future function is apparently specifically limited to an immediate
period which is not the case in other prospective languages such as
ENGLISH where present as future may cover a time sector coterminous with that covered by the formal future tense (consequently,
there is no question of gradation in the latter type).

In sum, the case for tense gradation can at this point only be
stated in the form of a statistical tendency:

Regarding tense gradation: retrospective languages tend
toward finer gradation in the past than in the future and
prospective languages tend toward no or equal gradation.

2.4 Obligatoriness of occurrence

Another indication of the more marked nature of the future in
retrospective languages is provided by the fact that at least in some

of them (GUARANÍ, ROTUMAN, KWAKIUTL and possibly TSIM-
SHIAN) the occurrence of future tenses is obligatory as opposed
to optional occurrence of past tenses in certain contexts. While
I have little in the way of definitive statements on the languages
sampled as to the optionality or obligatoriness of future or past
tenses, the few cases reported strongly suggest that:

> In retrospective languages, obligatory occurrence of an
> MOS past tense implies the same for an MOS future tense,
> the converse holding for prospective languages.

2.5 Neutralization

In addition to some of the neutralization features discussed
above, future tenses are often neutralized in certain sequential
and nontemporal environments in which the past-nonpast contrast
is maintained.

2.5.1 Subjunctive   The semantic range convered by the mode
generally dubbed subjunctive, i.e., representing uncertainty,
doubt, unreality, expectation, apprehension, etc. on the part of
the agent, is often defective in one or all of the MOS tenses. Thus
in MODERN GREEK, HAUSA, JAPANESE and RAROTONGAN
there are no temporal distinctions in the subjunctive. On the other
hand, in FRENCH, GEORGIAN, OLD IRISH, LATIN and FOX the
future is neutralized with the present (or nonpast) in the subjunctive
as opposed to the marked future of the indicative. While HAITIAN
CREOLE makes no formal distinction between indicative and subjunctive, in precisely those semantic contexts expressed by the
subjunctive in FRENCH, the major source language, the future is
neutralized with the present in the indicative. In LITHUANIAN
the temporal contrast is lost in the colloquial language but only the
future is neutralized in the literary language. The GERMAN subjunctive is exceptional among INDO-EUROPEAN languages in this
respect; it maintains the three-way tense contrast of the indicative,
albeit with certain restrictions. The only other language with a
future subjunctive was SOMALI. However, while Bell gives fairly
detailed information on both the indicative and the subjunctive as
well as on all tenses and aspects, he only once refers to the future
subjunctive (1953: 89) and provides no examples of its use. The
form cited is identical with that of the negative future indicative.
Since from a logical standpoint the very nature of the semantic
categories usually expressed by the subjunctive is such that a
future or posterior event or state is always implied, it is not surprising that the inherent category of future time tends to remain

unmarked. Inasmuch as we can compare them at all, we might say that future and subjunctive are in some ways "mutually inclusive," hence one or the other is superfluous. In any event I know of no case where a past but not a future MOS tense is neutralized in the subjunctive or a semantically comparable category or class of constructions. As demonstrated by the situation in LITHUANIAN above and also comparing the past-nonpast contrast in the subjunctive of CLASSICAL GREEK with the atemporal subjunctive of MODERN GREEK in conjunction with the semantic factors involved, there appears to be a strong likelihood of the existence of a diachronic universal:

> The chronological ordering of tense neutralization in a subjunctive or semantically comparable category is always unidirectional: the future-nonfuture contrast is neutralized first, the past-nonpast last.

2.5.2 Negative   In several of the languages examined the future tense is neutralized in negative constructions without a corresponding neutralization of the past. In HAITIAN CREOLE the continuous present replaces the future in negative clauses. In MENDE future merges with present in the negative conjugation. In RAROTONGAN the imperfect (incomplete, nonpast) is always substituted for the future after the negative particle. In TAGALOG the "modal" (unmarked) form of the verb replaces the future after a negative. In ONONDAGA future, but not past, is replaced by the indefinite in negative verbs. And in GEORGIAN the past-present-future contrast found in the positive participles is reduced to a past-nonpast contrast in the negative participles.

2.5.3 Gapping   The deletions found in conjunctive constructions, more recently referred to as "gapping,"[7] involving the loss of certain features from the noninitial or nonfinal verbs of a conjunctive series, also cast some light on the relatively greater markedness of future tenses in some of the languages studied. Thus, in HAITIAN CREOLE, ENGLISH, GERMAN and ROTUMAN,[8] noninitial verbs in conjunctive series are usually unmarked in the future but marked in the past; the same applies to DAKOTA except

---

[7]By Ross, for example, in "Gapping and the Order of Constituents," a paper presented at the 10th International Congress of Linguists, 1967.

[8] For ROTUMAN and DAKOTA the unmarked form of the verb is the same as the nonfuture (or aorist).

that it is the nonfinal verbs that are neutralized (DAKOTA is an
SOV language). The same is true for RAROTONGAN but with the
addition of an anaphoric particle to the verb to serve as a cross-
reference to the future-marked initial verb. In TAGALOG the
modal form of the verb may replace the future.   KWARA?AE,
which contrasts present and future imperatives, allows for optional
neutralization of noninitial serial future imperatives with present
imperatives. Such gapping is not permitted in FRENCH, KWA-
KIUTL and TSIMSHIAN. Since in all those languages in which
gapping occurs the future marker is a relatively loosely bound
particle or enclitic, or an auxiliary verb as in ENGLISH, TAGA-
LOG and GERMAN, one might suppose that the exceptions to gapping could be attributable to future constructions involving closely
bound affixes as with the simple future in FRENCH; but in KWA-
KIUTL the future is an enclitic and in TSIMSHIAN a preverbal
particle. However, the fact that past tenses on the whole tend to
be more bound in form than future tenses may help to explain why
they do not seem to lend themselves so readily to deletion in serial
constructions. Once again, barring evidence to the contrary, we
may propose the following:

Deletion of past tense in noninitial (or nonfinal) verbs of
conjunctive series implies deletion of future tense in the
same environment.

2.5.4 Subordinate clauses   There are a number of subordinate
clause types temporally located in the future that are found in
most languages. In some languages future is neutralized in these
environments, in others not. Due in part to the incompleteness
of the information for many of the languages sampled and in part
to the language-sensitive nature of many of these constructions,
it would be presumptuous to formulate any firm general statements
but the data are often suggestive of certain tendencies worth noting.
What follows, then, must be taken as very tentative indeed.[9]

Clauses referring to events always anterior to those of the corresponding main clauses (AFTER-clauses) are rarely marked by

---

[9] Factual statements are true for those languages sampled for
which adequate data was available and only in an MOS future context
except for posterior past and indirect discourse. Furthermore, only
temporal or sequential forms are considered here. Thus, for example, a present perfect denoting completion as well as anteriority as
in: When he has eaten I'll speak to him is excluded from consideration.

future; in retrospective languages they are usually unmarked or nonfuture and in prospective languages either present or past (indicative of perfect or anterior event).

Clauses referring to events anterior to (or near-simultaneous with) those of the corresponding main clauses (WHEN-clauses) are in most languages marked by future or present (or nonfuture in retrospective languages) tenses. Among prospective languages there are a few instances where an atemporal or present subjunctive is used (RAROTONGAN, TAGALOG, SOMALI).

Conditional clauses referring to probable events anterior to (or near-simultaneous with) those of the corresponding main clauses (IF$_1$-clauses) are marked principally by present or future tenses in prospective languages and are unmarked (or nonfuture), or more rarely marked by future or present, in retrospective languages.

Clauses referring to events always posterior to those of the corresponding main clauses (BEFORE-clauses) are usually marked by present or present subjunctive, more rarely by future or simply unmarked in prospective languages. Data on such clauses in retrospective languages is too limited to show any definite propensities.

Clauses denoting purpose and hence of necessity referring to posterior time are chiefly marked by present or present subjunctive in prospective languages but also less commonly by future or atemporal subjunctive. In retrospective languages future is the commonest marker.

Clauses that form the objects of certain verbs of perception or mental activity (expectation, fear, supposition, etc.) referring essentially to posterior events (OBJECT-clauses) are marked primarily by future in retrospective languages and by present, present subjunctive or future in prospective languages.

Comparing the ways in which tense is marked in these six clause types perhaps most striking is the fact that while AFTER-clauses are only rarely marked by future, all of the remaining five types are often, or at least more often, marked by future. Sequentially, AFTER-clauses fall into the same general class as WHEN and IF$_1$ clauses, anterior, while BEFORE, OBJECT and purpose clauses all refer to posterior events. Semantically, however, AFTER-clauses represent assumed facts or necessary preconditions, events whose occurrence is to be taken for granted, whereas the

other five types generally represent events that have a certain
measure of probability but perhaps not the certainty associated
with AFTER-clauses. In the latter there is an impression of
finality; in the former, of inconclusiveness.

2.5.5 Backshifting In addition to these there are three other
subordinate clause types and one main clause type which, when
neutralization occurs, show a strong tendency to do so not by
shifting to a present or unmarked tense, but rather to a past tense.

Clauses that refer to a future event in the MOS past (FP-clauses),
i.e., a posterior past, are most often marked by a combined future-
past marker (especially characteristic of most INDO-EUROPEAN
languages) or future (common in POLYNESIAN), less often by past
or past subjunctive in prospective languages. In retrospective
languages they are usually marked by future.

In indirect discourse corresponding to an MOS future of direct
discourse, the languages of the present sample mark the subordinate clause in much the same way they do an FP-clause: future
or, somewhat less widespread, future-past in prospective languages
and future in retrospective languages.

Clauses expressing contrary-to-fact or hypothetical condition
(IF$_2$ clauses) in prospective languages are chiefly marked by past
and less commonly by past or present subjunctive, a special "conditional" (hypothetical) verbal element or conjunctive (with an
unmarked verb), or future with or without a hypothetical adjunct
or conjunction. In retrospective languages these clauses are primarily marked by nonfuture with a hypothetical or other adjunct
or conjunction expressing impotentiality or low degree of potentiality
and less often by past or present subjunctive.

Main clauses used to indicate the result of a contrary-to-fact
condition (COND) (traditionally and confusingly dubbed "conditional
mode" in grammars of INDO-EUROPEAN languages) in prospective
languages are often marked by future-past or future plus hypothetical, sometimes solely by a hypothetical element, past, potential
or a subjunctive. In retrospective languages such clauses are
most often marked by future, with or without an additional element
(hypothetical, resultative, etc.), or future-past and somewhat less
often by hypothetical, potential or subjunctive.

The first two clause types, FP and indirect discourse, are
situated in a real posterior past while the last two are in a hypothetical

future; yet formally all four are often wholly (as in IF_2-clauses) or partially marked for past in prospective languages, rarely so in retrospective languages except in the case of COND clauses or sentences. This phenomenon, usually appropriately referred to as "backshifting" in the literature,[10] seems to be caused by two different sets of factors. In the case of indirect discourse and FP-clauses one important factor is undoubtedly a sort of assimilation to or attraction by the past tense of the main clause (cf. Jespersen 1965: 293-4 for ENGLISH and Cohen 1965: 131 for FRENCH). A second one is the logic of the situation, i.e., both subordinate clause types refer to some time in the MOS past. But in the case of IF_2 and COND clauses the governing factor would appear to be relative distant from reality as implied by tenses. Thus — and this is especially true of prospective languages where the present-future contrast in its simplest form may be neutralized-- the MOS present represents a more "real" time, a time closer to the speaker, and the past a time more remote, hence more "unreal."[11] There is an interesting contrast here between the "frontshifting" of historical tenses (cf. 1.3.2 above) which brings the past closer to the reality of the present and the opposite effect achieved by backshifting.

This argument receives some support from the existence of partially deictic tense systems in some languages. In RAROTONGAN, for example, the basic temporal contrasts are marked by a past (also perfective), present (zero) and future but superimposed on this system is a second one of a purely deictic nature, consisting of direction particles employed temporally to express various degrees of differentiation:

kua ?aere ?ua ake nei   te   pa?ī
"[pf] go   just here now[art] ship"
'The ship has only just sailed.'

---

[10] The term was apparently first used by Jespersen in reference to the effect produced when shifting from direct to indirect discourse in certain cases involving erroneous supposition and in the result of contrary-to-fact condition (in, for example, Essentials of English grammar, 260-3, but not in The philosophy of grammar, 292-5, where he speaks of it simply as "shifting of tenses"). Allen (1966: 171-6) expanded the range of the term to also include the same tense movement after "wish, as if," etc. and in nonfactual conditions (Jespersen's "preterite of imagination").

[11] Jespersen (1965:265-6 and 1966:255) attributes this to the implicit denial of present or future reality represented in these types of constructions.

The direction particle ake "indicates movement oblique to the
speaker, or refers to the place where the speaker will soon be or
will soon have left" (Buse 1963a: 164). Hence in this sentence ake
refers to movement from the past toward the present (i.e., speaker
time and place) and, in conjunction with kua, ʔua, and nei, forms
an immediate past. A similar situation exists in another MALAYO-
POLYNESIAN language, KWARAʔAE (Deck 1933), where the adverb
naʔa 'now (already)' apparently from the definite article na plus an
adjectival suffix -ʔa (cf. also neʔe 'this, here'), added to a present verb may be used to indicate immediate past and added to a
future verb to mark present action continuing into the future:

    nau   ku leka naʔa
    "[1 sg pres] go"
    'I'm going now.' (already left) (p. 38)

    nau   kui leka naʔa
    "[1 sg fut]   go"
    'I'm just going.' (p. 41)

    In several of the languages investigated the future marker is of
deictic origin. In many BERBER dialects originally without a
formal future, a future preverb has evolved from a demonstrative
particle. Thus in AHAGGAR TUAREG, for example, the relative
future preverb hé- is from the COMMON BERBER demonstrative
*ha- 'here it is' (Marcy 1939: 130-2). The future suffix -kess in
KOREAN is from an earlier kŏ '(over) there' + is 'be' (Kwon 1962:
75). The CLASSICAL LATIN future imperative -tō (OLD LATIN
-tod) is from *-tōd, the ablative of a demonstrative, lit. 'from
this (time)' (Kent 1946: 128-9). The future (positive) suffix -lɔ
(with tone 2 or 3) in MENDE appears to be related to a demonstrative verb lɔ₃ 'be this' which is also used as an auxiliary with
present continuous verbs (Aginsky 1935: 62-3, 73-5). And in SIUS-
LAWAN the future suffix -tŭx may contain a demonstrative element
tŭ 'that (one)' (Frachtenberg 1922: 528, 582).

    Backshifting in some languages serves other purposes than those
already mentioned. Of these perhaps the most notable is in marking polite requests. This is the case in ENGLISH:

    Would you see me tomorrow? vs. Will you see me tomorrow?

in FRENCH:

    Auriez-vous la bonté de me rendre un service?

and in TONGAN in prohibitions where past tense is used as a more polite form instead of the normal future tense (Churchward 1953, no example). Is it possible that this function of backshifting is simply another manifestation of the distance-from-reality principle, i.e., in the sense of being somehow removed from the ordinary, the here and now?

2.5.6 **Participles** Another grammatical category that is often prone to neutralization of future is that of participial constructions. Although I have reliable information on only two retrospective languages,[12] MANDAN and DAKOTA (both SIOUAN languages), future is neutralized in the participles resulting in a past-nonpast contrast. Among prospective languages, as one might expect, neutralization of future in the participial system is quite common. On the other hand I know of no case where past is neutralized but future retained. This can be restated as a universal:

A future participle implies both past and present participles but neither of the two converses is necessarily true.

2.5.7 **Subjunctive, negative and indefinite** The relatively high incidence of neutralization of future tenses in subjunctive and negative constructions is logically compatible with the measure of uncertainty, indefiniteness — the unknown quality — that is of necessity associated with the future inasmuch as the categories of subjunctive (see also note 13) and negative are perhaps to a certain extent inherently indefinite. At least the connection appears to be more than fortuitous and it would be of interest to look into the relationships that exist between future tenses and other semantically indefinite (or prone to indefiniteness) categories such as interrogatives, evidentials, certain determiners, etc.

3. **Semantics**

3.1 **General**

The range of meanings embodied in future tenses is a fruitful source for investigating their origins and patterns of historical development. In this section we will look at future tenses in some of the languages included in the sample from four standpoints:

---

[12]Discounting LITHUANIAN the classification of which is uncertain. However, a past-present-future contrast is retained for participles in LITHUANIAN.

1. their atemporal functions;
2. other grammatical categories particularly associated
   with future markers;
3. atemporal categories that may function as future indicators;
4. their etymologies.

For the most part the semantic features encountered in the
present sample fall into three major types: aspectual, modal and
goal-oriented. The last-named may be further divided into categories of spatial and nonspatial references. Thus the latter includes categories of cause, goal, purpose and result while the
former covers directionals such as allative or ablative case (or
preposition, postposition) or basic motion verbs meaning 'go' or
'come,' deictics, etc. In addition there is a small residue of
miscellaneous categories not readily classifiable with any of the
three major types.

3.2 Atemporal functions of future tenses

Of the aspectual categories that represent secondary functions
of future markers, gnomic or general truth was found to be the
most frequent (FRENCH, ENGLISH, CLASSICAL GREEK, LITHU-
ANIAN, TONGAN, DAKOTA, CLASSICAL MANDAIC, RUSSIAN,
HAUSA and perhaps KWARA? AE). However, this can hardly be
viewed as a general characteristic of future since a simple present
or unmarked tense is used even more often in this function. Furthermore, the application of one MOS tense to gnomic situations
in a given language does not necessarily preclude the use of another
for the same purpose (e.g. ENGLISH, FRENCH, GREEK). The
rationale for this semantic development could lie in the open-
endedness of gnomic time, that is, an event which was once true,
still is and (presumably) always will be.

Closely related to this function is the employment of a future
tense to mark customary or habitual event (HAUSA, LITHUANIAN,
RUSSIAN, ROTUMAN and TAGALOG). Note, too, cases like
ENGLISH would (FP) for customary past (He would brush his teeth
before breakfast). This use of a future tense to convey customary
or habitual event may be due to the inherent expectation of a recurrence of the event. Also in TAGALOG we find a rather interesting frequentative construction which produces agentive nouns. The
active future or occasionally present (punctual) theme is used as
such without any other derivational marker; magbabaká 'warrior'
(mag- act., CV-reduplicated stem marks future, baka *'fight').
A semantically similar construction resulting in frequentative

THE NATURE OF FUTURE TENSES   103

adjectives is formed from the passive future or modal (often marks
future event) stem with the potential or causative prefix: <u>maka</u>-
<u>kalimótan</u> 'forgettable' (<u>maka</u>- potent., CV-future, -<u>an</u> pass.,
<u>limot</u> 'forget').

The remaining examples of aspectual function are both inceptive
(ROTUMAN, KOREAN).

Goal-oriented functions were limited to two very closely linked
categories: purpose (GUARANÍ, KOREAN, KWARA?AE, MANDAIC,
CENTRAL SIERRA MIWOK, ROTUMAN, TSIMSHIAN, DAKOTA,
WINNEBAGO, HOPI, TAGALOG, TONGAN, BENGALI and HAUSA)
and result or consequence (KOREAN, TSIMSHIAN, KWAKIUTL).

Modal functions constituted the most diverse assemblage of
categories. In roughly descending order of certainty in those
languages for which information on such functions was available,
a future tense also served to mark:

Imperative (usually emphatic, often concomitant with a change
in intonation) in ENGLISH, GERMAN, ESKIMO, FRENCH, ISLAND
CARIB, CUNA, CLASSICAL JAPANESE, KOREAN, KWAKIUTL,
KWARA?AE, LITHUANIAN, MANDAIC, CENTRAL SIERRA MIWOK,
ONONDAGA, ROTUMAN, SIUSLAWAN, OLD PRUSSIAN, TAGALOG,
HAITIAN CREOLE, DAKOTA, HAUSA, HAIDA and TSIMSHIAN.
In GUARANÍ, HOPI, KOREAN, CENTRAL SIERRA MIWOK, SAN-
SKRIT and DAKOTA, it may indicate obligation or necessity. A
third imperative-related category marked by future was the polite
request (HAUSA, KOREAN, ENGLISH, FRENCH, WINNEBAGO,
FOX, RUSSIAN and COOS).

The next category in the scale of certainty or probability com-
prises the optative or hortative functions (LATIN, FOX, LITHU-
ANIAN, KOREAN, KWARA?AE, MANDAIC, CENTRAL SIERRA
MIWOK, RAROTONGAN, JAPANESE, ROTUMAN, DAKOTA and
OLD PRUSSIAN) and their antithesis, the cavetive (KOREAN).

A short step away are the desideratives (KOREAN, KWARA?AE,
LITHUANIAN, CENTRAL SIERRA MIWOK, SANSKRIT [future
participle], DAKOTA and perhaps TAIRORA). In PRE-CLASSICAL
GREEK an andative future composed of the active participle plus
i5n 'going' underwent fusion and reanalysis to become the desiderative suffix -seí5.

In CENTRAL SIERRA MIWOK, HAUSA, JAPANESE, SANSKRIT
and possibly ONONDAGA the future tense may also mark probability.

Another common function of future markers is to indicate possibility or potential as in SANSKRIT, OLD IRISH, KOREAN, LITHUANIAN, RUSSIAN, TSIMSHIAN, MODERN GREEK and GUARANÍ.

In some languages the future may mark supposition as in FRENCH:

Cet homme-là, il sera l'inspecteur?
'That man over there, (I suppose) he would be the inspector?'

or GERMAN:

Er wird der Mörder sein.
'(I guess) he is the murderer.'

This is also true of DUTCH, LITHUANIAN, ROTUMAN, DAKOTA and JAPANESE.

A future marker often serves to express a hypothetical condition or consequence. Thus the future tense may be used to mark hypothetical condition in LITHUANIAN and CENTRAL SIERRA MIWOK, and consequence in ROTUMAN, TONGAN and JAPANESE. Combined with a hypothetical mode or past tense marker the future tense is more commonly used to indicate the consequence of a contrary-to-fact condition (cf. 2.5.5) but in KWARA?AE and TAIRORA future + hypothetical may express the condition itself. This is also possible, although somewhat obsolescent, in ENGLISH with a FP: if he should come ... (as opposed to: if he came... or if he were to come...). Languages with FP for consequence are ENGLISH, DUTCH, FRENCH, OLD IRISH, KOREAN and CENTRAL SIERRA MIWOK; those with future + hypothetical are KWARA?AE, MANDAN, TAGALOG and TSIMSHIAN. In MENDE, a device semantically equivalent to hypothetical is used: future + negative hortative.

Wonder or amazement is sometimes conveyed by a future tense form as in RUSSIAN:

A on kak vskočít?
'But how could he jump up suddenly (like that)?'
(vskočít pres. perf. = fut. of vskákivaet) (Isačenko 1960: 86)

or KOREAN:

ilkkenil etči ttisil morir-io
'When (if) he can read, how does he not understand the meaning?'
(ilkkenil is a future perfect [anterior] participle) (Ramstedt 1939:97)

This kind of construction appears to exist in TSIMSHIAN also. All
examples of the type are questions. The underlying meaning seems
to be either potential or contrary-to-fact, hence, in conjunction
with the interrogative component of the sentence, expressive of
disbelief, surprise, etc.

Of the residual categories, two figure among the atemporal
functions of future tenses.

In RAROTONGAN the preverbal future particle ká is also used
with cardinals to produce a counting form:

ka ta?i, ka rua, ka toru
'one, two, three' (Buse 1963a:154).

Future here apparently refers to a prospective series extending to
some indefinite point in the future.

In TAGALOG the agentive noun and frequentative adjective constructions formed from future stems noted above appear to be
semantically related to either habitual or potential event.

These observations on some of the atemporal functions of future
tenses lead to at least two conclusions. First, while various kinds
of aspectual and modal categories may be represented by future
markers, only nonspatial (or nondirectional) goal-oriented categories may be so expressed. This lends support to the oft-noted
tendency for spatial categories to be semantically extended to
include analogous temporal ones but rarely (or never?) the converse. It would be interesting to see whether this also holds true
for the other basic tenses. And second, future tenses are far more
likely to be put to modal uses than to either aspectual or goal-
oriented ones. While I do not have nearly as much detailed information on the secondary functions of past tenses, it seems highly
probable that this is not the case with them except for the fairly
widespread use of past in backshifting due to hypothetical situations
or polite requests. The reason for the preponderance of modal
applications of future tenses must lie in the fact that most modal
categories refer to differing degrees of uncertainty, which correlates with the element of uncertainty inherent in any future event,

while past tenses generally refer to completed, hence certain,
events. The modal interrelations of future tenses often raise the
question as to whether "future" is best viewed as a temporal or as
a modal category. Certainly in some languages the evidence
strongly suggests the latter view. Thus in ENGLISH, for example,
the future auxiliary functions very much like the modal auxiliaries
(can, must, ought to, should, have to, etc.), is subject to similar
constraints and is homonymous with and descended from the volitional verb will. Sansom holds that the modern JAPANESE tense
system has evolved from one that contrasted degrees of certainty
and aspectual categories. Thus an original affirmative, completive
and definite form developed into a past tense, while one denoting
uncertainty or probability and incompleteness ultimately came to
mark futurity. Also, in colloquial JAPANESE the future tense is
normally used only when referring to an uncertain or probable
event, the present forms being used to represent other more certain future events. However, there are numerous cases where the
future tense functions analogously to the present and past tenses
and clearly serves primarily to mark temporal, not modal, relations as in FRENCH, for example.

3.3 Categories associated with future tenses

Although available data on categories either formally or semantically associated with future tenses was rather scanty, some of
it is illuminating and worthy of comment. Among the aspectual
categories several languages exhibited a special relationship between future and incompletive. Thus in INDO-EUROPEAN and
CLASSICAL MANDAIC, present and future (no contrast in MAN-
DAIC) were originally incompletive versus a completive past. In
JAPANESE the future is formed from the imperfect stem. Similarly in LITHUANIAN the imperfect (past), present and future stems
share the same base (the infinitive) but the perfect (past) has a
different one. In TAGALOG the future stem contains a marker of
incompleteness or continuous action. In HAUSA future verbs
always take the incompletive suffix. And in RAROTONGAN the
future marker is replaced (neutralized) by the imperfect (i.e.,
incompletive) in just those circumstances where the past is replaced by the perfect. On the other hand, in HUPA the future tense
forms are based on the present definite (punctual, completive)
stem. In RUSSIAN the present perfective, whose primary temporal function is to mark future events, generally represents
momentaneous or nondurative aspect. In much the same way the
GEORGIAN determinative preverbs, which constitute the commonest means of indicating futurity in the verb, are equally well

associated with momentaneous action. In AIKAMTHELI, a dialect
of ŠIRIŠANA, spoken in Northern Brazil and Venezuela, present
tenses are progressive while anticipatory (future, posterior) tenses
are punctual. The GEORGIAN preverbs just noted serve primarily
in most cases to specify goal-oriented activity.

While there appeared to be a few scattered examples of possible
modal associations with future tenses in some of the languages
investigated, the evidence was not decisive enough to rely on.
However, two miscellaneous categories were definitely associated
with future tenses.

In some INDONESIAN languages the future preverb and in others
the passive marker have the same origin, a preposition meaning
'to, towards.' Brandstetter (1916:165) offers a possible explanation. In INDONESIAN basic verbs of motion may often be omitted
leaving the following directional preposition to carry the semantic
burden. Thus a verb of 'going' in the function of an andative future,
once deleted, might have left the directional preposition with that
meaning whereas a verb of 'getting,' for example, as in 'I get into
the curse' would have left the preposition with a passive meaning.
In GEORGIAN the determined verb (corresponding to future) is
formed from a passive stem. In this case the connection between
passive and future seems to rest on the fact that passives often
connote possibility, hence desirability and ultimately eventuality.
In CHUKCHI the passive participle is identical in form with the
gerundive (i. e., obligatory future) of the KORYAK and KAMCHADAL
dialects.

The remaining associated category is indefiniteness. In ONON-
DAGA only future verbs can be indefinite and the indefinite prefix
replaces the future prefix when the verb is negated. In TLINGIT
the future and indefinite prefixes frequently cooccur. In TONGAN
the future preverb is sometimes used as a simple predicator in
relative clauses with indefinite antecedents, regardless of the MOS
time of the main clause:

na?e tātāha ha manu ?e mo?ui
"past be-rare indefinite-art. animal future live"
'Only here and there did an animal survive.'(Churchward 1953:234)

In TONKAWA future verbs, otherwise unmarked for tense, are
indefinite. For ENGLISH Allen (1966:157-8) points out that while
there is a formal contrast between identified (definite) and non-
identified (indefinite) past, preterite and present perfect respectively, the difference is neutralized in the future.

3.4 Atemporal categories used to mark future

Among the primarily aspectual markers that may also function as indicators of future time we found the following. In KOREAN there is a derivational suffix specifying inchoative state which also may occur in the sense of future existence.

In HAITIAN and MAURITIAN CREOLE, RAROTONGAN and CHUKCHI the durative or continuative may be used to designate future; in MODERN GREEK the simple present, which is durative vis-à-vis the aorist tenses, may be so used; in SOMALI the present continuous is used to mark an imminent future. Also in CHUKCHI the "derivational mode" (continuative) serves as a base for the formation of an intentive and two remote futures. Similarly in GEORGIAN the usual base for determined future verbs is the present (durative), although the addition of a determinative prefix generally results in a nondurative theme.

Representing the goal-oriented type, we have come across only a few scattered examples. Both QUILEUTE and KWAKIUTL have resultative affixes which are generally used instead of the temporal future markers in future situations construed as purposeful or consequential.

In CHUKCHI and RAROTONGAN allative-like constructions are used in certain contexts. In CHUKCHI verbal nouns that occur as complements of verbs of future implication (e.g. 'attempt, desire, prepare') take the allative case suffix, whereas in RARO-TONGAN there are a number of direction particles oriented in relation to the persons of the dialogue with both spatial and temporal values. One of these ake (see 2.5.5) refers to motion toward the speaker; in the following example it occurs with future reference:

    mē auē ake te   pēpe, e tāvarenga koe ki te mō'inā   u
    "if cry   [art] baby [impf] lull   you with[art] bottle milk"
    'If the baby cries (when I'm gone), keep him quiet with his bottle.'

Another refers to "...motion away from the speaker, or temporal progression away from the present (usually into the future)."

And a third, a?o "next to (usually just the other side of) the person addressed, happening next (the time or place being mentioned or understood)," as in:

mē kite a?o koe iā Tere, e ?akakite   kia   ?aere mai
"if see   you   [impf] inform [subjunc] come[to speaker]"
'If you should see Tere (where you are going), tell him to come
here.' (Buse 1963a:164-5)

A number of modals were found to have secondary future uses.
Thus in VEDIC SANSKRIT, AVESTIC and LITHUANIAN the injunctive was one means of indicating future time.

In BERBER and CHUKCHI the future may be expressed by the
optative or hortative. In SANTEE DAKOTA a desiderative or
optative particle ('would that...') is occasionally used instead of
the normal future in questions or statements involving uncertainty.

The inferential mode replaces the future in negative constructions in TAKELMA.

The subjunctive or a semantically equivalent mode replaces the
future in many languages, in particular when verbal or clausal
complements of verbs of future implication are involved.[13] This
is the case in FRENCH, GERMAN, ENGLISH (in the few constructions in which the old subjunctive survives, e.g. I demanded that
he come), the older GERMANIC languages, VEDIC SANSKRIT,
LATIN, LITHUANIAN, FOX, RAROTONGAN, AVESTIC, TAGALOG
(Modal), QUILEUTE, CHUKCHI, GEORGIAN, MODERN GREEK,
HAUSA, OLD IRISH and TONGAN (a subjunctive conjunction introduces the clause).

3.5 Future tense etymologies

The etymologies of future forms provide a great deal of insight
into the general semantics of the category. Starting again with
future tenses of aspectual origin, in the MORAVIAN contemporary
with OLD CHURCH SLAVIC the future tense was formed with an
inceptive auxiliary.

---

[13] Instructive in this regard are Hale and Buck's comment on the
LATIN subjunctive: "Each subjunctive tense has the force of the
indicative tense of the same name; and, in addition, each has a
future force" (1966:244); and Geary's on the subjunctive in FOX:
"In the subjunctive, the meaning is more theoretical or ideal than
factual. In the case of wishes and in temporal clauses there is a
strong future implication " (emphasis mine).

GOTHIC, GERMAN and CUNA have futures derived from in-
choatives and the ITALIC and CELTIC futures are from earlier
periphrastic constructions with auxiliaries meaning 'be' or 'become.' In UPPER CHINOOK the translative prefix ('become' with
intransitives, aorist with transitives) is formally identical with
the future of the KATHLAMET dialect (occurring only with intransitives in K. but with all verbs in EAST KATHLAMET).

The simple future suffix in TUNGUSIC is from an older durative
aorist.

Future formations originating in goal-oriented markers are
found in the RUSSIAN perfective and GEORGIAN determinative
prefixes.

In some languages purpose markers have evolved into future
tenses. Thus in the FRENCH CREOLES, FRENCH pour (+infini-
tive) has produced an immediate future in MAURITIAN and a future
imperative in HAITIAN. The OLD LATIN future infinitive (later
participle with esse) came from a periphrastic construction consisting of the supine (marking goal or purpose) + the auxiliary
'to be.' Paralleling the CREOLE example is the ITALIAN use of
a neutral verb of being followed by an original complement of
purpose:

Sta per mangiare.   'He's going to eat.'

Allatives sometimes develop into future tenses as already noted
in INDONESIAN (3.3). In GEORGIAN the preverb most frequently
used to mark future indicates motion toward the speaker or interlocutor.

An apparently widespread source of futures or intentives is a
basic verb of motion meaning 'go' which functions as an auxiliary.
Such constructions are found in ENGLISH, FRENCH and ANGEVIN
FRENCH, SPANISH, MODERN GREEK, CUNA, ARABIC, KWARA-
?AE (deferred future), CENTRAL SIERRA MIWOK, BASSA, GALLO-
ROMANCE and HAUSA. In LATIN and UMBRIAN a periphrastic
supine with auxiliaries meaning 'go' gave rise to a later future
passive infinitive. As noted above an earlier GREEK andative
future developed into a desiderative (3.2) and, in INDONESIAN,
the deletion of a verb meaning 'go' may have resulted in the association of future function with the following allative preposition
(3.3).

Semantically related to the andative futures are what we might call the "venitives," tenses that were originally verbs of 'coming.' Thus in SWEDISH, FINNISH (rare), EWE, SICILIAN and BASSA (one of the three intentives; the other two have andative auxiliaries), there are constructions that employ basic verbs of motion meaning 'come' as future auxiliaries. In ENGLISH and FRENCH the verb 'come' is used to mark future in temporal noun phrases:

dans les mois à venir   'in the months to come.'

In ENGLISH it may also be used in an inchoative sense: when you come to know him...; similarly in FRENCH, but denoting chance occurrence in the future:

si vous venez à le voir...   'if you should happen to see him...'

Perhaps also falling into this class of future markers is the KWARA?AE use of the direction particle ma?i 'hither' (toward the speaker) to indicate future or posterior event in noun phrases and the GEORGIAN common future determinative preverb mo- 'hither' (toward the speaker or interlocutor) (see 3.4).

An isolated but nonetheless interesting case is that of MODERN MANDAIC qa- + present participle, the common nonpast construction. In late CLASSICAL MANDAIC qa- was used to emphasize present event only but was extended in MODERN MANDAIC to include future reference and in some constructions, e.g. subordinate clauses introduced by 'before' or 'until,' to refer to future only. This proclitic was derived from the CLASSICAL MANDAIC preposition qam 'before, in front of.' In KONKOW, a CALIFORNIA PENUTIAN language, the regular future suffix has developed from a locative directional (LD) meaning basically 'down, downward motion' possibly through the intermediary of a common construction consisting of a continuative stem + the directional expressing action or state approaching a term, an end. Along with two other locative directions, the one under discussion forms an aspectual system. Thus -doJ 'up(ward)' but also inceptive -jeH 'hither, motion toward an unspecified point,' or progressive -kiT 'down-(ward)' or terminative, also future as in:[14]

---

[14] J, H and T are morphophonemic symbols representing j~ ˙, h ~ ˙ and t ~ ˙ respectively. Locative directionals and aspectuals occupy the same position class in the verb; future, a different one.

-doJ	-jeH	-kiT
LD ?ò·sa bódojtin	ný·msa síhje·n	čí·na· ?ýki·n
'He threw the rock	'The boat was	'He climbed down
up (into the air).'	floating along.'	the tree.'

Asp pédojpỳ	nìhaj ká·nohje·n	má·tmemènki·n
'Let's begin to eat.'	'I'm growing old.'	'Autumn is almost
		over.'(coming to an end)

Tense   nìhaj wó·notiki·n
                                      'I'll kill him.'

In several instances future tenses have evolved from deictic
elements. In addition to those already discussed in 2.5.5, there
is another example which, although not directly relevant to the
origins of future tenses, is worthy of mention in connection with
the general relationship between deixis and tense. In TONKAWA
what appears to be the locative auxiliary ('be in a certain place'),
when suffixed to the verb, marks the nonimmediate past; when
suffixed to a verb already containing the immediate future suffix,
the resultant form marks the nonimmediate future:

yagb - o?o· - ?
"strike [past] [1st]"
'I struck (him).'

yagb - a·dew -   o? - o
"strike [near fut][declar][1st]"
'I will/am about to strike (him).'

yagb - a·dew - o?o· - ?
"strike [near fut][past][1st]"
'I will strike (him).'

Modal categories provided the largest source class for future
markers. In many GERMANIC languages (at least ENGLISH,
DUTCH, EARLY HIGH GERMAN, SWEDISH, DANISH and ICE-
LANDIC), future auxiliaries evolved from PROTO-GERMANIC
*skal 'owes' or *skulan 'to owe.' In FRENCH and ITALIAN, the
analogous verbs from LATIN dēbēre are regularly used as auxiliaries of obligation, but at least in FRENCH, there is some
tendency to use devoir as a simple future, not necessarily involving any notion of obligation:

Il doit arriver dans quelques jours.
'He is to (is supposed to, or simply expected to) arrive in a
few days.'

In late LATIN or early ROMANCE another periphrastic construction indicative of obligation came into common use: infinitive +
habēre (cf. ENGLISH have to), eventually resulting in the para-
digmatic future (purely temporal) of most modern ROMANCE
languages. A parallel construction served the same purpose in
GOTHIC (haban+ infinitive) and a few examples of the same type
may be found in the OLD CHURCH SLAVIC New Testament texts.
Similar phenomena are found in ENGLISH: He is to arrive tomorrow, and the RUSSIAN durative future periphrasis, consisting of
the present perfective of 'be' + the infinitive. There was also the
UMBRO-SAMNITIC future perfect tense which was formed from
the perfect active participle + the injunctive of 'be' and the LATIN
first and second conjugation future in -bō from an earlier form of
the verb 'be.'

Two semantically near-identical categories, volitives and desid-
eratives, were particularly well represented in the present sample.
Languages with future auxiliaries from forms originally meaning
'want' included ENGLISH, DANISH, NORWEGIAN, RUMANIAN,
GALLO-ROMANCE, ANGEVIN FRENCH, ITALIAN (occasionally),
SERBO-CROATIAN, OLD CHURCH SLAVIC, MODERN GREEK,
ARABIC (immediate future), SOMALI and TAGALOG. In SOÛS
TUAREG (BERBER) one of the ways of expressing future is with
a preverb from an earlier volitional verb. Languages with orig-
inally desiderative futures included CLASSICAL MANDAIC and
TAKELMA (auxiliaries), CHUKCHI and FOX (prefixes), CUNA
and possibly CLASSICAL GREEK (suffixes). PROTO-INDO-
EUROPEAN *-syo, probably desiderative, was retained in SAN-
SKRIT, AVESTIC and LITHUANIAN (there is also a unique relic
in OLD CHURCH SLAVIC) as a future.

In AHAGGAR TUAREG (BERBER) one of the future preverbs
is the descendant of a verb meaning 'be able.'

Another major source of future tenses is represented by subjunctive or equivalent hypothetical or dubitative mode markers.
Thus in LATIN (third and fourth conjugation verbs), MIDDLE
IRISH, GOTHIC, OSCO-UMBRIAN and OLD JAVANESE, futures
have evolved from older subjunctives, while in MODERN GREEK
the future preverb is from a volitive (see above) plus the relative

that introduces subjunctive clauses. In TAGALOG the nonperi-
phrastic future is based on the modal (with subjunctive, imperative
and infinitive functions) stem.

Two miscellaneous types were encountered. In addition to the
-sy future, SANSKRIT had a periphrastic future formed from an
agent noun + the present of the verb 'to be.' This may be comparable to the TAGALOG frequentatives discussed above in 3.2.
In BERBER the indicative future is marked by a preverb that
derives from an earlier relative pronoun *ad 'that.' This type
of construction appears to be in part similar to the MODERN
GREEK relative just noted.

Thus the semantic categories that tended most to give rise to
future tenses were inceptive or inchoative aspectuals, a variety
of essentially spatial as well as nonspatial goal-oriented types and
quite a few modals, chiefly indicative of obligation, volition and
uncertainty or unreality. The conclusion drawn in Sec. 3.2 concerning the unidirectional nature of spatio-temporal metaphors,
namely that the evidence supports an extension of meaning from
spatial to temporal categories but not the reverse, is further
reinforced by the total absence of temporal sources for futures
as opposed to the relatively large number of spatial ones.

3.6 Summary findings

Summarizing our findings on the general semantics of future
tenses, we note first that application of the prospective-retrospective hypothesis to the various dynamic situations (i.e. atemporal
functions of future tenses, atemporal categories functioning as
futures, future tense etymologies) and semantic categories investigated uncovered no striking correlations between any of the latter
and either prospective or retrospective languages with the possible
exception of etymologies indicating an original verb of basic motion
('go,' 'come'), a volitive, or a hypothetical-dubitative. In general
the class of prospective languages accounted for more instances
of all major categories although among the atemporal future functions, the categories: purposive, imperative, optative, desiderative and potential were almost equally represented. The imbalances
noted could well be attributed to the fact that 23 languages were
identified as prospective and only 17 (including three doubtful cases:
ISLAND CARIB, LITHUANIAN and TAIRORA) as retrospective.

Secondly, the dynamic aspects of future semantics show certain
very definite correlations between the diachronic directions the

notion of futurity may take. If we compare the major categories
connected with the origins of future tenses (either atemporal categories functioning as futures or future etymologies) and those
connected with the directions in which future tenses may move
(atemporal functions of futures), we find that in both dynamic
situations the modal categories of obligation (and to a slightly
lesser extent the fairly closely related ones of imperative and
polite request), volitive-desiderative (and optative), and hypothetical-dubitative are of relatively high frequency of occurrence.
On the other hand, none of the major goal-oriented categories is
shared by both dynamic situations. The commonest type in terms
of origin was found to be the basic verbs of motion, followed at
some distance by deictics; in terms of deviation from future meaning the purposives constituted the only significant category. What
is true of the goal-oriented categories is also true of the aspectuals.
Common source categories were inchoative and durative; common
deviational ones were gnomic and customary event. The implications are obvious. While a basic verb of motion may evolve into
a future tense, the converse is not true, or at least is not likely.
The same logic would then apply to the remaining major goal-
oriented and aspectual categories:

deictic	>	future	but	future	⊅	deictic
inchoative	>	future	but	future	⊅	inchoative
durative	>	future	but	future	⊅	durative

and:

future	>	purposive	but	purposive	⊅	future[15]
future	>	customary	but	customary	⊅	future
future	>	gnomic	but	gnomic	⊅	future

However, the evidence for these six cases is somewhat more
limited than for the first. All in all the concept of future time as
primarily expressed in the verb and related future time as primarily expressed in the verb and related forms (e.g. participles,
infinitives) tends to be most closely associated with a large number
of modal notions which may be ranged along a scale of probability
(of occurrence of the event or state in question). Thus, listed in
descending order of probability, the modal categories we have
come across in the present study are:

---

[15] With the possible exceptions noted in Sec. 3.5.

obligation	probable
imperative	potential
polite request	inferential
optative	suppositional
cavetive	dubitative
volitive	hypothetical
desiderative	wonder, disbelief

Second in importance to the modals are a number of "open-ended" aspectuals (especially inchoative, durative and incompletive but also gnomic, actually timeless or infinite, and customary) that are essentially nonterminative in meaning, and the goal-oriented categories which are all potentially terminative. In fact, perhaps the one sense underlying all of these various categories in terms of future marking is goal-directed activity.

4. Conclusions

In the present paper we have proposed that the tense systems (excluding atemporal values) of most languages be classified as either prospective or retrospective. In the former case the present tense form(s) may often be used to mark future but not past time; in the latter the present may mark past but not future time. Notable exceptions to this categorization are gnomic and historical tenses.

Operating on the premise that future tenses are generally more marked than either past or present tenses, we investigated a number of features associated with tenses and a number of contexts in which tenses appear in most languages with the following findings:

4.1 General factors

1. Future tense forms may be less bound than present or past but never more so; hence a periphrastic MOS past implies a periphrastic MOS future but not the converse.

2. If the future is periphrastic, the auxiliary will always be a present tense or unmarked form.

3. Retrospective languages tend toward finer temporal gradation in the past than in the future and prospective languages tend toward no or equal gradation of past and future tenses.

4. In retrospective languages obligatory occurrence of an MOS past tense implies the same for an MOS future tense, the converse holding for prospective languages.

4.2 Neutralization

5. The loss of past-nonpast contrast in a subjunctive or semantically comparable category implies the prior loss of a future-nonfuture contrast in the same category.

6. Future tenses in some languages show a tendency not exhibited by past or present tenses to be neutralized in negative constructions.

7. Deletion of past tenses in noninitial (or nonfinal) verbs of conjunctive series implies deletion of future tenses in the same environment.

8. A future participle implies both past and present participles but neither of the two converses is necessarily true.

9. Retrospective languages tend to use R tenses (in subordinate clauses) as sequential markers whereas prospective languages do so to a lesser extent, i.e., some are used sequentially while others are used temporally (compare the predominant formal types used to mark WHEN, IF_1, purpose, OBJECT, FP, and indirect discourse clauses discussed in sections 2.5.4 and 2.5.5).

4.3 Backshifting

This phenomenon constitutes a special kind of neutralization; nonpast tenses are often replaced by past tenses in IF_2, COND, FP, and indirect discourse clauses in both prospective and retrospective languages. While backshifting in FP- and indirect discourse clauses is probably to be explained as resulting from assimilation of the R tense to the MOS tense of the main clause, in IF_2 and COND clauses distance from the relative reality of the present appears to be the primary factor. The "frontshifting" of historical tenses is the mirror image of backshifting in that a past event is rendered more real by marking it with a present tense.

4.4 Semantics

The semantic characteristics of future tenses were essentially examined from a dynamic standpoint: what were the original

meanings of the forms that came to be used as future tenses and
what atemporal functions do future tenses have? In answer to the
first part of the question, it was found that future tenses evolve
chiefly from modals, especially those expressing obligation, volition, uncertainty or unreality, and to a lesser extent from aspectuals or markers of goal-oriented categories. As to the second
part of the question, future tenses were most frequently found to
mark the same modal categories just noted and much less often
either aspectual or goal-oriented categories. This close connection between future tenses and modals is probably to be attributed
to the relative uncertainty inherent in both future event and most
of the categories subsumed under the general heading of modals.
The association between indefiniteness and futurity in several
languages also appears to be related to the feature of uncertainty
as is no doubt the neutralization of future tenses in negative and
subjunctive contexts noted above. While there were many cases
where a future tense evolved from an earlier spatial marker
(directional, deictic), there were no instances of a future tense
being used to refer to a spatial category. This is of more general
interest in support of the hypothesis that although spatial markers
may become or be used as temporal ones, the converse is not true.

BIBLIOGRAPHY

Abraham, R.C. 1959. The language of the Hausa people. London.

Aginsky, E.G. 1935. A grammar of the Mende language. Language
    Dissertation 20.

Albright, S.R. 1970. Kind of knowledge, information source,
    location and time in Širišana predicates. Department of Lin-
    guistics Seminar Paper No. 1, California State College,
    Fullerton.

Allen, R.L. 1966. The verb system of present-day American
    English. Janua Linguarum series practica 24. The Hague: Mouton.

Andrade, M.J. 1933-8. Quileute. Handbook of American Indian
    Languages, Bureau of American Ethnology, Bulletin 40 [HAIL]
    3. 149-292.

Bell, C.R.V. 1953. The Somali language. London.

Benveniste, E. 1959. Les relations de temps dans le verbe
    français. Bulletin de la Société de Linguistique de Paris [BSLP]
    54. 69-82.

Blake, F. 1925. A grammar of the Tagalog language. New Haven.

Boas, F. 1911a. Chinook. HAIL 1.599-677.

_____. 1911b. Tsimshian. HAIL 1.283-422.

_____. 1911c. Kwakiutl. HAIL 1.423-558.

Bogoras, W. 1922. Chukchee. HAIL 2.631-903.

Brandstetter, R. 1916. An introduction to Indonesian linguistics.
Asiatic Society Monograph 15. London.

Brugmann, K. 1888. Elements of the comparative grammar of the
Indo-European languages. New York.

Bull, W.E. 1960. Time, tense and the verb: a study in theoretical
and applied linguistics, with particular attention to Spanish.
University of California Publications in Linguistics 19. Berkeley
and Los Angeles.

Bunzel, R.L. 1933-8. Zuni. HAIL 3.385-514.

Buse, J.E. 1963a. The structure of the Rarotongan verbal piece.
Bulletin of the School of Oriental and African Studies [BSOAS]
26.152-69.

_____. 1963b. The structure of Rarotongan nominal, negative
and conjunctival pieces. BSOAS 26.393-419.

_____. 1963c. Rarotongan sentence structures. BSOAS 26.
632-45.

Chafe, W.L. 1970. A semantically based sketch of Onondaga.
IJAL mem. 25 (vol. 36, no. 2).

Churchward, C.M. 1940. Rotuman grammar and dictionary.
Sydney.

_____. 1953. Tongan grammar. Oxford University Press.

Clark, E.V. 1970. On the acquisition of the meaning of before and
after. Papers and Reports on Child Language Development 2.
Stanford.

Cohen, M. 1965. Sur le mode hypothétique en français. In:

Omagiu lui Alexandru Rosetti, 129-35. Bucureşti.

Deck, N.C. 1933-4. Grammar of the language spoken by the
Kwara'ae people of Mala, British Solomon Islands. Journal of
the Polynesian Society 42. 33-48, 133-44, 241-56 and 43. 1-16.

Ebeling, C.L. 1962. A semantic analysis of the Dutch tenses.
Lingua 11. 86-99.

Ebneter, T. 1966. Aviri a + infinitif et le problème du futur en
sicilien. Cahiers Ferdinand de Saussure 23. 33-48.

Ehrman, M.E. 1966. The meanings of the modals in present-day
American English. Janua Linguarum, series practica 45.

Faine, J. 1937. Philologie créole. Port-au-Prince, Haiti.

_____. 1939. Le créole dans l'univers. Port-au-Prince, Haiti.

Fillmore, C.J. 1970. Some thoughts about time and space in
semantic theory. Manuscript.

_____. 1971. Toward a theory of deixis. Manuscript.

Fourquet, M.J. 1959a. Le système verbal de l'allemand. BSLP
54. x xi -xxiii.

_____. 1959b. Le système verbal du néerlandais et du français.
BSLP 54. xlii-xlv.

Frachtenberg, L.J. 1922a. Coos. HAIL 2. 297-430.

_____. 1922b. Siuslawan (Lower Umpqua). HAIL 2. 431-630.

Freeland, L.S. 1951. Language of the Sierra Miwok. Indiana
University Publications in Anthropology and Linguistics mem. 6.

Geary, J.A. 1946. The subjunctive in Fox. IJAL 12. 198-203.

Goddard, P.E. 1911. Athabascan (Hupa). HAIL 1. 85-158.

Greenberg, J.H. 1966a. Universals of language (2nd ed.).
Cambridge.

_____. 1966b. Language universals. Current Trends in
Linguistics 3. 61-112. The Hague.

Gregores, E. and J.A. Suarez. 1967. A description of colloquial Guaraní. Janua Linguarum, series practica 27.

Hale, W.G. and C.D. Buck. 1966. A Latin grammar. Alabama Linguistic and Philological Series 8. University, Alabama.

Hobley, J. 1965. Bassa verbal formations. Journal of West African Languages 2. 39-50.

Hockett, C.F. 1967. The Yawelmani basic verb. Language 43. 208-22.

Hoijer, H. 1933-8. Tonkawa. HAIL 3. 1-149.

Holmer, N.M. 1946. Outline of Cuna grammar. IJAL 12. 185-97.

Isačenko, A. 1960. La structure sémantique des temps en russe. BSLP 55. 74-88.

Jakobson, R. 1957. Shifters, verbal categories, and the Russian verb. Russian Language Project, Harvard University.

Jespersen, O. 1965. The philosophy of grammar. New York.

_____. 1966. Essentials of English grammar. Alabama Linguistic and Philological Series 1. University, Alabama.

Johnson, O.E. 1936. Tense significance as the time of the action. Language Dissertation 21.

Jones, W. 1911. Algonquian (Fox). HAIL 1. 735-874.

Kent, R.G. 1946. The forms of Latin. Special Publications of the Linguistic Society of America. Baltimore.

Konow, S. 1938. Future forms denoting past time in Sanskrit and Prakrit. Norsk Tidsskrift for Sprogvidenskap 9. 231-9.

Kuryłowicz, J. 1964. The inflectional categories of Indo-European. Heidelberg.

Kwon, Hyogmyon. 1962. Das koreanische Verbum verglichen mit dem altaischen und japanischen Verbum. München.

Lakoff, R. 1970. Tense and its relation to participants. Language 46. 838-49.

Lehmann, W.P. and Lloyd Faust. 1951. A grammar of formal written Japanese. Cambridge.

Lotz, J. 1962. Semantic analysis of the tenses in Hungarian. Lingua 11. 256-62.

Macuch, R. 1965. Handbook of Classical and Modern Mandaic. Berlin.

Marcy, G. 1939. Observations sur le relatif futur en touareg Ahaggar. BSLP 41. 129-33.

Marr, N. and M. Brière. 1931. La langue géorgienne. Paris.

Miller, R.A. 1967. The Japanese language. Chicago.

Mirambel, A. 1956. Subordination et expression temporelle en grec moderne. BSLP 52. 219-53.

Paul, H. 1888. Principles of the history of language. London.

Pope, M.K. 1934. From Latin to modern French with especial consideration of Anglo-Norman. Manchester.

Potapova, N. 1947. Le Russe, manuel de la langue russe à l'usage des français. Moscow.

Ramstedt, G.J. 1939. A Korean grammar. Suomalais-ugrilaisen Seuran Toimituksia 92. Helsinki.

Renou, L. 1961. Le futur dans le véda. BSLP 56. 6-14.

Rosbottom, H. 1961. Different-level tense markers in Guaraní. IJAL 27. 345-52.

Sansom, G.B. 1928. An historical grammar of Japanese. Oxford.

Sapir, E. 1922. Takelma. HAIL 2. 1-296.

Schogt, H.G. 1965. "Temps et verbe" de Gustave Guillaume 35 ans après sa parution. Linguistique 1. 55-74.

_____. 1968. Le système verbal du français contemporain. Janua Linguarum, series practica 79.

Scur, G.S. 1963. Some remarks concerning the Germanic future.

Transactions of the Philological Society, 48-57.

Senn, A. 1966. Handbuch der litauischen Sprache. Heidelberg.

Swanton, J.R. 1911a. Tlingit. HAIL 1. 159-204.

_____. 1911b. Haida. HAIL 1. 205-282.

Sylvain, S. 1936. Le créole haïtien, morphologie et syntaxe. Wetteren, Belgium.

Taylor, D. 1951. Inflexional system of Island Carib. IJAL 17. 23-31.

Taylor, F.W. 1959. A practical Hausa grammar. Oxford.

Thalbitzer, W. 1911. Eskimo. HAIL 1. 967-1069.

Thumb, A. 1964. A handbook of the modern Greek language. Chicago.

Thurneysen, R. 1961. A grammar of Old Irish. Dublin.

Togeby, K. 1954-5. Les temps du français. Lingua 4. 379-93.

Ultan, R. 1967. Konkow grammar. Doctoral dissertation, University of California, Berkeley.

Vaccari, O. and E.E. 1937. Complete course of Japanese conversation grammar. Tokyo.

Vaillant, A. 1959. Le futur duratif en vieux-slave. BSLP 54. 1-17.

Valin, R. 1965. Les aspects du verbe français. In: Omagiu lui Alexandru Rosetti, 967-75. Bucureşti.

Vincent, A. and L. 1962. Introductory notes on Tairora verb morphology and syntax. Oceania Linguistic Monograph 6. 4-27.

Vogt, H. 1938. Esquisse d'une grammaire du géorgien moderne. Norsk Tidsskrift for Sprogvidenskap 9. 5-114 and 10. 5-188.

Wagner, G. 1934. Yuchi. HAIL 3. 295-384.

Weinreich, U. 1963. On the semantic structure of language. Universals of Language, ed. by J.H. Greenberg, 142-216.

Whitney, W.D. 1960. Sanskrit grammar. Cambridge, Mass.

Whorf, B.L. 1938. Some verbal categories of Hope. Language 14. 275-86.

Derivational Categories

YAKOV MALKIEL

ABSTRACT

This paper aims to accomplish three things: a) to delimit derivation — with full allowance for transitional cases — against such
other morphological processes as inflection and composition; b) to
distinguish, within the domain of derivation, between the most
characteristic variety, typologically, and the one best developed in
INDO-EUROPEAN, namely affixation (which, by definition, involves
a certain increase in the bulk of the given word) and several rival
varieties devoid of such increase: back-formation, clipping, con-
textually recognizable shifting to some other form class, rearrange-
ment of vowels, and the like; c) to isolate and analyze the most
sharply profiled varieties of affixes: prefixes, suffixes (a category
that offers particularly challenging classificatory problems), infixes,
interfixes, etc., beside suffixoids and interplays of pre- and suffixation ("parasynthesis"). Illustrations are offered from LATIN
and the majority of ROMANCE languages; also from ENGLISH,
GERMAN, RUSSIAN and a few other INDO-EUROPEAN languages,
plus SEMITIC by way of foil.

CONTENTS

1. Broad Contrast between Derivation and Composition

Derivation is one of the principal devices available to speakers
to produce a new word from one that already exists in their vocabulary. It is customary to cite, among its single most characteristic
features, the interplay of a root morpheme with at least one grammatical morpheme as the typical mechanism used to extract the
new word from the available resources. To that extent, derivation
at its purest clashes with composition at its purest. Compounding,
by definition, minimally involves two root morphemes. Thus,
SPANISH ¡adiós! '[I commend you] to God!' containing as it does
two free forms, namely the preposition a and the noun Dios, represents a compound. Conversely, SPANISH torero 'bullfighter'
falls into a root morpheme tor- 'bull' (corresponding to the free
form toro, under which the word is listed in dictionaries), plus
the masculine agentive suffix -ero 'one dealing with, acting on,
manufacturing, selling.' As a result of this structure, it constitutes a derivative.

2. Overlap between Prefixation and Composition

The line separating the two categories so far identified is not
all that neat. Thus, the vast majority of the GERMAN prefixes
occur also as prepositions and/or adverbs, e.g. durch- 'through,'
gegen- 'against,' über- 'above, beyond,' unter- 'under,' vor- 'before,' wieder- 'again,' zurück- 'back.' Consequently, one may
argue that a word architectured as is wiedersehen 'to see again'
is a compound, on the understanding that the prefix may be interpreted as being just a variety of the adverb-preposition. But the
four semantically pale elements underlying the prefixes be-, er-,
ge-, and ver-, as in behalten 'to keep,' erhalten 'to receive, obtain'
(beside halten 'to hold'), gerinnen 'to congeal' (alongside rinnen
'to flow'), and vertreten 'to represent' (flanking treten 'to tread')
are not used elsewhere as free forms— a state of affairs precluding
the classification of behalten, erhalten, gerinnen, and vertreten as
compounds. Similarly, the overwhelming majority of verbal prefixes (which French scholars label as "préverbes") in LATIN re-
appear in the ranks of adverbs and prepositions, e.g. ē-/ex- 'out,'
inter- 'between,' per- 'through,' prō- 'before,' sub- 'under,' a
situation which marginally justifies the analysis of exīre 'to go out'
and percurrere 'to run through' as compounds. But dis-, dī-
'asunder,' and re(d)- 'back, again' are strictly bound forms, and
the numerous verbs involving them qualify solely as derivatives.
Yet it is counterintuitive to separate all that strictly be-, er-, ge-,
and ver- from the remainder of GERMAN prefixes, with which they

interact, paradigmatically, or to establish a special isolative niche for LATIN dis-/dī- and re(d)-.

2.1 There is no dearth of other transitions from composition to derivation. Synchronically, one discovers words involving both processes, especially in GERMANIC; witness ENGLISH prizefighter, which contains one nominal component, another component which straddles the domains of nouns and verbs, plus an affix. One can similarly analyze GERMAN Bierbrauer 'beerbrewer' and LATIN agrimēnsor 'surveyor.' Diachronically, the transmutation of a "blurred" compound into an affixal derivative is an almost trivial phenomenon. The -wärts ingredient of GERMAN adverbs rückwärts 'back' and vorwärts 'forward, ahead' and the -ward segment of their ENGLISH counterparts afterward, inward, onward, toward are examples in point; the element at issue once meant something like 'turn, bent, slant,' being cognate to LATIN vertere. Under privileged circumstances, one can observe this metamorphosis step by step. Thus, LATE LATIN (ablative) laetā mente 'in a cheerful mood, with a cheerful mind' (a substitute for classical laetē) was clearly an adverbial phrase based on a compositional scheme. In contrast, FRENCH joyeusement 'cheerfully' is a derivative, in which -ment /mã/ represents little more than an average-sized suffix, particularly so in view of the elimination of ment from the lexicon. But OLD SPANISH miente (as against modern mente, clad in Latinized garb) involved an organic survival of mēns -tis 'mind,' and the original compositional design shines through, to this day, in such sequences as feroz y cruelmente 'fiercely and cruelly.'

2.2 It is equally vital to draw the sharpest possible line between inflection and derivation. Outwardly, the inflected word (i.e., typically, one placed in the context of declension, conjugation, or grading) is submitted to the same sort of formal adjustments -- chiefly affixational expansions — as one exposed to derivation; but the results are radically different. The derivational process leaves the word endowed with considerable syntactic leeway. ENGLISH commander (from command) or, for that matter, RUSSIAN sapóžnik 'shoemaker, boot-maker' (from sapóg 'boot') can be used as subjects, objects, or after prepositions — to be sure, with the necessary quota of foreseeable accommodations, such as (gen.) commander's, (dat.) sapóžniku, etc. Forms equipped with inflectional endings (ENGLISH he [she, it] commands, RUSSIAN sapogá 'of the shoe') have a much narrower range of contextual acceptability -- so narrow that sapogá, for instance, can be used after certain numerals ('two, three, four'), but not after others. To put it differently, a derivational affix grants its carrier a distinctly higher degree of syntagmatic

autonomy than does an inflectional affix. Understandably, where
rules of syntactic traffic are involved, the derivational element
is welded more closely to the primitive (or the root morpheme),
whereas the inflectional element represents the word's outer shell,
being thus left in closer vicinity to the other members of the clause
(phrase, sentence); cf. command-er'-s, sapóž-nik-u, above.

2.3 Important as this discrimination is, students of synchrony
and diachrony alike encounter situations where it is difficult to
trace a cogent border line. Take the case of the infinitive suffix
in ROMANCE. While an infinitive keeps performing its main function, it cannot be separated from the corresponding verbal paradigm. Thus, the segment -are of ITALIAN andare 'to go' can be
pitted against the -iamo of andiamo! 'let's go,' the -avo of andavo
'I used to go,' etc. But many infinitives are subject to nominalization; in the process, they become susceptible to pluralization and
combine with the definite and the indefinite article, the possessive
and the demonstrative adjective, etc.; cf. FRENCH le repentir
'the repentance,' un souvenir 'a remembrance, a keepsake,' son
pouvoir 'his [her] power,' ses devoirs 'his [her] duties or home-
work.' Once this stage has been reached, the nominalized infinitive
becomes contrastable with those derivational suffixes (and rival devices) that produce verbal abstracts. Thus, SPANISH pairs off
decir 'saying, say-so' and dicho 'saying, pledge, bright remark;'
correr 'running' (in the phrases a todo correr 'at full speed,' a todo
turbio correr 'no matter how bad things are') and correría 'excursion,
raid;' comer 'food' and comida 'eating, meal, dinner;' PORTU-
GUESE distinguishes between falar 'manner of speaking, parlance,
dialect,' fala 'talk, discourse,' and falada 'sound of voice, murmur,
rumor.' In this context the infinitive endings -ar, -er, -ir compete
visibly with miscellaneous markers of verbal abstracts and thus
deserve to rank as straight derivational elements. RUMANIAN
has gone one step further, by transmuting into nouns all of its
original infinitives (in -are, -ire, etc.) and developing, through
truncation, a new set of (sparingly used) infinitives; hence lucrare
'work,' durere 'pain,' întindere 'extension,' sosire 'arrival.'

3. Derivation through Affixation: Alternatives to the Pattern

The category of derivation best known from the modern EURO-
PEAN languages is affixation, so much so that in certain milieux
the two have been declared coterminous and, for all practical purposes, equated. The very label "affixation" suggests an increase
in size; it implies the attachment to the primitive of a segment
carrying the relevant grammatical message. Depending on the
locus where the insert is being made, analysts invoke prefixes,

infixes, suffixes, and occasionally ambifixes and interfixes. Sporadic examples of the more common varieties have already been supplied, and a more systematic treatment is offered below (see Sec. 5.1-5.5).

But even the more familiar modern EUROPEAN languages appeal to alternative procedures in helping speakers to produce one word from another in a manner compatible with the tag "derivation," and some of the exotic languages have gone very far indeed in advancing in unexpected directions.

3.1 Thus, in the GERMANIC languages, a noun can be placed alongside a verb — to denote an action or its results — in apophonic form, i.e. through vowel alternation entailing no lengthening of the primitive (cf. in ENGLISH <u>song</u> beside <u>to sing</u>). GERMAN is noted both for its wealth of such verbal abstracts and for the aesthetically pleasing variety of vocalic relationships:

Biß (beißen)	'bite'	Drang (dringen)	'urge'
Riß (reißen)	'tear'	Klang (klingen)	'melody'
Ritt (reiten)	'ride'	(Ge)sang (singen)	'song, singing'
Bruch (brechen)	'break'	Trank (trinken)	'drink'
Flug (fliegen)	'flight, flying'	Schwung	'swinging,
Schur (scheren)	'fleecing'	(schwingen)	élan'
Schwur (schwören)	'[sworn] oath'	(Über)schwang	'excess,
Trug (trügen)	'deceit'	(akin to schwingen)	ecstasy'
Zug (ziehen)	'draw, draft'	Sprung (springen)	'jump'

3.2 In the ROMANCE languages, presumably already at the archaic level of VULGAR LATIN, there developed two series — one masculine, the other feminine — of rhizotonic back-formations from many verbs, mainly those of the -<u>ar</u> class. Here too, one can hardly speak of any addition or elaboration. Consider the following examples selected from OLD PROVENÇAL:

a.
autrei (autreiar)	'grant, assurance'	gem (gemir)	'sigh'
		plaidei (plaideiar)	'pleading'
conort (conortar)	'consolation'	plor (plorar)	'weeping'
dol (doler)	'pain'	tornei (torneiar)	'tournament'
dopte (doptar)	'doubt, fear'	vol (voler)	'will'
esper (esperar)	'hope'		

b.
espera (esperar)	'hope'	perda (perdre)	'loss'
falha (falhir)	'fault'	venda (vendre)	'sale'
josta (jostar)	'joust'		

The ending of the masculine series is usually zero, or, in isolated cases — for phonic reasons — -e, a vowel which here carries
no semantic weight and thus fails to qualify for genuine suffixal
status. The -a of the second series stamps the words as feminine
singular, thus providing an inflectional rather than derivational
service.

A strikingly similar situation prevailed in OLD FRENCH; in
MODERN FRENCH the evolution went farther, through tendential
loss of the final consonant, so that cases of actual subtraction or
truncation, over against the older pattern of elaboration, are on
record. Consider from this angle the relationship of arrê(t) 'stop-
page, suspension' to arrêter; goû(t) 'taste' to goûter; je(t) 'cast(ing),
throw(ing)' to jeter; sau(t) 'jump' to sauter or, along a different
axis, of engrai(s) 'food for fattening, manure' to engraisser, and
of repo(s) 'rest, quiet' to reposer.

3.3   In familiar discourse, ENGLISH displays a quasi-deriva-
tional process which Anglists call "clipping;" it may be transparent
to the speakers involved, as in (air)plane, econ(omics), lab(oratory),
or the connection between (formal) primitive and (informal) derivatives may, with the passage of time, have become opaque, as in
pant(aloon)s, vamp(ire). In any event, clipping — by definition —
involves reduction rather than extension of the primitive. On a
smaller scale, clipping, as a characteristic trait of nursery language and student slang, is shared by various languages, being
everywhere peculiar to hypocoristics (cf. Johanna or Josephine →
Jo). In such a context, the shrinkage can be later balanced by
remedial or expressive reduplication, as in SPANISH (Jose)pe →
Pepe 'Joe.'

3.4   Still another variety of derivation unaccompanied by any
increase in sheer bulk can be illustrated with SEMITIC. That group
of languages has at its disposal a limited supply of prefixes and suffixes, of the type familiar from INDO-EUROPEAN. Thus, BIBLICAL
HEBREW used t- to extract nouns from verbs in conjunction with
certain vowel arrangements, cf. a) talmīd 'student' and b) the
sharply profiled series ta'^{a}wā 'desire,' ta'^{a}lā 'curse,' ta'^{a}nā
'heat, rut,' t^{e}busā 'destruction,' tablît 'annihilation,' t^{e}hil·ā 'glo-
rification, psalm,' etc. (a slightly later schema is represented by
talmūd 'doctrine' and targūm 'translation'). But far more common,
hence more typical, has been the selection of a particular arrangement of vowels and root consonants, including their lengthening.
A verbal abstract so derived from a triconsonantal root (KPR, say)
may then acquire this form: kip·ur (or plur. kip·urîm) 'atonement;'

the path from a biconsonantal root (DQ 'thin') may lead to diqduq
'grammar,' lit. 'refinement.' For the agentive HEBREW offers
the classical model of a lengthened central consonantal pillar,
flanked by the vowels a and ā: day·āg 'fisher,' day·yān 'judge'
(DYN), gan·ān 'gardener,' ḥay·āṭ 'tailor,' nap·āḥ 'smith,' qad·ār
'potter,' in rivalry with substantivated participles, some of them
supported by an m- prefix: mᵉlam·ed 'teacher,' with a few straight
suffixal derivatives in -ān or -ōn: ʿǣglōn 'driver, wagoner,' from
ʿagālā 'wagon' (cf. also ARAMAIC šad·ᵉkān 'marriage broker'),
and with such paraphrases as 'master of....' The lexico-morpho-
logical type ḥay·āṭ is equally well, if not better, represented in
ARABIC.

   3.5 Finally, there exists in many languages — in MODERN
ENGLISH possibly on a more generous scale than in most others
of comparable structure — the device of "internal derivation" (to
select one of several labels proposed), i.e. a device allowing
speakers to shift certain words from one form class to another
without the expected appeal to an affix. The context alone, then,
discloses whether a noun, an adjective, a verb, etc. is involved.
Examples include: fleet-, war-, in stylistic competition with naval,
military; to auction (off), to (pro)position, to service, as against
to (pro)pose, to fictionalize; to butcher, to waitress (unlike to
patron-ize, to victim-ize). FRENCH strongly favors such phrases
as le sérieux de la situation 'the seriousness of the situation,' le
ridicule de sa conduite 'the ridiculousness of his/her behavior,'
over ponderous derivatives — polysyllabic and sometimes fraught
with morphophonemic complications (*sériosité? *ridiculité?).
SPANISH tolerates, side by side, seriedad, ridiculez and the idiosyncratic construction lo serio de ..., lo ridículo de .... Certain
languages have recourse to a specific suffix to extract adverbs from
adjectives (witness LATIN -ē or -ter, ITALIAN -mente, ENGLISH
-ly, except in phrases like to talk fast); but other languages (e.g.
GERMAN, RUSSIAN, RUMANIAN, HEBREW) dispense with this
luxury.

4. The Three Typical Ingredients of an Affixal Relationship

   In affixal derivation at its simplest, the three irreducible elements forming the basic relationship are: a) the primitive, b) the
affix, and c) the link. Unfortunately, the morphological analysis
of primitives (as distinct from etymological inquiries into their
descent) has not been pursued with equal zest by all groups of linguists. To cite one instance of neglect, students of medieval and
modern languages, who have an excellent record of research in

prefixes and suffixes, have shown less alertness to the configuration of primitives (or roots) than Semitologists and paleo-Indo-
Europeanists. Yet it remains true that important quantitative and
qualitative features (phonic, accentual, syllabic, etc.) of the base
may exert a determining influence on the choice of a suitable affix
— or, under exceptional circumstances, may even prevent any
affix from joining a bizarrely structured primitive.

4.1 The feeling for neatness of formal contours may arise
rather unexpectedly. In LATIN two suffixes used for deriving
adjectival abstracts, -itia and -itiēs, were in competition with
each other: dūritia ~ dūritiēs 'hardness' (from dūrus 'hard'). In
SPANISH, until ca. 1600, the products of both survived side by side,
as -eza and -ez, with a modicum of overlap and with scattered
symptoms of semantic differentiation. Then, suddenly, one generation of influential speakers and writers began to draw a sharper
demarcation between the two, causing almost all derivatives from
trisyllabic bases to switch from -eza to -ez: delgadez(a) 'thinness'
(delgado), esquivez(a) 'shyness' (esquivo), redondez(a) 'roundness'
(redondo), robustez(a) 'strength' (robusto); also, altivez 'haughti-
ness' tended to crowd out -eza (altivo), without quite reaching the
goal. Conversely, in the majority of offshoots from mono- and
disyllabic bases, -eza continued to enjoy its previous vogue: alteza
'highness' (alto), bajeza 'lowness, meanness' (bajo), franqueza
'frankness, generosity' (franco), grandeza 'greatness' (grande),
nobleza 'nobility' (noble), vileza 'vileness' (vil), etc.; pereza 'idle-
ness' also survived, despite the early disappearance of its primitive
*pero < pigru. One recognizes a pattern of incipient economy: the
longer variant of the suffix, all other conditions being equal, joins
the shorter variety of stem.

4.2 A telling example of an affix's dependence on a favored
formal and semantic configuration of the relevant primitive is
offered by ENGLISH -ster. Strictly, one such affixal segment,
currently at the peak of its productivity, has overlaid its homo-
phone, nearly extinct. The older -ster, still observable in Webster
('weaver, weaveress'), spinster, and seamster (Brit. /sem-/),
referred to involvement in perfectly respectable domestic crafts
and focused referentially on the female agent, perhaps under col-
lateral pressure from sister. The debilitation of the older -ster
is visible in the formal and semantic wedges driven between Webster and weave; in the semantic distance separating spinster from
spin; and in enhanced explicitness of the reference to women in
seamster --> seamstress. The new wave of derivatives in -ster,
highly characteristic of urban life in America, encompasses such

words, of varying degrees of commonness, as dopester, funster, gamester, gangster, huckster, linkster, mobster, oldster, pollster, prankster, punster, rhymester, roadster, shyster, songster, teamster, tipster, trickster, youngster. The reference is still to human beings (since the car has, psychologically, almost become a member of the family, roadster is hardly an exception; cf. the ambiguity of speedster). But the persons alluded to are almost invariably male. Their professions are less than prestigious socially, or, at least, they operate at a lower ethical or aesthetic level, unless mere pastimes are involved. The lexical register is, clearly, either city slang or highly informal discourse bordering on slang. The primitives are invariably monosyllabic, with back and central vowels, as a rule, presiding over a word that typically — but not obligatorily — ends in a nasal or a bilabial. Old-ster — which simply echoes young-ster ; road-ster, and shyster — a folk-etymological reinterpretation of an obscene GERMAN word — clearly represent the outer rim of the entire group. By way of educated guess, let me add that lobster and monster, two words genetically unrelated and referentially diverse at face value, have, despite this distance, interacted with the members of the group — chiefly by virtue of their phonic proximity, and secondarily because lobster designates a funny-looking animal known for pinching, while (little) monster, used affectionately, and youngster undoubtedly belong together. The monosyllabicity of the primitives, then, has hardened into an unbreakable rule, and a certain playfulness of tone has also become a recurrent feature to the point of predictability, though the facetiousness need not reside in the primitive (cf. fun and pun with road and speed). Other features mark mere preferences, and exceptions are tolerated.

4.3 Depending on its broad architectonic design, a language may favor a certain affinity (or, if one views the situation in a diachronic perspective, a growing rapprochement) between root morpheme and affix, or it may, conversely, welcome their maximal differentiation. Vowel harmony as it functions in FINNISH, HUNGARIAN, and TURKISH represents the former tendency; the latter trend, less neatly grammaticized, pervades such LATIN and ROMANCE dissimilatory processes as are astride morpheme boundaries. Thus, mutual complementarity presides in LATIN over the distribution of two purely relational suffixes, -ālis and -āris. The first variant is the basic form (aequālis, causālis, nāvālis), doubly desirable in conjunction with any base that already exhibits one r (ministrālis, nātūrālis, rēgālis). The latter makes its appearance after -l- (cōnsulāris, salūtāris, singulāris), even if that -l- is in turn preceded by r- or -r- (rēgulāris, particulāris).

It has also been argued that the distribution of the diminutive suffixes -in and -(er)on in FRENCH, and of the ROMANCE descendants of LATIN -ānu and -īnu, -āceu and -īceu, -āmen and -īmen, -ātu and -ītu, -āculu and -īculu (i.e. of pairs of closely related derivational suffixes separated only by their stressed vowels) may have been at least in part controlled by varying reactions to the preceding nuclear vowels of the respective bases — the speakers' general proclivity being toward polarization.

5. Varieties of Affixes

5.1 Prefixes, which straddle inflection and derivation, are on the whole a self-defined category of grammatical morphemes. Though they are in general less widely appealed to than are suffixes, they can acquire extraordinary importance under certain circumstances. Such situations may crystallize in diffusion. Thus, while relatively few CLASSICAL GREEK suffixes have spread to other languages (starting with LATIN at the receiving end), most Western languages have, through one channel or another, inherited a profusion of GREEK prefixes. (Today's average speakers, weaned away in so many cultures from classical learning, may no longer be aware of their exact meaning, even if they are capable of grossly segmenting the words at issue.) ENGLISH at the collegiate level of education furnishes appropriate illustrations: a-rrhythmic, a-tonal (a- 'un-'); amphi-bious, amphi-theater (amphi- 'on both sides, around'); anti-ballistic, anti-climax (anti- 'counter'); apogee, apo-logy (apo- 'from'); hyper-tonic, hyper-trophy (hyper- 'above, super'); hypo-chondriac, hypo-dermic (hypo- 'beneath, sub-'); peri-patetic, peri-phery (peri- 'around, circum-'), etc. A different context in which prefixes may acquire exceptional prominence, as a result of a uniquely close enmeshment of aspect, tense, and prefixation within the verbal system, is observable in RUSSIAN. Thus, šël (which, through the agency of suppletion, relates to the infinitive idtí 'to go') means '[he, she, it] was going' — in a durative-imperfective key —, whereas po-šël (from pojtí) represents its perfective-inceptive-noniterative counterpart: '[he, she, it] started going, went [once].' As if to add to the intricacy, RUSSIAN prefixes, in their principal role as preverbs, also tend to establish a rapport with such quasi-homonymous prepositions as link the verbs at issue with their objects: vo-šël v les 'he entered (into) the forest,' a state of affairs difficult to imagine in a language such as FRENCH, where com- 'with,' dé- 'un-, dis-,' and r(e)- 'back' clash irremediably with avec, sans, and derrière. Still another partner in the RUSSIAN context is the case ending governed by the preposition in question.

In the INDO-EUROPEAN languages, there exist prefixes semantically very pale, not to say void, which either have survived by
inertia or else by providing certain subsidiary services of a rhyth-
mical or anti-homonymous nature (SPANISH a- and en- would fall
into this latter category). Normally, however, prefixes tend to
give a directional specification to the given word (particularly to a
verb) within a spatio-temporal universe. Thus, in LATIN ad- is
tantamount to 'to(ward),' ā-/ab(s)- to 'away from' (gentle removal),
contrā- to 'against,' dē- to 'down from,' dis- to 'asunder' (=GER-
MAN auseinander-, zer-), ē-/ex- to 'out,' inter- to 'between,' ob-
to 'in front of, approaching a clash with' (=GERMAN entgegen-),
praeter- and trā(ns)- to 'beyond,' retrō- to 'back,' sē- to 'away
from' (violent separation), sub- to 'below,' etc.

5.2 An analyst examining a representative slice of an older or
conservative INDO-EUROPEAN language will at once be struck by
the exceptional wealth of finely-graded derivational suffixes. In
this respect, INDO-EUROPEAN may very well come close to representing an extreme, with SEMITIC approaching the status of its
typological opposite. In some instances the elaborateness of forms
pressed into service will correspond to very refined conceptual
nuancing; then again, the conspicuous variety may simply mirror
a complex pattern of ethnoglottal stratification, traceable to wars,
settlements, broadly cultural fashions, and the like. Not infrequently, the abundance of available resources seems to have acted
as a stimulus, provoking a certain nicety of conceptual discrimination, and vice versa.

Thus, ENGLISH uses for its agentives the suffix -er, which
basically pertains to verbal stems (carri-er, kill-er), but has also
established contacts with the nominal domain via such relationships
as garden-er (garden, to garden), jobb-er (job, to job), lectur-er
(lecture, to lecture), merchandis-er (merchandise, to merchandise),
and even performs services for phrases (caretaker, ant-killer).
Nevertheless, there has sprung into existence a rarer, more sharply-
silhouetted rival suffix -eer, which refers to more aggressive,
typically masculine activities: auctioneer, conventioneer, moun-
taineer, pamphleteer, mutineer, and originally gazeteer ('one who
writes in a gazette'), profiteer, sloganeer. To these neatly segmentable words one may add buccaneer, at present 'pirate,' but
originally '(French) hunter of wild oxen in Haiti' and, of course,
engineer, which initially referred to the 'military engineer;' once
squeezed into this series, engineer almost inevitably developed
the secondary or tertiary meaning of 'clever manager, sharp oper-
ator.' Only the preëxistence of command-er and -ant seems to

have prevented <u>commandeer</u>, a Batavism, from infiltrating the
ENGLISH lexicon as a noun; it has penetrated that lexicon as a
verb, again with an ingredient of violence. The starting point
seems to have been names of military ranks of Continental back-
ground, such as <u>brigadier</u>, <u>cavalier</u>, <u>grenadier</u>; the decisive step
was the recognition of a peculiar human type (<u>condottiere</u> style):
bold, ruthless, vigorous, vociferous, which, once individuated in
real life, clamored for separate affixal characterization. Nothing
of the sort happened in GERMAN which, as a result of its apathy
to this challenge, borrowed from its "LATIN" neighbors both
<u>Offizier</u> 'army officer' and (obsol.) <u>Barbier</u> 'barber,' whereas in
ENGLISH *<u>officeer</u>, absorbed at the critical juncture, might have
inopportunely suggested a conduct unworthy of a gentleman and
*<u>barbeer</u> a degree of explosive virility seldom associated with the
trade of haircutters and beard-trimmers.

Again, a language abounding in suffixes, like RUSSIAN, will re-
serve at least one of them for the signaling of a strongly developed
anatomic feature, including varieties of hair growth: <u>borod-át</u>
'bearded' (<u>borodá</u>), <u>nos-át</u> 'with a protruding nose' (<u>nos</u>), <u>puz-át</u>
'with a thick belly' (<u>puz</u>), <u>usat</u> 'moustachioed' (<u>usý</u> [pl.]), <u>volosát</u>
'hairy' (<u>vólos</u>). Furthermore, on a racier level of discourse RUS-
SIAN has recourse to <u>-ást</u>, var. <u>-íst</u> which, as a result of being
placed on that plateau, tend to draw a caricature rather than a
portrait of the human being involved (upon occasion an animal will
also qualify for the cartoon): <u>brjux-ást</u> 'paunchy' (<u>brjúxo</u>), <u>glaz-</u>
<u>ást</u> 'wide-eyed' (<u>glaz</u>), <u>griv-ást</u> 'long-maned' (<u>gríva</u>), <u>koren-ást</u>/
<u>-íst</u> 'stocky' (<u>kóren'</u>), <u>lob-ást</u> 'with a protruding forehead' (<u>lob</u>),
<u>očk-ást</u> 'wearing funny eyeglasses' (<u>očkí</u> [pl.]), <u>rog-ást</u> 'long-
horned' (<u>rog</u>), <u>uš-ást</u> 'with long, usually drooping ears' (<u>úši</u> [pl.]),
<u>zub-ást</u> 'sharp-toothed' (<u>zub</u>); <u>kost-íst</u> 'big-boned' (<u>kost'</u>), <u>nogt-</u>
<u>íst</u> 'sharp-nailed' (<u>nógot'</u>), <u>pleč-íst</u> 'heavy-shouldered' (<u>plečó</u>),
<u>slez-íst</u> 'tearful' (<u>sleza</u>). There is no lack of -- weakly differen-
tiated -- doublets: <u>borodá(s)t</u>, <u>nosá(s)t</u>, <u>usá(s)t</u>, <u>volosá(s)t</u>, etc.
-- almost exactly the way SPANISH tolerates neutral <u>barb-ado</u>
'bearded' beside facetious <u>barb-udo</u> 'heavy-bearded.' Viewed
from the vantage of differently structured languages, this plethora
of competing anatomic suggestions, whatever the historical circumstances, borders on luxury.

5.2.1 In INDO-EUROPEAN the relation between primitive
and suffixal derivative can be of two sorts. Either the derivative,
rather than radically changing the semantic content of the primitive,
merely gives it a certain twist or coloring, as when the designation
of a person (including a proper name) is burdened with conveying

the additional message of the feelings that individual arouses in
the speaker himself and the speaker's group ('dear old...,' 'cute
...,' 'big...,' 'ugly...'). Designations of other living beings, of
objects, and — more sparingly — of abstracts ('light flirt,' 'violent
fit or outburst of jealousy') lend themselves to the same treatment.
This is the familiar ground of hypocoristics (diminutive, ameliora-
tive suffixes), augmentatives, etc., noted for the frequency of
gender switch (GERMAN: die Frau 'the woman' —➤ das Fräulein
'the young unmarried woman,' ITALIAN tavola (f.) 'table' —➤ tavo-
lino (m.) 'small table,' etc.). Where verbs are involved, size
becomes irrelevant, but a given action may often be sharply seg-
mented through adjunction of a suffix; the effect may be inchoative
('to begin to blanch or to redden'), terminative ('to stop talking'),
intensive, as when 'going' is transmuted into 'trudging,' and above
all, iterative, as when 'leaping' is fragmented into 'making a succession of small jumps' (witness FRENCH sautiller beside sauter,
SPANISH salticar beside saltar). The use of such a merely qualifying suffix normally precludes the switch of the given word from
one form class to another — except where the borderline is very
thin, as between nouns and adjectives.

Alternatively, a radical referential change may be aimed at,
with or without a concurrent switch from one form class to another.
Thus, without transcending the nominal domain, one may, by adding appropriate suffixes to the vernacular name of a locally important animal (fowl, fish), produce the designations of that animal's
female and its young (cubs, whelps); its lair (cave, stable, sty,
nest, etc.); the corresponding herd (pack, pride, swarm, school,
etc.); the animal's owner (herder, hunter, trapper, skinner, trainer,
seller); its hide, feathers, or fur; its meat, fat (or the respective
female's milk), etc.

Equally common in an average European language, if not more
so, are such suffixal derivatives as involve a clear-cut switch
from one form class to another. Thus, linguists set aside postverbal (or deverbal) nouns which typically involve either verbal
abstracts, names of the characteristic locales, labels for the tools
used (not infrequently weapons), or tags for the perpetrators of
the action ("agentives"). "Deverbal" refers strictly to grammatical
hierarchy; "postverbal" hints at the expected chronological sequence
of events. The two criteria should coincide in a correctly executed
analysis; but since our records are all lacunary, it happens that
the philological evidence for first appearances, disquietingly enough,
clashes with the internally postulated sequence of events.

For all its importance, the verb need not invariably represent the starting point ("primitive") in a suffixal relationship. Numerous languages, ENGLISH included, offer, for example, impressive series of (de)-adjectival verbs; consider the following set: blacken, (em)bolden, brighten, broaden, coarsen, dampen, darken, deepen, fasten (with semantic differentiation), fatten, flatten, harden, lighten, (en)liven, loosen, madden, moisten, neaten (up), redden, roughen, sharpen, shorten, sicken (rare), smoothen, soften, straighten, sweeten, thicken, toughen, tighten, weaken, whiten, widen. In MODERN ENGLISH, admission to this series seems to hinge, by way of concomitant condition, on the monosyllabicity and primary character of the base; for this reason no verbs in -en can be extracted from, say, bitter or heavy or narrow or yellow, let alone from dirt-y. Also avoided are adjectives ending in -n (brown, clean, fine, green, lean, thin, wan) or in a vowel or semiconsonant (blue, coy, dry, raw, shy). In a few cases, speakers seem to have preferred to derive a verb from an adjectival abstract: heighten, lengthen, strengthen. Other empty cases remain to be explained; for instance, why the absence of *wetten?

5.2.2 Granted the existence in a given language of a fine-meshed network of derivational suffixes (a fact that it might be hazardous to try to account for in mentalistic terms), the observer is entirely within his right in attempting to calibrate the impact of the given culture -- social structure, aggregate of folk beliefs, etc. -- on that independently established system of suffixes. Even after the operation has been so defined, great caution is mandatory; just because OLD FRISIAN has not served as the vehicle of a major philosophical literature or a school of allegorical poetry, it by no means follows that it has suffered from any dearth of abstract suffixes. As a matter of fact, OLD FRISIAN happened to display a plethora of just such morphemes: -e, -ene, -unge (-inge, -enge), -nisse (-nesse, -ness, -ens ~ -ense), -ithe (-ethe ~ -the, -de, -te), -elsa, -ath (-ad), -tha (-ta, -da), -ma, -îe, -hêde ~ -hêd (-heit), -skipi (-skipe ~ -skip, -schip), -dôm; a contingent fully comparable to the inventories that could be drawn up for MODERN ENGLISH and GERMAN, two cognates that have accommodated generations of philosophers. On the other hand, in a rural culture whose language exhibits abundant ramifications of suffixes, one's expectation of finding special morphemes reserved for isolable recurrent features of that peculiar life style and environment will seldom be frustrated. The languages of certain island cultures of less than easy access provide some telling examples. Thus, SARDINIAN, a fairly independent, if minor, ROMANCE language of archaic and bucolic "cut," has richly developed

ancestral -īle for the designation of all sorts of small yards, en-
closures, and stables for domestic animals -- with an amazing degree
of specificity: annile for lambs, bakkile for cows, berβeɣile for
sheep, brikkile for calves, kanile for dogs ('kennel'), krapile for
goats, kuβile for sheep or hares, etc. SARDINIAN has further
individuated a special suffix for the evocation of 'throngs, groups,
conglomerations': -adza, -alla, -aǧǧa (depending on the dialect);
has developed LATIN -īgine (which shrunk in the cognate languages)
into a neat marker of physical or mental defects, or else of temporary ailments, eruptions, irritations; has proliferated the descendants of -āmine, -īmine, -ūmine at the borderline of mass-nouns
('piles, heaps') and semi-abstracts; has cultivated -ondzu to convey the impression of a weakly-developed quality (pale color, mild
taste, and the like; cf. FRENCH -âtre, ITALIAN -ognolo); and
can boast a profusion of unique patterns of diminutives: those in
-adza, -udza, -idzɔne, -idzolu/ -idzɔla, etc. All in all, one immediately recognizes a wide range of daily vital experiences marked
by immediacy, and one senses throughout a down-to-earth attitude.

Changes in social attitudes can also, upon occasion, be effectively viewed through the prism of derivational suffixes. Thus, in
line with modern emancipatory trends, male and female agentives
are only minimally differentiated in the more progressive among
present-day ROMANCE languages; witness SPANISH director/-ora,
doctor/-ora, profesor/-ora; ambigeneric asistente, estudiante
'student,' gerente 'manager,' cajista 'typesetter,' florista 'flower-
vendor;' cajero/-a 'cashier,' camarero/-a 'servant,' etc. FRENCH
is similar in principle, if not in details, inasmuch as it makes a
precise distinction between (m.) assistant, étudiant and (f.) -ante,
while in other instances the sex-differentiating mechanism has been
shifted to the title, especially in direct address: Monsieur vs. Ma-
dame (l'ambassadeur, le docteur, le professeur); in yet other cases
one discerns a tendency, among sophisticated speakers, to distinguish between a) Mme le président in reference to the female first
executive and b) Mme la présidente with respect to the president's
spouse. All these frills, some of them perhaps otiose, characterize
the mid and late twentieth century. Medieval societies, in contrast,
leaned toward maximum differentiation of sexes and, consequently,
of genders in suffixally-derived agentives (and in closely-related
titles as well). Hence the otherwise inexplicable borrowing, by
speakers of ROMANCE, of BYZANTINE GREEK -issa for the labeling of females, a device which is still in full bloom in ITALIAN
(dottoressa, professoressa, studentessa) and which for centuries
flourished as well in FRENCH, leaving in its trail numerous deposits
in MIDDLE and MODERN ENGLISH (abbess, baroness, countess,

duchess, empress, marchioness, princess, and, with an extension
of the hypercharacterization to the females of "aristocratic animals": leopardess, lioness, tigress). On a distinctly lower social
level, among references to entertainers, one discovers an analogous
situation in older SPANISH where, by hook or by crook, radically
different suffixes were put to work for the designation of male and
female performers, cf. (m.) bail-ador or -arín vs. (f.) bail-adera
(in preference to *-adora or *-arina) 'dancer.' In PORTUGUESE,
a language spoken in one of Europe's most conservative countries,
fundamentally the same deep division prevails to this day, extending
to the realm of handicraft: serz-idor '(male) darner' vs. serzi-
ideira (rather than readily available *-idora) '(female) darner.'
In this corner of the lexicon, then, the degree of proximity to, or
distance between, the two relevant suffixes provides the perfect
mirror-image of a far-reaching change in attitudes.

5.2.3 Where speakers of a single language manipulate hundreds
of derivational suffixes, the issue of their most effective classification, for a variety of purposes (inventorying, analytical description,
reconstruction of events) will inevitably arise. Straight alphabetical
listing, useful for indexes and other reference tools, is hardly con-
ducive to deeper insights. Here is one concrete illustration of the
classificatory options available to analysts. Practically all RO-
MANCE linguists distinguish between the nominal and the verbal
domain. Beyond that level of agreement, each school of thought
goes its own way. Some of the older workers arrayed the suffixes
by a rigid formal criterion, namely in the alphabetic sequences of
the characteristic consonants (or consonant clusters) that presided
over the suffixes. More stimulating has been the semantic or functional approach which aims to bring together suffixes, whatever
their shapes, which perform more or less the same services. For
the language historian, the chief advantage of this alternative approach is the chance it affords to recognize at a glance rival morphemes; a not inconsiderable disadvantage lies in the resulting
fragmentation, when the same popular suffix appears in several
contexts. The positive side appears to prevail in a case like the
SPANISH names of fruit-trees derived from the corresponding
names of the fruits, not infrequently through the instrumentality
of such suffixes as -al (pera 'pear' → peral), -ero (Amer. Sp.
durazno 'peach' → duraznero), or -era (higo 'fig' → hig[u]era).
In other contexts a suffix may be dispensed with, and the same
word designates both fruit and tree (albérchigo 'clingstone peach,'
Penins. Sp. melocotón 'peach'), even though alberchig[u]ero and
melocotonero are also on record; yet other speakers experiment
with durazno as a dendronym. Still another way -- on balance,

the preferred — of short-circuiting the need for an explicit suffix
is the appeal to straight gender-switch, as in castaña 'chestnut' ~
castaño 'chestnut-tree.' The situation is further complicated by
the occurrence of -al, var. -ar in names of orchards: cerez-al
'cherry orchard' (beside cerez-a 'cherry,' -o 'cherry-tree'),
manzan-ar 'apple orchard' (beside manzan-a 'apple,' -o 'apple-
tree'). There is obviously a point in jointly listing and studying
these devices.

At least two more techniques have been tried out with promise
of limited success. For one thing, one is free to segregate suffixes
by provenience and mode of transmission. Thus, in ENGLISH,
-dom and -ship, -y and -ish (cf. serf-dom, hard-ship, worm-y,
ap-ish) are GERMANIC; -ance/-ancy, -al (as used in abstracts:
arriv-al, tri-al, withdraw-al), and -ice (as in coward-ice) beside
-ise (as in merchand-ise) are OLD FRENCH; the verbal suffix
-ize is a GREEK incrustation; -i — confined to ethnonyms (Israeli,
Iraqi) — is SEMITIC. In a language stratified like FRENCH, it is
relevant for cultural reasons to draw a line between instances of
vernacular and learned descent from LATIN: adjectival -el vs. -al,
abstracts in -tume (amer-tume 'bitterness') beside those in -itude,
etc. For another thing, in dealing with certain languages it is potentially useful to separate such suffixes as appear in clusters,
usually dominated by vocalic gamuts, from isolates. Thus, in
ITALIAN one encounters, on the one hand, -aggine, -iggine, -uggine;
-accio, -iccio, -occio, -uccio, etc. and, on the other, in adjectival
abstracts, -ezza and -ia, unaccompanied by any variants (bello
'beautiful' —→ bellezza; pazzo 'mad' —→ pazzia). If the given language has a sufficient number of tetradic and pentadic vowel gamuts
in its system of derivational suffixes, there is a good chance that
shorter series involving merely two or three paradigmatically contrastable vowels will tend to be expanded until they contain four or
five.

5.2.4 Not every segmentable phoneme or succession of phonemes at the end of a word is (or ever was) a suffix. One recognizes a motley residue of borderline cases. Take CATALAN (m.)
dupte 'doubt' beside dupt-ar 'to doubt' as against despatx (tx = /č/)
'office' beside despatx-ar 'to dispatch.' One senses that, although
the tolerance of CATALAN for consonants, including consonant
groups, in final position is considerable (cf. argent 'silver,' dolç
'sweet'), -pt apparently cannot be so collocated, a situation that
reduces the role of -e to making the entire word "pronounceable."
One's confidence rises as one notes that efecte 'effect, purpose'
alongside efect-iu (adj.) 'effective,' (subst.) 'cash' — against the

background of alt 'high, tall' ~ alt-iu 'haughty' — invites a similar
interpretation. In other contexts a final vowel may represent the
last remnant of an eroded case ending, i.e. of an inflectional morpheme, after the local collapse of declension; one could thus come
to grips with PORTUGUESE prim-o '(male) cousin' vs. prim-a
'(female) cousin,' where ill-defined ("fuzzy") -o and -a do not rank
as genuine suffixes. Semantically empty, submorphemic augments
involving an extra syllable are used in SPANISH to supply an accen-
tually more pleasing configuration for a given word, as in OLD
SPANISH murciego 'bat' (lit. 'blind mouse') → murciégalo ~ mur-
ciélago; observe that the speakers' playfulness here finds a second
outlet in folk etymology (hint of cielo 'sky'). Germanists speak of
"excrescents" where an additional consonant at the very end of a
word provides an aesthetically more satisfactory conclusion; contrast GERMAN (innovative) Axt, Habicht with ENGLISH (conservative) ax(e), hawk.

   5.3 "Infix" is a long-recognized label for a grammatical morpheme -- inflectional or derivational — which speakers wedge into
the root morpheme. Under optimal circumstances the insertion is
total; i.e. the infix is flanked on both sides by disrupted elements
of the radical. Thus, Indo-Europeanists operate with a nasal infix,
whichever its ultimate provenience, in cases like LATIN fingō 'I
shape, mould, arrange, imagine' vs. fictus 'shaped, etc.;' frangō
'I break, smash to pieces,' vs. frēgī 'I broke;' rumpō 'I tear,
break open, burst through' vs. rūpī 'I tore;' tangō 'I touch' vs.
te-tig-ī 'I touched.' The respective radicals are, in this order,
fig-, frag-, rup-, tag-, and the function of the infix seems to be
to set apart more vigorously than could otherwise be achieved the
present-tense (or infinitival) stem variant from its perfect-tense
or past-participial counterparts. The service thus furnished is
essentially inflectional. However, fingō likewise conflicts, as
regards the nasal infix, with fig-ulus 'potter, bricklayer' and the
latter's adjectival satellites: fig-ūlāris and fig-(u)līnus, also with
two better-remembered congeners: figmentum 'image, production,
fiction' and figūra 'shape, form, phantom' (the latter acts in turn
as the center of a small subfamily); frangō contrasts with frag-ilis
'brittle,' frag-men(tum) 'splinter,' frag-or 'crash, uproar, din,
clap,' and frag-ōsus 'a) broken, uneven, rough; b) crashing, roaring.'
To the extent, further, that rumpō stands in contrast to ruptor
'breaker, violator,' and that tangō can be placed in opposition to
tact-ilis 'tangible,' tactiō '(sense of) touch,' and tactus-ūs 'touch,
handling, influence' (as distinct from the nearly-homophonous past
participle tactus, -a, -um), one can state that certain categories
of verbal substantives and adjectives are kept at a desirable distance

from the most characteristic tier of the paradigm of the verb proper
through exploitation of the nasal infix, an ingredient which under this
novel set of conditions becomes a straight derivational device.

In certain exotic languages it happens, especially as a result of
metathesis, that the coda of the prefix or the opening segment of a
suffix is absorbed into the radical — a position from which the analyst can usually extricate it through study of the broader pattern.

5.4 Interfix — a term, introduced experimentally twenty or so
years ago, which is at present widely accepted in ROMANCE quar-
ters — serves as a handy tag for an "empty morph" intercalated
between an affix (usually a suffix) and the radical, as in SPANISH
carn-ic-ero 'butcher' (beside carne 'meat, flesh' plus agentive -ero)
and pan-ad-ero 'baker' (beside pan 'bread' plus, again, -ero). The
choice of -ic- (originally -iz-) and -ad- is traceable, as a rule, to
the existence of intermediate links which were later allowed to step
into the background, namely carn-iza 'slice of meat' and (em)-pan-
ada 'pie.' It is arguable that the elements -iz- and -ad- do not,
strictly, belong to the family of "-fixes" — as so far pieced together
— on account of their semantic voidness. It is further true that
alternative analyses are usually available. Thus, a skeptic might
posit the existence of two parallel bound forms for 'meat,' namely
carn- and carnic-, and stress the point that ambiguity, or at least
an excess of polysemy, is being avoided through indulgence of this
luxury, inasmuch as carn- joins -ero to produce carnero '(male)
sheep, mutton, battering ram,' while carnicero designates the person that slaughters animals and sells their meat. Similarly, panero
'baker's basket' can be conveniently pitted against panadero. This
approach resembles the analysis brought to bear on numerous GER-
MAN compounds, except that in that category free forms compete
with bound forms, cf. Herz 'heart' vs. Herzens-bildung 'senti-
mental education.' A third way of handling this situation would be
to extrapolate from the examples adduced the existence of such
semi-independent compound suffixes as -adero and -icero. The
matter, in essence, becomes one of practicality — primarily of
sheer economy. Assuming that in SPANISH (and its dialects) the
ingredient -ar- is found before ca. thirty genuine derivational suffixes: -ar-acho, -ar-ada, etc., one may hesitate to introduce
thirty new suffixes (or, for that matter, thirty new stem variants)
and prefer to compromise on the issue of inadequate semantic en-
dowment of the interfix. One more escape route would be to isolate
elements like -ar- and -ir-, and grant them a separate "status" in
the inventory, but in so doing to class them with submorphemic
"excrescents" (see 5.2.4 above). Other groups of linguists have

applied the term "interfix" to a semantically non-empty affix —
inflectional or derivational — that mediates between two roots constituting a compound or, possibly, between a root and an affix
hugging the word-boundary.

Derivational ambifixes — uncharacteristic of the major European
languages — would, within this general scheme, be such morphemic
elements as appear, be it in free alternation or according to some
distributional rule, either before or after the radical. One perceives a flavor of this situation by placing LATIN cum patre 'with
the (a, his, ...) father' alongside mēcum 'with me' — even though
cum in this context is hardly vested with affixal power. I have
been reminded that in other linguistic writings, e.g. in certain
descriptions of TAGALOG, the term ambifix has been used differently, referring to such affixes as comprise two discontinuous
parts, one of which is a prefix, the other a suffix.

5.5 At the periphery of the far-flung domain of these various
affixes, one discovers the corresponding affixoids which, to the
descriptivist, may be little more than pseudo-affixes, i.e. concatenations of sounds resembling those of a genuine affix and placed
in the same position vis-à-vis the radical, but lacking any recognizable semantic content or grammatical function of their own. At
first glance, they seem to involve chance resemblances. Thus,
in ENGLISH -er is analyzable as an inflectional suffix peculiar to
adjectives and signaling the comparative degree in larg-er, smart-er,
wet(t)-er (and by extension in bett-er, though one may question the
wisdom of isolating bett-). Independently, but with equally impressive frequency, -er occurs in agentives: danc-er, run(n)-er,
walk-er, without any distinction between references to males and
and to females (in contradistinction to GERMAN). In addition to
these two neatly circumscribed groups plus a small residue of differently segmentable nouns (saucer ~ sauce), one finds an ill-
defined -er as a concluding segment of the root morpheme in a
considerable number of nouns which by any standard form a motley
group: adder, cancer, hammer, hunger, lever, rudder, udder,
viper. This basic situation repeats itself in many languages.

Unlike the descriptivist, the historical linguist notices that the
lexical items endowed with nonsegmentable -er and its equivalents
often join in their affinities and other features of behavior those
equipped with homophonous genuine affixes. Thus, in SPANISH
the many transparently structured agentives in -ero are flanked by
derivatives in -ería indicative of the respective trade, craft, oc-
cupation, shop, etc.: cervec-ero 'brewer' (from cerveza 'beer')→

cervecería 'brewery.' Postrimero 'last' is not at all neatly segmentable and certainly does not function as an agentive, thus
involving -ero as a mere suffixoid; nevertheless, it follows the
lead of the agentives in casting off postrimería 'end.' Hence, in
historical linguistics affixoids cannot be disregarded in any study
of affixes.

5.6 There exist numerous interplays between affixes, including,
we recall, certain habitual or even obligatory concatenations of
interfix and suffix, or of two successive suffixes. Equally note-
worthy processes of interaction are observable where the joint
involvement of a prefix and a suffix is required to produce a derivative. This mode of derivation has sometimes been called
parasynthesis. The preliminary stage is the increasingly frequent
co-occurrence of certain prefixes and suffixes. The choice of possibilities is wide-meshed in the case of GERMAN -lich, an adjectival suffix which at rare intervals conjoins the straight verbal
stem (as in kläglich 'miserable,' from klagen 'to wail, complain'),
but usually accompanies a verb ushered in by one of a long series
of prefixes; hence ab-kömm-lich 'available,' an-geb-lich 'alleged,'
be-greif-lich 'understandable,' ein-träg-lich 'profitable,' ent-setz-
lich 'horrible,' er-sprieß-lich 'fruitful,' über-heb-lich 'arrogant,'
unsäglich 'ineffable,' unter-schied-lich 'distinctive' (strictly, from
the verbal abstract Unterschied), ver-läß-lich 'dependable,' ver-
mein(t)-lich 'presumed, presumable,' zer-brech-lich 'breakable,
fragile,' to the virtual exclusion of *geblich, *greiflich, *kömm-
lich, etc. A finer-meshed sifting is observable in SPANISH adjectival verbs. If the disyllabic primitive ends in -e or -o/-a,
the verb, as a rule, will waver between two clearly circumscribed
patterns: a-bland-ar ~ em-bland-ecer 'to soften' (blando), a-grand-
ar ~ en-grand-ecer 'to aggrandize' (grande), a-loc-ar ~ en-loqu-ecer
'to madden' (loco), a-trist-ar ~ en-trist-ecer 'to sadden' (triste).
Such adjectives of equal length as end in -io/-ia follow a different
path: en-fri-ar 'to chill' (frío), en-rubi-ar 'to bleach' (rubio),
en-suci-ar 'to dirty' (sucio), en-tibi-ar 'to make lukewarm' (tibio),
en-turbi-ar 'to muddy' (turbio). There remains a small residue
of individual cases defying clear classification: em-bot-ar 'to blunt,
dull' (boto), ens-anch-ar 'to widen' (ancho), oscur-ecer 'to darken'
(oscuro), a- ~ en-dulz-ar 'to sweeten' (dulce). Genuine parasynthesis, i.e. the speakers' practically simultaneous appeal to prefix
and suffix, underlies, in FRENCH, empellement 'sluice, dam'
(pelle 'showel'), enco(i)gnure 'corner, angle, corner-piece' (coin),
entre-colonnement 'distance between pillars' (colonne), all three
apparently arrived at without the mediation of any verb.

6. The Linkage of Affix to Root Morphemes

The linkage of affix to root morpheme may range from strict (and, as a consequence, highly predictable) to extremely loose. Under the category of linkage we can subsume, first of all, the various degrees of mutual predictability. Thus, in HISPANO-ROMANCE all of the learned proparoxytonic adjectives in -́ido are flanked by (fairly modern) abstracts in -ez, e.g. SPANISH acidez 'acidity,' calidez 'warmth, heat,' escualidez 'squalor, dreariness,' fetidez 'foulness,' floridez 'floweriness,' insipidez 'tastelessness,' palidez 'paleness,' timidez 'shyness,' etc.; POR-TUGUESE lepidez 'facetiousness,' tepidez 'lukewarmness,' etc.; there seem to be no exceptions on record. FRENCH has distinctly fewer such adjectives and, as a result, a commensurately smaller number of abstracts, but the degree of consistency remains the same, because all derivatives in harmony with the LATIN proto-types end in -ité: acidité, fétidité, insipidité, timidité. ITALIAN, conversely, is badly split; we can distinguish between molecules of formations in a) -ezza (squallidezza), b) -ità (callidità 'crafti-ness'), c) -ezza ~ -ità with all sorts of differentiating nuances (florid-ezza ~ florid-ità, insipid-ezza ~ insipidità, timid-ezza ~ timidità). In extreme cases, d) abstracts in -ezza, -ità, and mass-nouns ('matter') in -ume stand side by side, fanning out from such primitives as acido and fetido.

Another facet of the problem of linkage is the choice of the ap-propriate stem variant. Thus, FRENCH tolerates side by side nu- and nud- 'bare, naked,' sourd- and surd- 'deaf;' the more vernacular variants predominate in the free forms, in verbs de-rived therefrom (dénuer 'to denude,' assourdir 'to deafen'), even in verbal abstracts accompanying such verbs (assourdissement). In contrast, the learned counterparts emerge in adjectival abstracts: nudité, surdité. The extreme case of mutual estrangement, as il-lustrated with aveugle 'blind' vs. cécité 'blindness,' deserves to be labeled as a phenomenon of affixal suppletion; here predictability is perforce at its lowest.

7. Internal and External Diffusion of Affixes

Two vital preconditions for smooth transfer of an affix from one language to another are, first, the roughly simultaneous bor-rowing of several words equipped with that affix and, second, at least ideally, the preexistent parallel borrowing of some of the corresponding primitives. Thus ENGLISH in the late 'forties

adopted Israeli 'citizen of [the newly-created State of] Israel,'
distinguishing it from Biblical Israelite, on the model of Iraq /
Iraqi, Saud / Saudi, etc.; sophisticated speakers were also aware
of Ashkenaz / Ashkenazi, Sepharad / Sephardi, and the like. Even
where HEBREW and ARABIC lack actual prototypes, present-day
ENGLISH-speakers can freely derive such ethnonyms and adjectives
in -i from exotic names of countries in the Middle East. The absorption by older SPANISH of OLD FRENCH mer-, mar-chan(d)
as merchán and of mer-, mar-chand-i(s)e later made it easier
for that same speech community to adopt the ethnogeographic tags
picar(d) and Picardie, reinterpreting them as pícaro 'rogue, roguish'
and picardía 'knavery.' (There exist no native formations geared
to -día, as distinct from -d + ía.)

    The borrowing process can energize or stunt the growth of a
suffix. Thus GERMAN, in taking over adjectival -el(l) from
FRENCH, gave it an unforeseen impetus; cf. finanziell, kommer-
ziell, maschinell, devoid of any immediate FRENCH models.
Innovatively enough, GERMAN also split certain words into two
variants, depending on their use either as free forms or as opening segments of compounds; witness originell vs. Originalgenie,
reell vs. Realpolitik. In other instances further growth has been
thwarted by lexical migration. Thus -ise, peculiar to mass-
nouns and to adjectival abstracts, picked up momentum in FRENCH,
while in ENGLISH merchand-ise has, in course of time, become
an isolate, in part through defection of coward-ice -- influenced by
malice?

BIBLIOGRAPHY

Ahlsson, Lars-Erik. 1960. Die alt-friesischen Abstraktbildungen.
    Diss. Uppsala: Almqvist & Wiksells.

Chantraine, Pierre. 1933. La formation des mots en grec ancien.
    Paris: Klincksieck.

Hasselrot, Bengt. 1957. Étude sur la formation diminutive dans
    les langues romanes. Uppsala Universitets Årsskrift.

Koziol, Herbert. 1937. Handbuch der englischen Wortbildungslehre.
    Heidelberg: Winter.

Leumann, Manu. 1944. Gruppierung und Funktionen der Wortbild-
    ungssufixe des Lateins. Museum Helveticum 1. 129-151.

(Absorbed into the author's Kleinere Schriften, 1959.)

Malkiel, Yakov. 1957. Los interfijos hispánicos; problema de lingüística histórica y estructural. Miscelánea "Estructuralismo e historia" 2.107-99. Tenerife: Universidad de la Laguna.

_____. 1966. Genetic analysis of word formation. Current Trends in Linguistics 3: Theoretical foundations, 205-264. The Hague: Mouton.

_____. 1970. Patterns of derivational affixation in the Cabraniego dialect of East-Central Asturian. University of California Publications in Linguistics 64. Berkeley and Los Angeles.

Marchand, Hans. 1969. The categories and types of present-day English word-formation; a synchronic-diachronic approach. München: C.H. Beck (rev. 2nd ed.).

Meyer-Lübke, Wilhelm. 1960. Historische Grammatik der französischen Sprache 2: Wortbildungslehre, revised by J.M. Piel. Heidelberg: Winter.

Paul, Hermann. 1920. Deutsche Grammatik, Vol. 5: Wortbildungslehre. Halle: Niemeyer.

Wagner, Max Leopold. 1952. Historische Wortbildungslehre des Sardischen. Romanica Helvetica 39. Bern: Francke.

Respect Degrees
in Pronominal Reference

BRIAN F. HEAD

ABSTRACT

This study examines the social meaning of variation of pronominal categories and types of pronouns used in reference. Comparison of alternation of pronominal reference in more than one hundred
languages leads to the following generalities or hypotheses of linguistic universals: (1) variation of pronominal categories and of
types of pronouns to show degrees of respect or social distance is
more common in address than in reference to the other participants
in discourse; (2) variation of number is the most widespread process
for showing degrees of respect or social distance; (3) when variation
of number is used in reference to convey social meaning, the non-
singular typically indicates greater respect or social distance than
does the singular in any person in which both are used in reference
to individuals; (4) variation of the categories of person to show
degrees of respect or social distance in address typically co-occurs
with variation of number for the same purpose; (5) alternation of
person indicates greater differences in degree of respect or social
distance than does alternation of number, while alternation of both
categories shows greater difference in social meaning than does
change of only one of them; (6) reduction and substitution of nouns
or nominal expressions are common ways of introducing use of
third person pronouns into address systems; (7) when employed so
as to convey social meaning, the categories distant or non-proximate,
exclusive, and indefinite or impersonal usually indicate greater
respect or social distance than do the respective opposing ones,
while those of inanimate and non-human typically indicate less respect
than do their counterparts; (8) when used to convey social meaning in
reference, demonstrative and reflexive pronouns, as well as common
nouns and nominal expressions used instead of pronouns, typically
indicate greater social distance than do personal pronouns.

I am grateful to Charles A. Ferguson and Joseph H. Greenberg
for their valuable suggestions and for calling my attention to some
relevant data, and to Aryon Dall'Igna Rodrigues, Frank R. Brandon,
and Yara Frateschi Vieira for helpful comments on an earlier version of this study. Remaining shortcomings are of my responsibility.

CONTENTS

1. Introduction

The features of language commonly used to show degrees of respect or social distance in reference include personal pronouns, titles, proper names, common nouns and nominal expressions used instead of pronouns. Several recent studies have dealt with social factors in the use of pronouns and other forms in reference to the addressee. These studies have usually emphasized description of the social conditioning of variation of address in a given language, or occasionally in more than one.[1]

Instead of examining the social factors which condition variation of address or of reference in general, the present study deals with the relationship between (a) variation of grammatical categories and (b) degrees of respect or social distance in pronominal reference.[2] The strategy adopted here is the common one of establishing

---

[1]Much of the recent work on address has been influenced by the important early study by Brown and Gilman (1960), who surveyed pronominal address in several languages, principally French, German and Italian. Brown and Gilman state that, as a convenience, they propose to use "the symbols T and V (from the Latin tu and vos) for a familiar and a polite pronoun in any language" (p. 254). This convention is often cited and has been adopted by authors of studies of address in various languages. But the convention can be misleading, for the differences in categories between alternate "polite" and "familiar" address pronouns is not always the same in other languages as that found in the Latin model for T and V (i.e. the difference between singular and plural in the second person of the personal pronoun). Brown and Gilman of course recognized this, as is shown by their discussion of the address pronouns in Italian and German. Many of the authors of subsequent studies on address, however, fail to state clearly which categories are involved in alternation between pronouns, and some do not even identify the word classes of alternate address forms (e.g. noun as opposed to pronoun). The recent studies have concentrated almost exclusively on description of the influence of relevant social factors, and, apart from statements on usage, characterization of the language data has received little attention.

[2]In this study, I have tried to avoid use of such terms as "familiar" and "polite," "intimate" and "formal" to characterize the social meaning of personal pronouns according to their usage

typological classifications as bases for assertion of universal
properties. Accordingly, data from several languages are examined in the attempt to identify general processes and limitations in
the use of variation of pronominal categories and types of pronouns
in reference to show degrees of respect or social distance.[3]

(ftnt. 2 cont.)

in reference. Although widely employed in studies on address
(e.g. Brown and Gilman, as cited in the preceding footnote), such
terms often misrepresent the difference in meaning between alternate forms. If the use of a pronoun (such as French second person
singular tu) may be considered "familiar" in certain circumstances,
use of the alternate form (second person plural vous) in the same
situation is not necessarily "polite": it may be aggressive, authori-
tative, insulting, or perhaps simply non-familiar or non-intimate.
The difference in meaning between alternate forms of reference is
not the same from one situation to another, and thus is not faithfully
captured by the general use of pairs of descriptive terms. Moreover, marking theory does not support the use of such terms: reference usage may be considered to be normally unmarked, in that
the form commonly employed is devoid of semantic content different from that of the primary defining features of the situation; it is
marked only in the relatively small proportion of instances in which
the form actually encodes content information (Geoghegan 1969,
1970). Use of a descriptive term would seem appropriate only in
the special instances where reference is marked. In view of the
relative nature of the difference between alternate usages in reference, I have given preference to the notions of degree of respect
and social distance for the present study.

[3]The present study is based principally on published language
materials rather than on data obtained from informants. However,
an expression of gratitude is due to M. Israel, J. Tomazczyk, A.
Trofin, R. de Bleser, A. Sen, R. Bhatnagar, A. Mathai and M.
Esztergar for their kind assistance in clarifying data from the
following languages, respectively: Tamil, Polish, Rumanian,
Dutch, Bengali, Hindi, Malayalam and Hungarian. Because this
study deals with questions of usage, grammatical descriptions
(structural sketches and the like) have not been very helpful to me
in my search for relevant data. Indeed, many descriptions of
pronoun systems contain no reference to variation in usage. Thus,
I have often relied on data from practical grammars or handbooks.
The materials from which relevant language data (that is, data on
variation in usage of pronouns to show different degrees of respect

Although most of the material used for the present study provides information only on modern varieties of the languages considered, the analysis given here is not confined to synchronic
perspectives: historical data have been taken into account when
available, in order to clarify the relationships between alternate
forms of reference in the same language.

Processes in the use of pronominal features to show degrees of
respect or social distance differ from one language to another in
terms of their grammatical domains and extent of variation. Alternation of reference to convey social meaning may involve only one
grammatical category (such as number or person), a combination
of categories (such as both number and person), classes or types
of pronouns (such as personal pronouns or demonstrative ones), or
a combination of types or pronouns along with pronominal categories (for example, alternation between a personal pronoun in the
second person and a third person reflexive pronoun). The language
material considered in the present study is arranged so that the
simpler processes of variation are described before the more complex ones. The data are also organized in accordance with a relevant universal: the assertion that all pronominal systems include
the categories of person and number (Greenberg 1963, 96; Ingram
1971, P13). Thus, variation within these categories as a means of
indicating different degrees of respect or social distance will be
examined prior to consideration of other processes of alternation
in pronominal reference to convey social meaning.

The scope of the present study is limited to cases of alternation
in reference to convey social meaning which involve types of pronouns or pronominal categories, but this is not intended to imply
that variation of categories does not occur in other word classes to
show degrees of respect or social distance. On the contrary, variation of number -- for example -- to show degrees of respect or
social distance in reference to individuals is not restricted to pronouns: it is manifested in the noun system in some languages
(e.g. Amharic, Hebrew, and Hausa) or in the verb system. Variation of features not found in the pronoun system also may be used
in other word classes to convey social meaning: examples include

---

(ftnt. 3 cont.)

in reference) were obtained in the survey for the present study are
listed in the bibliography. Many other materials consulted do not
provide information on variation in pronominal reference to convey
social meanings.

alternation between different forms of imperatives, or between imperatives and other verb forms used with the same function, and the use of augmentative and diminutive noun suffices.

2. Degrees of Respect and Variation of Number

Variation of number to show degrees of respect or social distance is found in pronominal reference to each of the three participant roles in discourse: the speaker, the addressee, and the one spoken about. In the materials surveyed for the present study, it is more frequently reported in pronouns of the second person that in those of the first or third.

2.1 Variation of number in second person pronouns [4]

Of the languages on which information is available to this study, the following are reported to employ variation of number with second person pronouns as a means for showing degrees of respect or social distance:[5]

---

[4]As used in this section, the term "second person reference" indicates reference to the addressee by use of a personal pronoun in the second person only, "first person reference" is to the speaker by use of a personal pronoun in the first person, and "third person reference" is to the person spoken about by use of a personal pronoun in the third person. In subsequent sections, however, it is necessary to distinguish carefully between the name of the category and that of the role in discourse, since, in some languages, the grammatical category of person shows variation in reference to the same role as participants in the speech act (see sec. 3).

[5]The sources used for information on the languages in this list and on others cited as examples in this study are given in the bibliography (see also n.2). In several other languages mentioned in the material consulted, number is apparently used to indicate different degrees of respect or social distance in reference to the addressee, but the information provided is insufficient to justify including them in this list: Jain (1969, 88) mentions Kashmiri and Punjabi, among other Indian languages -- both Indo-Aryan and Dravidian -- in his discussion of use of the plural in Hindi to show respect in address; Swift (1963, 107) indicates that in Kituba the use of a suffix of plurality "adds an element of politeness to the imperative"; Samarin (1967, 138-139) mentions Gbaya as an example of the African languages which use "a plural pronoun in referring to a

Singular - Plural

Amharic	Ila	Papiamento
Arabic	Indonesian	Persian
Basque	Indo-Portuguese	Philippine Spanish
Bengali	Creole	Creole
Bulgarian	Italian	Polish
Catalan	Java Portuguese	Portuguese
Chagatay	Creole	Provençal
Changana (Tsonga)	Kanarese	Romanian
Chinyanja	Kannada	Russian
Chitumbuka	Kapampangan	Sango
Czech	Kefa	Sanskrit
Danish	Khasi	Serbo-Croatian
Dari	Lala	Shona
Dutch	Lamba	Sindhi
Eastern Pomo	Latin	Spanish
Estonian	Latvian	Sukuma
Faroese	Lithuanian	Swedish
Fijian	Malagasy	Tagalog
Finnish	Malay	Tamil
French	Malayalam	Telugu
Galla	Mandarin Chinese	Tigrinya
Gbaya	Mande	Tulu
German	Marathi	Turkish
Gilyak	Moré	Urdu
Greek	Nepali	Welamo
Gujarati	Norwegian	Welsh
Harari	Nsenga	Wisa
Hindi	Nyamwesi	Yiddish
Icelandic	Nyanja	Yoruba

(ftnt. 5 cont.)

single individual when that person is held in respect"; Garvin and Riesenberg (1952, 204-205) mention use of a plural marker in Ponape as an honorific in greetings; Codrington (1891, 232), cited by Frazer (1910, II, 77) and Freud (1953, 10), reports that on Leper's Island, one of the New Hebrides, a mother changes from the use of the singular to "more distant plural forms" in addressing her son once his puberty ceremonies have begun. These languages have not been included in the preceding list of languages exemplifying use of number to show degrees of respect or social distance in second person reference, because the information available to this study does not contain sufficient detail on the various pronominal categories and types of pronouns used in reference.

Singular - Dual

Navaho   Mota   Tikopia

The languages in this list, as well as the ones given in subsequent lists of examples, are grouped together in the present study only because the same grammatical features are found to alternate in them in pronominal reference showing different degrees of respect or social distance. Placing the above languages in the same list does not mean that the details of variation of number in second person pronouns are identical in them. On the contrary, languages differ widely with regard to the extent to which alternation of number to show degrees of respect or social distance occurs in different varieties, the periods of which it is most characteristic, the social features which condition it and their relative importance, and the range of relative social meaning of the pronouns of address which differ in number. (A good example of a language in which major varieties differ greatly with regard to their address systems is Spanish, particularly in Latin America; see Kany 1951, 55-98, and Paez-Urdaneta 1976.)

There are, however, important similarities between the languages listed above with regard to use and general social meaning of variation of number in second person pronouns. First, alternation of number to show degrees of respect or social distance appears to be restricted to reference to individuals: in the material surveyed, there are no reports of variation of number to convey any sort of social meaning in reference to more than one person. Moreover, in all of the languages in the preceding list, variation of number in second person pronouns has the same general social meaning when used in pronominal reference to an individual addressee: the non-singular (plural or dual) shows greater respect or social distance than does the singular. In view of its genetic and geographic range, the list suggests that this semantic process -- use of the non-singular for polite address of an individual -- is neither a characteristic of particular groups or families of languages nor limited to a single area of the world (although it seems to be rare in indigenous languages of North and South America): it appears to be a universal tendency.[6]

---

[6]Other studies have also suggested that use of the non-singular to show greater respect or social distance than the singular in addressing an individual is a general tendency, or language univer-

Although greater respect or social distance is shown by the non-
singular in almost all languages in which alternation of number is
used to convey social meaning in pronominal address, a few exceptions have been reported: in Bemba "the paramount chiefs ... are
said to be addressed with you (singular) despite the fact that all
other adults are addressed in the plural (either second or third
person)" (Gregersen 1974, 53), while in both Chukchee and Koryak
it is reported that the plural forms of the second person are often
used in place of the singular without conveying the idea of respect
(Bogoras 1922, 722).

Since variation of number of convey social meaning in address
is so widespread among different languages and areas of the world,
it is appropriate to consider whether there are any conditions
which prevent, or tend to prevent, its occurrence in a language.
An obvious limitation is lack of distinction between singular and
non-singular in the system of pronouns. Although no language is
reported to lack distinction of grammatical number in the first
person, there are a few in which it is reported not to occur in the

---

(ftnt. 6 cont.)
sal, not to be accounted for by a particular historical motivation.
According to Gregersen (1974, 53), the development of an honorific
use of you (plural) in African languages is "less obviously motivated"
than in European languages. Brown (1965, 54) states that plurality
seems to be a natural metaphor for social power. He points out
that, although honorific use of the second person plural in Latin may
have served as a model for the plural of respect in many European
languages (as posited by Brown and Gilman 1963, as well as by
several earlier studies on language history), the likelihood that
metaphor directed usage is increased by the fact that languages
unrelated to Latin have independently developed such a form of
address. (In this connection, he refers to "some of the Indian
languages of California," citing Kroeber 1925.) Having noted that
in several languages the plural is used in address to show greater
social distance than the singular, Bean (1970, 564) states that
"... in languages that use number in the pronominal system to
express the presence or absence of social distance, it appears to
be universal that the plural communicates the presence of social
distance and the singular its absence." Bean also argues that the
notion of distance is inherent in the plural because plurality refers
to a triad (of the speaker and more than one addressee), while
intimacy is inherent in the singular because it refers to a dyad (of
the speaker and one addressee).

second: Siouan (according to Boas 1911, 41), Korean, Kamanugu,
Malay and Chitkuli (Forchheimer 1953, 65-66, 79, 114).[7]

The special social conditions in which a language is formed or
in which some speakers are found can also lead to lack of variation
of number or other categories to represent social distinctions in
address. Speakers of pidgins and creoles use forms of address
that they receive from speakers of other languages. During early
stages in the formation of a pidgin or creole, often only one form
of address is used, and that form is likely to be derived from one
that is non-deferential in its original language. A similar limitation can occur when speakers belonging to a single class become
isolated from the rest of their language community, like low caste
speakers of Hindi in Trinidad, who also have no deferential pronouns of address among themselves (Durbin 1972).

In later stages, during decreolization, the process used in
reference for showing degrees of respect or social distance is likely
to be variation between forms of different origins, rather than
between pronominal categories or types of pronouns. In Philippine
Creole Spanish, the Spanish-derived pronouns are used in both
numbers in address for showing greater respect than native Philippine ones (Frake 1971, 227). The difference is in accordance with
distinctions in usage generally found in recent relexification processes (Molony 1977). Similar variation between address forms of
different origins is found in other language contact situations: in
both Javanese and Sundanese the non-Austronesian forms of self-
reference typically indicate greater respect or social distance than
the Austronesian ones (Wallace 1976, 22).

-----

[7]Alternation of number in reference to the addressee is also
found in languages in which third person pronouns are used in
address (examples are given in sec. 3.1). With the exception of
Siouan (said to have "only a very imperfect distinction between the
third person singular and plural"), the languages reported not to
distinguish number in the second person also lack this distinction in
the third. Although many speakers of English use only one second
person pronoun both for an individual addressee and for more than
one, English is not considered here to be an example of a language
without number distinction in the second person: not only is this
distinction currently employed in various dialects, particularly in
Northern England (Evans 1977), as well as in special styles (Foster
1976), it is a common feature of the standard language of earlier
periods.

The most respectful form of address in a Creole language is typically the most recent one adopted from a more prestigious language, regardless of its social meaning (which is often non-deferential) in the language of origin. A good example of this is found in Portuguese creoles, many of which initially adopted vós, the second person plural pronoun, as a general form of address, and more recently adopted você. The latter indicates greater respect or social distance than does the earlier term in the creoles in which both occur. Alternation between these two forms of address, with the same relative social meaning as found in the creoles, is not attested in any other variety of Portuguese. (In all major dialects você is non-deferential, in contrast with the Spanish cognate Usted, while vós is no longer current in most varieties of Portuguese as a form of address to individuals, although it is some-times used in prayer.)

Since the non-singular commonly shows greater respect or social distance in address than does the singular, and there may be more than one non-singular category (e.g. dual and plural), it is necessary to determine how many degrees of distinction in social meaning are possible in variation of number in pronominal refer-ence. Although alternation between both singular and dual and singular and plural are attested examples of variation of number in address to show degrees of respect or social distance, only one relative difference in social meaning is found to occur in variation of number in address in the materials surveyed here: there is no example of a scale with three degrees of social distance or respect corresponding to the sequence singular/dual/plural, but only cases of alternation conveying two general relative meanings.

In the evolution of address systems, however, a different sort of sequence based on variation of number is sometimes found. In some languages, plural pronouns used formerly in polite address of individuals have acquired general usage in address, losing both their earlier social meaning and their original number, only to be repluralized later. The repluralized or new plural form may then come to be used like the original one was earlier: for showing greater respect or social distance than the opposing form, with the difference that the new distinction is between a new plural form and an archaic one, while the former one was between the now archaic plural and the singular. When used in reference to indivi-duals, repluralized forms always show greater respect or social distance than the earlier ones. Examples of this diachronic se-quence in the use of variation in number to convey social meaning are found in Turkish, Basque, and Bengali and several other lan-

162   Brian F. Head

guages in India, in which "double plural" forms are found in
respectful address: archaic plural pronouns with a new plural
marker. (If, as is sometimes reported, "you all" is employed in
respectful address to individuals, Southern American English is
also an example of the sequence of evolution from plural to respectful singular, then to general singular, followed by addition of a
new plural marker and use of the new "double" plural as respectful
singular.)

2.2 Third person reference

The materials surveyed in this study report that variation of
number is employed to show different degrees of respect or social
distance in third person pronominal reference in the following
languages:[8]

Singular - Plural

Amharic	Kanarese	Persian
Bengali	Kannada	Russian
Chinyanja	Kefa	Shona
Dari	Khasi	Syriac
Efatese	Kwatiutl	Tagalog
Galla	Malagasy	Tamil
German	Malay	Tigrinya
Gura	Malayalam	Tulu
Hadiyya	Mandarin Chinese[9]	Welamo
Haida	Marathi	Wisa
Harari	Moré	Yoruba

---

[8]This list is comprised only of languages in which variation of
the grammatical category of number in the third person pronouns
is used to convey social meaning in reference to the "notional"
third person (someone other than the speaker or the addressee).
Alternation of number in third person pronouns to convey social
meaning is also found in some of the languages in which the third
person is used in address. Examples of the latter are discussed
in sec. 3.1.

[9]There is perhaps some doubt as to whether Chinese belongs in
this list. Chao (1956, 219) mentions honorific forms Nin for nii
(second person singular) and Tan for Ta (third person singular), and
states that the origin of Nin is probably nii.men >niim > niin >

With regard to both use and meaning of variation of number to convey social meaning in reference to the notional third person, the above languages show similarities among themselves equivalent to the ones previously found among languages in which variation of number is used for showing degrees of respect or social distance in reference to the addressee. Variation of number to convey social meaning in the third person occurs only in reference to individuals (there are no reports of use of the singular with any type of social meaning in reference to more than one person), and use of the non-singular typically indicates greater respect or social distance than does use of the singular.

Variation of number as a means of showing degrees of respect or social distance is less common in the third person than in the second. However, even if one considers only reference to the notional third person (but not to the addressee, for which the third person is also used in some languages, as discussed in sec. 3.1), the genetic and geographic range of the languages in which this process of conveying social meaning is found is sufficiently great to indicate that it is not to be accounted for by some specific motivation in each language community in which it occurs, nor by particular circumstances in one language or another, followed by diffusion to others. Thus, not only in the second person, but also in the third, use of the non-singular in pronominal reference to show greater respect or social distance than the singular appears to be a universal tendency. But this is not to say that a particular social feature cannot serve to motivate use of the non-singular in third person reference: it has been reported that in Munda-Koh "it is considered indecent to speak of a married woman except in the dual: she is, as it were, not to be imagined as being without her husband" (Jespersen 1924, 194).

2.3 First person reference

Variation of number to show different degrees of respect or social distance is also found in first person reference. The use of a "plural of majesty" is found at one time or another in the history

---

(ftnt. 9 cont.)

nin. Nii.men is the second person plural, while the third person plural is ta.men. Thus, although Chao does not mention it, the origin of Tan seems likely to parallel that of Nin· both are probably modified plural forms.

of most, if not all, languages of Western Europe.[10] In addition to
the widespread uses of the plural of the first person for self-reference in Indo-European languages (in Sanskrit, Hindi, Bengali,
Greek, Latin, German, English, Danish, Norwegian, Swedish,
Icelandic, French, Spanish, Italian, etc.), variation of number in
first person pronominal reference is reported in the following
languages by the materials surveyed in the present study:

Amharic	Kanarese	Navaho
Arabic	Kannada	Nsenga
Auca	Lala	Nyamwesi
Chinyanja	Lamba	Tagalog
Haida	Luo	Tigrinya
Hebrew	Moré	Turkish

---

[10]The "plural of majesty, " the "plural of modesty" (as used by
the Pope) and "editorial we" are sometimes mentioned as contrasting uses of the first person plural. For example, Bean (1970, 564)
states: "In English, an individual of very high rank sometimes
speaks in the first person plural (e.g. the "royal we"). The speaker
makes himself symbolically plural, precluding dyadic relationships,
and establishing distance between himself and his audience. In this
way he indicates that deference is expected. The "editorial we"
may also be seen as an introduction of social distance ... In this
case, however, the distance serves to deemphasize the personality
of the writer." Similarly, Muller (1914, 68) states that the social
meaning of the pluralis reverentiae used in address is the opposite
of that of the pluralis modestiae used by the speaker to refer to
himself, although Grimm, Diez and Meyer Lübke all attribute the
origin of the "plural of respect" in address to use of the "plural of
modesty" by the speaker. Jespersen (1924, 193) and Brunot (1953,
273) also distinguish differences in meaning between uses of the
plural of the first person in self-reference. Parallel contrasting
uses (of modesty and of authority or superiority) are not said to
occur in the case of the plurals of the second and third person;
their alleged occurrence in the first person of self-reference should
be carefully examined.

The status of the plural is no doubt unique in the first person:
unlike its use in pronouns of the second and third persons, the
plural in the first person does not normally refer to several people
with the same role in the speech act. Except in the rather uncommon
case of several people speaking in unison, it does not refer to
several speakers, but to one, by himself or along with whomever

As in second and third person pronominal reference, variation of number in the first person to convey social meaning is restricted to reference to an individual, and the distinction is between singular and non-singular, with the non-singular -- usually the plural -- implying greater respect or social distance than the singular.[11] Use of the dual for this purpose has been reported in Navaho (Sapir and Hoijer 1960, 752A) and in Auca (by Peeke 1973, 41, who states that "...'honorific' includes dual or plural exclusive in first person ...").

In the languages mentioned above, use of the non-singular (plural or dual) for self-reference implies greater respect due to the speaker (when it indicates power or authority, for example) or greater social distance between him and others. In some languages, however, use of the non-singular for self-reference does not serve to convey these social meanings. In Chukchee and Koryak, the plural of the first person is reported to be used often to refer to the speaker, but without the idea of respect (Bogoras 1922, 722).

(ftnt. 10 cont.)

else he elects to include. The differences between exclusive and inclusive uses of the plural in the first person perhaps underlie the alleged distinctions in meaning between "royal we," "editorial we" and the "plural of modesty." "Royal we" is normally exclusive, referring only to the speaker, while "editorial we" and the "plural of modesty" tend to be inclusive, associating the speaker with the addressee(s), the notional third person or both. Use of the first person plural to show greater respect or social distance is exclusive, while inclusive use indicates proximity between the speaker and the other referent(s).

On the other hand, "royal we," "editorial we," and the "plural of modesty" have features in common. All three can call attention to the special status of the speaker as king (or other authority), writer or Pope (or some other spokesman for a group). Special status is inherent in use of the first person plural in self-reference in speech communities in which such use is not appropriate for all speakers. Thus, all three can serve to indicate a greater degree of respect or social distance than is implied by the more common use of the singular.

[11]Turkish may be an exception. Lewis (1967, 35) states that the first person plural is "sometimes used colloquially for 'I'," but does not indicate the social meaning of this usage.

In Nyamwesi, the plural of the first person is used in self-reference
by adults when speaking with someone who is addressed in the plural;
in this case, employment of the plural is a general feature of discourse, and its use in the first person does not convey special
social meaning per se. For African languages, Gregersen (1974,
52) describes a distinction between royal use of the singular and
plebian use of the plural: "... a widely found distinction requires
that my people, my village, and so on be appropriate only in the
mouths of chiefs, commoners saying our people, our village, etc.
Such is the case for Zande, Hausa, and Nyamwezi, and many,
many others."

Use of the singular rather than the plural in self-reference for
showing greater power or importance of the speaker or social distance between him and the addressee(s) is also exemplified by the
reply attributed to God in telling Moses how to refer to him: "I AM
THAT I AM: and he said, thus shalt thou say unto the children of
Israel, I AM hath sent me to you" (Exod. 3.14). The absolute
respect and devotion required of the Israelites in worship of a
single divinity is implied by use of the grammatical singular. The
absoluteness of the singular is particularly striking in view of the
polytheism of the Egyptians.[12] (On the other hand, the name for
God in the Hebrew Scriptures [Elohīm, literally "gods"] is like a
plural of respect, since plural nouns also occur in Biblical references to important individual persons. That this use of the grammatical plural does not imply notional plurality, but is merely
another example of the widespread use of the non-singular to signify respect, is shown by the co-occurring use of the singular in
pronominal reference and in verb forms.)

Use of the first person plural in self-reference is closely related
to use of the plural for showing respect or social distance in
addressing an individual. Use of the plural to show greater social
distance than the singular in reference both to self and to an individual addressee is widespread among Indo-European languages,
but use of the plural to refer to a notional third person is not so

---

[12]Use of the plural in self-reference is attributed to God on at
least two occasions, both when speaking to himself: the creation of
man (Gen. 1.26) and the confusion of tongues at Babel (Gen. 11.7);
but the plural is never used in the Bible in pronominal references
to God as notional third person (cf. Gen. 1.27 and Matt. 19.4), nor
in address. The singular is also attributed to God in self-reference
when speaking to others (e.g. Gen. 12.7).

common, although it is found in some languages (see sec. 2.2 for example). Similarly, in almost all (at least fifteen out of eighteen, excluding perhaps Auca, Hebrew and Luo) of the languages of the above list of examples of languages in which the non-singular of the first person is used in self-reference to convey a different social meaning from that of the singular, the non-singular of the second person is employed with similar meaning in address, but the plural of the third person is used in a like way in only about half of them for referring to someone other than the speaker or an addressee (in Amharic, Chinyanja, Haida, Kanarese, Kannada, Moré, Tagalog and Tigrinya, according to the materials surveyed here).

3. Degrees of Respect and Differences in Person

The materials surveyed in this study include mention of several languages in which different categories of person are used in reference to the same participant role in discourse. Variation of person in reference appears to be most common in address, but it is also found in reference to the speaker or to someone other than the addressee or the speaker. Moreover, use of the third person for either the addressee or the speaker also appears to be more common than use of either the first person for reference excluding the speaker, or the second for someone other than the addressee.

3.1 Third person for reference to the addressee

Use of personal pronouns in the third person for reference to the addressee has been reported in several languages, including the following:

Amharic	Harari	Norwegian
Bemba	Italian	Nsenga
Danish	Janger	Sotho
Eastern Pomo	Kashmiri	Swedish
Efatese	Kefa	Tagalog
German	Lala	Welamo
	Lamba	

It is usually reported that the third person is used for showing greater respect or social distance in address than the second. Bemba appears to be an exception, in that the paramount chiefs are addressed in the second person singular, although other adults are addressed in the plural of the second or the third person (Gregersen 1974, 53).

Among languages in which personal pronouns in the third person
are used in address, one should distinguish between (a) those in
which this form of reference to the addressee is used only to replace nouns or nominal expressions in the same piece of discourse,
and (b) those in which its use does not depend in this way on verbal
context.

In all of the languages given in the preceding list, use of the
personal pronoun in the third person for address does not occur
merely in replacement of other items used in the same discourse
to refer to the addressee -- at least presumably, since the materials from which information on this form of address in the languages listed above was obtained do not mention such a restriction.
In some languages, however, personal pronouns in the third person
are employed in reference to the addressee only when replacing
nouns or nominal expressions. In contemporary French, for example, use of the third person pronouns (masc. il, fem. elle) to refer
to the addressee depends on discourse context, as is shown in the
following instances of anaphora: Sa Majesté veut-elle?, Monsieur
veut-il? (cf. Brunot 1953, 20).

Endophoric (discourse-bound) use of third person pronouns in
reference to the addressee is not often mentioned in descriptions
of address usage, but there is reason to believe that is is more
widespread in the history of languages than is exophoric (discourse-
free) use, since the latter has often been derived from the former.
Among the languages of the preceding list on which adequate historical information is available, exophoric use in address of existing
third person pronouns commonly developed from the use of these
pronouns as endophoric substitutes for nouns or nominal expressions employed to refer to the addressee: this is true of German,
Danish, Norwegian, Swedish and Italian.

Since the third person is generally used with personal pronouns
which replace nouns or nominal expressions, it is also commonly
used with personal pronouns when they replace proper nouns,
common nouns or nominal expressions as forms of address.[13]

---

[13]Substitution of nouns and nominal expressions is not the only
mechanism which serves to introduce use of the third person of
personal pronouns into address systems: reduction of nominal
forms of reference can lead to the formation of new "pronouns."
This process has occurred in Spanish (in which Usted evolved from
Vuestra Merced, "Your Grace"), Dutch (U from Uwe Edelheid,

Since pronouns in the third person are used to replace nouns and nominal expressions employed for reference in the same context, use of the third person of personal pronouns in address and self-reference is especially common in the speech of adults to young children. In his survey of baby talk as a special way of speaking to infants in several languages, Ferguson (see vol. I) points out that every study that mentions special features in the use of pronouns in this form of language notes that those of the first and second person are often replaced by nouns. This is presumably in order to facilitate comprehension, as well as to teach role relationships between the speaker and the addressee. Nouns designating the adult as speaker and the child as addressee may of course be repeated throughout discourse, but they tend to be replaced, at least occasionally, by personal pronouns in the third person. Thus, in forms of language used in speaking to children, employment of personal pronouns in the third person for reference to the speaker or to the addressee is a feature of discourse in baby talk, and does not have the same social meaning that it does in other types of language (namely, to indicate greater respect or social distance than use of the first or second person, respectively).

Languages in which personal pronouns in the third person are employed in address can be divided into two groups according to their use of the grammatical categories of number: those in which the singular is used and those in which a non-singular is used, for deferential address to an individual.

In varieties of Italian in which a third person pronoun is used to show greater respect or social distance than one in the second, the singular is employed for deferential address to an individual. The

---

(ftnt. 13 cont.)
"Your Nobility") and other languages (see sec. 5.4 for discussion of pronominalization of nominal forms of address).

Introduction of third person pronouns into the address system through (a) substitution of other address terms by existing personal pronouns and (b) reduction of nominal expressions so as to create new pronominal forms, are clearly distinct processes, but the difference is sometimes overlooked: a recent study dealing with acquisition of polite forms in Italian states that "terms such as La Vostra Signoria 'Your Lordship' ... were shortened to the feminine pronoun lei ..." (emphasis added).

same is true in the use of third person personal pronouns for address in Harari, Kashmiri, Kefa, Sotho and some varieties of Swedish. The singular of third person personal pronouns was formerly used for respectful address to an individual in German, Norwegian and Danish, but the plural of the third person is employed for this purpose in contemporary forms of these languages. The plural of the third person is also employed in respectful address to an individual in Amharic, Bemba, Eastern Pomo, Efatese, Janger, Lala, Lamba, Nsenga, Tagalog, and some forms of Swedish.[14]

Apart from the natural tendency of grammatical number to correspond to notional or objective number, two factors appear to determine which number is used with third person pronouns in deferential address to an individual: agreement with replaced forms (nouns or nominal expressions), and generalization of use of the non-singular to show higher degrees of respect or social distance than the singular in pronominal reference.

Pronouns usually agree in number with the nouns or nominal expressions that they replace, in address and elsewhere. In addition to the general tendency for grammatical number to coincide with notional number, agreement with replaced forms helps to account for use of the singular for an individual and the plural for more than one person in deferential address during earlier periods in German, Norwegian and Danish, as well as in some contemporary varieties of Swedish and Italian: the nouns or nominal expressions which the third person personal pronouns replaced also varied in grammatical number in accordance with the notional distinction between one and more than one. (In Italian, agreement with the replaced nominal expression accounts also for use of the feminine of the third person singular in deferential address to individuals of both sexes; see sec. 4.1 for discussion of the social meaning of variation of gender in pronominal reference.)

Use of non-singular number with the third person in deferential address appears to be more likely in languages in which the non-singular is also used, or has been used, for showing greater degrees of respect or social distance in pronominal reference in

---

[14]Use of the third person plural in address has also been reported in Agni, where it appears to be merely a feature of discourse context, not to convey social meaning: once the plural of the second person has been employed, it can be replaced by the third person plural (Delafosse 1900, 52).

the other grammatical persons, whether to the addressee or to the other participants in discourse. In most, if not all, of the languages listed above in which the plural of the third person is used for deferential address to an individual, this number is, or has been, employed with similar social meaning also in first or second person reference to individuals. This is the case in Amharic, Danish, Eastern Pomo, German, Lala, Lamba, Norwegian, Swedish and Tagalog. Further information is needed in order to determine whether it is also true of Efatese, Janger and Welamo.

3.2 Use of the third person for reference to the speaker

Personal pronouns in the third person are commonly used in reference to the speaker in two kinds of discourse: (1) autobiography and (2) baby talk, as the form of language used by adults in speaking to small children. In both cases, the third person of the personal pronoun is usually introduced into self-reference through substitution of nominal forms -- proper names, common nouns or nominal expressions -- which also identify the speaker in the same piece of discourse. In autobiography, use of nominal forms of self-reference serves to give the impression of objectivity, while adults employ them to refer to themselves when speaking to small children in order to facilitate understanding (cf. Jespersen 1924, 217).[15]

Since the replacement of nouns by pronouns is largely a matter of textual style, alternation between nominal forms and third person pronouns in self-reference does not in itself serve to indicate different degrees of respect or social distance. It is rather the use of the nominal form by the speaker or writer to refer to himself that conveys a different social meaning from that of the more commonly used personal pronoun in the first person. Once the nominal form of self-reference has been employed, its replacement

---

[15]Use of the third person in self-reference by writers is sometimes considered a form of modesty, or to be "self-effacement in order to produce the impression of absolute objectivity" (Jespersen 1924, 217). However, since this use is typical of important personages, whether in autobiography (e.g. Caesar in De Bello Gallico and Captain John Smith in his memoires) or in literature (Marlowe's Faustus, Shakespeare's Julius Caesar, Cordelia and Richard II, Lessing's Saladin, etc.), it is actually an indication of special status, and hence implies greater social distance than does the more commonly used first person singular.

by a third person pronoun is determined by style and the require-
ments of textual cohesion.

When used in exophoric pronominal reference to the speaker
(not merely to replace nouns or nominal expressions used in self-
reference), the third person shows greater social distance between
the speaker and others than does the first.

Third person pronouns referring to the speaker typically occur
in the singular, unlike the use of the third person in address, in
which the singular and the non-singular are both attested in several
languages in deferential reference to individuals.

Use of the third person for self-reference is more likely to
occur when the speaker is also addressed in the third person by
those with whom he is communicating.

3.3 Use of the first person for reference to someone other than the speaker

In analyzing the social meaning of the first person when employed
for reference to discourse participants other than the speaker, it
is necessary to distinguish between (a) use of the first person singular or non-singular to refer exclusively to either an addressee or
a notional third person so as to convey social meaning, and (b) the
common use of the first person non-singular to refer to the speaker
along with an addressee and/or notional third person, without
special social meaning.

Use of the first person to refer exclusively to the addressee is
found in many languages, including, among others, English, German, Danish, Swedish and French (Jespersen 1924, 217-218;
Paulston 1975, 7-9). A typical example is to show similarity of
interests with the addressee, as when doctors ask, "And how are
we today?"

Use of the first person in address is widespread in forms of
language used in speaking to babies and small children. Reference
may be either to both the speaker and the addressee, in order to
encourage participation of the latter in a mutual activity, or only to
the addressee, as a means of showing interest or as an order. Because of this variable range of inclusiveness, the use of "we" in
addressing small children can be ambiguous (Wills 1977, 279).

The non-singular is used in almost all languages in which the
first person is employed for addressing children, whether reference

is to both the speaker and the addressee or to only the latter. An interesting exception is found in modern Japanese, in which small boys are sometimes addressed by their mothers and other adults with a form which is appropriate in ordinary language as first person singular, that is, for use by a speaker to refer to himself.[16]

Occurrences of the first person in address in other forms of speech are found in many languages. In general, they appear to be similar to the use of the first person by adults in addressing children, not only in that the non-singular is widely used, but also in that the first person often indicates less social distance than do other forms of address, or is downward directed, denoting superior status of the speaker. In English, the condescending nature of the first person plural to refer to the addressee is such that, under certain general conditions, its use in any declarative or interrogative is to be interpreted as a command (Ervin-Tripp 1976, 47-49). Such cases exclude the speaker: although the first person plural is used, reference is only to the addressee. In contrast, use of the first person dual inclusive in Hawaiian is considered a polite form of address for greeting an individual (Kahananui and Anthony 1970, 7).

Use of the first person to convey special social meaning in address is probably more widespread than is indicated by mention of this form of address in the materials surveyed here, especially in baby talk (a form of communication not discussed in most of the bibliography on pronominal reference available for the present study).

---

[16]In discussing differences between boys and girls in the use of forms of personal reference in Japanese, Ide (1977, 18) states: "Some boys ... begin using boku as a self referent from the beginning. It is because mothers who are close to their sons often use boku instead of you or boys' name in referring to them as second persons. When a mother say(s), for example, "Ken-chan, boku mo iku? (Ken, are you coming along?), " boku which is a word for "I" is used for "you" ... Boku, a first person pronoun, does have boyhood connotation ... There is no parallel use for girls, since watashi, which could be the counterpart for boku, is never used as early as boku is." Although the author refers to boku as a "first person pronoun, " it is actually a noun (meaning "slave") which is used instead of a pronoun (see also sec. 5.4). But regardless of the word class, use of the singular is an unusual feature in this type of address, since the non-singular is usually employed when forms normally used to refer to the speaker are used in address.

Use of pronouns in the first person to refer exclusively to a
notional third person (someone other than the speaker or the
addressee) is rarely mentioned. In a literary example sometimes
cited by works on the French language, an honored poet is referred
to in the first person plural by his proud patron, who declares,
when introducing him, "Nous sommes lauréat" (Le Bidois and Le
Bidois 1935, 181; Sandfeld 1965, 35). The implication is clearly one
of social proximity between the speaker and his esteemed referent.

3.4 Use of the second person for reference to someone other than the addressee

Use of the second person for reference to someone other than
the addressee appears to be limited to cases in which it is employed
as a generic term.[17] Both the singular and the non-singular occur
in use of the second person as a generic. Sometimes both are used
for generic reference in the same language, as in French. When
the second person is used generically, the reference can include
the addressee along with others, or it can be merely to people in
general, not necessarily including the addressee.[18]

Use of the second person as a generic does not in itself clearly
indicate degrees of respect or social distance, but is rather a

---

[17]Use of the second person by the speaker to refer to himself in
monologue is not a valid example of use of the second person to
refer to someone other than the addressee, for in this case the
speaker is merely addressing himself and the second person is
grammatically and notionally appropriate.

[18]The use of "you" in generic reference can give rise to misinterpretation by the addressee, since this pronoun can be ambiguous as to range of inclusion. This is exemplified in an amusing way
by Jack London in Martin Eden (quoted at length by Jespersen 1924,
216). When Miss Ruth asks Martin what "booze" is, he tells her
that it means "whisky and beer -- anything that will make you drunk."
This causes her to admonish him: "Don't use you when you are impersonal. You is very personal, and your use of it just now was not
precisely what you meant." "I don't just see that." "Why, you said
just now to me, 'whisky and beer -- anything that will make you
drunk' -- make me drunk, don't you see?" "Well, it would, wouldn't
it?" "Yes, of course," she smiled, "but it would be nicer not to
bring me into it. Substitute one for you, and see how much better
it sounds."

question of style. The second person commonly alternates with other forms of generic reference, such as plurals of personal pronouns in the first and third person, and indefinite or impersonal pronouns.

4. Respect Degrees and Variation of Other Pronominal Categories

In addition to categories in terms of the universal features of person and number, pronominal systems may include other types of categories, according to features of gender (e.g. masculine/feminine or masculine/feminine/neuter), humanness (human/non-human), proximity (proximate/non-proximate), extension or range of inclusion (inclusive/exclusive with regard to speaker or hearer), etc.[19]

For showing degrees of respect or social distance, use of categories other than those of person and number appears to be much less common. Relatively few examples are found in the materials surveyed for this study.

4.1 Gender

As previously mentioned (sec. 3.1), the third person feminine singular is used in some forms of Italian for showing greater respect toward an addressee of either sex than is indicated by the use of a second person pronoun. The fact that the feminine pronoun is employed for this purpose should not be interpreted as use of gender for showing degrees of respect or social distance: variation of the category of gender is not involved, since the feminine is used

---

[19]Buchler and Freeze (1966) mention the following pronominal categories in their study of the distinctive features of pronoun systems: formal features -- minimal/nonminimal membership, inclusion/exclusion of speaker, inclusion/exclusion of hearer, maximal membership (range of inclusion)/nonmaximal membership, maximal membership (specified number)/nonmaximal membership; social and cultural features -- solidary/nonsolidary, male/nonmale, persons/nonpersons, proximate/nonproximate. Although Altmann and Riška (1966) have formulated a general typology of courtesy in language, there are no previous studies, insofar as I know, which examine general relationships between grammatical and semantic features of pronominal reference through analysis of data from numerous languages.

for both male and female addressees. The feminine is not in itself considered more respectful than the masculine, but rather the pronoun which is used for respectful address merely agrees in gender (and number) with the nominal expression it has replaced. In this case, the pronominal variation which is used to show degrees of respect or social distance is that of the category of person, with the third person showing greater respect or social distance than the second.

But this is not to say that variation in gender is never used to show degrees of respect in pronominal reference. Cohen (1936, I, 136) indicates that there are several languages, including Amharic, in which the feminine gender is used instead of the masculine in disrespectful reference to a man. Hoben (1976) points out that use of the feminine in Amharic to address a man can be either disrespectful or affectionate. Ferguson (1964, 106) mentions that in baby talk in both Arabic and Marathi shifts of gender are used to show endearment: a feminine noun, pronoun, adjective, or verb form is used for reference to a boy or a masculine one for a girl.

In Zuara Berber, it is reported that a man will refer to his wife by use of the third person masculine plural when speaking to his mother, although he may use the third person feminine singular to refer to her when speaking to a sister (Mitchell 1975, 159). The difference in social meaning conveyed by the alternation of reference forms in this case cannot be attributed solely to variation of gender, since the category of number also varies, in accordance with the widespread use of the non-singular for showing greater respect or social distance than the singular.

In Sinhalese, it is reported that a pronoun used by older people only in feminine address is employed as a polite form of address among younger ones, while the polite form of address for males among the older is said to have a slightly impolite connotation among younger speakers and not to be normally used by them for addressing females (Karunatillake and Suseendirarajah 1974, 92). It appears that younger urban speakers have adopted the feminine pronoun as the polite form of address, while using the "neutral" (neuter?) one for showing lack of respect or social distance in addressing both men and women. (However, this example should be accepted with caution, for the only description available to the present study does not state clearly whether variation of categories of gender is involved, or usage merely varies in accordance with the sex of the addressee.)

Alternation of gender in reference is not limited to the sex-based categories of masculine and feminine, but also is found in variation involving the category of neuter and those of animate/inanimate and human/non-human.

In Danish, the sex-indicating pronouns are used to refer to human beings and to animals in which the speaker has a personal interest (Jespersen 1924, 237-238). Similarly, in English, the greater the interest of the speaker in a child or animal, the less likelihood that the it for inanimate gender will be used, while animals or things may be referred to as he or she to show interest (Jespersen 1924, 235). It can also be used for showing lack of respect in reference to a person.

In Mohawk, the non-masculine genders -- feminine, indefinite and neuter -- are combined in two morphological categories: the feminine/indefinite, used in part for female human beings who are regarded in some prestigious or respectful way by the speaker, and the feminine/neuter, which may be derogatory in reference to a woman, but is not necessarily so (Bonvillain 1973, 86-87).

In addition to neuter, categories such as non-human and inanimate can be used for showing lack of respect in reference to a person, as in Grebo (Innes 1966, 52-53) and Yao (Gregersen 1974, 52).

4.2 Proximity

Data on Ticuna suggest that the categories of proximity occur in third person singular pronouns and that the one with the category meaning "near" is used for familiar reference, while "distant" is used for general, non-familiar reference, so that the distinctions in proximity are used to show different degrees of social distance (or of respect), as well as differences in physical distance or in discourse context (Anderson 1962, 54-55 and 362).[20] Even if this interpretation of the rather complex and incomplete data from Ticuna is correct, use of categories of proximity for showing

─────────────────────────

[20]This analysis, based on a partial reinterpretation of Anderson's examples, is not entirely certain: it depends on particular hypotheses where the description of third person forms is incomplete, namely in characterization of the meaning of alternate forms as "general," "distant," "previously referred to" and "familiar" (see p. 362).

degrees of respect or social distance in pronominal reference does not appear to be widespread among different languages.

4.3 Definiteness

The third person pronouns of Navaho are reported to differ in terms of definiteness, with the "less definite ... used in polite conversation, and ... considered a deferential form between certain relationships" (Young and Morgan 1964, 3).

Similar use is found in a late fashion in ancient Egyptian, in which it was customary for the Pharoah to speak of himself with an impersonal and to be addressed in the same way (Gregersen 1974, 53).

In contrast, use of the indefinite <u>on</u> in French instead of the first person plural of the personal pronoun is usually considered a feature of familiar language, and thus reflects lack of social distance. (Detailed recent discussions of this usage are found in Grafström 1969 and Muller 1970.)

In English, the use of "someone" in address or reference to a notional third person is typically downward directed, as in "It's past someone's bedtime."

4.4 Inclusiveness

Variation between categories of inclusiveness sometimes accompanies that which is used between categories of number, or of both person and number, for showing degrees of respect or social distance.

In self-reference in Auca, the exclusive first person dual or plural is used as an honorific (Peeke 1973, 41). Similarly, the <u>pluralis maiestatis</u> which is widespread in European languages, is used in an exclusive sense, although there is no formal indication of a difference in grammatical category. Thus, it appears that "exclusive" indicates greater social distance, while "inclusive" indicates less, although exceptions are known: in greetings in Hawaiian, the inclusive first person dual is considered a polite form of address (Kahananui and Anthony 1970, 7).

4.5 Respect affixes

A few languages are reported to show degrees of respect or social distance in pronominal reference by use of affixes without any categorical meaning (such as number, person, gender, etc.) other than a social one.

For Nengone, Tryon (1967) lists "normal" and "respectful" forms for the personal pronouns in all persons and numbers. The same suffix serves to distinguish all of the "respectful" forms from the corresponding "normal" ones.

Classical Nahuatl is reported to have both honorific and pejorative suffixes (Andrews 1975, 178).[21]

For Kusaiean, Lee (1975, 105-106) gives two sets of polite forms of the pronouns: one is composed of the personal pronouns plus both a "respect marker" and the plural marker, the other consists of the personal pronouns with an affix "whose meaning is not clear."

In some languages, the use of "honorific" affixes can be more a matter of overall style than a particular feature of pronominal reference: this appears to be the case in both Javanese and Japanese.

In view of the widespread use of alternation of grammatical categories to show degrees of respect or social distance, as well as the employment of lexical items for this purpose, the existence of affixes with autonomous categories of social meaning seems doubtful: the ones used for showing social meanings are likely to be grammatical or derivational in nature, or perhaps the remnants of historical compounds, although in both cases the original meanings and forms may no longer be retained.

5. Degrees of Respect and Alternation Between Personal Pronouns and Other Forms

5.1 Reflexives

Alternation between reflexive and personal pronouns so as to indicate different degrees of respect occurs in several of the languages considered here.

---

[21]Descriptions of Nahuatl differ with regard to this point: Andrews reports both honorific and pejorative pronominal suffixes in the classical language, but Molina (1571, 21-22) mentions only the honorific one, as does Buchler (1967), when describing address in a modern variety. Other languages -- such as Tagalog (Kess 1973) and Indonesian (Kridalaksana 1974) -- have particles used as honorific affixes to forms other than pronouns.

In Hungarian, use of the reflexive in the third person indicates
greater respect or social distance in address than does use of a
personal pronoun in the second person (Moravcsik 1971, A46).
According to Hall (1938, 89), there are two forms meaning "self"
which are used to convey social meaning, one for "formal" address,
the other for "semi-intimate" address.

In some varieties of Basque, the reflexive form ber- is employed,
in combination with a demonstrative, for showing greater respect
or social distance in address than is indicated by personal pronouns
(Azkue 1925, 433).

In Hindi and Urdu, a reflexive form ap is also used for the
addressee, in addition to the second person singular and plural
personal pronouns. As a reflexive, it occurs in all categories of
person and number; in reference, it is used only for individuals
in the role of addressee, and is considered the most respectful
form of address by pronoun (Bailey 1974, 28-32; Jain 1969, 88-91).

Use of the reflexive as an honorific for reference to the addressee
has spread to Bengali, where the pronominal form in which it
occurs (apni) is more respectful than either the second person
singular personal pronoun ("inferior" address form) or the second
person plural personal pronoun ("common" address form). When
used as the reflexive "self," Bengali apni is invariable for all persons and numbers, but when used for address the plural form apnara
is obligatory. Thus, variation of number, in accordance with the
widespread pattern previously discussed (sec. 2.1), combines with
variation of type of pronoun to show degrees of respect or social
distance in address.

Use of the reflexive to show greater respect or social distance
than personal pronouns in address is also found in Marathi and
Nepali (Hudson 1965, passim; Southworth 1974, 183-184).

Honorific use of reflexive forms also occurs in Tamil and several
other Dravidian languages, where third person reflexive pronouns
are used to replace second person personal pronouns in address
showing greater respect or social distance.[22] The singular, the

---

[22]The high incidence of honorific use of a reflexive among the
languages of India, including non-related ones (Indo-European and
Dravidian), suggests that this is an areal feature. Although some
borrowing has clearly occurred on the Indo-Aryan side, there is no
indication in the material available for this study that borrowing of

plural or the double plural (i.e. the reduplicated form of the
plural) of the reflexive pronoun may be used, according to the
amount of respect intended. Use of the reflexive form in pronominal reference is limited to individuals in the role of addressee
(Caldwell 1913, 395-406).

In the Dravidian languages, the reflexive pronoun has also been
prefixed as a possessive so as to form honorifics which are used
for reference either to the addressee or to the person spoken
about. Usually the plural, which indicates greater respect than
the singular, is found as the first member of the compound, although in some cases either the base form or the singular occurs.

Considering its limited occurrence in the languages surveyed
for the present study, alternation between reflexive and personal
pronouns does not appear to be widespread, but rather to be
largely a feature of respectful language in India. In the languages
in which it occurs, the reflexive pronoun -- regardless of its
number -- typically indicates a greater degree of respect or social
distance in address than do the personal pronouns with which it
alternates.[23]

(ftnt. 22 cont.)

the feature in question has taken place between unrelated languages.
Moreover, the Dravidian and the Indo-Aryan reflexives reported to
occur in somewha t similar honorific usage differ with regard to
formal and categorical features. It is possible, however, that
diffusion of the process has occurred without borrowing of forms.
Among the languages of India, diffusion of a different process for
showing degrees of respect or social distance in reference is implied by Bray (1909, 76): "The plural of respect has no place in
Brahui; if used at all, it is used only by those who have learnt its
force in other languages."

[23] Use of reflexive pronouns for emphasis or contrast occurs of
course in English. "It's John himself" is more emphatic -- and
thus may serve to attach more importance to the referent -- than
"It's John." The reflexive form in "Himself, the Champion, " used
as an introduction, stresses importance and thus may indicate
greater respect than would the introduction without the reflexive in
the same circumstances. The social meaning of the reflexive is
evidenced by the incongruency of "Himself, the Village Idiot" as
opposed to "Himself, the Champion." Use of reflexives for emphasis is found in many languages, but is not usually considered a
means of showing degrees of respect or social distance.

5.2 Demonstratives

Some examples of use of demonstratives to show degrees of respect or social distance are found in the materials surveyed for this study.

In Egyptian, an expression translated literally as "the servant there" is found as a form of self-reference for showing humility and respect toward the addressee (Gardiner 1957, 121). Use of the demonstrative for distance reinforces the notion of social separation between speaker and addressee, or of respect toward the latter, which is implied by use of the lexical item meaning "servant" in self-reference.

In Greek, pejorative or depreciative use of demonstratives occurs in several places in the New Testament. The demonstrative is employed without a noun head, and contrasts with the ordinary use of the personal pronoun. The false witness, in referring to Jesus, says, "This [fellow] said, I am able to destroy the temple ...," (Matt. 26.61). Similarly, the scribes and the Pharisees use demonstratives in their accusations: "Why does this [man] speak blasphemies ...?" (Mark 2.7) and "This [man] receiveth sinners ..." (Luke 15.2). The demonstrative is also used in depreciative reference to others besides Christ. In the parable of the prodigal son, the elder brother refers to the prodigal as "this thy son," when complaining of unjust treatment to their father (Luke 15.30).

Both demonstratives, the one for proximity and the one for showing distance, are used in depreciative reference in New Testament Greek. The one for proximity occurs in the preceding examples, but the one for distance is also used, as when Jesus foretells his betrayer at the last supper: "He (literally, that) it is, to whom I shall give a sop ... And after the sop Satan entered into him (lit., that) ..." (John 13.26-27).

In Latin, the demonstrative of the second person, iste, came to have a pejorative meaning. Its frequent use in reference to an adversary in tribunal language led to general use in depreciative reference. (Examples include: Cicero, In Lucium Catilinam 1,1, and De Deorum Natura 1,44,122.) In contrast, the third person demonstrative, ille, used to indicate something or someone distant from both speaker and addressee, often a model or example worthy of being followed, came to indicate respect or admiration. (For example: Cicero, De Oratore 2,14,58 and Tusculanae Disputationes 5, 103.) For showing degrees of respect or social distance, both demonstratives came to be used in reference to other participant roles in discourse, notwithstanding their original categories of second and third person.

In French, Portuguese and other Romance languages, use of any of the demonstratives in personal reference often indicates less respect or greater social distance than does use of a personal pronoun or a nominal form of reference, such as a title or name. The demonstrative may be employed to convey social meaning only in exophoric reference, not in textual reference. An example is the depreciative use of celui-là, "that one," in French to refer to to a notional third person.

Use of the demonstrative to show degrees of respect or social distance is also found in contemporary variaties of Basque in which the deferential form of address for an individual is berori, a compound pronominal form consisting of the intensive or reflexive ber- plus the second person demonstrative -ori (Gavel 1929, 212).

In view of the extensive material surveyed for the present study, the few examples given above seem to constitute scant indication of use of the demonstrative in personal reference. It should be re-called, however, that in many languages there is no clear distinc-tion between demonstratives and third person personal pronouns, and that the latter often have their origin in the former. (See Benveniste 1966 for a discussion of the nature and origin of pronouns.)

The uses exemplified above do not manifest a clear pattern; on the contrary, variation of usage for conveying social meaning differs from one language to another. The demonstrative can be used for depreciative reference or for showing respect; relative degrees of respect may be shown by alternation between different demonstra-tives, or the use of one of the demonstratives can have a constant general social meaning; the categories of person in the demonstra-tives do not manifest a uniform relationship to the relative degrees of respect or social distance, nor to the respective participant roles in discourse when used to convey social meaning. The only feature common to the various examples noted above of use of demonstratives instead of personal pronouns is that the demonstra-tive generally indicates greater social distance (but not necessarily more respect) than does the personal pronoun usually employed.

5.3 Possessives

The use of possessives is common in languages in which nominal expressions are employed in address and reference to the speaker or the notional third person.

Possessives in the second person are found in reference both to the speaker and to the addressee in expressions used for showing respect toward the latter, as in terms equivalent to "thy slave" or "thy servant" for the speaker and "thy Majesty" or "thy Grace" for the addressee. The singular second person possessive occurs in the traditional form of respectful address in Roumanian (dumneata, "thy Lordship"), while the plural one is found in deferential forms of address in French (Votre Majesté), Spanish (Vuestra Majested), Portuguese (Vossa Excelência, "your Excellency," Vossa Senhoria, "your Lordship") and many others.

In forms of reference consisting of possessives and nouns, the degree of respect or social distance is indicated principally by the semantic features of the noun head, with the possessive merely showing personal deixis. However, variation in person of the possessive can serve to indicate differences in social meaning not conveyed by the noun head without the possessive. When Mary Magdalene greets Jesus after he has arisen from the tomb, she addresses him as Rabboni, 'my great Master." Use of the term for "Master" or "Teacher" is respectful, and even more deferential with the augmentative suffix, while the possessive indicates her personal submission. Similarly, the first person singular is used by Jesus when he cries out to God from the cross (Matt. 27,46; Mark 15.34) and by David when he prays in great distress (Ps. 22.1). In contrast, the scribes and Pharisees use the second person possessive in querying the disciples about Jesus, to whom they attribute faults and from whom they disassociate themselves (and thus would not use a first person possessive in reference to him): e.g. "Why eateth your Master with publicans and sinners?" (Matt. 9.11).

Although use of a nominal expression in reference often tends to attenuate or neutralize the force of the social meaning conveyed by the deixis of the possessive, distinctions in degree of respect or social distance can sometimes be found in contrastive uses of person: e.g. "my Majesty," by a counselor or other member of the court, as opposed to the more general "your Majesty" or "his Majesty." Use of the possessives in all three persons with an epithet meaning "Majesty" is found in Egyptian (Gardiner 1957, 121 and 415), and in several other languages.

5.4 Pronominalized nouns[24]

The third person of the personal pronouns was introduced into Italian as a respectful alternate to the second person in address by replacement of an honorific expression formed by noun with a possessive (Lei replacing La Vostra Signoria, "Your Lordship," and similar nominal expressions). In other major Romance languages, nominal expressions composed of possessives and nouns employed in address in former times either came to be used as pronouns, with greater or lesser formal change (Spanish, Portuguese, Rumanian), or fell into disuse without being replaced by a personal pronoun (French).[25] In Spanish and Portuguese honorific expressions (Vuestra Merced and Vossa Mercê, meaning "Your Grace") were shortened and generalized in usage, forming alternates (Usted and Você, respectively) to the second person personal pronouns for showing degrees of respect or social distance in address. These pronominalized forms are third person in both origin and contemporary predicate agreement, although they are used only to refer to the addressee(s).[26]

---

[24]It is not uncommon for nouns and nominal expressions to undergo pronominalization in the sense that they come to be generally used as noun replacements and acquire features characteristic of pronouns (e.g. lack of modifiers). Grammarians often treat such forms simply as pronouns. In order to emphasize both synchronic and diachronic differences between such forms and personal pronouns, I have adopted the term "pronominalized noun."

[25]Use in French of the personal pronoun in the third person as a substitute for a nominal expression referring to the addressee is exemplified by La Fontaine's fable Le loup et l'agneau: "Sire, répond l'Agneau, que Votre Majesté ne se mette pas en colère; mais plutôt qu'elle considère ..." Neither the nominal expression nor the third person pronoun (except as a substitute for an epithet in the same piece of discourse) is common in general address usage in contemporary French.

[26]Agreement is relevant to the present study only to the extent that it reveals the categories involved in variation of pronominal reference to show degrees of respect or social distance. Grammatical implications of variation in number as a means of showing respect or social distance are discussed by Moravcsik (1971, esp. pp. A45-A46) and Comrie (1975).

In Rumanian, the replacement of personal pronouns by pronominal forms derived from expressions consisting of nouns and possessives was more general than in Spanish and Portuguese: new reference forms came into being for all categories of person and number. The process exemplified by joining the second person singular possessive -ta to domnia "Lordship" to form dumneata, used for showing greater respect or social distance in address than the second person personal pronoun, served to create new pronominal forms for reference to participants in all roles of discourse. Although these forms replaced expressions with noun heads, verbal agreement corresponds in person to that of the possessive modifier. Use of the form with the second person plural possessive (dumneavoastră) for reference to an individual addressee is a more recent development, due to the influence of French (Pop 1948, 205; Mota 1972, 161).

Similar evolutions are found in the address systems of other languages. In Dutch, a third person singular pronominal form (U) for respectful use in address also evolved from an honorific expression consisting of a possessive and a noun (Uwe Edelheid, "your Nobility") as an alternate to the second person singular or plural. Verbal inflection with the pronominalized form (U) in reference to an individual addressee is usually third person singular, although the second person singular is also used (Koolhoven 1961, 25).

In all of the cases mentioned above, the pronominal forms derived from nominal expressions composed of nouns and possessive pronouns were introduced into the language to show greater respect or social distance in reference than the existing personal pronouns.

Nouns without possessives or other modifiers also occur as pronoun substitutes in reference. Differences are found from one language to another with regard to both (1) degrees of pronominalization among the nouns employed in reference, and (2) the extent to which nouns are used as pronouns, in terms of the number, semantic range and frequency of lexical items used like pronouns for reference, in any given language.

Highly pronominalized nouns are found in both Polish and Portuguese: pan and o senhor ("gentleman"), respectively, and related feminine and plural forms are used in all grammatical functions for showing greater respect or social distance in address than the second person pronouns. In Portuguese, many other nouns are also found in address, but they are employed less frequently, and they show little pronominalization, since they are commonly used only

as vocatives, not in the other grammatical functions in which pronouns freely occur (Head 1976, 343).

In some languages, alternation occurs between several pronominalized nouns in address, or in reference to any of the participants
in discourse. Wide ranges of degrees of respect or social distance
are covered in address by alternation between numerous reference
forms in Burmese, Cambodian, Hausa, Japanese, Korean, Malay,
Thai, Vietnamese and other languages, especially in Asia. The
forms used in address are often called "pronouns, " but many of
them (in some cases, probably all) are obviously pronominalized
nouns, which have -- or originally had -- lexical meaning apart
from their use as pronominals.

Use of pronominalized nouns is not limited, of course, to any
of the roles of discourse. A widespread means of showing respect
to an addressee is to humble oneself in self-reference by use of
terms equivalent to "sl ve" or "servant": this process is exemplified by Persian, Kmer, Malay, Javanese, Sundenese, Thai, Burmese,
Cambodian and Vietnamese (see also Wallace 1976, 21). In many
Asian languages, such words have become the common form for
indicating the speaker (see also Müller, cited by Jespersen 1924,
217).

In view of the numerous processes of variation of pronominal
categories and types of pronouns, as well as alternation between
true pronouns and other forms of reference, which are found to
show degrees of respect or social distance, the existence of genuine pronouns with only social meaning seems doubtful. Most
honorific "pronouns" are actually nominal forms which have acquired
pronominal functions; close examination, where adequate historical
information is available on the lexicon, may often reveal others.

6. Relationships Between Different Processes of Variation
   in Pronominal Reference

As shown by data previously discussed (secs. 3, 5.1, 5.2),
more than one process of variation in pronominal reference to
indicate degrees of respect or social distance may occur in the
same language. It is therefore of interest to consider the relative
degrees of respect or social distance shown by forms representing
different processes. Since the data on reference to the addressee
are more plentiful than those on reference to the speaker or to
someone other than the speaker or the addressee, the following
discussion of relationships between different processes is based

largely on examples found in address. This limitation does not
affect the results of the analysis, since no combinations of different
processes of variation are found in pronominal reference to Speaker
or Other that are not also attested in address. In fact, the latter
often shows a greater variety of forms from different processes
than does reference to the other participants in discourse.

The material surveyed in this study has frequent mention of
only one combination of variation of different pronominal categories
in reference to show degrees of respect or social distance: number
and person.

6.1 Differences in number and person

Comparison of the lists of languages showing variation of number
and those showing variation of person to indicate degrees of respect
and social distance in address (secs. 2.1 and 3.1) shows that both
processes often occur in the same language.

In Italian, the two types of variation of categories used in
address -- alternation of number in the second person, and alternation of person, between the second and the third -- constitute a
major difference between dialect areas: in general, the former is
characteristic of Southern Italy, the latter of Central and Northern
Italy (Hall 1948, 18). When both processes occur in the same dialect, the hierarchy of increasing degree of respect or social distance in reference to an individual addressee is said to be second
person singular/second person plural/third person singular
(Speight 1975, 28). Moreover, in dialects in which alternation of
person is the only process currently in common use for showing
degrees of respect or social distance, the third person singular
has replaced the second person plural as a form of polite address,
having been introduced to substitute a nominal expression with a
possessive pronoun in the second person plural (Bourciez 1956,
533-534). Thus, the data from Italian, whether viewed diachronically or synchronically, exhibit a single hierarchy of degrees of
respect or social distance in address: second person singular/
second person plural/third person singular. The same hierarchy
is manifested by the pronouns of address in Swedish, in which a
similar difference between dialects with regard to their systems of
address is also found (Paulston 1976).

In summary, variation of person to show degrees of respect or
social distance in address often occurs in languages in which variation of number is found with the same function, either synchroni-

cally or diachronically. From the synchronic point of view, variation of number and of person may occur separately and independently
in different dialects (as in Italian and Swedish) or conjointly in the
same dialect (as in German, Danish, Norwegian and Tagalog).
When both occur diachronically, the attested sequences follow the
order of second person plural, then third person (singular or plural,
or singular and then plural) in the evolution of alternates to the
second person singular for showing greater respect or social distance. (Comparison of the lists in secs. 2.1 and 3.1 reveals several
other languages in which variation of both number and person in
address is found. According to very limited data, the same hierarchy of social meaning in variation of number and of person also
occurs, at least in a few languages, in reference to the speaker:
use of the plural in the first person indicates greater social distance than does the change of number in the first person.)

6.2 Differences in number and in type of pronoun

The language data of this study exhibit only a few different combinations of variation of both a pronominal category and the type of
pronominal form used in reference for showing different degrees of
respect or social distance. All involve variation of number in the
person pronoun, along with variation of the type of pronoun used,
between (a) personal pronouns and (b) demonstrative pronoun,
reflexive pronoun or pronominalized noun.

In Basque, pronominal reference to an individual addressee may
be by use of the second person singular of the personal pronoun,
the second person plural of the personal pronoun, or a third person
singular demonstrative-reflexive pronominal form, with increasing
degree of respect or social distance.

In Hindi, Urdu and Bengali, the hierarchy of social distance or
respect in pronominal address is second person singular personal
pronoun, second person plural personal pronoun and reflexive pronoun. In several Dravidian languages, it is reported to be second
person singular personal pronoun/second person plural personal
pronoun/second person double plural personal pronoun/third person reflexive pronoun (usually double plural, as in Tamil), with
the possibility of further distinction between singular, plural and
double plural in the reflexive, in the hierarchy of increasing respect
(Caldwell 1913, 395-403). In Malayalam, however, the hierarchy
from least to greatest respect or social distance is somewhat different: second person singular personal pronoun/third person singular reflexive pronoun/second person plural personal pronoun/third
person plural reflexive pronoun (Chandrasekhar 1972, 248).

Variation of number in the second person personal pronoun and alternation between personal pronouns and pronominalized nouns is found in address in several of the languages represented by the material surveyed in this study, including Polish, Dutch and some of the Romance languages. In Dutch, Polish, Spanish and Portuguese, the hierarchy of respect or social distance, according either to contemporary use or to the evolution of the address system, is second person singular personal pronoun/second person plural personal pronoun/singular pronominalized noun. A somewhat different situation is found in Rumanian, in which the hierarchy is second person singular personal pronoun/pronominalized nominal expression with second person singular possessive pronoun (dumneata "thy Lordship")/pronominalized nominal expression with second personal plural possessive pronoun (dumneavoastră "your [pl.] Lordship") (Ştefănescu-Drăgăneşti and Murrell 1974, 54-55).

7. Conclusions

In view of the limited number of languages, language families and geographic areas represented by the material used in this study, as well as the rather modest amount of detail on usage found in much of the source material, all conclusions presented here are clearly partial and tentative. Further research should lead to additional assertions and to refinement of some of the ones made here.

Based on the material analyzed in the present study, the following hypotheses of universal properties of pronominal reference showing degrees of respect or social distance are presented:

1. Number is the pronominal category most widely used among different languages in alternation of reference by personal pronoun to show degrees of respect or social distance.

2. Variation in number to show degrees of respect or social distance is used in pronominal reference only to individuals, never to groups.

3. In variation of number in pronominal reference showing different degrees of respect or social distance, the non-singular typically indicates a higher degree of respect toward the referent, or greater social distance between him and other participants in the speech act, than does the singular.

4. A repluralized or a double plural pronominal form indicates greater respect or social distance than an original, archaic

or simple plural, when the two are found in alternation showing different degrees of respect or social distance.

5. Variation of more than one pronominal category may occur in
the same language in reference showing different degrees of
respect.

The combination of variation of different pronominal categories
to convey social meaning that is most common in the material surveyed here is that of number and person. Although there are no
obvious reasons for other combinations to be impossible (and a few
are actually attested), no other one can be so likely to occur, since
number and person are the only universal categories in pronoun
systems.

6. Variation of the category of person in personal pronouns so
as to show degrees of respect or social distance usually
occurs in synchronic or diachronic combinations with variation of number for the same purpose.

7. In languages in which variation of person in pronominal
reference is used to show degrees of respect or social
distance, the third person indicates greater social distance when used in reference to either the addressee or
the speaker than do the pronouns of the second and first
person, respectively.

8. Variation of person in pronominal reference indicates greater
differences in degree of respect or social distance than does
variation of number.

Thus, in languages in which variation of number and of person
are both employed to indicate social meaning in address, the hierarchy in order of increasing social distance is: second person
singular, second person plural, third person singular, third person
plural.

9. Use of the third person personal pronoun to show greater
respect or social distance than the second person pronoun in
reference to the addressee is usually introduced into languages by substitution of nouns or nominal expressions used
in respectful address.

This assertion is not intended to exclude or deny the possibility
of diffusion between languages.

10. If the gender of a third person personal pronoun does not
vary when used in reference to the addressee(s), in a language which has distinctions of gender in the third person
personal pronouns, then it corresponds to that of the noun
or the head of the noun phrase which the pronoun replaced.

11. Variation of gender so as to employ one which does not
correspond to the notional category of the sex of the referent
is not used for showing greater respect than reference with
the usual gender.

In the examples noted in this study in which variation of gender
is employed for showing degrees of respect or social distance, use
of a gender which does not correspond to the notional category of
the referent is often disrespectful or pejorative, although it sometimes shows affection.

12. In a language in which categories of proximity are employed
to show degrees of respect or social distance, the one used
to indicate greater physical distance or distance within discourse is also used to indicate greater respect or social
distance.

13. In a language in which categories of definiteness are employed
to show degrees of respect or social distance, the one used
as indefinite or least definite is also used to indicate greater
respect or social distance.

14. Reflexive pronouns, demonstrative pronouns, and pronominalized nouns or pronominalized nominal expressions used
in reference, usually indicate greater respect or social distance than do personal pronouns of the same number.

It appears that reflexive and demonstrative pronouns are more
likely to indicate high degrees of respect or social distance than
are pronominalized nouns, which are sometimes disrespectful or
pejorative.

15. Variation between different sorts of third person pronouns
is not a common means of showing degrees of respect or
social distance.

Reflexive and demonstrative pronouns seem to alternate rarely
with personal pronouns in the third person, or among themselves,
for showing degrees of social distance or respect in reference.

This assertion applies only to true pronouns, not to pronominalized nouns, which in some languages are numerous and alternate extensively among themselves.

16. The use of variation of any pronominal category to show degrees of respect or social distance is more widespread among different languages (and thus more likely to occur in any given language) in reference to the addressee than in reference to the speaker or to someone else.

The category of number is a possible, though not likely, exception to this assertion, since it is conceivably employed more widely in reference than to the speaker than in address. Although language materials usually provide more information on processes for showing social meaning in address than to those used in self-reference, variation of number in the first person for self-reference is clearly widespread. Some language historians consider variation of number in the first person as a means of signalling social distance to antecede that of the second: Bourciez (1956, 252), for example, attributes use of the plural in the second person for respectful address in Latin to analogy with like use in the first person for self-reference. Moreover, universal features of pronominal systems tend to favor use of the plural of the first person over its use in the second, since all known systems show number distinctions in the first person, but not all do in the second. Unfortunately, processes of self-reference have received much less attention in works on languages than have those of address, and the data provided in the material surveyed here are insufficient for clarification of the relative extent among different languages to which variation of number occurs in reference to the speaker, and the relationship of this process to variation of number in reference to the addressee.

17. Processes of variation of the type of pronoun used in reference for showing degrees of respect or social distance are more common in address than in reference to the speaker or to someone other than the speaker or addressee.

18. Processes of pronominal reference for showing degrees of respect or social distance occur more commonly in reference to individuals than in reference to more than one person.

19. Honorific affixes to pronouns are more common than pejorative ones; if a language has pejorative pronominal affixes, it also has honorific ones.

20. In languages in which categories of proximity, inclusiveness and definiteness are employed to convey social meaning, non-proximate, exclusive, and indefinite or impersonal usually indicate greater respect or social distance than do the opposing ones; inanimate and non-human typically indicate less respect than do their counterparts, when used with social meaning.

21. A pronominal form used for showing greater respect or social distance is never eliminated from the system of reference in favor of one for showing less respect or social distance.

When two or more pronominal forms alternate among themselves so as to show degrees of respect or social distance, and one of them comes to be generally used in reference without special social meaning, the one adopted for general use is always one formerly employed in polite or respectful reference.

In addition to the above assertions, the present study points to some perspectives for further investigation or processes for showing social meaning and reference. Briefly, more information is needed on all of the following: (1) usage in particular languages, especially those which appear to be exceptional with regard to features previously identified or which represent linguistic groups on which little study has been done concerning the social meaning of alternate forms of reference, (2) historical developments, both for identifying the origins of processes for showing social distance in reference and for comparing diachronic patterns with synchronic ones, (3) usage in special kinds of language, such as baby talk and creoles, and (4) reference usage in other grammatical classes (e.g. use of verbal categories).

Now that some of the universal features of the processes used in pronominal reference to show degrees of respect or social distance have been identified at least tentatively, it is desirable to begin to seek their explanation. Analogies between notional and grammatical categories appear to offer a possibility.

Physical distance in personal interaction can often be shown to be correlated with the social distance or degree of intimacy between the participants in communication, in accordance with the norms for using space in the respective society (see, for example, Hall 1959 and Fast 1971). Analogies between physical and social distance can readily be represented symbolically through the use of grammatical categories. The third person in personal pronouns and demonstratives is notionally more distant than the second, the identity of the individual more remote in the non-singular than in the singular. Through analogy, the former member of each of these opposing categories can be used to represent greater social distance than the latter. Moreover, the plural seems a natural metaphor for greatness. Symbolic use of other categories is readily conceivable on the basis of analogy between their notional properties and the concepts attached to social relationships: inanimate and non-human are considered inferior to animate and human and thus are likely to be used for showing disrespect in reference.

Other analogies can be found, but this type of explanation is precarious for several reasons. Semantic distinctions are not clearly and consistently delimited by grammatical categories. Moreover, the grammatical features available for symbolic representation differ from one language to another, and social distance itself is conceived differently from one society to another, or even from one community to another within the same society. Although it is tempting to explain linguistic universals simply as the manifestations of conceptual or cognitive ones, language does not correspond simply and uniformly to thought. Even if there are conceptual universals, their existence is not sufficient cause for linguistic ones. Finally, any attempt to explain presumably universal features of respect degrees in pronominal reference is hampered by the simple lack of information on some aspects of usage. It has now been shown that some features of the processes of pronominal reference for showing degrees of respect have universal scope, but further knowledge is needed with regard to apparent exceptions, and further understanding is required in cases of variation in pronominal reference to convey social meaning which do not appear to manifest a well-defined pattern.

BIBLIOGRAPHY

Aaltio, M.-H. 1971. Finnish for foreigners. Helsinki: Kustannusosakeyhtiö Otava.

Alexander, W.D. 1968. A short synopsis of the most essential points of Hawaiian grammar. Rutland, Vt.: Charles E. Tuttle.

Altmann, G. and A. Riška. 1966. Towards a typology of courtesy in language. Anthropological Linguistics 8. 1-10.

Anderson, Doris G. 1962. Conversational Ticuna. Yarinacocha, Peru: Summer Institute of Linguistics.

Andrews, J.R. 1975. Introduction to classical Nahuatl. Austin: University of Texas Press.

Armbruster, C.H. 1908. Initia amharica. An introduction to spoken Amharic. Part I: Grammar. Cambridge: The University Press.

Austerlitz, R. 1959. Semantic components of pronoun systems: Gilyak. Word 15. 102-109.

Azkue, Resurrección María de. 1925. Morfología Vasca. Bilbao: Editorial Vasca.

Bailey, T.G. 1974. Urdu. Teach yourself books. Edited by J.R. Firth and A.H. Harley. London: The English Universities Press.

Bates, Elizabeth. 1976. Language and context: The acquisition of pragmatics. New York: Academic Press.

Bates, Elizabeth and Laura Benigni. 1975. Rules of address in Italy: a sociological survey. Language in Society 4. 271-288.

Bean, Susan S. 1970. Two's company, three's a crowd. American Anthropologist 72. 562-564.

Beaulieux, Léon. 1950. Grammaire de la langue bulgare. Paris: Institut d'Études Slaves.

Bender, Marvin L., J. Donald Bowen, Robert L. Cooper and Charles A. Ferguson (eds.). 1976. Language in Ethiopia. London: Oxford University Press.

Bengali language and literature. Encyclopaedia Britannica. 1960. Chicago, London and Toronto: William Benton.

Benveniste, E. 1966. La nature des pronoms. Problèmes de linguistique générale, vol. I. Paris: Gallimard, 251-257.

Bhatt, Sooda L. 1971. A grammar of Tuḷu (a Dravidian language). Unpublished Ph.D. dissertation. Madison: University of Wisconsin.

Bickerton, Derek. [1977]. Creoles and language universals. Mimeo. University of Hawaii. 31 pp.

Boas, Franz (ed.). 1911-22. Handbook of American Indian languages. Washington, D.C.: Government Printing Office.

Bogoras, Waldemar. 1922. Chukchee. Handbook of American Indian languages, ed. by Boas, Part 2, 631-903.

Bonvillain, Nancy. 1973. A grammar of Akwesasne Mohawk. Ottawa: National Museum of Man.

Bourciez, Édouard. 1956. Éléments de linguistique romane. Paris: Klincksieck.

Bowen, J.D. 1965. Beginning Tagalog. A course for speakers of English. Berkeley: University of California Press.

Bray, Denys de S. 1909. The Brahui language. Part I. Introduction and grammar. Calcutta: Superintendent, Government Printing.

Bridges, James E. 1915. Burmese grammar. Rangoon: British Burma Press.

Briggs, Elinor. 1961. Mitla Zapatec grammar. Mexico: Instituto Lingüístico de Verano and Centro de Investigaciones Antropológicas de Mexico.

Brown, Roger. 1965. Social psychology. New York: The Free Press.

_____ and A. Gilman. 1960. The pronouns of power and solidarity. Style in language, ed. by T.A. Sebeok. Cambridge, Mass.: MIT Press, 253-276.

Buchler, Ira R. 1967. The analysis of pronominal systems: Nahuatl and Spanish. Anthropological Linguistics 9. 5. 37-43.

_____ and R. Freeze. 1966. The distinctive features of pronominal systems. Anthropological Linguistics 8. 8. 78-105.

Brunot, Ferdinand. 1953. La pensée et la langue. Paris: Masson et Cie.

Brunot, Ferdinand and Charles Bruneau. 1956. Précis de grammaire historique de la langue française. Paris: Masson et Cie.

Buxó Rey, María Jesús. 1973. Procesor de cambio y regresión en formas apelativas: Un modelo analítico en Cataluña. Etnica (Barcelona) 5. 17-59.

Caldwell, R. 1913. A comparative grammar of the Dravidian or South-Indian family of languages. London: Kegan Paul, Trench, Trübner and Co.

Campión, Arturo. 1884. Gramática de los cuatro dialectos literarios de la lengua euskara. Tolosa: Eusebio Lopez.

Cardona, George. 1965. A Gujarati reference grammar. Philadelphia: University of Pennsylvania Press.

Cerulli, Enrico. 1936a. La lingua e la storia de Harar. Studi Etiopici I. Roma: Istituto per l'Oriente.

_____. 1936b. La lingua e la storia dei Sidamo. Studi Etiopici II. Roma: Istituto per l'Oriente.

_____. 1938. Il linguaggio dei Giangerò et alcune lingue Sidama dell'Omo (Basketo, Ciara, Zaissè). Studi Etiopici III. Roma: Istituto per l'Oriente.

_____. 1951. La lingua caffina. Studi Etiopici IV. Roma: Istituto per l'Oriente.

Chandrasekhar, A. 1972. Personal pronouns and pronominal forms in Malayalam. Anthropological Linguistics 12. 7. 246-255.

Chao, Yuen Ren. 1956. Chinese terms of address. Language 32. 217-224.

Chart, Ira E. 1943. The "voseo" and "tuteo" in America. Modern Language Forum XXVIII. 17-24.

Chatelain, Émile. 1880. Du pluriel de respect en Latin. Revue de Philologie IV. 129-139.

Churchward, C.M. 1964. A new Fijian grammar. Fiji.

Codrington, R.H. 1885. Melanesian languages. Oxford: Clarendon Press.

Cohen, Marcel. 1971. Matériaux pour une sociologie du langage.
Paris: Maspero.

_____. 1936. Traité de langue amharique (Abyssinie).
Paris: Institut d'Ethnologie.

Comrie, Bernard. 1975. Polite plurals and predicate agreement.
Language 51. 406-441.

Cooke, Joseph R. 1968. Pronominal reference in Thai, Burmese
and Vietnamese. University of California Publications, Linguistics 52. Berkeley and Los Angeles: University of California Press.

Curme, George O. 1905. A grammar of the German language.
New York: Macmillan.

Darby, Alfred. 1933. A primer of the Marathi language. Bombay:
Tatva-Vivechaka Press.

Dalgado, Sebastião Rodolpho. 1900. Dialecto Indo-Português de
Ceylão. Lisboa: Imprensa Nacional.

Das, Sisir Kumar. 1968. Forms of address and terms of reference
in Bengali. Anthropological Linguistics 10. 4. 19-31.

Das Gupta, Bidhu Bhusan. 1928. Learn Hindi yourself. Calcutta:
Das Gupta Prakashan.

Delafosse, Maurice. 1900. Essai de manuel de la langue agni.
Paris: J. André.

Desgranges, M. 1845. Grammaire sanscrite-française. 2 vols.
Paris: L'Imprimerie Royale.

Destaing, E. 1925. Interdictions de vocabulaire en berbère.
Mélanges René Basset. Paris: Ernest Leroux, II, 177-210.

Diez, Frédéric. 1876. Grammaire des langues romanes. Trad.
Alfred Morel-Fatio and Gaston Paris, Paris.

Diguet, Édouard. 1905. Éléments de grammaire annamite. Paris:
Imprimerie Nationale.

Dunn, C.I. and S. Yanada. 1958. Teach yourself Japanese.
London: The English Universities Press.

Durbin, Mridula A. 1973. Formal changes in Trinidad Hindi as a result of language adaptation. American Anthropologist 75. 1290-1304.

Eckmann, János. 1966. Chagatay manual. Bloomington: Indiana University.

Ervin-Tripp, Susan. 1976. Is Sybil there? The structure of some American English directives. Language in Society 5. 25-66.

Evans, William. 1977. "You and Thou in Northern England. Papers in language variation, ed. by David Shores and Carol P. Hines. SAMLA-ADS Collections. University: University of Alabama Press.

Eys, W.J. van. 1879. Grammaire comparée des dialectes basques. Paris: Maisonneuve.

Fast, Julius. 1971. Body language. New York: Pocket Books.

Ferguson, Charles A. 1977. Baby talk as a simplified register. Talking to children, ed. by C. E. Snow and C. A. Ferguson. 209-235.

_____. 1964. Baby talk in six languages. American Anthropologist 66. 103-114.

_____. 1978. Talking to children: A search for universals. Universals of Human languages, vol. I, ed. by J.H. Greenberg, C.A. Ferguson and E.A. Moravcsik. Stanford: Stanford University Press.

Filbeck, David. 1973. Pronouns in Northern Thai. Anthropological Linguistics 15. 8. 345-361.

Firth, Raymond. 1963. We, the Tikopia. A sociological study of kinship in primitive Polynesia. London: Allen and Unwin.

Forchheimer, P. 1953. The category of person in language. Berlin: W. de Gruyter.

Fortune, G. 1955. An analytical grammar of Shona. London: Longmans, Green and Co.

Foster, John F. 1976. Linguistic universals and the tenacity of

thou. Paper presented at the 75th Annual Meeting, American
Anthropological Association, Washington, D.C., 21 Nov. 1976.

Frake, Charles O. 1971. Lexical origins and semantic structure
in Philippine Creole Spanish. Pidginization and Creolization of
languages, ed. by Dell Hymes. Cambridge: University Press,
223-242.

Frazer, Sir James George. 1938-39. Anthologia anthropologica.
4 vols. London: P. Lund Humphries.

Freud, Sigmund. 1953. Totem and taboo and other works.
London: Hogarth Press and the Institute of Psycho-Analysis.

Friedrich, Paul. 1964. Semantic structure and social structure:
An instance fr om Russian. Exploration in cultural anthropology, ed. by Ward H. Goodenough. New York: McGraw Hill.

_____. 1972. Social context and semantic feature: The
Russian pronominal usage. Directions in sociolinguistics. The
ethnography of communication, ed. by John I. Gumperz and
Dell Hymes. New York: Holt, Rinehart and Winston. 270-300.

_____. 1967. Structural implications of Russian pronominal
usage. Sociolinguistics, ed. by William Bright. The Hague:
Mouton, 214-253.

Gage, William W. (ed.). 1974. Language in its social setting.
Washington, D.C.: The Anthropological Society of Washington.

Gardiner, Alan. 1957. Egyptian grammar. London: Oxford
University Press.

Garvin, P.L. and S.H. Riesenberg. 1952. Respect behavior in
Ponape: An ethnolinguistic study. American Anthropologist
54. 201-220.

Gavel, H. 1929. Grammaire basque. Tome I: Phonétique,
parties du discours autres que le verbe. Bayonne: Courrier.

Geoghegan, W.H. 1970. A theory of marking rules. Working
Paper no. 37, Language-Behavior Research Laboratory.
Berkeley: University of California.

_____. 1969. The use of marking rules in semantic systems.

Working Paper no. 26, Language-Behavior Research Laboratory. Berkeley: University of California.

Góral, José Joaquim. 1953. Gramática elementar da língua polonêsa, com diversos exercícios compostos. Curitiba: Tipografia "Lud."

Gorgoniyev, Y.A. 1966. The Khmer language. Moscow: "Nauka" Publishing House.

Grafström, Åke. 1969. On remplaçant nous en francais. Revue de Linguistique Romane 33. 131-132, 270-298.

Greenberg, J.H. 1966. Language universals with special reference to feature hierarchies. The Hague: Mouton.

_____ (ed.). 1963. Universals of language. Cambridge, Mass.: MIT Press.

Gregersen, Edgar A. 1961. Luo: A grammar. Unpublished Ph.D. dissertation. New Haven: Yale University.

_____. 1974. The Signaling of social distance in African languages. Language in its social setting, ed. by Gage. 47-55.

Grimm, J. 1819-37. Deutsches Grammatik. Göttingen.

Hall, Edward T. 1959. The silent language. Garden City, N.Y.: Doubleday.

Hall, Robert A. 1938. An analytical grammar of the Hungarian language. Baltimore, Md.: Linguistic Society of America.

_____. 1948. Descriptive Italian grammar. Ithaca, N.Y.: Cornell University Press and Linguistic Society of America.

Haugen, Einar. 1975. Pronominal address in Icelandic: From you-two to you-all. Language in Society 4. 323-339.

Head, Brian F. 1976. Social factors in the use of pronouns for the addressee in Brazilian Portuguese. Readings in Portuguese linguistics, ed. by J. Schmidt-Radefeldt. Amsterdam: North-Holland. 289-348.

Hoben, Susan J. 1976. The meaning of the second-person pro-

nouns in Amharic. Language in Ethiopia, ed. by Bender et al.,
281-288.

Hopgood, C.R. 1953. A practical introduction to Tonga. London:
Longmans, Green.

Huart, M.Cl. 1899. Grammaire élémentaire de la langue persane,
suivie d'un petit traité de prosodie, de dialogues, de modèles
de lettres et d'un choix de proverbes. Paris: Ernest Leroux.

Huber, Joseph. 1929. Katalanische Grammatik. Laut- und
Formenlehre, Syntax, Woltbildung. Heidelberg: Carl Winter.

Hudson, D.F. 1965. Bengali. Teach yourself books. London:
The English Universities Press.

Ide, Sachiko. 1977. Women and language. Mimeo. University
of Hawaii. 46 pp. (To appear in Contemporary Japanese
Women.)

Ingram, David. 1971. Typology and universals of personal pronouns. Working Papers on Language Universals 5. P1-P35.

Innes, Gordon. 1966. An introduction to Grebo. London: School
of Oriental and African Studies.

Jain, Dhanesh K. 1969. Verbalization of respect in Hindi.
Anthropological Linguistics 11. 3. 79-97.

Jespersen, Otto. 1922. Language. Its nature, development and
origin. London: Allen and Unwin.

_____. 1924. The philosophy of grammar. London: Allen
and Unwin.

Josephs, Lewis S. 1975. Palauan reference grammar. Honolulu:
University Press of Hawaii.

Kachru, Braj B. 1973. An introduction to spoken Kashmiri.
Urbana, Ill.: University of Illinois.

Kahananui, Dorothy M. and Alberta P. Anthony. 1970. Let's
speak Hawaiian. Honolulu: University of Hawaii.

Kany, Charles E. 1951. American-Spanish syntax. Chicago:
University of Chicago Press.

Karunatillake, W.S. and S. Suseendirarajah. 1974. Pronouns of
address in Tamil and Sinhalese--A sociolinguistic study.
International Journal of Dravidian Linguistics 4. 83-96.

Kess, J.F. 1973. Respectful address in Tagalog: A preliminary
study. Cahiers linguistiques d'Ottawa VII. 17-24.

Kiddle, Lawrence. 1953. Some social implications of the voseo.
Modern Language Forum 3-4. 50-54.

Kocher, Margaret. 1967. Second person pronouns in Serbo-
Croatian. Language 43. 725-741.

Koefoed, H.A. 1975. Danish. Teach yourself books. London:
The English Universities Press.

Koolhoven, H. 1961. Dutch. Teach yourself books. London:
Hodder and Stoughton.

Kraft, Charles H. and A.H.M. Kirk-Greene. 1973. Hausa. Teach
yourself books. London: The English Universities Press.

Kridalaksana, Harimurti. 1974. Second participant in Indonesian
address. Language Sciences 31. 17-20.

Kroeber, Alfred L. 1925. Handbook of the Indians of California.
Washington, D.C.: Bureau of American Ethnology.

Lambert, Wallace E. and G. Richard Tucker. 1976. Tu, vous,
usted. A socio-psychological study of address patterns.
Rowley, Mass.: Newbury House.

Le Bidois, Georges and Robert Le Bidois. 1935-38. Syntaxe du
français moderne. 2 vols. New York: G.E. Syechert.

Lee, Kee-Dong. 1975. (With the assistance of Lyndon Cornelius
and Elmer Asher.) Kusaiean reference grammar. Honolulu:
The University Press of Hawaii.

Lehr, Marianne, J.E. Redden and Adama Balima. 1966. Moré
basic course. Washington, D.C.: Foreign Service Institute.

Lewis, G.L. 1967. Teach yourself Turkish. London: The English
Universities Press.

Lewis, M.B. 1954. Teach yourself Malay. London: The English Universities Press.

Lind, Gerald. 1971. A preliminary study of the pronouns of address in Swedish. Stanford Occasional Papers in Linguistics 1. 101-130.

Lindenburg, T.W.H. 1953. Kleine niederländische Sprachlehre für Schul-, Privat- und Selbstunterricht. Heidelberg: Julius Groos Verlag.

Macdonald, Donald. 1907. The oceanic languages, their grammatical structure, vocabulary and origin. London: H. Frowde.

MacDonald, R. Ross and Soenjono Darjowidjojo. 1967. A student's reference grammar of modern formal Indonesian. Washington, D.C.: Georgetown University Press.

Macdonell, Arthur A. 1927. A Sanskrit grammar for students. London: Oxford University Press.

Mace, John. 1964. Teach yourself modern Persian. London: The English Universities Press.

Madan, A.C. 1906. Wisa handbook. A short introduction to the Wisa dialect of North-East Rhodesia. Oxford: Clarendon Press.

Marm, I. and Alf Sommerfelt. 1947. Teach yourself Norwegian. London: The English Universities Press.

Marsack, C.C. 1962. Teach yourself Samoan. London: The English Universities Press.

Martin, Samuel E. and Young-Sook C. Lee with the assistance of Elinor Clark Horne. 1969. Beginning Korean. New Haven and London: Yale University Press.

McClean, R.I. 1963. Teach yourself Swedish. A grammar of the modern language. London: The English Universities Press.

McCormack, William, with the assistance of M.G. Krishnamurthi. 1966. Kannada. A cultural introduction to the spoken styles of the language. Madison: University of Wisconsin Press.

McGovern, William. 1968. Colloquial Japanese. London: Routledge and Kegan Paul.

McNeill, David. 1971. Are there specifically linguistic universals?
Semantics: An interdisciplinary reader in philosophy, linguis-
tics and psychology, ed. by Danny D. Steinberg and Leon A.
Jakobovits. Cambridge: University Press, 530-535.

Meile, Pierre. 1945. Introduction au tamoul. Paris: G. P.
Maisonneuve.

Mercier, Henry. 1957. La politesse arabe au Maroc. Tanger:
Éditions Eurafrique.

Meyer-Lübke, W. 1890-1902. Grammatik der romanischen
Sprachen. Leipzig.

Mirikitani, Leatrice T. 1971. Speaking Kapampangan. Honolulu:
University of Hawaii Press.

Mitchell, T. F. 1975. Covert matters best disclosed. Principles
of Firthian Linguistics, ed. by T. F. Mitchell. London:
Longman, 154-166.

Molina, Fray Alonso de. 1571. Arte de la lengua mexicana y
castellana. Mexico. Facsimile edition: Madrid: Ediciones
Cultura Hispánica, 1945.

Molony, Carol H. 1977. Recent relexification processes in
Philippine Creole Spanish. Sociocultural Dimensions of
Language Change. New York: Academic Press.

Moravcsik, Edith. 1971. Agreement. Working Papers on Language
Universals 5. A1-A69.

Mota, Atico F. Vilas Boas da. 1972. Fórmulas de tratamento nas
línguas românicas: português e romeno. Unpublished Ph. D.
dissertation, University of São Paulo.

Muller, Ch. 1970. Sur les emplois personnels de l'indéfini on.
Revue de Linguistique Romane 34. 133-134, 48-55.

Muller, H. F. 1914. The use of the plural of reverence in the
letters of Pope Gregory I. The Romanic Review 5. 68-89.

Nandris, Grigore. 1953. Colloquial Rumanian. Grammar, exercises, reader vocabulary. London: Routledge and Kegan Paul.

Nguyên Dình Hoà. 1974. Colloquial Vietnamese. Carbondale, Ill.: Southern Illinois University Press.

O'Leary, De Lacy. 1965. Colloquial Arabic. London: Routledge and Kegan Paul.

Paez-Urdaneta, Iraset. 1976. Dialectologia del voseo hispano-americano. Unpublished Master's thesis. Stanford University.

Palakornkul, Angkab. 1975. A socio-linguistic study of pronominal usage in spoken Bangkok Thai. Linguistics 165. 11-41.

Paulston, Christina Bratt. 1975. Language universals and socio-cultural implications in deviant usage: Personal questions in Swedish. Studia Linguistica XXIX. 1-15.

_____. 1976. Pronouns of address in Swedish: Social class semantics and a changing system. Language in Society 5. 359-386.

Peeke, M. Catherine. 1973. Preliminary grammar of Auca. Norman, Okla.: Summer Institute of Linguistics.

Peng, Fred C.C. 1974. Communicative distance. Language Sciences 31. 32-38.

_____ and Iunko Kagiyama. 1973. La Parole of Japanese pronouns. Language Sciences 25. 36-39.

Pop, Sever. 1948. Grammaire roumaine. Berne: Franke.

Price, Thomas. 1966. The elements of Nyanja for English-speaking students. Blantyre: Church of Central Africa Presbyterian.

Roberts, H. 1891. A grammar of the Khassi language. London: Kegan Paul, Trench, Trübner.

Robinson, Joy L. 1977. Verbal deference in Catalan: A sociolinguistic investigation of the pronouns of address. Unpublished Ph.D. dissertation. Stanford: Stanford University.

Rowlands, E.C. 1969. Teach yourself Yoruba. London: The
    English Universities Press.

Samarin, William I. 1967. A grammar of Sango. The Hague:
    Mouton.

_____. 1966. The Gbeya language. Grammar, texts, and
    vocabularies. Berkeley and Los Angeles: University of
    California Press.

Sandfeld, Kr. 1965. Syntaxe du français contemporain. I: Les
    pronoms. Paris: Honoré Champion.

Sansom, George. 1946. An historical grammar of Japanese.
    Oxford: Clarendon Press.

Santandrea, Stefano. 1946. Grammatichetta Giur. Roma:
    Italica Gens.

Sapir, Edward and Harry Hoijer. 1960. American aboriginal
    languages. Encyclopaedia Britannica. Chicago, London and
    Toronto: William Benton, vol. 1, pp. 750-753.

Scovel, Thomas. 1973. pronominal substitutes in Thai. Paper
    read at the summer meeting, Linguistic Society of America,
    Ann Arbor, Michigan.

Shewan, A. 1913. The PLVRALIS MAIESTATIS in Homer.
    Classical Quarterly 7. 129-131.

Shores, David and Carol P. Hines (eds.). 1977. Papers in lan-
    guage variation. SAMLA-ADS Collections. University: Uni-
    versity of Alabama Press.

Silverberg, William. 1940. On the psychological significance of
    Du and Sie. Psychoanalytic Quarterly IX. 509-525.

Slobin, Dan I. 1963. Some aspects of the use of pronouns of
    address in Yiddish. Word 19. 193-202.

Smith, Edwin W. 1907. A handbook of the Ila language (commonly
    called the Seshukulumbwe) spoken in north-western Rhodesia
    South-Central Africa. London: Oxford University Press.

Snow, C.E. and Charles A. Ferguson. 1977. Talking to children.
    Cambridge: Cambridge University Press.

Southworth, Franklin C. 1974. Linguistic marks for power: Some relationships between semantic and social change. Anthropological Linguistics 16. 5. 177-191.

Speight, Kathleen. 1975. Italian. Teach yourself books. London: The English Universities Press.

Spencer, Harold. 1950. A Kanarese grammar. With graduated exercises. Mysore City: The Wesley Press.

Stanner, W.E.H. 1937. Aboriginal modes of address and reference in the North-West of the Northern Territory. Oceania VII. 300-315.

Ştefănescu-Drăgăneşti, V. and Martin Murrell. 1974. Romanian. Teach yourself books. London: The English Universities Press.

Stevens, Alan M. 1965. Language levels in Madurese. Language 41. 294-302.

Stevick. Earl W. 1965. Shona basic course. Washington, D.C.: Foreign Service Institute.

_____ and L. Hollander. 1965. Chinyanja basic course. Washington, D.C.: Foreign Service Institute.

Suseendirarajah, S. 1973. Pronouns in Battiwala Tamil. Anthropological Linguistics 15. 4. 172-182.

Swanton, John R. 1911. Haida. Handbook of American Indian languages, ed. by Franz Boas. Part 1, 205-282.

Swift, L.B. and E.W.A. Zola. 1963. Kituba basic course. Washington, D.C.: Foreign Service Institute.

Tanner, Nancy. 1967. Speech and society among the Indonesian elite, a case study in a multilingual community. Anthropological Linguistics 9. 3. 15-40.

Thompson, Laurence C. 1965. A Vietnamese grammar. Seattle: University of Washington Press.

Tisdall, William St. Clair. 1961. A simplified grammar of the Gujarati language, together with a short reading book and vocabulary. New York: Frederik Ungar.

Tripathi, K.B. 1957. Western Oriya dialect. Indian Linguistics. Bagchi memorial volume, ed. by Sukumar Sen, 76-85.

Tryon, D.T. 1967. Nengone grammar. Linguistic Circle of Canberra Publications, Series B - Monographs, no. 6. Canberra: The Australian National University.

_____. 1968. Dehu grammar. Canberra: The Australian National University.

Ullrich, Helen E. 1976. The Kannada verb: Sociolinguistic implications. International Journal of Dravidian Linguistics 5. 327-337.

Van Wagoner, Merrill Y. 1949. Spoken Iraqi Arabic. New York: Henry Holt.

Wallace, Stephen. 1976. Pronouns in contact: Aspects of pronominal change in Southeast Asia. Mimeo. Cornell University. 35 pp. ("Prepared for a Festschrift to honor Charles F. Hockett on his 60th birthday.")

Westermann, Diedrich. 1960. A study of the Ewe language. Translated by A.L. Bickford-Smith. London: Oxford University Press.

Whitney, Arthur H. 1968. Teach yourself Finnish. London: The English Universities Press.

Williams, W.L. and H.W. Williams. 1965. First lessons in Maori. Revised by W.W. Bird. London: Whitcombe and Tombs.

Wills, Dorothy D. 1977. Participant deixis in English and baby talk. Talking to children, ed. by Snow and Ferguson. 271-295.

Wittermans, Elizabeth P. 1967. Indonesian terms of address. Social Forces 46. 48-51.

Yates, Alan. 1975. Catalan. Teach yourself books. London: Hodder and Stoughton.

Yegorova, R.P. 1971. The Sindhi Language. Moscow: "Nauka" Publishing House.

Young, Robert W. and William Morgan. 1964. The Navaho language. Salt Lake City: Deseret Book Co.

Zamarripa y Uraga, Pablo. 1928. Gramatica Vasca. Bermeo:
Gaubeka.

Zamora Vicente, Alonso. 1960. Dialectología Espanõla. Madrid:
Gredos.

Typology and Universals
of Personal Pronouns

DAVID INGRAM

ABSTRACT

Personal pronouns are examined from three different directions
to observe typological and universal characteristics. First, they
are analyzed in terms of the persons that may appear in the lexicon
of a language. The resulting systems are referred to as person
systems. They are then subdivided into number systems and person feature systems. Secondly, the rules that are needed to generate the underlying deictic features of personal pronouns are
presented along with typologic findings about them. Last, the case
systems of personal pronouns are analyzed and feature assignment
rules are suggested to account for the resulting typology.

Reprinted from Working Papers on Language Universals 5,
May 1971, pp. P1-P35. This paper is a revised version of Chapter
4 of my doctoral dissertation The Role of Person Deixis in Underlying Semantics (Stanford University, 1970).

CONTENTS

1. Introduction

This study presents three distinct ways to look at personal (or henceforth person)[1] pronoun systems. The first of these examines the lexical marking of their deictic features. That is, what are the roles or combination of roles in the speech act that each language considers to be of sufficient importance to mark by a separate lexical form? For example, ENGLISH has a five-way system.[2]

1. I we
 you
 he[3] they

I shall refer to such systems as person systems. The four most frequent person systems are outlined along with the theoretical implications. As will be seen, the ENGLISH system is highly atypical. Universals are discussed.

The second aspect to be considered concerns the rules for generating the deictic features of person pronouns. I shall discuss the rules in 2., and suggest that they are needed for a general account of the deictic characteristics of person pronouns.

2. i. Rule Schema
  ii. Deictic Incorporation
  iii. Deictic Categorization
  iv. Coordinate Collapsing

Types of languages will be distinguished in terms of their rule systems. Language specific rules are distinguished from language universal rules in an attempt to formulate that set of rules needed to capture the person pronouns of any language.

---

[1]The term 'personal' will be replaced in this discussion by 'person,' a more accurate term for the phenomenon.

[2]That is, there are five roles or combinations of roles of the speech situation that can be expressed lexically. The nature and formalism of person deixis will be more completely explained in Sec. 2.1.

[3]Gender and case do not come into consideration when person deixis is observed in isolation. He is just a marker for a reference to a single person who is neither speaker nor hearer.

The third systematic aspect of person pronouns treated is the often talked about one of pronoun distribution, or case.[4] Given that certain deictic features of person are mapped to surface structure by specific rules such as those in 2., there are additional constraints on the surface distribution. I shall refer to those pronoun cases as sets of pronouns, and discuss set systems. Set systems have been studied in terms of ergative systems, accusative systems, active systems, etc. No one, however, has looked at the rules that operate on person deixis which are required to generate any of these sets. Therefore, besides the typology of such systems, there are some suggestions on how they may be accounted for in generative grammar.

This tripart analysis attempts to give an overview of person pronouns, and particularly their deictic features, along with some suggestions on the theoretical apparatus behind them. The typologies presented are tentative, and not given as the last word on the subject. They are based on samples from approximately 60 languages and more data will need to be considered before stronger statements can be made.

2. Person Systems [5]

I use the following method to mark person systems. The ENGLISH subject pronouns are used with added markers when needed. The base system is given in 3.

3. I   we
   thou   you
   he   they

Since I am considering here only person roles, I ignore features such as gender and case. To mark any number systems such as 'dual' or 'trial,' a number will be placed after the appropriate

---

[4]I will discuss case, though not gender, because case effects entire sets of pronouns, as distinct from gender which only affects individual forms, and only in some languages.

[5]While I will refer to these as person systems, they are more specifically deictic person systems. There are other person systems which I do not examine. These would be syntactic person systems which look at the agreement constraints between nouns and verbs.

plural form. An example of a dual pronoun is you-2.[6]   The
distinction of exclusive-inclusive will be shown by following the we
pronoun with the abbreviations 'excl.' or 'incl.'   The one major
study that has been done so far along these lines is The category
of person in language by Forchheimer (1953).   In that study he gives
the types of pronoun systems based on person.   His typology, however, is based on morphological considerations.   His types are:

4. a. Languages with morphological plural of pronouns (i.e.
        those that form plural pronouns by attaching a plural
        affix to the singular pronouns).

    b. Languages without morphological but with lexical plural,
        at least in the first person (i.e. a separate lexical entry
        such as we in ENGLISH).

    c. Languages with lexical and morphological plural in the
        first person.

    d. Languages with morphological or lexical and composite
        plural (the latter consisting of compounding two singular
        pronouns, e.g. 'I + he' to mean 'we').

    e. Languages with two composite forms for inclusive and
        exclusive plural of first person.

    f. Languages with variants of one form used to express in-
        clusive and exclusive plural of first person.

    g. Languages with variants of second person plural for inclu-
        sive first person plural.

    h. Languages with complete sets of pronouns plus composite
        forms.

    i. Languages with less than three distinct plural forms.

The systems I will explain are based on Forchheimer's data.   My
approach, however, differs from his in two important ways.   First,

---

[6]It is important to note that this notation does not imply that this
is the morphological representation of these features.   Morphological aspects of personal pronouns are beyond the present goals and
may be seen in Forchheimer (1953).

I did not concern myself with morphological marking. Whether the person we-inclusive, for example, is marked by one lexical entry or by an 'I' form plus a morphological affix was not considered. The thing that was important was that the language used some distinct way to mark that particular person. Since his typology was based on such morphological considerations, such a change results in a more straightforward system of person. His typology is not really one of person, but of person marking in terms of the distribution between separate lexical entries and affixation processes.

Instead, I have used the common approach of counting the surface forms of the person pronouns and using that number to designate the system. Such a method is commonly used to describe vowel systems, like a three-vowel system vs. a four-vowel system etc. (e.g. Sedlak 1969). ENGLISH is then a five-person system, (but note footnote 5). The second difference from Forchheimer's study is that I attempt to consider the frequency of certain systems. That is, instead of just showing which systems exist, I also want to distinguish common systems from uncommon ones. These statements are typical of many of Greenberg's statements on universals (e.g. Greenberg 1963).

The data from Forchheimer revealed 21 different deictic person systems from 71 languages.[7] The amount of variety can be accounted for by the fact that Forchheimer was presenting a study of person and included all the unique types he found. The systems, their subtypes and the frequency of occurrence of each is shown in Table 1. The sub-types state that while the number of deictic forms was the same, the systems contained different deictic units. For each language the set of pronouns (e.g. nominative vs. accusative when such distinctions existed) that contained the most person pronouns was considered.

Table 1.   The person systems of 71 languages from data
           presented by Forchheimer (1953)

Systems	No. of languages
1. Four-person system	2
2. Five-person system (A)	1
3. " " " (B)	1
4. Six-person system (A)	19
5. " " " (B)	2
6. " " " (C)	1

---

[7]See comments introducing the Appendix.

(Table 1 cont.)

Systems	No. of languages
7. Seven-person system (A)	1
8. " " " (B)	10
9. Eight-person system (A)	2
10. " " " (B)	1
11. " " " (C)	2
12. Nine-person system (A)	5
13. " " " (B)	1
14. " " " (C)	1
15. Ten -person system (A)	1
16. " " " (B)	1
17. Eleven-person system (A)	15
18. " " " (B)	1
19. " " " (C)	1
20. Twelve-person system	1
21. Fifteen-person system	2

                                      Total   71

The representations of all of these along with the individual languages
are given in the Appendix.

Setting a criterion of at least three languages for each system
reveals four systems that are more frequent than the others. These
are:

5. a. six-person system (A)   19
   b. eleven-person system (A) 15
   c. seven-person system (B) 10
   d. nine-person system (A)   5

These four systems account for 71% of the sample. I shall look at
these four individually.

The six-person system (A) is by far the most common system
in languages, as looking also at other language data revealed. This
is the system in 6.

6. six-person system (A)
   I   we
   thou you
   he   they

It is the system of such diverse languages as CHINESE, SUMERIAN,
SHILH, FINNISH, HAUSA, HOPI, LATIN, etc.

The other three systems reveal two features applied with complete generalization to this base system. These two features are
dual and exclusive-inclusive.   System 5.b has both, 5.c the latter,
and 5.d the former.   The second most frequent system in the sample,
the eleven-person system (A), is shown in 7.

7. eleven-person system (A)
    I   we-2-incl.   we-incl.
            we-2-excl.   we-excl.
    thou   you -2   you
    he   they-2   they

We see the features dual and inclusion-exclusion applying across
all forms.   This system is characteristic of POLYNESIAN languages
(e.g. HAWAIIAN) and several AMERINDIAN languages (e.g. SHO-
SHONE, CHINOOK, IROQUOIAN).   It is also recorded for some
AUSTRALIAN languages (e.g. DYIRRINGAN, KAMILAROI).

The third system in 5. is the seven-person system (B).   This
system differs from the six-person system (A) by the addition of an
inclusion-exclusion distinction.

8. seven-person system (B)
    I   we-incl.
            we-excl.
    thou   you
    he   they

This system is represented by diverse languages such as FUL
(NIGER-CONGO), TAMIL (DRAVIDIAN), ALGONQUIAN (AMERIN-
DIAN), and SOMALI (CUSHITIC).

The last system is the nine-person system (A), which deviates
from the base system of 6. by the feature dual.

9. nine-person system (A)
    I   we-2   we
    thou   you-2   you
    he   they-2   they

The frequency of this system was lower than the other three and
three of its representative languages were of the FINNO-UGRIC
group.   It is in this regard perhaps not on the same level as the
other three in terms of occurrence.

As can be seen, the ENGLISH system presents an atypical picture of the way languages tend to mark person deixis. In comparison
to the most common system shown in 6., one might predict ENGLISH
to re-acquire a form for the second person plural. This is particularly interesting in the light of dialects of ENGLISH where forms
such as you all and you-s are common, depending on the area.
Historical observations could reveal some interesting facts about
the direction of deictic person systems, but they are beyond the
goals of this study.

2.1 Sub-systems

2.1.1 Number systems   Each language's deictic person system
can be characterized by its number system. This marking can be
captured by the following formalism. A deictic person number system consists of a left to right linear sequence of integers showing
the specific references for the system. Take the system in 6. Its
number system is shown in 10. The device '>' is an arbitrary symbol to mean 'greater than.'

10. 1,   1 >

10. states that the person pronouns subdivide into two groups in terms
of number, those that mark one referent, and those that mark more
than one. I will call this the 'more-than-one' system. Notice that 8.
is also a more-than-one system.

Both 7. and 9. include the number 'dual.' Their number system
is given in 11.

11. 1, 2, 2 >

This will be called the 'more-than-two' system. An examination of
the other data revealed one other number system, that one which
includes trial number. This will be referred to as the 'more-than-
three' system. These three systems are shown in 12.

12. a. more-than-one system: 1, 1 >
    b. more-than-two system: 1, 2, 2 >
    c. more-than-three system: 1, 2, 3, 3 >

We can now use the deictic person systems and the number systems to formulate one way to characterize the person deixis of any
language. A person pronoun system can be shown as its number

system with the number of person forms of each number set.   Take,
for example, the system in 6.   This system can be represented as
13.

13.   1, 1>
         3   3

This states that the number system is more-than-one, and that
three person forms represent one referent per form, and three
represent more than one.   The system in 6. can be shown as different from the system in 10. in this way; 8 will be 14.

14.   1, 1>
         3   4

The more-than-two systems are 7. and 9.   They are shown as
15.a and b respectively.

15.a.   1, 2, 2>   b. 1, 2, 2>
        3   4   4   3   3   3

There is one additional factor that needs to be added before this
approach can be used to characterize any language's person pronoun
system.   These are languages that have forms that are unmarked as
to number, such as the ENGLISH you.   The ENGLISH system would
be characterized as a sub-type of the more-than-one system, with
the following system.

16.   1, 1>, u
         2   2   1

The 'u' represents unmarked forms as to number.   The total set of
number systems found in the sample are then:

17.a.   1, 1>
   b.   1, 1>, u
   c.   1, 2,   2>
   d.   1, 2,   2>, u
   e.   1, 2,   3,   3>

2.1.2 Person feature systems The analysis of person can also
be reduced to discuss the individual person features that make it up.
Elsewhere (Ingram 1970) I have suggested a formalism for capturing
the deictic features of person pronouns.   There I propose that in
addition to syntactic and semantic features, linguistic theory needs

a third formal feature, specifically the deictic feature. It is set off from the other two features by a different formal device, this being the use of curly brackets.

I offer three features of person deixis which are given in 18.

18. a. Speaker   b. Hearer   c. Other

They capture the fact that the speech act has three basic roles, the speaker, the hearer, and the one talked about.

These three features formally comprise the person deictic unit. This is shown in 19.

19.
$$\left\{ \begin{array}{l} \pm \text{ sp} \\ \pm \text{ hr} \\ \pm \text{ X} \end{array} \right\}$$

Here X refers to Other. The plus or minus choice with each allows for person pronouns that represent combinations of roles. So, for example, we-exclusive is $\{+\text{sp}, -\text{hr}, +\text{X}\}$. The pronoun 'I' does not consist of a combination, so it would be $\{+\text{sp}, -\text{hr}, -\text{X}\}$.

Since there may be more than one Hearer or Other, the unit has the convention that there are as many pluses as there are roles. 'They,' for example, would consist of more than one plus. They-3 would be as in 20.

20.
$$\left\{ \begin{array}{l} - \text{ sp} \\ - \text{ hr} \\ + \text{ X} \\ + \text{ X} \\ + \text{ X} \end{array} \right\}$$

Since this device becomes awkward when higher numbers are introduced, the convention is that each feature is F^n where n = number of pluses. 20. would now be as 21.

21.
$$\left\{ \begin{array}{l} - \text{ sp} \\ - \text{ hr} \\ + \text{ X}^3 \end{array} \right\}$$

A last characterization of the person deictic unit concerns roles where it is known that there are more than one, but the number is not known. When this is indefinite number, such as people in

The people stormed the castle, I suggest X^n where n is plural but unknown. When there is reference to the entire class membership of an object, such as <u>dogs</u> in <u>Dogs are animals</u>, this will be $X^{\bar{n}}$. This means that all the members of n are referred to, although that exact number is unknown.

With this brief outline of the features of person deixis, we can now characterize the features of the above systems. Let's take the system in 6. as an example. Using fully specified deictic person distinctions, this system would be as in 22.

22. a. $\left\{\begin{array}{l} + sp \\ - hr \\ - X \end{array}\right\}$ b. $\left\{\begin{array}{l} - sp \\ + hr \\ - X \end{array}\right\}$ c. $\left\{\begin{array}{l} - sp \\ - hr \\ + X^1 \end{array}\right\}$

      I   thou   he

    d. $\left\{\begin{array}{l} + sp \\ +\left[\begin{array}{l}\pm hr\\ \pm X^n\end{array}\right] \end{array}\right\}$ e. $\left\{\begin{array}{l} - sp \\ + hr \\ + X^n \end{array}\right\}$ f. $\left\{\begin{array}{l} - sp \\ - hr \\ + X^{1>} \end{array}\right\}$

      we   you   they

With the information on typology, however, we can capture general-izations about deictic person systems and refine 22.

First, we know that there are universal systems of number. We can then assume that any language's pronouns will fall under one of these three systems. This will be a 'universal constraint.' With each language, we then state its own system. By convention, this will divide its person pronouns into the appropriate number of num-ber distinctions. For system 6. this convention states that a lan-guage with 1, 1> will have two sets of pronouns for number.

To mark this, each deictic of the lexicon will have the form:

23. $\{D\}^n$ where D = deictic unit, n = number

The choice of n in 23. for the more-than-one system, for example, will be 1, or 1>. We can now do away with the X feature in the lexicon. The n convention will state that the number of pluses in the deictic unit must fall within the range of n, and if the X is needed, it will be introduced by a 'redundancy rule.' The entries for 22.a to c are now:

24. a. $\left\{\begin{array}{l} + sp \\ \propto hr \end{array}\right\}^1$ b. $\left\{\begin{array}{l} - sp \\ + hr \end{array}\right\}^{1>}$ c. $\left\{\begin{array}{l} - sp \\ - hr \end{array}\right\}^{1>}$

     we   you   they

The plural forms will be represented in a similar manner. There is the convention that any feature <u>not</u> in the deictic representation can be marked if the number system calls for it. Thus, in 24.c, X will be plus since the number system calls for a plus, and there is none specified. This general convention captures the marking of 'we' in those languages that do not have the inclusive-exclusive distinction marked lexically. The plural forms of 6. as shown in 22.d to 22.f are now shown as 25.

25. a. $\left\{\begin{matrix}+ \text{sp}\\ \alpha\,\text{hr}\end{matrix}\right\}^{1>}$ b. $\left\{\begin{matrix}- \text{sp}\\ + \text{hr}\end{matrix}\right\}^{1>}$ c. $\left\{\begin{matrix}- \text{sp}\\ - \text{hr}\end{matrix}\right\}^{1>}$

     we   you   they

We now have, by collapsing 24. and 25., three feature units. Using these we can now complete the characterization of this pronoun system as shown in 13. There we had:

26. (=13.)   1, 1>
           3 3

Now we include the feature units.

27.   1, 1>   with the features $\left\{\begin{matrix}+ \text{sp}\\ \alpha\,\text{hr}\end{matrix}\right\}^{n}$ $\left\{\begin{matrix}- \text{sp}\\ + \text{hr}\end{matrix}\right\}^{n}$ $\left\{\begin{matrix}- \text{sp}\\ - \text{hr}\end{matrix}\right\}^{n}$
     3 3

Filling in the number systems for n will result in the conventions noted above and the final system as shown in 6.

Let us now look at 7. That system has been re-defined as 15.a., which is:

28. (=15.a)   1, 2, 2 >
            3 4 4

Using the conventions of lexical representation, the pronouns will be given as in 29.

29. a. $\left\{\begin{matrix}+ \text{sp}\\ - \text{hr}\end{matrix}\right\}^{1}$ b. $\left\{\begin{matrix}- \text{sp}\\ + \text{hr}\end{matrix}\right\}^{1}$ c. $\left\{\begin{matrix}- \text{sp}\\ - \text{hr}\end{matrix}\right\}^{1}$

     I   thou   he

d. $\left\{\begin{matrix}+ \text{sp}\\ + \text{hr}\end{matrix}\right\}^{2}$ e. $\left\{\begin{matrix}+ \text{sp}\\ - \text{hr}\end{matrix}\right\}^{2}$ f. $\left\{\begin{matrix}- \text{sp}\\ + \text{hr}\end{matrix}\right\}^{2}$ g. $\left\{\begin{matrix}- \text{sp}\\ - \text{hr}\end{matrix}\right\}^{2}$

   we-2-incl.   we-2-excl.   you-2   they-2

h. $\left\{\begin{matrix}+ \text{sp}\\ + \text{hr}\end{matrix}\right\}^{2>}$ i. $\left\{\begin{matrix}+ \text{sp}\\ - \text{hr}\end{matrix}\right\}^{2>}$ j. $\left\{\begin{matrix}- \text{sp}\\ + \text{hr}\end{matrix}\right\}^{2>}$ k. $\left\{\begin{matrix}- \text{sp}\\ - \text{hr}\end{matrix}\right\}^{2>}$

   we-incl.   we-excl.   you   they

We have four feature units. Combining these with 28., we get the characterization of the deictic person system in 7.

30. $\begin{matrix} 1, & 2, & 2 > \\ 3 & 4 & 4 \end{matrix}$ with the features $\begin{Bmatrix} +sp \\ -hr \end{Bmatrix}^2 \begin{Bmatrix} -sp \\ +hr \end{Bmatrix}^n \begin{Bmatrix} -sp \\ -hr \end{Bmatrix}^n \begin{Bmatrix} +sp \\ +hr \end{Bmatrix}^n$

The third system I discussed, the seven-person system (B) of 8. will be 31.

31. $\begin{matrix} 1, & 1 > \\ 3 & 4 \end{matrix}$ with the features $\begin{Bmatrix} +sp \\ -hr \end{Bmatrix}^n \begin{Bmatrix} -sp \\ +hr \end{Bmatrix}^n \begin{Bmatrix} -sp \\ -hr \end{Bmatrix}^n \begin{Bmatrix} +sp \\ +hr \end{Bmatrix}^n$

Compare it with 27. and 30. It differs from 27. by having different features., In regard to 30. they have the same features but differ in number system.

The fourth system, 9., has the units of 27. but the number system of 30.

32. $\begin{matrix} 1, & 2, & 2 > \\ 3 & 3 & 3 \end{matrix}$ with the features $\begin{Bmatrix} +sp \\ \alpha hr \end{Bmatrix}^n \begin{Bmatrix} -sp \\ +hr \end{Bmatrix}^n \begin{Bmatrix} -sp \\ -hr \end{Bmatrix}^n$

Comparing these four most frequent systems reveals a striking generalization about the way people use and mark person deixis by person pronouns. What we have are two number systems and two acts of deictic features that can characterize well over the majority of person deixis systems in languages. These are:

33. a. <u>number systems</u>

    i. more-than-one system: 1, 1 >
    ii. more-than-two system: 1, 2, 2 >

   b. <u>features</u>

    i. three-unit-system: $\begin{Bmatrix} +sp \\ \alpha hr \end{Bmatrix}^n \begin{Bmatrix} -sp \\ +hr \end{Bmatrix}^n \begin{Bmatrix} -sp \\ -hr \end{Bmatrix}^n$

    ii. four-unit-system: $\begin{Bmatrix} +sp \\ -hr \end{Bmatrix}^n \begin{Bmatrix} -sp \\ +hr \end{Bmatrix}^n \begin{Bmatrix} -sp \\ -hr \end{Bmatrix}^n \begin{Bmatrix} +sp \\ +hr \end{Bmatrix}^n$

These seven sets of features and the five number systems in 17. can be used to characterize the pronouns of any language. For atypical systems, the only change necessary is to specify the n for the features of that language. Take, for example, ENGLISH. I have shown ENGLISH as 16.

34. (=16.) 1, 1>, u
           2, 2   1

The final characterization of the system is as in 35.

35. 1, 1>, u   with the features $\left\{\begin{matrix}+\mathrm{sp}\\ \propto\mathrm{hr}\end{matrix}\right\}^{n}$ $\left\{\begin{matrix}-\mathrm{sp}\\ +\mathrm{hr}\end{matrix}\right\}^{u}$ $\left\{\begin{matrix}-\mathrm{sp}\\ -\mathrm{hr}\end{matrix}\right\}^{n}$
     2   2   1

The 'u' on the second feature means that that feature only occurs as unmarked, i.e. it does not take a number. This typology can characterize the systems in the Appendix.

2.2 Universals

Greenberg (1963) presents Universal 42 in regard to the number and person systems of person pronouns. "Universal 42. All languages have pronominal categories involving at least three persons and two numbers" (p.96). The above discussion has corroborated this universal with more specific findings. We can now expand this universal to include the above results.

Concerning the person system analysis, we can make the tentative statement that every language designates at least four persons -- 'I,' 'thou,' 'he,' and 'we.' The upper range was found at 15 (see Appendix).

In regard to number systems, we found that there were three possible number systems. Comparing them, we can see that every language has at least two number sets, 'I,' and 'greater than I.'

The feature analysis in 33. showed that there are two possible feature sets. The one contains three features, and the other four. The latter is distinct from the former in containing the feature of exclusion vs. inclusion. These are summarized in 36.

36. a.   Person systems

          Universal 1: there are at least four persons in every language:

          I   we
          thou
          he

36. b. number systems
        Universal 2: there are three number systems:
        i.   more-than-one   1, 1 >
        ii. more-than-two   1, 2, 2 >
        iii. more-than-three 1, 2, 3, 3 >

    c. feature systems
        Universal 4: there are two feature systems:
        i.   three-unit system
        ii. four-unit system

3. Rule Systems

3.1 Deictic rules

    In this section I shall look at four rules for deriving person pro-
nouns from underlying deictic features. These four rules are:

37. a. Rule schema   c. Deictic categorization
    b. Deictic incorporation   d. Coordinate collapsing

    First, I will briefly discuss how these four rules operate. The
grammatical model of underlying semantics[8] provides the domain
for these rules and consists of a semantic component and a syntactic
component which are closely related. Their relation is similar to
the one now being discussed between syntax and phonology. In this
case the output of the semantic component is the input to the syntactic one. This is shown in 38.

    38. semantics → syntax → phonology

The first two rules in 37. apply in the semantic component, the latter
two in the syntactic component. It is important, however, to mention and emphasize that this model does not have to be accepted for
the rules in 37. to apply. All these rules require is a model where
there is an abstract level where semantic and deictic information
is contained, and a point where categorization takes place. Current
popular models that may satisfy these conditions include Fillmore's
(1968) case grammar and McCawley's generative semantics (1968).

_____

[8]For more detail of underlying semantics and a general review
of current semantic theories (e.g. generative semantics), see Chapter 2, "On the role of semantics," in Ingram 1970.

In the first specification of deixis in the semantic (or abstract level) component, there are some implicit universals. The assignment of person deictic units is universal for those semantic categories that are OBJECT. I will assume for the moment the over-simplified generalization that there are two primitive categories, OBJECTS and PREDICATES. Also, person deictic specification is universal.

39. Person deictic specification
Every OBJECT is by convention specified as to its role in the speech act, i.e. speaker, hearer, other.

This principle automatically marks the pluses and minuses of the deictic unit. Consequently, the assignment of roles in generating sentences is not arbitrary, but based on the notion of a discourse involving speakers, hearers and others. It is at this point that the four rules above begin to apply.

Rule schema operates after the principle of reference. The latter determines referential indices.

40. Principle of reference
Every '+' of a deictic unit is matched by a referential index.

This places an index with an integer which refers to an object in the real or imaginary world so that reflexivization and other rules for co-reference will be possible.

As a consequence of person deictic specification, there may be more than one role in the deictic unit. If there is more than one role, rule schema applies.

41. Rule schema
Category C (either NP or OBJECT depending on the model of grammar) will be rewritten into as many categories as there are referential indices. Each new category will contain a deictic unit with one of the pluses of the original category, and one referential index.

Rule schema is needed in any language that marks more than one role at a time in the speech act. A language that would not require rule schema, for example, would be one where only one role can be specified. That is, one could only refer to the speaker or the hearer, or one other person who is neither speaker nor hearer. I know of no such language, and finding one outside of the world of fiction appears unlikely. Our first rule then, rule schema, is universal. This is required by the evidence Greenberg (1963) has mentioned that every pronoun system has a plural number.

I would like to exemplify how this process occurs. First, there is the generation of a category C (which in this discussion is OBJECT) with its person deictic unit. Person deictic specification operates to mark the speech roles. Below, 39. is thus exemplified, marking the unit for we-inclusive.

42. $\qquad$ C $\qquad$ Person deictic specification $\qquad$ C

$$\begin{Bmatrix} \pm\,sp \\ \pm\,hr \\ \pm\,X \end{Bmatrix} \qquad\qquad \longrightarrow \qquad\qquad \begin{Bmatrix} +\,sp \\ +\,hr \\ -\,X \end{Bmatrix}$$

The <u>principle of reference</u> assigns referential indices. In this case there are two, shown as x and y.

43. $\qquad$ C: x, y $\qquad$ <u>Principle of reference</u>

$$\begin{Bmatrix} +\,sp \\ +\,hr \\ -\,X \end{Bmatrix}$$

Rule schema applies, and generates as many categories as there are referential indices.

44. $\qquad$ C: x, y $\qquad$ <u>Rule schema</u>

$$\begin{Bmatrix} +\,sp \\ +\,hr \\ -\,X \end{Bmatrix}$$

a.　$C \rightarrow C^n$　　　where n = number of

b.　$C^n \rightarrow C_1 \dots C_n$　　referential indices

C: x
$$\begin{Bmatrix} +\,sp \\ -\,hr \\ -\,X \end{Bmatrix}$$

C: y
$$\begin{Bmatrix} -\,sp \\ +\,hr \\ -\,X \end{Bmatrix}$$

The next rule is <u>deictic incorporation</u>. We might first suggest that it is a universal rule that maps the person deictic unit of a category under that category. On the surface, however, such a rule does not appear to adequately account for languages that have person markers (e.g. NAVAHO).[9] 45. gives ENGLISH paraphrases for these two types.

---

[9]Commonly these are affixes that are obligatory constituents of the verb.

45. a. John went home.   Language A (without person markers)
    b. John he-went home.   Language B (with person markers)

It might be suggested that <u>deictic incorporation</u> be a language spe-cific rule, and that language A undergoes it whereas language B does not. Since it would not occur in the latter, the deictic unit would undergo syntactic categorization. A deeper look into lan-guage B type languages, however, reveals that this analysis is inadequate and needs to be rejected.

First of all, it was based on the assumption that person pronouns and person markers fulfill the same syntactic role. This, however, is false. Though both contain deictic features, they do not contain the same syntactic features. Specifically, the latter are not affected by <u>first mention</u>.

Let us take 45. as the initial sentences of a discourse for these two language types. The first features specified in the syntax is [±first mention], i.e. whether or not an item has been mentioned yet in the discourse. 'John' in both sentences will be thus marked [+first mention]. Now, let us look at what a subsequent set of sen-tences might be.

46. a. he wanted to   Language A
    b. he-wanted to   Language B

The language A, a segment that is [-first mention] can become a pro-noun. This has occurred in 46.a. The 'John' segment therefore must have had an underlying deictic unit. The underlying structures of that segment in 45.a and 46.a are shown in 47.a and b, respectively.

47. a. AGENT   b. AGENT

$$\begin{pmatrix} \begin{bmatrix} \begin{Bmatrix} -sp \\ -hr \end{Bmatrix}^1 \\ +X^1 \end{bmatrix} \\ [+FM] \end{pmatrix}$$
   'John'

$$\begin{pmatrix} \begin{bmatrix} \begin{Bmatrix} -sp \\ -hr \end{Bmatrix}^1 \\ +X^1 \end{bmatrix} \\ [-FM] \end{pmatrix}$$
where FM = first mention
   'he'

This occurs regardless of whether or not the person pronoun is obligatory. In ENGLISH it is obligatory. In ITALIAN, however, it is optional. We can now define the nature of a person pronoun.

48. <u>Person pronoun</u>
    A person pronoun is a syntactic segment with the feature
    [- first mention] that substitutes for a semantic category
    or categories and represents that category's deictic unit.

This rough definition approximates the traditional definition of person pronouns as noun substitutes.[10] In this case, however, it does
not represent a noun, but an entire semantic category.   Thus,
AGENT in our example may not just be John or boy, but also the
tall boy, the boy who ran to school, etc.   This captures the fact
that pronoun replaces entire NPs, not just nouns.   Other arguments
against the traditional definition have been based on the grounds
that forms such as I and you are not noun substitutes.   They are,
however, in the theory of first mention when Ross' (1970) performa-
tive analysis is considered.   These are segments that are always
[- first mention], and therefore always are substituted.   So all person pronouns can be the result of anaphoric processes.

Person markers differ from person pronouns in that they are not
affected by first mention.   The person marker occurs in 45.b, even
though it is the first mention in the discourse.   Person markers are
primarily person deictic markers.

49.   Person marker [11]
      A person marker is a syntactic segment in most cases un-
      affected by first mention that overtly marks the person
      deictic features of a semantic category.

These two can be further distinguished by their derivation.   The
person deictic features of a person pronoun result from deictic
incorporation.   That is, a person pronoun is isomorphic with the
segment for which it substitutes, or conversely, it does not result
from a segmentalization process.   Person markers, however, do
not result from deictic incorporation for they are not isomorphic
with the segment they represent.   Another rule is needed for these,
which I will tentatively call deictic copying.

We can now observe the nature of these two rules by looking at
language B.   On the surface 46.a and b look similar.   This, however,

---

[10]However, they are not substitutes in any true sense.   Pronouns
consist of features that were already present in the noun phrase.
The pronoun then is replacing the whole segment by only part of the
original feature matrix.   The features that are retained in person
pronouns are primarily deictic.

[11] That they are unaffected by second mention turns out to be not
completely true, thus the use of the phrase 'in most cases.'   Akmajian and Anderson (1970) provide an interesting discussion of
person markers in NAVAHO and how they vary from third to fourth
person dependent on the ambiguity introduced by pronominalization.

is misleading. The 'he-' in 46.b is not a person pronoun, but a
person marker, the same one presented in 45.b. What about the
person pronoun in language B? These languages typically have
optional person pronouns. Thus, 46.b can also be stated as 50.

50.   HE he-wanted to.

The 'HE' segment is the pronoun, with the feature [-first mention].
It is only required when the segment is stressed. Languages such
as language B, then, have a process of first mention whereby a
subsequent rule deletes all pronouns that are [-FM]. This process
is also retrievable for other pronouns. In these languages 51. can
be paraphrased by 52.

51.   I-went home.
52.   I I-went home.

Because of these considerations, the status of deictic incorporation as a language specific rule is inadequate. Since most segments
in a language can undergo anaphoric processes, each segment requires deictic specification. So deictic incorporation is universal.
What this means is that the native speaker is aware of the person
deictic roles of any segment in the utterance, and can substitute for
it.

Language A and language B both share deictic incorporation.
They differ, however, because language B contains person markers.
The rule that distinguishes language B from language A will be one
that copies the person deictic unit of a semantic category onto the
predicate category (or from OBJECT to PREDICATE). I will refer
to this rule as person deictic copying. It is a language specific rule,
i.e. some languages undergo it and others do not. We thus have our
first typological distinction. Language A and language B represent
two basic types of languages as to person marking.

53. a.   Language A = Non-person deictic copying languages
    b.   Language B = Person deictic copying languages

The latter type, person deictic copying languages, are distinguished
by having person deictic features on the verb. In the literature this
type in the past has been referred to as 'incorporating languages.'
Because of the current use of that term in semantic theory, I have
avoided using it in this latter sense.[12]

---

[12]For an example of the use of this term in this latter sense, see
Boas 1966.

I will discuss aspects of <u>person deictic copying</u> in more detail
in Sec. 3.2. Before leaving it for now, however, I would like to
make a few comments about it in general. The typological distinction in 53. suggests a general process that is present in many languages. In terms of the child who is innately equipped to learn any
language, this means that every child potentially has this capability,
and does not realize it if his language does not have such a rule.
There is, in fact, child language data that suggests such a process.

ENGLISH is a language A type language; that is, it does not have
<u>person deictic copying</u>. The child learning ENGLISH, therefore,
must suppress such a rule. Data from children show that they often
use constructions that indicate <u>person deictic copying</u>. Below are
some examples.

     54. a. I Adam drive.
         b. Mommy get it my ladder.

The question arises, why does the child use such forms? One source
is the child's linguistic environment. We can rule this out, however,
because such irregular forms do not occur in the adult language.
Another source of children's anomalies is over-generalization of
rules. An example is the past affix <u>-ed</u> which will be over-generalized to produce forms like <u>goed</u> and <u>comed.</u> But what rule would
be over-generalized to account for the above forms? My suggestion
for this anomaly is that its source lies in the child's innate disposi-
tions. Every child is capable of learning a linguistic behavior that
can be characterized by <u>person deictic copying</u>. In ENGLISH this
rule must be suppressed. In each case it is, but not before occasionally manifesting itself in forms of those in 54.

    55. a. I + you   ———→ we (opt)
        b. I + he   ———→ we (opt)
        c. you + he ———→ you (opt)
        d. he + she ———→ they (opt)
        e. he + he ———→ they (ob)

This is obligatory for 'he +he' (55.e) and optional in the other cases.
There are also sequence restriction, such as she + he ─→ he + she,
and I + you ─→ you + I. I will not, however, go into these.

The way languages collapse pronouns varies from one to another.
Grammars rarely discuss this, but Chao (1968: 631-2), for example,
mentions the following distinctions for CHINESE (+means here absence of connective).

56. a. you + I   ———→ we (opt)
    b. you + I + he ———→ we (opt)
    c. I + you + he ———→ we (opt)
    d. I + he   ———→ we (ob)

Here I + he which is permissable in ENGLISH he and I is not allowed
in CHINESE (under normal conditions where the pronouns are juxta-
posed without conjunction), and must undergo coordinate collapsing.
I cannot at present claim that coordinate collapsing is universal,
although it may be. In any case, it is a widespread phenomenon in
many languages.

57. a. Rule schemata (universal)
    b. Deictic incorporation (universal)
    c. Deictic copying (language specific)
    d. Deictic categorization (language specific)
    e. Coordinate collapsing (widespread)

3.2 Systems of person deictic copying

Above I mentioned the kinds of languages, language A and language B, that differ as to person deictic copying. There are many
languages that represent each. The language A kind represents
those languages that do not have person deictic copying. Examples
are ENGLISH, BARI, CHINESE, FINNISH, FULANI, JAPANESE,
NEPALI, PALAUNG, PASHTO, TURKISH, URDU, etc. For the
rest of this section I will be concerned with those that do, i.e. language B types. From the actual language data I will attempt to get
an overview into the process.

We can tentatively divide language B types into three sub-types.
These are based on the number of categories to which copying may
apply. For example, in the example 'John he-went home' there is
one category copied. In 'John he-hit-it the ball,' there are two.
There seems a constraint of three upon the number of categories
that can be copied. Below are the types.

58. a. Single deictic copying languages
    b. Dual deictic copying languages
    c. Trial deictic copying languages

There are three categories that are used when copying occurs.
These are the three basic syntactic functions -- subject, object and
indirect object.

59. a. Subject   b. Object   c. Indirect object

These can be used to characterize a copying rule. Thus we can
have 'subject person copying,' 'object person copying,' or 'indirect
object copying.' This captures how the phenomenon has been discussed in the literature.[13]

Taking the three subtypes in 58 and describing the particular rules
by the syntactic categories in 59. reveals the following typology.

60. a. <u>Single person deictic copying languages</u> (A)
        i.   Subject copying rule (or)
        ii. Object copying rule

    b. <u>Dual person deictic copying languages</u> (B)
        i.   Subject copying rule (and)
        ii. Object copying rule

    c. <u>Trial person deictic copying languages</u> (C)
        i.   Subject copying rule
        ii. Object copying rule
        iii. Indirect object copying rule

This results in three possible systems which I have labelled A, B
and C. I will give a sample language of each along with what the
system looks like.

<u>System A</u> is one where only the subject is copied. A language
like this is ATESO, a NILO-HAMITIC language. An ENGLISH
paraphrase of this language system is shown in 61. 61.a shows a
[+first mention] of the subject <u>John</u>, 61.b the second mention unstressed, and 61.c the second mention stressed form. I ignore the
other features of the verb.

61.   ATESO (VSO)   ENGLISH (SVO)
    a. he-hit John ball   = John hit a ball.
    b. he-hit ball   = He hit the ball.
    c. he-hit HE ball   = Hé hit the ball.

---

[13] There is a problem as to whether or not these are deep or
surface categories that <u>copying</u> operates upon. Since that decision
does not affect the following typological findings, I do not include a
discussion of it here. Those more interested in that topic are referred to Chapter 4 of my dissertation where I discuss it at some
length.

I have not found a language that only has object copying, but I leave
the possibility open at the present time. A hypothetical sample of
such a language based on the above sequences in ATESO would look
like 62.

```
62.    ? (VSO)              ENGLISH (SVO)
    a. hit-it John ball     = John hit a ball.
    b. hit-it John          = John hit it.
    c. hit-it John IT       = John hit ít.
```

System B, which has both subject and object copying, was a relatively common system. An example is ACOOLI, a CHARI-NILE
language. 63.a shows the first mention of both subject and object.
63.b is the unstressed second mention of both, and 63.c the stressed.

```
63.    ACOOLI (SVO)             ENGLISH (SVO)
    a. John he-hit-it ball       = John hit a ball.
    b. he-hit-it                 = He hit it.
    c. HE he-hit-it              = Hé hit it.
       (or) he-hit-it IT         = He hit ít.
```

The last system, System C, copies all three categories onto the
verb. An example of this is SUMERIAN which has a complicated
series of affixes on the verb.

```
64.    SUMERIAN (SOV)
    a. John ball to-me it-to-me-he-hit
    b. he it to-me it-to-me-he-hit

       ENGLISH (SVO)
    a. John hit a ball to me.
    b. He hit it to me.
```

From this overview of the derivation of person pronouns and
person markers, I have tried to show the difference between the
two. The former result from a theory of first mention and represent the replacement of a category. Person markers, on the other
hand, directly specify the person deictic unit of a particular category. Since they both contain person deictic features, they are
similar in their nature. They derive, however, from different
rules.

The person markers result from what I have referred to as
person deictic copying. I have given the three systems that languages manifest in that regard. As for person pronouns, they
result from a theory of first mention. I have already discussed

the process of feature marking (i. e. [-FM] [+pro]) that results in
them. As is common in languages, these can be optional (e.g.
ITALIAN) or obligatory (e.g. ENGLISH). To account for this, we
need a late rule in the syntax, a language specific one, of person
pronoun deletion. I will not go into this rule in any detail, though
its operation is obvious. It would be interesting to look at the conditions that are necessary for it to operate. For example, it operates for subject pronouns in ITALIAN, and this can be explained
on the grounds that the verb distinguishes all the persons. Perhaps
this is the constraint that dictates its operation. In any case, that
rule further distinguishes person pronouns from person markers,
as the latter does not undergo such a rule.

4. Set Systems

4.1 Introduction

The last typological aspect of person deictic systems that I will
look at concerns distribution or case systems. As deictic features
are marked and derived by rules to the surface structure, there
is a point where lexical insertion occurs. A typical segment for
insertion might have the features of 65.

65.   AGENT
$$\begin{pmatrix} [S] \\ \begin{Bmatrix} -sp \\ -hr \\ +X^1 \end{Bmatrix} \\ [-FM] \\ [+def] \\ [+pro] \end{pmatrix}$$

      (e.g. he)

There need to be, however, other aspects to consider because such
a specification as 65. would still not be adequate for most languages.
That is, most languages have sets of pronouns based upon various
aspects of the derivation. We therefore need a formalism of universal scope that can derive these various sets. I will first describe
the types of person pronoun set systems that have been described in
the literature, and then suggest one way to account for them.

4.2 Set systems

These systems consist of five fundamental types that have been
outlined by Sapir (1917) and recently by Fillmore (1968). The latter

refers to these as pronominal systems. This study suggests that there are various kinds of 'pronominal' systems, and that a finer distinction is necessary. Earlier I discussed deictic person systems (2.1), and deictic rule systems (3.1). In this section I will refer to Sapir's pronominal systems as deictic person set systems. So we present three typological systems of person deixis.

66. a. Person systems
    b. Rule systems
    c. Set systems

Fillmore presents names for only three of the five possible SET systems. In my review of these types I will attempt to provide a broader nomenclature for them.

As a preliminary, Fillmore (1968: 53) discusses these systems in terms of the semantic categories of AGENT and OBJECT. He proposes three possible sentences with these.

67. a. Verb + Agent — intransitive sentences with active 'subjects'
    b. Verb + Object + Agent — transitive sentences with agents
    c. Verb + Object — intransitive sentences with inactive 'subjects'

Using these distinctions I shall present these systems in a slightly different manner, using ENGLISH paraphrases of each.[14] The paraphrases correspond to 67. are 68., respectively.

68. a. PRO_1 runs
    b. PRO_2 hits PRO_3
    c. PRO_4 is tall.

68. allows for four possible pronoun sets for these four positions. Each slot is marked PRO with a numeral.

The Sapir typology reveals five types under three categories. These three categories are:

69. a. One set system
    b. Two set system
    c. Three set system

The two set system has three possible kinds. I will present each in turn.

---

[14] Lyons (1968) uses this approach in discussing these.

The one set system has one PRO[15] set for all the possible slots in 68. This system occurs in YANA.

70. <u>One set system</u> $(PRO_1, PRO_2, PRO_3, PRO_4)$ = set
    a. he runs
    b. he hits he
    c. he is tall

Lexical insertion in such a system can occur without further features.

The two set systems consist of three kinds. Fillmore calls these accusative ergative, and active systems. The one thing in common is the fact that all three have two sets of PRO. What is different, however, is the PRO_n that these two sets replace. The first of these, the accusative system, is that which we have in ENGLISH.

71. <u>Two set system:</u> <u>accusative</u> (PRO_1, PRO_2, PRO_4) = Set 1
    a. he runs (PRO_3) = Set 2
    b. he hits him
    c. he is tall

The constraint on this type appears to be one of surface position. The ergative system has received much attention of late. It has because of the way it marks semantic agent in transitive sentences. Languages with this kind of system include BASQUE, CHINOOK and many others.

72. <u>Two set system:</u> <u>ergative</u> (PRO_1, PRO_3, PRO_4) = Set 1
    a. him runs (PRO_2) = Set 2
    b. he hits him
    c. him is tall

This system has position constraints in terms of whether or not it occurs with a transitive verb. The third two set system has the most obvious semantic constraints. This system, represented in 70., is found in DAKOTA. It is the active system.

73. <u>Two set system:</u> <u>active</u> (PRO_1, PRO_2) = Set 1
    a. he runs (PRO_3, PRO_4) = Set 2
    b. he hits him
    c. him is tall

---

[15] Since these systems apply to person features, they affect both person pronouns and person markers. I will use the form PRO to refer to both.

The lexical insertion here appears to be purely based on semantic categories of AGENT-OBJECT.

The last system is Sapir's example of TAKELMA. This system has three sets for the four possible ones in 68. These are:

74. <u>Three set system</u> (PRO_1, PRO_4) = Set 1
    a. he runs (PRO_2) = Set 2
    b. HE hits him (PRO_3) = Set 3
    c. he is tall

It has a distinct form for agent when there is a transitive verb.

4.3 <u>Feature rules</u>

Given the five types of set systems in Set. 4.2, how do we generate each kind? This possibility needs to be formulated in an adequate general theory of grammar. The problem to do it, however, is troublesome because there seems to be different motivations (syntactic and/or semantic) for the various types.

First, let us look at the sets of PRO in 70. to 74. to see what factors are contributing to the distinctions. In the one set system there are no distributional constraints. This means that the way to mark these case distinctions in the other types is not universal. That is, set systems do not have to occur in every language.

The accusative system has two sets of PRO. Set 1 represents three PRO's, all of which occur in the subject position. Set 2 has one PRO, that one which does not occur in the subject position. We can look at set marking as a process whereby a segment is specified by some feature of its derivation. In this case the feature is whether or not that category is the surface subject or not. We can account for this by a late rule of PRO marking, which we will call the <u>subject rule.</u> It would state that all PRO's should be marked for whether or not they are subject. This would assign to 65., for example, the feature [± subject].

The next set system is the ergative system. It contains two sets, but these two differ from the two of the accusative system. A look at the two sets shows that the second one (Set 2) only has one PRO member. That one represents the subject of a transitive verb. The subject of a transitive verb has been referred to as an ergative. This system can then be marked by the <u>ergative rule.</u> Such a rule states that any PRO is marked for whether or not it is the subject of a transitive verb. The feature assigned would be [± ergative].

The active system contains two sets of two PRO's each. Set 1 has PRO_1 and PRO_2 which are both agents or actors. Set 2 has PRO_3 and PRO_4 which are both objects or inactives. The marking reveals the syntactic marking of a semantic category. The rule of segment marking can be referred to as the <u>actor rule</u>, and it would specify the feature $[\pm active]$.

The last system is the three set system. 74. shows these three sets. Set 1 has the subject of intransitive verbs. This could result from the <u>subject rule</u>. Set 2 has subject of the transitive verb marked by a different feature. What appears to occur is that the <u>ergative rule</u> has also applied. This system can be explained by the operation of both of these feature markings.

These five systems are accounted for by three optional segment structure rules. These rules are:

75. a. Subject rule
     b. Ergative rule
     c. Active rule

They occur singly, and 75.a and b can apply together. 76. shows the sets of PRO for these five systems with their appropriate feature markings.

76. a. One set system: Set 1

     b. Two set system - accusative: Set 1   Set 2
                                      [+ subject] [- subject]

     c. Two set system - ergative: Set 1   Set 2
                                      [- ergative][+ ergative]

     d. Two set system - active: Set 1   Set 2
                                      [+ active]   [- active]

     e. Three set system: Set 1   Set 2   Set 3
                          [+ subject] [+ subject]   [- subject]
                          [-ergative][+ ergative] [- ergative]

APPENDIX

The data for the person systems are taken directly from Forch-heimer (1953). Consequently, they are based on a secondary source that used grammars which were available in or about 1950. Due to

more recent work and alternative grammars not used by Forchheimer,
a more recent study may well result in different systems for certain
languages than those given by Forchheimer and consequently shown
below. I found the introduction of these potential inaccuracies a
small price to pay for the overview of person systems available
from Forchheimer's large amount of data.

Four-person system		Languages (page no. in Forchheimer)
I	we	KOREAN (65)
thou		KAMANUGU (66)
he		

Five-person system

A.	I	we	BURMESE (43)
	thou	you	
	he		

B.	I	we	ENGLISH
	thou		
	he	they	

Six-person system

A.	I	we	CHINESE (42)	TURKISH (54)
	thou	you	JAPANESE (43)	EAST SUKETI (55)
	he	they	KOTTISH (48)	CHUKCHEE (56)
			SUMERIAN (49)	KHASI (61)
			SHILH (50)	MASAI (67)
			TSHIMSHIAN (75)	AKKADIAN (68)
			LATIN (76)	AZTEC (74)
			HAUSA (71)	TLINGIT (78)
			HOPI (73)	WIYOT (105)
			FINNISH (53)	

B.	I	we-incl.
		we-excl.
	thou	you
	he	

C.	I	we-2-incl. we
		we-2-excl.
	thou	
	he	

Seven-person system

A.	I	we-2	we	CARRIER (78)
	thou		you	
	he		they	

Seven-person system (cont.)   Languages (page no. in Forchheimer)

B. I   we-incl.   TAGALOG (80)   ALGONQUIAN (104)

           we-excl.   OLD NUBIAN (94)   SOMALI (104)

     thou   you   FUL (95)   GÂRÔ (112)

     he   they   TAMIL (101)   PURIK (113)

                           ORDOS MONGOL (103) NYUL-NYUL (126)

Eight-person system

A. I   we-2   we   WEST GREENLAND ESKIMO (50)

     thou you-2   you   GOTHIC (77)

     he   they

B. I   we   ARABIC (70)

     thou you-2   you

     he   they-2   they

C. I   we-2-incl. we-incl. SOUTHERN PAIUTE (88)

                      we-excl.

     thou   you

     he   they

Nine-person system

A. I   we-2   we   MAIDU (45)

     thou you-2   you   OSTYAK (52)

     he   they-2   they   MORDWINISH (53)

                          LAPPONIAN (53)

                          TONKAWA (58)

B. I   we-2-incl. we-incl. MAYA (106)

              we-2-excl. we-excl.

     thou   you

     he   they

C. I   we-2-incl. we   LOWER KANAURI

              we-2-excl.

     thou you-2   you

     he   they

Ten-person system

A. I   we-2-incl. we   COOS (108)

               we-2-excl.

     thou you-2   you

     he   they-2   they

B. I   we-2-incl. we-excl. KANAURI (116)

              we-2-excl. we-incl.

     thou you-2   you

     he   they

Eleven-person system

Languages
(page no. in Forchheimer)

A. I   we-2-incl.   we-incl. HAWAIIAN (81)
         we-2-excl.   we-excl. SHOSHONE (89)
    thou you-2   you   CHINOOK (91)
    he   they-2   they   SIUSLAWAN (109)
                                   IROQUOIAN (111)
                                   CENTRAL KANAURI (116)
                                   MANDARI (120)
                                   OTOMI (121)
                                   DYIRRINGAN (124)
                                   KAMILAROI (125)
                                   SAIBALGAL (127)
                                   BONGU (128)
                                   KÂTE (128)
                                   YOKUTS (131)
                                   KIOWA (131)

B. I   we-2-incl.   we   EWE (132)
         we-2-excl.
    thou you-2   you
    he   they-2   they
                         he-they

C. I   we-2-incl. we-3-incl. we-incl. KELE (133)
         we-2-excl.   we-excl.
                                we
    thou   you
    he   they

Twelve-person system

I-incl. we-2-incl.   we-incl. ROTUMAN (95)
I-excl. we-2-excl.   we-excl.
thou   you-2   you
he   they-2   they

Fifteen-person system

I   we-2-incl. we-3-incl. we-incl. NOGOGU (81)
        we-2-excl. we-3-excl. we-excl. WORORA (126)
thou   you-2   you-3   you
he   they-2   they-3   they

Languages

The language material for certain sections is taken directly
from secondary sources and is so cited (e.g. Forchheimer 1953,
Sapir 1905). The languages that were examined from other sources
are listed below alphabetically. The appendix deals with language
data given in Forchheimer (1953).

ACOOLI	Malandra 1955	JAPANESE	Harada 1966
A TESO	Hilders and	NAVAHO	Young and Morgan 1967
	Lawrence 1957	PALAUNG	Milne 1921
BARI	Spagnolo 1933	PASHTO	Shafeev 1964
CHINESE	Chao 1968	SUMERIAN	Bertin 1888
FINNISH	Olli 1958	TURKISH	Lewis 1967
FULANI	Taylor 1953	URDU	Catchpole 1946

BIBLIOGRAPHY

Akmajian, A. and S. Anderson. 1970. On the use of fourth person
    International Journal of American Linguistics [IJAL] 36.1-8.

Bertin, G. 1888. Languages of the cuneiform inscriptions. London.

Boas F. 1966. Introduction to the Handbook of American Indian
    languages. Lindoln: University of Nebraska Press.

Catchpole, H. 1946. Elementary Urdu. Ipswich, England.

Chao, Y-R. 1968. A grammar of Spoken Chinese. Berkeley:
    University of California Press.

Fillmore, C. 1968. The case for case. Universals in linguistic
    theory, ed. by E. Bach and R. Harms. New York.

Forchheimer, P. 1953. The category of person in language. Berlin.

Greenberg, J. 1963. Some universals of grammar with particular
    reference to the order of meaningful elements. Universals of
    language, ed. by Greenberg, 73-113. Cambridge, Mass.: M.I.T.
    Press.

Harada, T. 1966. Outline of modern Japanese linguistics. Tokyo:
    Nihon University.

Hilders, J. and J. Lawrence. 1957. An introduction to the Ateso language. Kampala.

Ingram, D. 1970. The role of person deixis in underlying semantics. Doctoral dissertation, Stanford University.

Lewis, G. 1967. Turkish grammar. Oxford.

Lyons, J. 1968. Theoretical linguistics. London: Cambridge University Press.

Malandra, A. 1955. A new Acholi grammar. Kampala.

McCawley, J. 1968. Lexical insertion in a transformational grammar without deep structure. Papers from the Fourth Regional Meeting of the Chicago Linguistic Society.

Milne, L. 1921. An elementary Palaung grammar. Oxford.

Moravcsik, E. 1971. Agreement. Working Papers on Language Universals [WPLU] 5. A1-A69. Stanford University.

Olli, J. 1958. Fundamentals of Finnish grammar. New York: Northland.

Ross, J.R. 1970. On declarative sentences. Readings in English transformational grammar, ed. by R. Jacobs and P. Rosenbaum, 222-272. Waltham, Mass.

Sapir, E. 1917. Review of C.C. Uhlenb ck. IJAL 1. 82-86.

Sedlak, P. 1969. Typological considerations of vowel quality systems. WPLU 1. 1-40a.

Shafeev, D. 1964. A short grammatical outline of Pashto. IJAL 30.3, Part III, Pub. 33.

Spagnolo, L.M. 1933. Bari grammar. Verona: Missioni Africane.

Taylor, F.W. 1953. Fulani grammar. Oxford.

Young, R. and W. Morgan. 1967. The Navaho language. Salt Lake City.

Generalizations About Numeral Systems

JOSEPH H. GREENBERG

ABSTRACT

This paper contains 54 generalizations about numeral systems of the languages of the world. Most of them pertain to the most "unmarked" series, the cardinals in attributive construction with nouns. The mathematical structure of such systems in terms of arithmetical operations, the order of elements in the numeral phrases and its syntactic relation to the noun head are the main topics considered. In addition, there are brief discussions of other syntactic functions of cardinals, their relation to other series such as ordinals, and numeral systems in relation to language contact and cultural evolution.

CONTENTS

1. Introduction

In this study a number of generalizations concerning numeral systems are proposed. Many, but not all of them, are stated here for the first time. The existing literature on this topic can be divided into several quite different sorts of studies. There are first, particularly in the earlier period, general or regional surveys of numeral systems, such works as those of Pott (1849), Conant (1896), Fettweis (1927), Thomas (1897-8, on Mexico and Central America), Dixon and Kroeber (1907, on California), Schmidt (1915, on Africa) and, above all, the immense worldwide collection of Kluge (1937-42). These studies are useful in showing the typological variety and areal distribution of numeral systems in regard to their basic mathematical structure. However, none of these studies are recent. In addition, they give no information regarding the syntax of numeral constructions which constitutes the basis for many of the generalizations presented here. A second class of works is by mathematicians concerned with the history and evolution of numerical systems, such as Wilder (1953), Smeltzer (1958) and Menninger (1969). These works contain valuable ideas regarding the mathematical aspects, but they tend to concentrate on the development of written notations in the Near East and Europe, and to be cursory and superficial regarding spoken languages, particularly in non-Western and preliterate societies. Finally, there are studies by linguists in the relatively recent period. Brandt Corstius (1968) has edited a collection of formal grammatical analyses of particular systems, most of them transformational generative. An important contribution is that of Hurford (1975), a generatively oriented study which aims at greater generality and considers a number of diverse systems. A number of Hurford's formulations cover some of the same ground as mine, although expressed in a different framework. He notes, for example, that "in languages it is often the case that M's have the properties of nouns" (p. 51)(an M is a base of a numeral system). With this, compare the discussion under generalization 20. His rule of 1-deletion is contained in generalization 36, and his switch rule in my 26 and 27. His "packing principle" is related in a complex way to generalizations 37 and 38 of this paper.

Among non-generative treatments, the pioneer article of Salzmann (1950) deserves to be mentioned. I had already completed most of the present research when Stampe (1977) came to my attention: this article, which is similar in approach to mine, contains a number of generalizations and explanatory suggestions almost all of which, it is gratifying to report, independently corroborate my own conclusions. Among the more significant points are the following: that

cardinal numbers are basically defined by their order in counting,
that a system based only on addition suffers from "the stringent
limit that memory plays on such a counting procedure," that smaller
numerals are adjectival in nature and larger nominal, that the preferred order in addition is larger preceding smaller, particularly
for larger numbers, that the preferred order in multiplication is
multiplier preceding multiplicand, and that this preference is related
to the worldwide favoring of QN (quantifier-noun) order as against
NQ order, a fact which, as Stampe notes, was earlier stated by
me. He also observes the tendency for the smaller, more frequent
numbers to be expressed by combinations which are more unified
phonetically. On a few relatively minor points, however, his generalizations are not borne out by my evidence. Readers of this
article are urged to consult Hurford's book and Stampe's article
also.

This study will mainly be concerned with a synchronic treatment
of the most unmarked system, cardinal numbers in the attributive
construction. Later sections also take into consideration the relation between attributive and other uses of cardinal numerals (e.g.
counting, predication) and between cardinal and other series such
as ordinals. There is also a section on language contact and one
on evolutionary factors in the development of numeral systems.

2. Cardinal Numerals in the Attributive Construction

2.1 The scope of cardinal numeral systems

By the scope of a cardinal numeral system will be meant the set
of numbers which can be expressed in it. It is important to distinguish, as is usually done, between a number and a numeral expression. Numeral expressions are always in some particular
spoken language or system of written notation. Thus, 'the square
root of sixteen,' vier, six moins deux, and '2^2' are all numeral expressions which designate the same number. We must be able to
represent numbers as such in abstraction from the numerical expressions by which they can be designated.[1] Hurford (1975) uses
strokes for this purpose; thus the number referred to in the above
examples would be represented as ////. For larger numbers, this
is obviously impractical. Hence like him I will, as a practical
device, employ Arabic numerals for this purpose.

---

[1] In the text of the paper I have tried to distinguish carefully between number and numeral, but I have sometimes used phrases like
the 'number n' in place of such clumsy expressions as 'the numeral
expression designating n' when the meaning was clear from the context.

It is important to distinguish among numerical expressions in any natural language a special subset, the numerals proper, which constitute the numeral system of the language. Thus, in ENGLISH 'sixteen' is a numeral expression which is also a part of the numeral system, whereas 'the square of four,' which designates the same number, is a numeral expression which is not. The system of numerals is described by a specific part of the grammar. In general its bounds are clear, but doubts may occasionally arise. For example, is 'nineteen hundred and seventy' as an alternative expression for 'one thousand nine hundred and seventy' part of the numeral system in ENGLISH? Further examples from ENGLISH are 'dozen' and 'score.' Reasons for considering expressions of this kind as not part of the system will be mentioned later.

The set of numerical expressions is obviously broader than that of the numerals in any language. The following generalization regarding numeral systems has already been stated by Merrifield (1968):

1. Every language has a numeral system of finite scope.

Thus, corresponding to each of the "grammars for numeral names" contained in Brandt Corstius (1968), there is a specific number which is the largest for which a numeral is generated, and this is true of all formalized treatments which I have examined. Given this result, it will be convenient to define the limit number L for each system as the next largest natural number after the largest expressible in the system. The reason for adding 1 is that this will often give us a convenient round number. Thus, for AMERICAN ENGLISH $L = 10^{36}$, assuming that, as in most dictionaries of AMERICAN ENGLISH, the lexical item with the highest numerical value is 'decillion.'

As contrasted with the much larger body of numerical expressions, the numerical system proper is generated by the act of counting. We do not normally count 'one, two, three, the square root of sixteen, five...' in ENGLISH. Further, this helps us to eliminate such marginal expressions as 'dozen,' 'score,' etc. By and large, the numerals used in counting are the same as the set which has been mentioned above as the primary object of the present study, namely cardinal numbers in the form they take when they qualify nouns. In some languages, however, they differ from counting forms. However, they always exhibit the same mathematical structure. For example, we never have a language in which the counting forms are decimal while the forms which qualify nouns are vigesimal. This topic will be discussed under

generalization 53, at which point this identity of mathematical
structure will be shown to extend to other numeral sets as well.

Of course, counting is a matter of competence rather than performance, since presumably nobody will ever count to some very
large number. As long as there is a procedure such that given a
numeral expression for any number, speakers can produce the
next higher number, this is sufficient.

It is a corollary deducible from generalization 1 that no natural
language has a place system with the zero principle, such as found
in the written system of Arabic numerals. The possibility of
expressing an infinity of natural numbers in this way derives from
the theorem that for an arbitrary base $\underline{b}$ (in ENGLISH, of course,
$b = 10$), every natural number N can be written in just one way in
the form:

$N = a_n b^n + a_{n-1} b^{n-1} \ldots a_1 b + a_0$ where a_n, $a_{n-1} \ldots a_1$, a_0

designate numbers from a set $0, 1 \ldots b-1$.

MANDARIN has a term ling which means zero and indicates an
empty place (in fact it means 'empty'), but it is redundant, is not
used consistently and, more importantly, the numbers b^n, $b^{n-1}, \ldots$
i.e. 10,000; 1,000 etc. are indicated by a finite set of unanalyzable
lexemes rather than by the place principle.

It is not asserted here as a generalization, but it is possible that
all natural languages can designate any number, however large, by
using numerical expressions which are not part of the numeral system. All that is required is a recursive mechanism involving 'one.'
However, what is needed, then, for practical purposes, is some
way of keeping track of the 'ones,' and this can only be done by
counting them, so we are back to the numerical system.

2. Every number $\underline{n}$ $(0 < n < L)$ can be expressed as part of the
numerical system in any language.

We may call this the thesis of continuity. Considering the relation of the cardinal numeral system to the act of counting, we may
consider this, strictly speaking, a tautology, since if any numerical
expression names a number $\underline{n}$, the next by definition names $n+1$.
If there is no next numeral, then $n+1 = L$, the limit number.

However, it is worth stating because contrary assumptions have
sometimes been made. For example, Lichtenstein (1811-12: I.668)

stated that Van der Kamp could not find a XHOSA word for 8, although he stayed among them a long time and he himself could not
discover BECHUANA words for 5 or 9. In more recent times,
some Indo-Europeanists have claimed that numerals for the higher
decades, since they are not reconstructible, did not exist while a
word for 100, which is reconstructible, did (Szemerényi 1960). As
we shall see later, there is a relation between historical stability
and markedness. In general the higher the numeral, the more
marked, but units of the system have a special status and are less
marked than would be deduced from their number value alone.

3. Zero is never expressed as part of the numeral system.

Instances in which reference is made to a class with zero members
are normally dealt with by negative constructions in natural languages.

This might again be viewed as a tautology, since the numeral
system is based on counting, and counting begins with 'one;' we do
not count a set without members. However, it is worth stating
since a linguistic extension of the numeral system to include 'zero'
is not logically excluded. It is also of interest to note that in Peano's
famous system of axioms for numbers, the very first postulate is
"zero is a number" (Peano 1908: 27).

2.2 Systems without operations or with addition only

    In this and subsequent subsections, along with certain generali-
zations regarding numerical systems, we will develop pari passu
the notion of the arithmetical analysis of such systems. The most
basic concept is the generalized mathematical notion of function.

    Every numeral expresses a number as a function with one or
more numbers as arguments. For example, in ENGLISH 'twenty
three' expresses 23 as a function $(a \times b) + c$ in which the argument
a has the value 10, b has the value 2, and c has the value 3. A
limiting case is the identity function with takes on the same value
as its single argument, e.g. 'three' in ENGLISH which designates
3 as the value of the identity function with the argument 3. When
this is so, we may say that a particular number receives simple
lexical representation.

4. In every numerical system some numbers receive simple
    lexical representation.

No matter how high L is, it is possible to have a system in which
no number receives simple lexical representation. Thus we might
construct a system as follows: (2-1, 3-1, 2+1, 2+2, etc.). Such

a system requires the use of subtraction, or perhaps some other non-additive function, at least once, to express 1. Every system, then, has one or more numerals which receive simple lexical expressions. Salzmann (1950) calls the set of such numerals the 'frame' of the system. We shall call them here the atoms. Atoms are of two kinds, simple atoms and bases.

5. No number is ever expressed in any numerical system by means of a function any of whose arguments is $\geq$ L.

For example, in a system which only goes up to 7 (i.e. L−8), we could not express 6 by (9−3), since 9 > L.

We can typologize systems into those which use only the identity function and thus consist solely of atoms, and those which also employ other functions such as addition or multiplication. Those of the former type are reported from South America, Australia, New Guinea and South Africa (Bushman).

6. The largest value of L in systems with only simple lexical representation is 5 and the smallest is 2.

An example of L = 5 is GUANA, an ARAWAKAN language (Kluge 1937-42: III.40) with the system 1, 2, 3, 4, 'many.' Such systems are uncommon. There is a single instance of a system L = 2, namely BOTOCUDO, a MACRO-GE language in Brazil with only two terms: 1, 'many.' The most common values for L are 3 and 4. However, even systems with L = 4 often express 3 as 2 +1. It seems that 2 is never 1 +1, although rarely, 2 may be the dual of 1. It is of interest to note that these simplest systems parallel that of number in the noun. Corresponding to L = 2 is a singular/plural distinction, and to L = 3, singular/dual/plural. This relationship is graphically illustrated in WORORA, an AUSTRALIAN language in which there is only a simple numeral root which means 1 in the singular, iaruŋ, 2 in the dual, iaruŋandu and 3 or more in the plural, iaruŋuri (Love 1933).

It is characteristic of all of these systems and of some with addition only that there is a term which is usually glossed 'many,' with the indefinite value $\geq$ L.

7. The smallest value for L in systems with arithmetical operations is 4. This is a surprisingly low value. An example of a language with this limit is PORT ESSINGTON, Tasmania, with 1, 2, 2+1, 'many.'

This upper limit is rather uncertain for reasons which will soon appear. An example of L = 11 is the language of DAGUR and VA-TAI in New Guinea (Frederieci 1913: 41), with the following system: 1, 2, 2 +1, 4, 4 +1, 4 +2, 4 +(2 +1), 4 +(2 +2), 4 +(2 +1)+2, 10. The parenthesized sums are represented by single words.

Two instances have been encountered of systems in which counting can be carried on up to 30 and which could be interpreted as involving addition only. These are MULLUKMULLUK in Australia (Tryon 1974) and AGHU in New Guinea (Drabbe 1957). In the former, for example, 20 is expressed as 'hand one, one, foot, foot' which could be analyzed as (5 +5 +5 +5). This reflects, of course, the common method of first counting on the hands and then on the feet. However, since 5 is itself expressed as 'hand one,' this could be interpreted as (5 x 1), and the above analysis might be amended to ((5 x 1)+5 +5 +5). For AGHU in New Guinea, however, an account in which any of the numbers are represented by a function which involves multiplication seems to be excluded. In this system, also, counting on the fingers and toes is involved. A typical example is the term for 11: kito wodo, which means 'big toe.'

In these and similar instances it seems that numerals are never used without the accompanying gestures, and the gestures are often used without verbalization. It seems doubtful that such expressions are used attributively to nouns in sentences. There are other indications that some of the numerical systems recorded in the literature are simply the names for gestures used in counting. For example, for AUETÖ, a Tupian language, Steinen (1894: 536) gives the same numeral expression for 4 and 9. This is probably the word for 'index finger.' Even more strikingly, the following "system" is reported by Koch-Gruenberg from the Kaliana in South America, meyakan 1, meyakan 2, meyakan 3, (meyakan 'finger').

Another source of uncertainty is revealed by Douglas' statement regarding the WESTERN DESERT LANGUAGE in Australia (1958) in which numerals up to seven are given, the higher ones being formed by addition of 1, 2, or 3. "...originally, it appears, these compounds implied only a vague number."

2.2.1 The arithmetical operations in general

9. Of the four fundamental arithmetical operations -- addition and its inverse, subtraction, and multiplication and its inverse, division -- the existence of either inverse operation implies the existence of both direct operations.

This is one of a series of generalizations which point to the marked status of the inverse operations.

10. The existence of multiplication implies the existence of addition.

This is a near universal. I have encountered just one instance in which a numerical system has multiplication without addition, whereas there are many examples of addition without multiplication. In one subgroup of the YUMAN languages, which are affiliated to the HOKAN stock, we find systems in which L =11 and the numerals may be analyzed as follows: 1, 2, 3, 4, 5, 3 x 2, 7, 4 x 2, 3 x 3, 10.

The only arithmetical operation beyond the four fundamental ones is one which might be called the "going-on" operation.[2] It is found in the MAYAN group and in a few FINNO-UGRIC languages. An example is OSTYAK in which 18 is expressed as 8, 20, that is, '8 going-on 20.' Such constructions often involve an ordinal inter-pretation, as is clear, for example, in ESTHONIAN when this same number is to be interpreted as '8 of the second decade.' In other instances, however, the meaning is in fact something like 'going-on,' e.g. VOGUL 23 vat-nupəl xurm 'thirty-towards three.' In functional notation the 'going-on' operation may be expressed as follows: $f(x, y, z) = (x - 1) y + z$. Then, OSTYAK 18 is the value of this function for the arguments $x = 2$, $y = 10$, $z = 8$.

One might argue that exponentiation is also an operation utilized in natural languages, but I believe this is erroneous. For example, ENGLISH 'hundred' is not to be analyzed as 10^2 with 10 and 2 as arguments in a function $f(x, y) = x^y$, since, unlike the representation of 200 as 2 x100, 2 is not expressed overtly. A marginal case is ENGLISH 'billion,' 'trillion,' 'quadrillion'... in which, if we go by the LATIN etymology, we can analyze these in their British interpre-tation as $10^{2.6}$, $10^{3.6}$, $10^{4.6}$ ....

11. Subtraction is never expressed by the mere sequence of the subtrahend and minuend.

In standard arithmetical terminology the subtrahend is the num-ber subtracted, the minuend the number from which subtraction takes place, and the remainder is the result.

---

[2] This operation is called "overcounting" by Hurford (1975: 235), following Menninger 1969.

As contrasted with subtraction, simple juxtaposition is common
for addition and multiplication, e.g. GERMAN 13 drei-zehn 'three,
ten.' There are instances in which subtraction might seem to occur
without overt expression, but such instances are generally to be
interpreted as involving deletion. For example, in TARAHUMARA,
a UTO-AZTECAN language, ki-makoi is 9 and makoi is 10. One
might wish to interpret ki therefore as 1. The ordinary word for 1
is bire and hence ki would be a suppletive allomorph. However,
the correct analysis is that ki expresses subtraction and bire has
been deleted. There are three reasons for making this kind of interpretation a general rule. First, the apparent subtrahend is generally
suppletive. Secondly, the element to be deleted is always one of a
limited set, essentially 1 or the bases of a system, and these are
precisely the elements which are subject to deletion, as will be
indicated in a later generalization. Thirdly, there are examples
in which such a deletion is clearly indicated by the meaning of the
element which remains. For example, in EFIK 9 is usuk-kiet in
which kiet is the ordinary word for 1, while 10 is edip, a base of
the system. In this case usuk cannot be an allomorph of edip, 10
since it is derived from suk 'to be left over.' However, in TAMIL
and other DRAVIDIAN languages, 9 appears to be 'one, ten' and
this may be a genuine exception.

12. When a number is expressed by subtraction, or when a sub-
    traction occurs as a constituent of a complex expression,
    the subtrahend is never larger than the remainder.

This generalization would be violated if a language expressed 2
as 10-8, since the subtrahend 8 is larger than the remainder 2.
It would not be violated, however, if 8 was expressed as 10-2,
which in fact is found quite often. Note that in the former instance
we would be using 8, which had not occurred in the counting series,
up to that point to express 2. This is one example of the general
tendency to construct numerals on the basis of those which have
occurred earlier in the series. Of course, if we are to have subtraction at all, the minuend must not yet have occurred in counting,
e.g. 10 in the above example. There is also the fact that in counting a sequence subtractively, we seem to be going backward, a
factor noted by Stampe (1976). This may be one reason for the un-
popularity of subtraction. Amasoye (1972: 34), a speaker of KALA-
BARI IJO which has a vigesimal system that makes extensive use
of subtraction, in advocating a more "rational" decimal system with
addition only, says regarding subtraction: "The effect of this manner of counting is that we progress in our counting not by actually
advancing but by retrogressing."

13. A subtrahend is always a simple lexical expression.

As noted earlier, a simple lexical expression is one which does
not involve any except the identity function. An example of a violation would be the expression of 17 in a language as 20-(2+1). There
is no corresponding limitation for addition. For example, in WELSH
pedwar ugain ac un ar bumtheg 'four twenty and one on five-ten,'
i.e. (4 x 20) +[1+(5 +10)], both addends are complex. Whereas the
subtrahend may not be complex, the minuend may be. For example,
in YORUBA 65 is [(20 x 4)-10]-5 in which there are two complex
minuends, (20 x 4) and (20 x 4)-10.

14. If a number n is expressed by subtraction as y-x, then
     every number z(z>y>n) is also expressed subtractively
     and with y as the minuend.

For example, in LATIN 18 is duodēvīginti, that is 'two from
twenty.' Here n = 18 and y = 20 and x = 2. The only number z
smaller than y (20) and greater than n (18) is 19. Hence, 19 also
will be expressed subtractively with 20 as the minuend, i.e. 20-1.

A marginal exception is ZAPOTEC, as described in Córdova's
Arte del Idioma Zapoteco, reproduced in Thomas (1897-8) in which
55 is (60-5), but 56 is either (60-4), as predicted by generalization
14, or (60 +1)-5, and correspondingly for 57, 75, 76, 95 and 96.
In MONTAGNAIS, an ATHABASKAN language, 7 is expressed as
either (10- 3) or (8 -1), although 9 is (10 -1) and 8 is (4 x 2). Hence
this is also an exception.

15. Every minuend is a base of the system or a multiple of the
     base.

This is evidently what is intended by Salzmann when he states
(1950: 82): "Subtractive operation is usually of the Latin type undē-
vīginti and is bound to the cycle boundary." That is, in LATIN 19
expressed as (20 -1), and 20 -- the minuend -- is a member of what
Salzmann calls a cycle, since at regular intervals of ten we get
multiples of ten while the intervening numbers are expressed by
operating on, i.e. adding to or subtracting from, them. Later
base will be defined, but for the moment we will consider it as
generally understood.

The above quoted example of ZAPOTEC is obviously an exception to this generalization also, since in the expression of 57 as
(60 +2)- 5 the minuend 62 is not a base or a multiple of a base.

There are two further exceptions, one is ARIKARA, a CADDOAN language in which, as reported by Prince Maximilian von Wied, 7 is (8-1), 9 is (10-1) and 11 is (12-1) in a decimal system. The exceptions here are, of course, 7 and 11. The other is MONTAG-NAIS in which, as noted under generalization 14, 7 may be expressed as (8-1).

16. Division is always expressed as multiplication by a fraction. Only units or multiples of units are dividends, and the denominator of the fraction is always 2 or a power of 2.

Division is even more "marked" than subtraction and subject to severe limitations. Almost all examples are 50 expressed as $(\frac{1}{2} \times 100)$, usually in a vigesimal system. In ORIYA, an INDO-ARYAN language, 275 is <u>pau ne tini šata</u> 'quarter from three hundred,' i.e. $(3 \times 100) - \frac{1}{4} *(100)$, with the occurrence of 100 which is multiplied by $\frac{1}{4}$ being deleted. [3] 'Half' is the "unmarked fraction" and is almost always a simple lexical item, often derived from 'to split,' or 'to break' or the like. Even where a full system of fraction is found, the expression of half as 'one second' is excessively rare.

2.2.2 <u>The commutative and associative laws of addition and multiplication</u> As we move from subtraction and division to addition and multiplication, it becomes necessary to consider, in a more systematic way, the procedures involved in analyzing numerical systems. This is mainly because of complications related to the commutative and associative laws which apply to addition and multiplication, but not to subtraction and division.

Given that a certain numeral expression in a language designates 8 and that it does so as a function of 10 and 2, we can deduce that subtraction is involved. Whether there is an overt morpheme meaning 'to take away' or the like or not, the minuend is unambiguously 10, the subtrahend 2, and the remainder 8. In regard to addition and multiplication, however, a certain ambiguity obtains, which has no parallel in the corresponding inverse operations. To begin with addition, a distinction is made in arithmetic between the augend, that which is added to, and the addend, that which is added. The result is the sum, and any term of the sum is called a summand, whether it is the augend or the addend. According to the commutative law of addition, a +b = b +a, and this principle can be generalized

---

[3] The asterisk, here and elsewhere, denotes a deleted expression.

to any number of summands. Hence in addition, given a language
in which 7 is expressed as a function of 5 and 2, we can deduce
that the arithmetical function is addition, but these numerical values are insufficient to determine which of the two summands is the
augend and which is the addend. These two interpretations correspond to two different pragmatic situations, e.g. putting two objects on an already formed pile of five objects, as against putting
five objects on a pile of two objects. Since the numerical result
by the commutative law is the same, it might be thought that linguistically this makes no difference. But, as the subsequent discussion will show, there are various indications as to which of the
two possible analysis is the correct one and this leads to generalizations regarding the construction of numerical systems.

A similar situation obtains in regard to the commutative law of
multiplication. That which is multiplied is called the multiplicand,
and that which multiplies, the multiplier. The result is the product,
and the term factor is applied both to the multiplicand and the multiplier. The commutative law of multiplication states that a x b =
b x a, and this result can be extended to any number of factors. If,
in 3 x 10, 3 is the multiplicand, we are to think of ten piles with
three objects on each pile, while if 10 is the multiplicand, we have
three piles of ten objects each.

Because of the commutative law by which the order of summands
or factors does not matter for the final result, standard arithmetical
notation does not provide a means for symbolizing these distinctions.
Parenthesization is introduced here as a method. In 5 (+3) = 8, 5 is
the augend and 3 is the addend, whereas in (5 +) 3, 5 is the addend
and 3 is the augend. Similarly, for multiplication, in 3 (x 10), 3
will be the multiplicand and 10 the multiplier, whereas in (3 x) 10,
3 will be the multiplier and 10 the multiplicand.

Hierarchization will be used as a cover term for the process of
determining the augend/addend or the multiplicand/multiplier. The
augend and multiplicand are the passive members and the addend
and multiplier the active ones.

Where there are three or more addends or factors, an additional
process enters, namely grouping. The associative law of addition
(a +b) + c = a + (b + c) tells us that whether we combine b with a to
produce a first sum or b with c, the result is the same. Mutatis

mutandis the same analysis applies in relation to the associative law of multiplication (a x b) x c = a x (b x c). Grouping distinctions both for addition and multiplication once more have pragmatic correspondents. Thus, given that x = 3, b = 5 and c = 6, [a(+b)](+c) can be interpreted as follows. We first have a pile of three objects (a = 3), to which we add five (b = 5). We then take six objects (c = 6) and add it to the resulting pile of eight objects to obtain fourteen. Both associative laws can be generalized to n summands or factors. In other words, order of operation does not affect the mathematical result.

2.2.3 Steps in the analysis of numerical systems It is not the purpose of this section to give a detailed set of procedures for analyzing numerical systems. However, something like at least a partial ordering of procedures and of definitions seems necessary to provide sufficient clarity in regard to some of the terms to be used in the generalizations. For example, the notion of augend and addend involves a relationship between two numerical expressions, but until grouping has been carried out, we will not be able to apply these concepts to sequences of three or more addends.

The first step in analysis has already been briefly considered in Sec. 2.2.2. To each numeral is assigned one or more numbers based on morphemic identifications, and the arithmetical functions are inferred. For example, in ENGLISH 'two hundred and three,' the numeral which designates 203, is analyzed as containing the arguments 2, 100, 3 and the arithmetical function inferred is (a x b)+c, in which a = 2, b = 100 and c = 3. In the limiting case of simple lexical expression, say 'six,' which designates 6, the function is the identity function f(a) = a, where a = 6.

At this stage, we do not as yet have hierarchization or grouping of summands or factors, but we can automatically infer some parenthesizations from the arithmetical functions themselves. This is so for subtraction and division as well as for combinations of multiplication with addition or subtraction. In the above example of ENGLISH 'two hundred and three,' to derive the correct numerical value we must parenthesize (2 x 100) + 3. If we did not, we would get 2 x (100 + 3) = 206.

The identification of phonologically different stretches as representing the same number is of three different kinds. One of these is agglutinal-fusional, as when ENGLISH fif- in fifteen is taken to represent the same number as five in twenty-five. A second is

suppletion, as when in CHRAU, an AUSTRO-ASIATIC language,
mat indicates 10, but for 20 we find var jat where var means 2.
This leads us to deduce that jat is a suppletive alternant for 10.
A further type, portmanteau expression, can be illustrated by RUS-
SIAN sorok 40. An analysis into (4 x 10) without specific subse-
quences being assigned meanings 4 and 10 is suggested by the facts
about the RUSSIAN numeral system, but this requires the notion of
base, which has not yet been defined.

We next note that in certain numerical expressions in languages,
the arithmetical operations themselves are represented by overt
morphemes. Reverting to the earlier ENGLISH example of 'two
hundred and three,' we can deduce that 'and' designates the operation of addition. Such an overt morphemic expression of an operation will be called a 'link,' in this case a link for addition. Such
'links' are not the only way in which operations are expressed.
Word order, prosodic phenomena, inflection or some combination
of them are other methods. In MANDARIN 32 is expressed as
3, 10, 2 in which the order is significant. For example, 2, 10, 3
would represent 23. In CLASSICAL SANSKRIT aṣṭāçatam 8́, 100
is 108, but aṣṭaçatám 8, 100´ is 800. The use of accent alone, in
this case pitch accent, is extremely rare, and I cannot quote any
instance outside of SANSKRIT. However, accentual phenomena
often accompany other methods, but are so sparsely reported in
the literature that I refrain from generalizing about them.

An example of inflection is the following. In CLASSICAL ARABIC
5 is represented as xams^{un} (the feminine nominative singular indefinite is used here as the citation form). The plural xamsūna,
cited in the nominative, represents 50. There are corresponding
relations between other digits and the corresponding tens. Here
the inflection -ūna represents at the same time the operation of
multiplication and the multiplier 10. Later it will be shown that
there is good reason in instances like this to assume a deletion of
'ten.'

For some links, their very meaning virtually compels a particular hierarchization. Consider addition first. It frequently involves
no overt expression, e.g. ENGLISH 'twenty-five.' Almost as common is a formative, often affixed meaning 'and' or 'with.' In many
languages a single morpheme means both 'and' and 'with.' We may
call this a comitative link. Since the basic meaning is association,
it may, on occasion, go with either of the two addends. For example,
in GALLA 103 is ḍibbā-f sadi 'hundred-and three,' whereas in
CLASSICAL ARABIC the same number is mi'at^{un} wa-thalāthat^{un}

'hundred and-three.' Later we shall see that in such expressions the augend is universally the hundreds expression while the digit is the addend. It will also appear that the decisive factor here is whether the language is prepositional or postpositional, not the arithmetical relation.

A third type is far less popular, but is still widespread. This is a word or affix meaning 'upon.' It will be called a superessive link. By its very meaning it would seem to go with the augend. If we add three items to ten, then the three are put on the heap of ten and not vice versa. 'Under' never occurs as a link. Unlike the comitative link, the superessive link shows consistency across languages in regard to the numeral with which it is in construction, regardless of the word order of the numerals or whether the language is prepositional or postpositional. For example, in OLD CHURCH SLAVIC 11 is jedinŭ na desęte 'one on ten' in which the syntactic connection of 'on' with 'ten' is shown by the fact that it is a preposition which governs the locative case of desęti, just as it does with other nouns. In LOGBARA, a CENTRAL SUDANIC language which is postpositional, 11 is moodri dri-ni alo 'ten on-it (lit. its head) one.' We see that once more it is 'one' which is on 'ten,' and not vice versa. An invariant relation also holds with the rather rare 'possessive link,' e.g. QUECHUA 11 which is čunka ukni-yuq 'ten one-having' which exactly parallels the far-off MOUN-TAIN NUBIAN, an EASTERN SUDANIC language with 11 'ten one-having,' i.e. 'ten' which possesses a 'one.'[4]

These facts might be stated as one or more generalizations. However, a more powerful statement becomes possible after we have introduced another fundamental operation, namely serialization. This determination is independent of the semantics or syntax of overt links that we have just been considering, since it depends only on the mathematical structure of the numerical system. In fact it will be applicable whether there are links or not. Whenever there are at least two successive number, x, $x+1$..., such that

---

[4] In addition to the modes of expressing addition described in the text, there are others. One of these involves the meaning 'to be extra,' 'to be added,' or the like. An example is KOLOKUMA IJO 11 oi keni fini 'ten one is-extra.' Another is a form meaning 'to be left,' 'remain,' as in ANGLO-SAXON 12 twā-lif 'two remain,' MODERN ENGLISH 'twelve.' In both of these the identity of the augend is given by the semantics. In the latter method, the unit is perhaps always deleted.

each is expressed as the sum of some constant y and z, $z+1 \cdots$,
respectively, we will say that y is an augend by serialization. We
may illustrate this from ENGLISH. Let x be 'twenty-one,' $x+1$
be 'twenty -two,' etc. They are expressed as $(2 \times 10) + 1$, $(2 \times 10)+2$,
etc., respectively. Hence 20 is the augend by serialization in these
expressions, and 1, 2... are the addends. The augend may have
either simple lexical expression or be internally complex, as with
$20 = 2 \times 10$ in this example.

There are some instances in languages in which addition occurs
without being part of such a series. An example is MANDJAK, a
language of the West Atlantic branch of NIGER-CONGO in which
7 is $6 + 1$, but 8 receives simple lexical expression. Such non-
serialized sums will be said to be sporadic.

Augends identified by serialization for any particular sum never
disagree with those identified by superessive, possessive or other
links which lend themselves to interpretation in this regard. The
first notion is, however, the broader one. Further superessive
or possessive links never occur in sporadic sums. This probably
also holds for the other methods mentioned in footnote 4. We have
therefore the following generalization.

17. Every superessive or possessive augend is a serialized augend.

We can see that this is an empirical generalization by noting what
a language would have to be like to violate it. Let us suppose that
in a particular language 8 was expressed as '3 on-5,' but 9 was a
single lexical expression. We would have a superessive augend 5
which was not a serialized augend.

18. A serialized augend is always larger than its addends.

The reader may have noticed that in all the examples given, the
augend was larger than the addend. Note that serialization was defined without reference to the relative size of the numbers. For
example, if in a language 8 was $2 + 6$, and 9 was $2 + 7$, then 2 would
be a serialized augend which was smaller than its addends. In the
above statement, a restriction was made to serialized augends to
the exclusion of sporadic sums. There is sometimes no way in
which the augend can be identified. Even with sporadic augends,
however, there are no convincing counter-examples.

Up to now nothing has been said in regard to grouping, a process
which becomes relevant where there are more than two addends.

Generalizations 17 and 18, which relate to hierarchization and thus assume two addends, will be found to hold for each successive pair of constituents after grouping is carried out.

19. Whenever there are three or more summands and at least one is a product, parenthesization starts by separating the summand with the largest numerical value from the rest. The same rule then applies to the remainder, if it consists of more than two summands, and so on.

For example, in ENGLISH 3423 with the summands 3 x 1000, 4 x 100, 2 x 10, and 3, since at least one summand is a product, generalization 19 applies. Since 3000 is the largest numerical value, we first parenthesize (3 x 1000)+[(4 x 100) +(2 x 10) + 3]. We then parenthesize within the second member: (4 x 100)+[(2 x 10)+3]. Since the remainder has only two summands, the process is complete.

In every generative account of numerical systems I have seen, the phrase structure tree which results assumes a constituent structure which is in accordance with this generalization.

There are a number of empirical indications which support the preceding generalization and no strong counterevidence. a) Word order in languages like GERMAN which for numbers like 325 dreihundert-fünf-und-zwanzig [(3 x 100) +(5) +(2 x 10)] would require discontinuous constituents, were we to group the hundreds and tens as one constituent distinct from the digits. b) The absence of 'and' in ENGLISH between twenty and five in the corresponding expressions 'three hundred and twenty-five' tells in favor of (3 x 100) + [(2 x 10)+5] rather than [(3 x 100) +(2 x 10)]+ 5, since coordinating conjunctions generally join constituents. c) The existence of morphologically fused forms or unification in a single word by accent, for the lower values. As an example of the former we may note in HINDI that complex numerals lower than 100 are all single words whose morphological elements are so irregularly fused that morphemic analysis becomes difficult, whereas multiples of one hundred, one thousand, etc. are separate words. For example, 273 is dō sau ti-hattar 'two hundred seventy-three' in which we may compare ti with tin 'three,' and hattar with sattar 'seventy,' and sāt 'seven.' This supports a parenthesization {(2 x 100)+[(7 x10)+3]}. In ESTHONIAN multiples of 10 and 100 are written as single words united by the word accent whereas the thousands are written separately.

The proviso in generalization 19 that at least one of the sums
be a product was made for the following reason: there are instances
like WELSH dau ar bum-theg 'two on five-ten,' i.e. 2 + (5 +10),
which grouping clearly does not involve taking the largest value
first. The analysis of 17 here as 2 + (5 +10) is further supported,
since, in accordance with generalization 17, (5 + 10) is a serialized
augend. Thus, 16 is un ar bumtheg 'one on five-ten.' It is characteristic of expressions such as this involving three simple addends
that two of them always form a complex which is serialized. This
is expressed in the following generalization.

20. The maximum number of sporadic addends is two.

This principle may be further illustrated by the following example.
In KATO, an ATHABASKAN language of California, 9 is bun-naka-
naka 'five-two-two.' However, bun 'five' is a serialized augend,
as can be seen from 6 which is 'five-one' and 7 which is 'five-two.'
Hence the analysis of 9 here is 5 + (2 + 2). In fact 4 is naka-naka
'two-two.'

We now turn to hierarchization and grouping in multiplication.
The analysis will in general be parallel to that for addition, but
with some important differences. Corresponding to the augend in
addition is the multiplicand. Here also, there are instances in which
the semantics determines the hierarchization. Unlike addition,
overt expression of the operation of multiplication is relatively
infrequent, with most examples from North America. A clear type
of semantic determination is the use of an adverbial numeral, i.e.
a member of the series 'once,' 'twice,' etc., which is then obviously
the multiplier. For example, in CLASSICAL GREEK 2000 is dis-
khílioi 'twice-thousand' in which dis is the same as the numerical
adverb for 'twice.' This immediately suggests an analysis (2 x)1000,
i.e. 1000 taken twice, not, obviously, 2 taken a thousand times.
There are instances in which syntactic considerations play a rôle.
Whereas the chief extra-numerical model for addition, namely coordination, is, as we have seen, non-hierarchical, this does not
hold for the main syntactic models for multiplication, the numeral-
noun construction and the partitive. Thus, if in a language we find
30 expressed as 'three-ten(s),' we usually find a general syntactic
resemblance to construction such as 'three houses.' We shall see
later that, in particular, multiplicands are often treated like nouns
and multipliers like numerals or like noun modifiers in general.
Hence, it is reasonable to equate the multiplicand with the noun
and the multiplier with the adjective. In the partitive construction,
the multiplicand may be identified with the noun in the partitive as

in WOLOF 200 ɲar-i temer 'two-of hundred,' which is completely
parallel to ɲar-i nag 'two-of cow.'

As with addition, we have the independent criterion of serialization. If we find successive products of the form n x m and n x
(m +1), we say that n is the multiplicand by serialization and m,
m + 1 are multipliers. However, the definition of a serialized
augend is not completely parallel to that of a serialized multiplicand. One of the ways in which it differs is that we do not require
that n, m, m + 1, etc. in the above expression should always have
overt lexical expression. Consider, for example, SWAHILI in
which 2, 3, 4 are mbili, tatu and nne, respectively, whereas 20
is ishirini, 30 thelathini and 40 aroba'ini, with similar lack of
morphological relations between digits and tens up to and including
9 and 90. This is because the tens have been borrowed from ARA-
BIC. Still, we wish to say that ishirini is (2 x 10), thelathini (3 x 10),
etc., since, it would be generally agreed, we are dealing with a
decimal system. In other words, we allow a "portmanteau" analysis
here. Let us call expressions like 'twenty' and 'thirty' in ENGLISH
serialized products. To allow for instances like SWAHILI we say
that a serialized product may have simple morphemic expression.
On the other hand, as with the augend, the multiplicand itself may
have an arithmetically complex internal structure. For example,
in ADYGE, a NORTHWEST CAUCASIAN language, 40 is (2 x)(10 x 2),
60 is (3 x) (10 x 2), and 80 is (2 x) (10 x 4). We are evidently dealing
here with a vigesimal system in which the base 20 is expressed in
a mathematically complex way.

We need one more proviso, namely that every one of our serialized products should be a serialized augend or minuend also. Without this limitation, we could analyze ENGLISH 'four,' 'six,' 'eight'
as portmanteaus of (2 x 2), (2 x 3) and (2 x 4), respectively. But,
of course, they are not augends. We may recapitulate our somewhat
complicated definition of a serialized multiplicand as follows. A
serialized multiplicand is a number whose successive multiplication
by at least two other numbers results in serialized products which
are either expressed as simple lexemes or as a product of the multiplicand and multiplier, and such that each serialized product is also
a serialized augend or minuend.

Parallel to the earlier generalization 17 regarding augends, we
have one regarding multiplicands:

21. All adverbially or partitively expressed multiplicands are
    serialized multiplicands.

That is, in a case like that of CLASSICAL GREEK dis-khilioi 'twice
a thousand,' it will always be found that the adverbially expressed
multiplicand is also a serialized multiplicand. The situation is
similar in regard to partitive expressions.

Incidentally, in defining serialized multiplicand, we have also
defined the notion of base which up to now has been the sole method
of typologizing numeral systems. A serialized multiplicand is a
base. Since both multiplication and addition are involved in this
definition, a system without these operations cannot have a base.
There can be, however, and commonly is, more than one base, e.g.
10; 100; 1000; 1,000,000 in ENGLISH. The smallest base will be
called the fundamental base. If all the bases are powers of the
fundamental base, the system will be called "perfect." There are
only four numbers which figure as fundamental bases in perfect
numeral systems of the world in order of frequency: 10, 20, 4 and
12. Most systems with 20 as a fundamental base have 100 as the
next highest base rather than $400 = 20^2$.

   21. All the bases of a system are divisible by the fundamental
   base.

A violation of this produces a very complicated system. At least
two such systems do seem to exist, that of COAHUILTECO, a
HOKAN language, as reported in Swanton 1940, which has 3 and 20
as bases, and SORA, a MUNDA language, with 12 and 20 (Stampe
1977: 601).

The multiplicands which are not serialized multiplicands by the
above definition, and therefore not bases, fall into two types. There
are first those which fail because they are not augends, even though
they are multiplied by successive numbers. The multiplicand
here is usually two, and they can be called 'pairing systems.' As
far as I know, all examples are from North America. One example
is the WINTUN branch of California PENUTIAN. For example,
the Central WINTUN numerals from 1 to 10 can be analyzed as
follows 1, 2, 3, 4, 5, 2 x 3, 7, 2 x 4, 10 - 1, 10. Because of the
existence of the successive products 2 x 3 and 2 x 4, 2 is a multiplicand, but does not conform to the earlier definition of a serialized
multiplicand. We will call it a pseudo-base. It has a further characteristic, namely that the multiplicand is smaller than the multiplier, whereas generally the opposite holds, e.g. ENGLISH 'twenty'
which is (2 x) 10.

   22. A multiplicand in a pseudo-base is always smaller than its
   multiplier.

In a true base, this may also hold for individual numeral expressions. There are decimal systems, e.g. KERES (Kluge 1937-42: III.486) in which, for example, 120 is $[(10 + 2) x]10$. However, in such cases numbers smaller than the base are also multipliers. Hence we have the following implicational relation.

23. If a serialized multiplicand is a factor in some product in which the multiplier is larger than the multiplicand, it is also a factor in some product in which it is smaller than multiplicand.

The other case in which a multiplicand is not a base by the definition given here is that of sporadic products. For example, in BRETON, 18 is <u>trixwek</u> 'three six.' Neither 3 nor 6 are ever multiplied by any other number in the numeral system. We can posit that 3 is the multiplicand because BRETON has QN word order.

Parallel to generalization 20 about sporadic addends, we have the following:

24. The maximum number of sporadic factors is two.

Whenever three or more numbers are multiplied, it will always be found that all except one, the multiplier, form a complexly expressed serialized multiplicand, i.e. a base. For example, in HUASTEC 200, expressed as 2 x 5 x 20, 5 x 20 is a complex expression for 100 which is a base, as can be seen from 300 which is 3 x 5 x 20, etc. This, incidentally, gives us a grouping and hierarchization $[(2 x)(5 x 20)]$.

There is one other interesting fact about multiplication which has no parallel with addition. This is the rôle of the number 1 itself. Structurally, it parallels zero in addition, being what is called in mathematical group theory a 'unity,' i.e. just as $\underline{n + 0 = n}$ for any $\underline{n}$, so $\underline{n \times 1 = n}$ for any $\underline{n}$.

While 0 is, as we have seen, never expressed, 1 sometimes is. Since multiplication of any number by 1 is redundant, it is not usually expressed. However, 1 is always part of the numeral system, while 0 never is. Hence the possibility of its employment always arises. The following will be found to hold:

25. Only a base is ever multiplied by 1.

Thus, in ENGLISH one says either 'one hundred' or 'a hundred,' and similar expressions exist in many languages. It is not difficult to see why this is so. Bases which are often called units are in effect being counted, hence one starts with 'one.' The base is sometimes expressed by some ordinary noun in the language, e.g. 'road' in YUCHI. In some societies when large numbers are counted, the units are represented by stones or some other material object which themselves are counted. For example, Tönjes (1910: 62) in his grammar of OVAMBO, a SOUTHWESTERN BANTU language, notes: "If someone has the task of counting a herd of 37 oxen, one proceeds as described above and if asked regarding the total, he answers: 'ēngobe odi li omilongo nhatu nengobe nhano na mbali.' That is, these cows are three tens and seven cows." Similar facts are described in Araujo 1975 regarding the BASQUE counting of sheep. An interesting confirmation of the rôle of counting in the expression of 1 as a multiplier is the fact that in GUJARATI 100 is ek so 'one hundred' in counting, but simply so 'hundred' in context.

2.3 Order of elements in numerical expressions

The most important principle underlying the order of addends is that when in a language there are instances of both the larger addend preceding the smaller and of the smaller preceding the larger, the latter construction is found in the smaller numbers, and there is a definite number or a free variation interval at which the order shift takes place. The order is never reversed again for higher numbers.

For example, given in ITALIAN that 16 is expressed as (6 +) 10 se-dici in which the smaller precedes the larger, we will predict that all smaller numbers expressed by addition will have the same order, e.g. quindici (5 +)10, quattordici (4 +) 10, etc. Given that 17 is diciasette 10 (+7), we will predict that in all higher numbers expressed by addition, the larger will precede the former. For example, 18 is diciotto 10 (+8) and 23 is ventitre 20 (+3).

Sometimes there is a free variation interval in which either order occurs. For example, in WELSH, as described by Bowen and Rhys (1960), for numbers up to and including 59, the smaller precedes the larger. From 61 to 99 both orders occur, while over 100 the larger precedes the smaller. In view of generalization 18 which states that a serialized augend is always larger than its addend, the statements in this section could be as easily made regarding augends and addends.

Note that generalization 19 regarding the grouping of addends is logically prior to those of this section. In languages like GERMAN

in which a number like 243 is <u>zweihundert-drei-und-vierzig</u> with
the order 200, 3, 40, we can only say that the larger addend precedes the smaller in this expression because it has already been
parenthesized as $200 + (3 + 40)$.

In order to express the additional regularities regarding the
free variation interval, the earlier loosely expressed generalization is broken up into two as follows:

26. If in a language, in any sum the smaller addend precedes
    the larger, then the same order holds for all smaller num-
    bers expressed by addition.

27. If in a language, in any sum the larger addend precedes the
    smaller, then the same order holds for all larger numbers
    expressed by addition.

That these two generalizations are logically independent can be
shown from a logically possible but in fact nonexistent type of language which conforms to one and violates the other. Consider a
language in which the numerals 11-17 are analyzed as follows:
$1 + 10$, $2 + 10$, $3 + 10$, $4 + 10$, $5 + 10 \sim 10 + 5$, $6 + 10$, $10 + 7$. Such a language would conform to generalization 26 but violate 27.

It will be convenient to define the upper cut-off number for addition as the largest number with the order smaller-larger + 1, and
the lower cut-off number as the smallest number with the order
larger-smaller − 1. The free variation interval will consist of all
the numbers expressed by addition, which are at once less than or
equal to the upper cut-off number and greater than or equal to the
lower cut-off number.

For example, in ITALIAN where the upper cut-off number is 17
and the lower cut-off number is 16, the cut-off interval will be null.
In the WELSH example the upper cut-off number is 100, the lower
cut-off number is 60, and the free variation interval is 61-99.

It will then be a corollary deducible jointly from generalizations
26 and 27 that all numerals formed by addition in the free variation
interval are in free variation in regard to the order of their summands.[5]

---

[5] I have found just one exception to the generalizations about cut-
off numbers, namely TRUMAI, an Equatorial language (Steinen 1894:
542) in which 'three' is $(2 + 1)$ but 'six' through 'nine' and 'eleven'
through 'fourteen' are $(5 + 1)...(5 + 4)$ and $(10 + 1)...(10 + 4)$. The
highest numeral given is 'twenty.' However, the expression for
'one' in $(2 + 1)$ is suppletive.

Languages in which for all numerals formed by addition, the
larger precedes the smaller are extremely common. Those in
which the smaller always precedes the larger are extremely rare.
MALAGASY is an example. In CLASSICAL ARABIC it was possible for all numbers but in free variation with an order in which
only digits preceded tens. There is thus a world-wide favoring of
the order larger + smaller. In the history of both INDO-EUROPEAN
and SEMITIC, there has been a constant drift towards lowering both
the upper and lower cut-off numbers. For example, in LATIN the
lower and upper cut-off numbers were 20 and 100, while for SPAN-
ISH they are 15 and 16, respectively. It may be stated as an intra-
genetic diachronical universal that for any language in either family
at t_1 and t_2, where t_2 is later than t_1, both the upper and lower
cut-off at t_2 is less than or equal to the upper and lower cut-off
numbers at t_1.

There is evidently a cognitive principle involved in the favoring
of the order larger + smaller. If I express a large number, say
10,253 in the order 10,000; 200; 50; 3; the very first element gives
me a reasonably close approximation to the final result, and every
successive item gives a further approximation. The opposite order
leaves the hearer in the dark till the last item is reached. He may
not know even then, till a noun or an inflection on the last item of
a substantivized numeral informs him that the numeral construction
is closed. In light of this, we can see also why natural languages
do not adopt a place system with zero. Either the powers are in
ascending order with the attendant cognitive problem just described,
or they are in descending order, in which case the hearer has exactly the same problem, since an initial 6 may indicate 6,000 or
600,000 or 60, and this will not be known till the numeral expression is completed. In natural languages the existence of separate
lexical terms such as 'thousand' for powers of the base soon orients
the hearer.

28. If there are any numerals in which the expression of the
multiplier follows that of the multiplicand, the language is
one in which the numeral follows the noun.

It will be convenient in discussing ordering within a product,
since in most instances the multiplicand is a unit of the system, to
use the symbols M for multiplier and U for unit, and talk of MU
or UM order. Since, as we have seen, the most common syntactic
treatment of multiplication is to equate it with the QN (quantifier-
noun) construction, i.e. <u>three tens</u> like <u>three houses</u> and <u>tens three</u>
like <u>knives three</u> in most languages, the two orders harmonize, MU

with QN and UM with NQ. Where there are numeral classifiers,
it is the order numeral + classifier that is fundamental and conforms
to this generalization and not classifier phrase + noun (cf. Greenberg
1963). Wherever the above harmonization is broken, it is always
in favor of MU order which occurs in a number of instances with
NQ order, e.g. LHASA TIBETAN and MAORI. Thus, as noted
by Stampe, MU order is highly favored over UM in languages of
the world, being even stronger than the preference for QN order
in relation to NQ. The only example encountered of a language with
the disfavored order relationship both for addition and multiplication,
i.e. smaller before larger and UM is TIMUCUA, an extinct language of Florida (Pareja 1886). Even here, for numerals over
'twenty' the order larger before smaller prevails.

29. If the multiplier follows the multiplicand in a particular
    numeral, it follows in all higher numerals which are ex-
    pressed by multiplication. Where there is this variability
    in multiplicand-multiplier order, the language is always
    one in which the numeral follows the noun.

More frequently in NQ languages than the disharmonic relation
with MU permitted by generalization 28 is variability which always
takes the form described in the above generalization. The point at
which MU is replaced by UM might be called the cut-off point for
multiplication, analogous to that for addition described earlier.
Here also, there may be a free variation interval.[6]

MARGI, a CHADIC language of Nigeria which has a decimal
system, may serve as an example. The order with multiplier of
ten is 2 x 10, 3 x 10, etc., but for hundreds it is 100 x 2, 100 x 3,
etc. In this language the numeral follows the noun. Another example which shows that the cut-off point need not be one at which a
new base occurs is NANDI, a SOUTHERN NILOTIC language of
the NILO-SAHARAN stock. In this language we have 2 x 10, while
from 30 through 50 there is free variation, and from 60 on the order
is 10 x 6. Here again, the numeral follows the noun. In these and
other languages of this type, we have a diachronic process by which
starting with the highest units, a former MU construction is changing to UM to harmonize with QN order. The general principle

---

[6] Strictly speaking, because of the free variation interval, this
generalization as well as 35 and 46 should be split into two generalizations, as was done with the cut-off for addition stated in generalizations 26 and 27.

which underlies this and a number of other generalizations is that
the larger the number value of a numeral, the more it resembles
the noun in its syntax. In some instances it can be shown that
there has been a shift from QN to NQ, which precipitated a change
from MU to UM, starting with the highest numerals.   A detailed
discussion of this phenomenon is reserved for a separate publication since space limitations preclude a fuller treatment here.

30. A link for addition is never initial in a numeral.

31. If a link for addition is final, the language is postpositional.

32. If a link for addition occurs medially, it always goes with
     the following numeral in a prepositional language and with
     the preceding numeral in a postpositional language.

These three generalizations may be taken together. It was noted
earlier that addition in languages where there is overt expression
of this relationship is frequently 'comitative,' and is similar in its
syntax to nominal coordination. However, although probably all
languages have overtly expressed markers of coordination, many
languages simply juxtapose numerals without overt coordination,
e.g. TURKISH.

Where coordinators are found, their order properties are clearly
related to whether the language is prepositional or postpositional.
Of the two most common types of links, the superessive is itself
an adposition, while words for 'and' are the same as for 'with' in
many languages. The kinds of deletion, on the whole, parallel those
of coordinators in languages of the same adpositional type.

However, generalization 30 seems to transcend this relationship
in that initial links might be expected in prepositional languages,
and because we have initial coordinators in instances like LATIN
et...et... and ENGLISH 'both...and.'

The patterns commonly encountered where there is an extended
set of addends is shown in the table below, separately for prepositional and postpositional languages. A much more detailed investigation of noun and other coordinate constructions in relation to
numeral construction is required than was attempted for this study
and would probably yield further generalizations.[7]

---

[7] The patterns for the expression of coordinators could of course
be considered a kind of gapping, and the results of a fuller study
might be fruitfully considered in the light of recent work on this

Prepositional languages	Postpositional languages

Prepositional languages

1. W C-X C-Y C-Z
2. W   X   Y C-Z

Postpositional languages

1. W-C X-C Y-C Z
2. W-C X-C Y-C Z-C
3. W   X   Y   Z-C
4. W-C X   Y   Z

In the above table, W, X, Y, Z stand for numeral expressions and C indicates an overtly expressed coordinator. I have considered fused expressions to be single numeral expressions, e.g. fourteen in ENGLISH. Sometimes a coordinator is found in petrified form within a complex numeral, e.g. CLASSICAL GREEK 13 treiskaídeka, i.e. three-and-ten.

The importance of the adpositional factor is shown vividly by BEDAUYE, a NORTHERN CUSHITIC postpositional language which has borrowed wa 'and' from ARABIC, a prepositional language. Whereas in ARABIC prepositional pattern 1 is found for wa which is prefixed, e.g. CLASSICAL ARABIC 355 thalāthu mi'atin wa-xamsu wa-xamsūna 'three hundred and-five and-fifty,' in BEDAUYE we find variation between patterns 1 and 2 of the postpositional kind for the same element, e.g. 31 məhei taman-wa gal-(wa) 'three ten-and one(-and).'

33. When there is word order variation in addition between larger and smaller, and one order has an overt link and the other has not, it is always the order smaller +larger which has the link.

This is one further indication of the primacy of the order larger + smaller in addition.

The following are examples. In LATIN 21 was either ūnus et vīginti or vīginti ūnus (i.e. 'one and twenty' or 'twenty one'). In the later style of BIBLICAL HEBREW (e.g. Chronicles) the same variation existed. In ARAUCANIAN, an Andean language of South America, 11 is either mari quiñe 'ten, one' or quiña huente mari 'one on ten.'

34. If a link for subtraction is final, the language is postpositional.

(ftnt. 7 cont.)
phenomenon, e.g. Sanders 1976. As far as I know, however, all kinds of gapping considered up to now consider coordinations in which the deleted elements are always the non-coordinators, e.g. John likes fish and Mary meat.

This is, of course, analogous to generalization 32. Unlike addition, subtraction may have an initial link, e.g. earlier BIBLICAL
WELSH, as described by Hurford (1975). Subtraction is expressed
finally in SOMALI, a postpositional language, e.g. 19 <u>labaton mid-la</u>
'two-ten one-not.'

2.4 Some characteristics of bases

We have already had one generalization, no. 25, which refers
specifically to the bases of a numerical system and which states
that only a base is ever multiplied by 1. Further investigation of
multiplication by one indicates a further regularity.

> 35. If 1 is expressed as a multiplier with a particular base,
> it is expressed with all higher bases.

For example, in ENGLISH we do not say 'a ten' or 'one ten,' but
given that we do have 'a hundred' or 'one hundred,' we predict on
the basis of this generalization that we will have 'a thousand,' 'one
thousand.' There are many confirmatory instances. There may
be a free variation interval. For example, in MAORI for 10, 'one-
ten' is in free variation with 10, whereas for 100, it is stated to
be "generally required." One exception was encountered, ULITHI,
an AUSTRONESIAN language, in which 1 is expressed with 10,
100 and 1000 but not with 10,000 and 100,000.

> 36. The only numeral expressions deleted are those for 1 and
> for bases of the system.

In the discussion of generalization 11 regarding the overt expression of the operation of subraction, it was noted that 1 is often deleted as a subtrahend. In reference to generalization 25 and 35,
both of which refer to 1 as a multiplier with bases, one might
choose to regard its omission found in most languages, as involving
deletion.

Bases also are frequently deleted. An example was noted earlier
in the discussion of generalization 16, referring to division where
the example of ORIYA was cited, in which 100 is deleted in the expression of 275 as $(3 \times 100) - \frac{1}{4} *(100)$. The lowest base is often deleted in all its occurrences from $\underline{b+1}$ up to but not including $\underline{(2 \times) b}$.
This will only occur where there is an overt link for addition and
particularly when, as is often the case, this link is different from
that employed for higher numbers. This process is at present going
on in HAUSA in which 11 - 17 may be expressed according to the

model góomà šáà dáyá 'ten plus one' for simply šáà dáyá, with
the latter being increasingly favored. This does not apply to 18
and 19 because they are expressed by subtraction from 20. In such
cases, when the process of deletion is complete, the former link
will be reinterpreted as a suppletive variant of 10, thus involving
a drastic semantic change. Bases are also deleted as multiplicands,
particularly where the digits have number agreement with plural
multiplicands. An instance is EFIK, with a vigesimal system.
Here 20 is édíp, but 40 is àbà (2 x) *20, 60 is àtá (3 x) *20, etc.;
àbà is the plural of ìbà 'two,' àtá of ìtá 'three,' etc. In SIDAMO,
an EASTERN CUSHITIC language, 50 - 90 are the plurals of 5 - 9.
In the light of these examples, the SEMITIC expression of 30, 40,
etc. as the plurals of 3, 4, respectively, which has puzzled Semit-
ists, becomes clear. Originally, 20 was the dual of 10, but has
everywhere except in ETHIOPEAN SEMITIC, in analogy to the other
decades, become the plural of 10, whereas in ETHIOPIC the dual
was generalized from 20 to the remaining decades.

There are also examples of the deletion of bases where the
"going-on" relation occurs, e.g. ESTONIAN, in which for 11 - 19
we have expressions which can be interpreted as '1 of the second
*10,' etc.

2.5 Some general organizing principles of numerical systems

The preceding 36 generalizations obviously put powerful constraints on what constitutes a possible numeral system. Nevertheless, they fail to account for some very general regularities. For
example, given the complex mathematical structure and morphological irregularities of the expression of 72 as soixante douze,
i.e. 'sixty-twelve' with each component further susceptible of a
more complex analysis as (6 x 10) and (10 + 2), respectively, we
would be quite surprised if we found 372 in FRENCH was not trois
cents soixante douze but say *trois cents septante dix deux. Yet
this is not forbidden by any of the generalizations thus far. Many
conventional grammars describe the numeral system by a relatively
small series of translation equivalents, giving, for instance, just
one example of a complex numeral > 100 and < 1000 in a decimal
system and assuming that the reader will be able to form all the
others from this single example. This suggests that certain overall consistencies are being taken for granted.

37. If a numeral expression contains a complex constituent,
    then the numerical value of the complex constituent itself
    in isolation receives either simple lexical expression or

is expressed by the same function and in the same phonological shape, except for possible automatic phonological
alternations, stress shifts, or overt expressions of coordination. This principle will be called the principle of
incorporation.

This generalization, of course, presupposes an analysis into
immediate constituents on the basis of generalization 19. A complex constituent contains at least two numerals. The application
to the FRENCH example is as follows. In 372, to be analyzed as
$[(3 \text{ x}) 100][+((6 \text{ x}) 10)(+(10 (+2)))]$, $((6 \text{ x}) 10)(+(10 (+2))$ is a complex
constituent, since it contains four numerals. It has the value 72.
In FRENCH 72 is expressed exactly the same way as in 372.

There is a still stronger principle which holds for all numerals
above a particular base in systems which have more than one base.
Such a base may be called the base for predictable expression. Put
informally, there are no "surprises" in numerals larger than this
base. Thus, in FRENCH, we should be surprised when we get to
70 and find that it is expressed soixante-dix and not *septante
(which occurs in some forms of FRENCH). Above 100 there are no
such surprises except that we can never predict at what point a new
higher base will appear, or when we will reach L, the limit. Since
I have not found it possible to state this principle in a very simple
way, instead of stating it in its entirety, followed by explanations
and illustrations, it will be given in steps. Those statements which
are intended as part of the generalization are underlined.

38. In systems with more than one base, there is a base, the
    base for predictable explanation, above which in all num-
    erals certain regularities hold. Such numerals, when
    analyzed into their two principal constituents, will fall into
    two types, simple and complex. In the simple numeral
    we have a product, or rarely a quotient. In the complex
    numeral the two constituents are summands. An example
    of a simple numeral is 'five hundred,' of a complex num-
    eral is 'three hundred and forty-five.' By generalization
    19 concerning groupings in a sum, the principal constituents
    are 'three hundred' and 'forty-five.' In the simple consti-
    tuent the factors or elements in a division are expressed
    in the same way as when they occur in isolation. For exam-
    ple, in ENGLISH 'five hundred' conforms to this, but 'fifty'
    does not. Hence the base for predictable expression in
    ENGLISH cannot be 'ten.' Complex expressions fall into
    two parts, a product and a remainder. For example, in

ENGLISH 'three hundred and seventy-two,' 'three hundred' is a product and 'seventy-two' is a remainder. The remainder has the two following properties. It never has a larger value than the next lower base of the total expression. For example, in 'three hundred and seventy-two,' the remainder 'seventy-two' has a value 72, which is smaller than the next lower base of the total expression 'three hundred seventy,' i.e. 100. This does not hold for FRENCH soixante-douze in which the remainder 12 > 10. Finally, the remainder is expressed by the same mathematical function as when it occurs in isolation. For example, in 'three hundred and seventy-two,' the remainder 'seventy-two' is expressed in the same way as in the numeral expression for 72 in isolation both in its mathematical analysis and phonological expression. In RUSSIAN 140 sto sorok 'hundred forty' the remainder 40 is expressed in the same way as 40 in isolation. This is not required by the preceding generalization (37) and, along with other facts, shows that 100 is the base for predictable expression in RUSSIAN. In decimal systems the base for predictable expression is usually 100. In MANDARIN it is 10.

39. The degree of morphological fusion varies inversely with the size of the numerical value.

One of the overall characteristics which we observe in numerical systems is that in general the smaller the numeral, the more we encounter morphological irregularities. This is conformity with the marking hierarchy in that the larger the numerical value, the more marked, and morphological regularity is a property of marked expressions. This principle is consistent with the two preceding in that it also involves the notion that the greater the predictability in formation, the higher the numerical value.

The foregoing generalization has been stated quite vaguely. It could have been broken down into a whole series of implicational generalizations, e.g. if a product containing a particular base is a single word, so is every product containing a smaller base.

This hierarchy is often finely graded. The following are examples. In YAKUT, a TURKIC language, süürbe 'twenty' shows no resemblance to ikki 'two' and otut 'thirty' only a vague one to üs 'three.' Above 'thirty' all the tens are clearly the digits followed by uon 'ten,' but 'forty' and 'fifty' show sandhi phenomena not reflected in the orthography, i.e. tüörduon and biehuon (cf. tüört 'four,' bies 'five'),while above 50 there are no sandhi phenomena. In EFIK there are two links for addition, è and yè. The former is used up to 20. For 21 - 23, ye is in free variation with y- and > 24 only yè occurs. Many more examples could be cited.

2.6 The syntax of numerical expressions

A full-fledged study of the syntax of numeral systems which can on occasion reach heights of complexity (e.g. RUSSIAN, CLASSICAL ARABIC) would require a full-length study in itself. Here only a few of the more obvious regularities are pointed out. The syntax of numeral construction can be divided at least roughly into those of the internal syntax of complex numeral expressions and the external syntax of the numeral expressions as whole in the QN constructions. The following discussion is confined essentially to external syntax.

It is well known that in many languages with singular/plural distinction in the noun, e.g. TURKISH, the noun itself is in the singular with numerals designating numbers larger than 1. A more detailed study of this problem reveals certain further regularities.

40. In languages in which the expression of plurality is facultative in the noun, the singular may be used with numerals designating numbers >1.

In most instances the use of the singular is, in fact, compulsory. One of the characteristics of unmarked categories, in this case the singular, is that in many instances it stands for the category as a whole, and hence may be used with the plural, while the marked category of the plural is restricted to actual plurality. Whenever this holds, the cardinal numeral designating numbers > 1 are included in the situations in which a singular form of the noun may, or usually must be used.

41. In languages with singular/dual/plural systems in the noun, if the plural is used in any instances where a set of two objects is designated, the plural may be used with the numeral for 2.

This is the counterpart of 40 for systems with duals, in which the dual-plural distinction is neutralized and the relatively unmarked plural appears in the position of neutralization. The best known examples are INDO-EUROPEAN and SEMITIC. For example, in Homeric GREEK the plural is freely used where the dual might be expected and among these instances is that of constructions with dúō 'two.'

42. If numeral expressions for the smallest addends take the plural of the noun when they designate numbers >1, then complex numerals with 'one' as an addend will take the plural of the noun if 'one' is not a separate word.

For example, in ENGLISH 'two,' 'three,' etc. take the noun in the plural. So does 'eleven.' When 'one' is a separate word, the whole expression may (e.g. BANTU languages in general) or may not (e.g. ENGLISH 'twenty one') take the singular.

43. Where there is rule-governed variation between the use of the singular and plural with numerals, the use of the singular is favored with higher numbers, in measure construc- tions, in indefinite constructions, and with nouns which are inanimate or impersonal.

The following are some examples. In ERZA MORDVIN the plural is used after 2 - 10, the singular >10. In MODERN ARABIC dialects in general the same rule holds, but for 3 - 10 in some dialects rather than 2 - 10 because of the existence of a dual. For AMHARIC, Armbruster (1908) gives the following complex rule. For animate nouns after 2 - 99, either the singular or plural is used, over 99 the singular only. For inanimates the singular or plural is used with 2 - 9, whereas >9, the singular only is used. This evidently combines a preference for the singular both with higher numbers and inanimates. Trumpp in his grammar of PASHTO (1873) states that masculine animate nouns are in the plural with numerals >1, whereas for other nouns the singular may occur, although the plural is more usual. In TLAPPANEC, a HO- KAN language of Nicaragua, personal nouns are in the plural with numeral >1, impersonal in the singular only. In this case imper- sonal nouns do not have plurals. It is in fact clear that the rule with regard to numeral constructions is in accord with this ten- dency in nouns themselves. The following implicational universal probably holds here. Wherever a language has plural forms for any impersonal nouns, it has them for personal nouns, and simi- larly for inanimates and animates.

The other factors enumerated in generalization 43 can be illus- trated from the following examples. In AKKADIAN the singular of nouns is used with measure expressions while the plural is used with countables. In KANARESE either the singular or plural is

used with measures, the plural only with nonmeasures (cf. ENG-
LISH 'six foot tall,' etc.). In MODERN WESTERN ARMENIAN
the singular is used with indefinite numeral construction, the plural
with definite. The same rule holds for EWE, a NIGER-CONGO
language.

44. The order noun-numeral is favored in indefinite and approxi-
    mative constructions.

Variations in QN order is of two general types. In some languages either QN or NQ may occur with any numeral. The contrast of order may then have a semantic or syntactic function. In
the second type, certain numerals precede and others follow the
noun.

Illustrations of generalization 44 include the following. In BEN-
GALI when the classifier phrase follows the noun the construct is
definite, when it precedes it is indefinite. In certain ARABIC dialects, e.g PALESTINIAN and HASSANIYA of Mauretania, QN is
usual, but when NQ occurs, it is with the definite construction.
Similar facts hold for BANGGAIS and SAMOAN, both AUSTRONE-
SIAN languages, the former having classifiers. In TAMIL, NQ is
favored when the noun is definite. It is worth noting that sometimes
this order preference occurs in constructions of descriptive adjectives with nouns. For example, in BEDAUYE, AN order occurs
when the phrase is definite, NA when it is indefinite.

In RUSSIAN and in ZYRYAN, a FINNIC language, QN is the
usual order while NQ order is associated with an approximative
meaning. In BENGALI within the numeral classifier construction
Q-Cl is usual, but Cl-Q is approximative.

45. If a language has NG order in the possessive construction,
    it has QN order in the partitive construction.

We have seen the partitive is the second major type of construction in QN constructions, the other being adjective-noun. In most
languages with partitive constructions, it is assimilated to the
genitive construction of the noun in its possessive subtype. In such
cases NG generally goes with QN, i.e. 'house of the man' is like
'three of the oranges,' and GN with NQ. However, QN is favored
over NQ in that there are languages like LITHUANIAN in which,
while the genitive order is GN, the partitive has QN.

46. If there is variation in NQ order depending on the identity
    of the numeral, one of the two orders is used with a

continuous series of numbers beginning with 'one,' or 'one' and the bases of the system are used with one of the orders. If there is free variation with a particular numeral x, the next higher is also in free variation or is in the opposite order to that of x with the noun.

The reason for specification of bases in the system as an alternative is based on a very small number of instances like IGBO in which the order is NQ, except for 'one,' 'twenty' and 'four hundred.'

Diachronically viewed, I believe the generalization holds that it is the lowest and most unmarked numerals (sometimes 'one' alone) which show the earlier order. In regard to instances in which the numerals with the lowest values follow the nouns, some of the evidence has been discussed in Greenberg 1975. I believe this principle also holds when the lowest numbers precede the noun, and thus lead to the hypothesis that there has been a shift from QN to NQ with the lowest numerals as the survivers of the earlier order. In the discussion of generalization 29, it was noted that variation of MU order in which UM occurs with higher numerals is also evidence of a shift from QN to NQ. The case for both interpretations is strengthened by instances in which both of these infrequent phenomena occur in the same language, e.g. ADYGE and KABARDIAN, closely related NORTHWEST CAUCASIAN languages, and MASAI, an EASTERN NILOTIC language. In the case of MARGI which has MU-UM switch, some closely related languages of the BATA group have QN order for the lowest numerals.

47. If a language has both partitive and adjectival QN constructions, the smallest number which employs the partitive is larger than the largest number which has the adjectival construction.

In general there is a preference for the partitive with larger numbers. The following are a few representative examples. In some dialects of BERBER in Morocco (Laoust 1921), 'one' and 'two' are adjectives. Above 'two' all numerals are in a genitive-like construction with the noun and may have the genitive particle n. In RUMANIAN from 20 all numerals are followed by de 'of, from' with the substantive. WELSH has both constructions, but the partitive is preferred with higher numbers. In NEW EGYPTIAN the construction numeral + n 'of' +noun is used particularly with larger numbers. In LITHUANIAN 1 - 9 are adjectives, while with larger numbers the genitive plural is used. In RUSSIAN and some other SLAVIC languages, in the direct cases numbers larger than 'four' govern the genitive plural. This generalization is subject to the following limitation. In some languages in complex numbers the construction is determined by the smallest addend, particularly if it is adjacent to the noun. Thus, in RUSSIAN 'twenty-one' has the same construction as 'one.'

The preference of the partitive for higher numbers is in accordance with some other generalizations we have already encountered. The higher the number, the more likely it is to be treated as a noun, and the basic noun-noun construction is of the genitive type.

48. The construction with the interrogative 'how many?' is usually the same as that with the highest block of numerals.

For example, in ENGLISH 'how many?' governs the plural. In RUSSIAN <u>skol'ko</u> takes the genitive plural when the whole phrase is in a direct case. In AMHARIC, as we saw in the discussion of generalization 43, there is a complex rule which involves a preference for the singular of the noun with higher numerals. The singular is also found with the interrogative. A minor exception is CLASSICAL ARABIC. The interrogative <u>kam</u> governs the accusative singular like numerals 11 - 99, not the genitive singular like those larger than 99.

3. Cardinal Contextual Numerals and Other Numeral Series

The main section of this paper has been restricted to what may be considered the most unmarked series, namely, cardinal numerals as qualifiers of nouns. The overall uses of cardinal numerals may be classified as follows. We may first distinguish discourse uses from nondiscourse uses. The nondiscourse use is in counting which may in turn be divided into concrete and abstract counting. In the former specific items are involved, whereas in the latter the numerals are abstracted from such contexts as when we simply count 'one, two, three....' Such counting is done even in technologically simple societies. There are also sometimes guessing games in which numbers figure as such. The distinction between concrete and abstract counting is particularly clear in numeral classifier languages. If, for example, bananas are being counted, the appropriate classifier is used with each numeral. In abstract counting, the general classifier may be used or no classifier at all. There are a fair number of languages in which there are distinct counting and discourse forms. In such instances we may call the former absolute and the latter contextual. That the absolute forms are the marked category can be seen from the following generalizations.

49. Absolute forms of cardinal numbers may have overt markers added to the contextual forms, but not vice versa.

50. Where there are contrasting forms for the absolute and contextual uses of cardinal numerals, there is always neutralization for some numerals, in which case the contextual form appears.

51. The existence of a separate absolute form for a particular numerical value implies its existence for the next lower value.

The following are examples. In CHUVASH two sets of forms exist for 1 - 10, the absolute being longer, e.g. pĕr 'one' (contextual): pĕrre (absolute). Above ten, the longer form only occurs with the digits in complex numerals. In GÃ, a KWA language of the NIGER-CONGO family, eko is the contextual form for ekome, the absolute. The following exceptions have been noted. In MOROCCAN ARABIC from 11 -19 the contextual forms are longer, e.g. ḥdašel 'eleven' (contextual), ḥdaš 'eleven' (absolute). Another exception is HUNGARIAN két 'two' (contextual), kettő 'two' (absolute). Here the exception is not in the overt marking which is regular, but that in violation of generalization 51, there is no separate absolute form for 'one.' A similar exception exists in regard to the MANDARIN forms for 'two.'

52. Where the distinction between absolute and contextual cardinal numerals exists, the use of contextual form as a multiplier with a lower base implies its use with all higher bases.

For example, in MANDARIN there are two forms for 'two,' èr (absolute) and liǎng (contextual). Of these, èr is used as a multiplier of 'ten,' where liǎng is the usual but not exclusive form with 'hundred,' 'thousand' and 'tenthousand.' A similar relation exists in PALAUNG with ŭ 'one' (contextual) and hlɛh 'one' (absolute) in that ŭ is used with bases from 100 up. The use of the contextual form with bases is once more to be referred to the general principle that bases behave like substantives, and the larger their numerical value, the more substantive-like they are.

Within discourse, one may distinguish ordinary from arithmetical discourse. In the latter, so far as I can see, the absolute forms are used when a distinction of contextual and absolute exists. In non-arithmetical discourse, the main uses besides that as noun qualifiers are substantivized forms and predications. In the former a noun is deleted. This is a universal possibility in numeral classifier languages, in which case the classifier is always retained. In case languages, the numeral seems almost always to acquire a case marker if it did not already have it in the non-deleted form. In predication, if a separate absolute form exists, it is used. For more detailed discussion, reference may be made to Greenberg 1974, in which what is there called the A form corresponds to the contextual and the B form to the absolute.

The generally marked character of the ordinals and other numeral series in relation to the cardinals is discussed in Greenberg 1966. The chief phenomena to be noted are overt marking of ordinals in comparison to cardinals, the neutralization of the distinction for higher numbers with the cardinal form appearing in the position of neutralization, and the suppletive irregularities commonly found in the lowest ordinals, e.g. ENGLISH 'first,' 'second,' .... This latter may be stated implicationally in a form analogous to generalization 52. Other marked series include the adverbial ordinal 'the first time,' 'the second time,' and distributives 'one at a time,' 'one each.' These show relationships to the unmarked cardinals resembling that of the ordinal.

The basic generalization by which the discussion in the body of this paper confined to cardinal forms qualifying nouns becomes valid for all numeral series is the following.

53. All numeral series have the same mathematical structure.

A further distinction not mentioned above is that between specialized and generalized numerals, some languages have terms with meanings such as KHASI bhar '32 oranges.' It might be thought that these are exceptions. However, they merely behave like nouns to which the usual numeral system is applicable, as in ENGLISH 'one dozen,' 'two dozen,' etc.

4. Numeral Systems and Language Contact

It is a well-known phenomenon that higher numerals are more commonly borrowed than lower ones, usually in a sequence starting at a certain number. There are, however, occasional exceptions, e.g. SWAHILI which borrows the numerals for 6, 7 and 9 from ARABIC, but retains the BANTU term for 8. It is not, however, so much that the terms for numbers over a certain value are borrowed, but rather that the atoms of the source language are borrowed in this order. It will be recalled that by atoms are meant the lexically expressed numbers, and that these in turn can be divided into bases and non-bases. The following is an example. In TUPI indigenous numerals are found for 1 - 3 and PORTUGUESE terms for 4 - 20.[8] However, 21 is vinte mocoi cembyra 'twenty (Port.), one (Tupi), on-top (Tupi)' and so for all complex numerals over 20, with PORTUGUESE borrowing for the digits 4 - 9 only. An almost completely parallel case is that of KUI, a DRAVIDIAN language in which INDO-ARYAN numerals are borrowed from ORIYA for 3 - 20, while above 20 the odd numbers for 'one' and 'two' continue to be DRAVIDIAN. Thus, suppletion does not arise in these instances. We therefore have the following diachronic near-universal.

54. If an atomic numeral expression is borrowed from one language into another, all higher atomic expressions are borrowed.

In other instances of contact, the result is the replacement of an old system by a new one, with or without borrowing. An interesting example is that of a number of PLATEAU BENUE-CONGO languages in Nigeria with an earlier duodecimal system which is being replaced by a decimal system through the influence of HAUSA. The process is similar in all these languages. They had atomic expressions up to 12. It might be thought that the old expression for 11 and 12 would simply be eliminated and a decimal system constructed, either using the old word for 10 or borrowing its HAUSA equivalent. However, what happens is that the old word for the unit 'twelve' is reinterpreted as 10, and the old expressions for 10 and 11 eliminated. Similarly, the old word for $12^2 = 144$ is reinterpreted as 100, or in some languages the HAUSA word for 100 is borrowed.

This seems to show that for the speakers there is a certain psychological reality attached to the notion base. There are instances in which related or borrowed words for one base are used with the value of a different base. For example, in ADAMAWA FULANI, the HAUSA dubu 'thousand' is borrowed in the meaning 'million.' In northern East Africa there is a widespread root tam, tom, which sometimes means 10 and sometimes 20. An intricate history of

---

[8] "Atom" in this connection is meant in terms of the borrowing language in which fused forms analyzable in the source language may be treated as individual lexical items, e.g. PORTUGUESE 11 - 19 in TUPI.

successive replacements of decimal by vigesimal systems and vice-
versa can be largely reconstructed, but this is not discussed here.

A further indication of the psychological reality of the notion of
base as such is that in some languages terms for higher bases are
formed from that of a lower base by the addition of a qualifier meaning 'large' or the like. This is also an indication of the relatively
marked character of the higher bases. Examples include NAMA
HOTTENTOT in which 100 is 'large 10,' and YUCHI in which 100
is the word for 'road,' thousand is 'road large' and million is 'road
large old.'

Another interesting possibility is that a complex numeral expression of the older system is reinterpreted as a unit of the new system. An example is ABKHASIAN, a NORTHWESTERN CAUCASIAN
language in which an older decimal system is being replaced by a
vigesimal system. The expression for the first six decades are as
follows: 10, 2 x 10, 3 x 10, 2 x (2 x 10), 2 x (2 x 10) + 10, 3 x (2 x 10),
etc. Once more, we note the relative stability of the lower numerals, the vigesimal system having only penetrated down to 40.
Here and elsewhere in language contact, we see that the relative
marking hierarchy founded on the largeness of the numerical values
is as potent as in the internal structure of numerical systems. This
principle is also involved in generalization 54 in that the more
marked the number, the more likely that its numeral expression
will be borrowed. There is further confirmation of this principle
in that there are instances in which an irregular ordinal 'first' is
borrowed, while 'one' is not. In fact, I do not know of a single
instance in which the latter has occurred. It was also shown earlier that the absolute (counting) form is marked as against the contextual form. There is at least one example of borrowed numerals
being used in counting, while the indigenous ones are retained in
context. This is MALTO, a DRAVIDIAN language in which ARYAN
terms for 1, 2 are borrowed for counting, while the indigenous
terms are retained in contextual uses.

5. Numeral Systems and Cultural Evolution

There has recently been a revival of interest in the evolutionary
aspects of language, stimulated principally by the well-known work
of Berlin and Kay (1969) on color terminology. Cecil Brown has
discussed botanical and body-parts terminology from this point of
view (1976, n.d.) and recently, Webb (1977) has discussed the existence of a verb 'to have' in its possible connection with cultural
evolutionary factors. The study of numeral systems would seem

to have a special value from this point of view for two reasons.
Unlike the areas just mentioned, the existence of a connection is
not in dispute. Moreover, it is also clear what it consists of,
mainly but not exclusively, the size of L, the limit number. Yet
as far as I know, there has been no recent work on numeral systems
from this point of view. Here, only a few observations are offered.

The typological divisions between systems without bases and
those with at least one base has at least a gross correlation with
technological level. The building up of systems with more than
one base shows a variety of processes, as has been seen at various
points in the exposition. Higher bases are sometimes formed from
internal linguistic resources. The example of 100 as 'large 10'
has already been cited. Another internal method, that of multiplication, can be illustrated from KUTENAI in which yitwu is 10,
yitwunwu (*yitwuyitwu) is 100, yitwul-yitwunwu 1000 and yitwul-
yitwul 10,000. The external method of borrowing is, of course,
well-attested and certain terms for higher bases have a vast geo-
graphical spread, e.g. IRANIAN hazar for 'thousand.'

The process of building up of higher units is, however, subject
to much fluctuation. At a certain middle cultural level, say with
agriculture but without writing, the upper portions of the system
may be seldom used. One symptom is variability. Different informants give different versions often with differing upper limits.
The existence of such a penumbra of the system will also appear
in the variation from language to language within the same family
in that only lower numerals may be reconstructible, even though
each individual language may go well above these smaller numbers.
As in INDO-EUROPEAN and elsewhere there may be gaps in what
is reconstructible. For example, in BANTU 'ten' is easily reconstructible and in general the systems are decimal, but the numerals
6 - 9 are not, presumably because they are less frequent than the
base. There may be actual regression where a people changes its
mode of life through external circumstances. For example, the
BUSHMAN languages of South Africa usually have no numeral higher
than 3, yet at least 4 seems reconstructible for the larger stock,
KHOISAN, as a whole suggesting 'secondary primitivity.'

One final observation regarding this aspect of numeral systems
may be offered. Less "progressive" methods may for a time out-
perform more progressive ones. In parts of New Guinea gesture
methods based on body parts starting with the fingers of one hand
and then going up to wrist, elbow, etc., and around back to the
other hand provide a way of expressing numbers as high as 20 at

a point where the spoken language does not go beyond three or four. In regard to writing, something similar holds. In an interesting paper, Boyer (1944) distinguishes iterative methods of graphic symbolization from ciphering. The Roman numerals involve iteration in that 300, for example, is CCC. On the other hand, the Ionian system based on the GREEK alphabet in which α symbolized 1, β 2 etc. is a ciphering method. The Egyptian Hieroglyphic method and other ancient methods were iterative at a time when spoken language utilized the ciphering principle. It would seem that, as elsewhere in evolution, a new structure which is basically more progressive than an older one may not immediately realize its potential which requires a period of time for its unfolding.

BIBLIOGRAPHY

Amasoye, Boma I. 1972. The future of the Ijo language and its dialects. Vienna: Amasoye Private Printing Press.

Araujo, F. 1975. How the Basque count sheep. Anthropological Linguistics 17.4.

Armbruster, Carl Hubert. 1908. Initia Amharica. Cambridge University Press.

Berlin, Brent and Paul Kay. 1969. Color terms: their universality and evolution. Berkeley and Los Angeles: University of California Press.

Bowen, John T. and T.S. Rhys. 1960. Teach yourself Welsh. London: English Universities Press.

Boyer, C.B. 1944. Fundamental steps in the development of numeration. Isis 35.153-168.

Brown, Cecil H. 1976. General principles of human anatomical partonomy and speculations on the growth of partonomic nomenclature. American Ethnologist 3. 400-424.

_____. (n.d.) Folk botanical life forms: their universality and growth. Manuscript.

Conant, L.L. 1896. The number concept. New York: Macmillan.

Corstius Brandt, H. 1968. Grammars for number names. Dordrecht: D. Reidel.

Córdova, J. de. 1578. Arte del idioma zapoteca, ed. by Nicolas León (1886). Morelia.

Dixon, R.B. and A.L. Kroeber. Numeral systems of the languages of California. American Anthropologist 9. 663-690.

Douglas, W.H. 1958. An introduction to the Western Desert Language of Australia. Oceanic Linguistic Monograph 4. University of Sydney.

Drabbe, P. 1957. Spraakkunst van het Aghu-Dialect van de Awju-Taal. The Hague: Martinus Nijhoff.

Fettweis, E. 1927. Das Rechnen der Naturvölker. Berlin.

Frederieci, Georg. 1913. Wissenshaftliche Ergebnisse einer amtlichen Forschungsreise nach dem Bismark-Archipel im Jahre 1908. Mitteilungen aus den deutschen Schützgebieten, Ergänzungsheft 7. Berlin.

Greenberg, Joseph H. 1963. Some universals of grammar with particular reference to the order of meaningful elements. Universals of language, ed. by J.H. Greenberg, 58-90. Cambridge, Mass.: M.I.T. Press.

_____. 1966. Language universals. The Hague: Mouton.

_____. 1972. Numeral classifiers and substantival number problems in the genesis of a linguistic type. Working Papers on Language Universals [WPLU] 9. 1-39.

_____. 1974. Studies in numerical system I: double numeral system. WPLU 14. 75-89.

_____. 1975. Dynamic aspects of word order in the numeral classifier. Word order and word order change, ed. by Charles N. Li, 27-46. Austin and London: University of Texas Press.

Hurford, James R. 1975. The linguistic study of numerals. Cambridge: Cambridge University Press.

Kluge, Theodor. 1937-42. Die Zahlenbegriffe. Berlin.

Laoust, Emile. 1921. Cours de berbère marocain; grammaire, vocabulaire, textes. Dialectes du Sous, du Haut, et de l'Anti-Atlas. Paris: A. Challamel.

Lichtenstein, Heinrich. 1811-12. Reisen im südlichen Africa, in den Jahren 1803, 1804, 1806. Berlin: C. Salfield.

Love, J.R.B. 1933. An outline of Worora grammar. Studies in Australian linguistics, ed. by A.P. Elkin. Australian National Research Council, Science House, Sydney.

Menninger, Karl. 1969. Number words and number symbols. Cambridge, Mass.: M.I.T. Press.

Merrifield, William R. 1968. Number names in four languages of Mexico, in Brandt Corstius 1968: 91-102.

Pareja, Francisco de. 1886. Arte de la lengua Timuquana (original 1614). Bibliothèque Linguistique Américaine 11. Paris: Maisonneuve.

Peano, Giuseppe. 1908. Formulario mathematico. Turin: Bocca.

Pott, A. F. 1849. Die quinäre und vigesimale Zählmethode bei Völkern aller Weltteile. Halle.

Salzmann, Zdenek. 1950. A method for analyzing numerical systems. Word 6. 78-83.

Sanders, Gerald A. 1976. A functional typology of elliptical coordinations. Reproduced by the Indiana Linguistics Club.

Schmidt, Marianne. 1915. Zahl und Zählen in Afrika. Anthropologische Gesellschaft in Wien. Mitt. 45. 165-209.

Smeltzer, Donald. 1958. Man and number. New York, (2nd ed.).

Stampe, David. 1977. Cardinal number systems. S.S. Mufwene et al. ed., Papers from the Twelfth Regional Meeting, Chicago Linguistic Society, 594-609.

Swanton, John Reed. 1940. Linguistic material from the tribes of southern Texas and northeastern Mexico. Bureau of American Ethnology, Bulletin 127. Washington, D.C.

Steinen, Karl von den. 1894. Unter den Naturvölkern Zentral-Brasiliens. Berlin: D. Reimer. (2nd ed. 1899)

Szemerényi, Oswald. 1960. Studies in the Indo-European system of numerals. Heidelberg: Winter.

Thomas, C. 1897-8. Numeral systems of Mexico and Central America. Nineteenth Annual Report, Bureau of American Ethnology, part 2, 853-956. Washington, D.C.

Tönjes, Hermann. 1910. Lehrbuch der Ovambo-Sprache Osikuanjama. Berlin: D. Reimer.

Trumpp, Ernest. 1873. Grammar of the Pašto, or language of the Afghans. London: Truebner.

Tryon, D.T. 1974. Daly Family languages, Australia. Canberra: The Australian National University.

Webb, Karen. 1977. An evolutionary aspect of social structure and a verb "to have." American Anthropologist 79. 42-49.

Wilder, Raymond Louis. 1953. The evolution of mathematics.

Reduplicative Constructions

EDITH A. MORAVCSIK

ABSTRACT

The paper is a study of the form properties, of the meaning
properties, and of the intralingual and interlingual distribution of
reduplicative constructions. Some generalizations that have proved
to be exceptionless within a limited cross-linguistic sample are
proposed as tentative language universals. An attempt is made to
relate some of these generalizations to other facts about languages
outside the domain of reduplication.

This paper was written as part of my work for the Stanford
Project on Language Universals. I am grateful for comments that
I received on a preliminary oral presentation from Charles Ferguson,
Joseph Greenberg, Joan Kahr and Merritt Ruhlen; and for the in-
formation on reduplication in MANDARIN to Sandra Thompson.

CONTENTS

1. Introduction

A language is a means whereby meanings can be expressed and understood. It follows, therefore, that a language has to provide for the differential expression of different meanings: at least some of the meaning distinctions have to be matched by distinctions in the form of utterances. Given the class of natural human languages, and given in particular the special medium of expression employed in such systems, which is orally and nasally produced sounds, there are two logically possible elementary ways in which linguistic forms can differ from each other: quantitatively and qualitatively. Qualitative differences may stem either from differences in sound properties or from differences in the temporal relations of sound properties. Thus, for example, the two sound strings pa and ba differ from each other in some of the sound properties that are involved in their pronunciations; the two sound strings pa and ap, however, do not differ in this manner, since all sound properties involved in the pronunciation of one of them are also involved in the pronunciation of the other; they are nonetheless distinct by token of the differential temporal precedence relation that the simultaneous property clusters p and a bear to each other. Quantitative differences, on the other hand, pertain to the duration of the production and perception of a sound property. Thus, the two sound forms ab and abb differ neither in their sound properties nor in the temporal relations of their sound properties: their distinctness stems from the fact that the bb of abb has a duration that extends over a larger number of time units than the duration of the b of ab, whether due to prolonged articulation or to repeated articulation.[1]

This paper is a study of the ways natural human languages utilize one of these two basic types of sound differences that are available for the differentiation of different meanings in language: quantity. Its more specific purpose is to contribute to the eventual explanation of the role of quantitative sound differences in linguistic expression by contributing to the definition of those two sets whose

---

[1] There is one particular kind of distinctness of sounds whose classification within the present scheme is unclear to me. This is the kind resulting from differential intensities of articulation, such as "tenseness" or "stress." Depending on the actual physical correlates of such intensity differences, they may involve either quality only, or quantity only, or both quality and quantity; but it will certainly not be the case that they involve neither and thus fall outside the present scheme.

particular inclusion relation is the basic explanandum. These two
sets are the set of ways in which quantitative form differentiation
could in principle be used in natural human languages in the expression of meanings; and the set of ways in which quantitative
form differentiation is so used.[2] A more precise delimitation of
the subject matter of the paper is possible by the following definition of those utterance sets that will be investigated:

> Utterance 1:   ...A... = ...X...
> Utterance 2:   ...B... = ...Y...,

where A and B are non-null interpretable semantic representations
that have some elements in common, X and Y are non-null syntactic, phonological, or phonetic representations, the equation sign
stands for symbolic equivalence; and where Y either properly or
improperly includes all of X, and a proper or improper part of X
repeated n times, but B does not include a matching reduplication
of A. The only additional a priori restriction that will be assumed
is that such utterance pairs will fall within the scope of this study
only if a particular meaning distinction thus paired off with a quantitative form difference in one utterance pair is also paired off with
the same quantitative form difference in another utterance pair of
the same language. I take this schema to semi-formally define the
familiar linguistic concept of reduplication, with a reduplicative
construction being what is represented above as Utterance 2.[3]

Reduplicative constructions thus delimited may be exemplified
by any of the following (where the sound form of the reduplicative
construction is underlined):

---

[2] For a parallel discussion of that subclass of qualitative sound
differences that consists in the differential temporal relations of
identical sound properties, see Moravcsik, forthcoming. For a
survey of the possible qualitative sound differences in language
stemming from different articulatory movements, see Catford 1968.

[3] The terms "reduplication" and "reduplicative construction"
are of course infelicitous, since they make vague reference to
there being only two copies of the same thing in the construction
in question. A more properly suggestive term would be "reiteration," or "repetitive construction." Since, however, the term
"reduplication" is widely used and the other two are not, I will
continue to use the former.

a. ENGLISH: He is <u>very very</u> bright.

b. MOKILESE: ...<u>roarroarroar</u>...
                     'to continue to shudder' (Harrison 1973: 426)

c. SAMOAN: <u>mamate</u> 'They die.'   (Pratt 1862)

d. SUNDANESE: ...<u>sakalikali</u>...
                     'not even once'   (Robins 1959: 363)

In the ENGLISH example, emphasis is paired off with the simple
repetition of a modifier; compare the form and meaning difference
between a. and <u>He is very bright</u>. That the sound-meaning correspondence is recurrent in the language is shown by additional
examples such as <u>He is an old old man</u> versus <u>He is an old man</u>.
In the MOKILESE example, continued action is expressed by the
triplication of the verb; compare <u>roar</u> 'to shudder.' The intralingual recurrence of the sound-meaning correspondence is indicated by the existence of additional examples, such as <u>rikrikrik</u>
<u>sakai</u> 'to continue to gather stones' versus <u>rik sakai</u> 'to gather
stones.' In the SAMOAN example, repetition of the penultimate
syllable of the verb is correlated with the plurality of the subject;
compare <u>mate</u> 'he dies.' Another example is <u>taooto</u> 'they lie,'
versus <u>taoto</u> 'he lies.' In the SUNDANESE example, the meaning
'not even one X' is associated with the repetition of X and the
p refixation of <u>sa</u> to X, which is <u>kali</u> 'time' here; compare also
<u>sahǒlayhǒlay</u> 'not even one mat' versus <u>hǒlay</u> 'mat.' Some ex-
amples of what may at first appear to be reduplicative constructions
but that are excluded by our definition from this class of linguistic
objects are words such as <u>papa</u> 'father' and <u>ásás</u> 'digging' in
HUNGARIAN. <u>Papa</u> 'father' is not a reduplicative construction
since there is no meaningful form <u>pa</u> in the language; and <u>ásás</u>
is not a reduplicative construction since — even though there is a
form <u>ás</u> in the language to mean, among others, 'dig$_v$' — nominalization is not recurrently paired off with the reduplication of
the verb; compare, for instance, <u>áll</u> 'stand$_v$,' <u>állás</u> 'standing,'
*<u>állńll</u> 'standing.'[4]

---

[4] Two other classes of constructions characterized here as non-
reduplicative by our definition may be pointed out. One is the class
of onomatopoeic expressions — i.e. expressions that describe sus-
tained sounds that are not linguistically interpretable — which in
many languages do include repetitions of sound sequences; compare

Given now a precise definition of the utterance sets that we will be concerned with, and given the general rationale of the study of such utterance sets, I will turn to the consideration of the specific questions that have to be asked and answered about reduplicative constructions. All such questions appear to me to pertain either to the particular form properties of reduplicative constructions, to the particular meaning properties of such constructions, and to the conditions that determine the distribution of such constructions within and across languages. More specifically, we want to know the following:

1. Given the total set of utterance pairs in natural human languages that fit the schema above, which of the various form-related sub-patterns that are within the bounds of the definition actually occur and which do not? In other words, exactly what occurs reduplicated; how many times; how are the reduplicated copies ordered; and is the meaning difference correlated with reduplication by itself or is there also some additional form difference?

2. Given, again, the total set of utterance pairs in natural human languages that fit our definition, what are the particular semantic properties of reduplicative constructions? In other words, are there any generalizations to be made about the particular meaning distinctions that are conveyed by quantitative form differences and

---

(ftnt. 4 cont.)
ANCIENT GREEK barbaros 'foreign-speaking,' HUNGARIAN kakukk '(sound of the cockoo,' TZELTAL cinucinucin '(sound of guitar being strummed)' (Berlin 1963: 215f); see cross-linguistic data in Emeneau 1969 and relevant data for ENGLISH in Thun 1963. Such constructions do not qualify as reduplicative unless the unreduplicated form is meaningless, which is not the case for the great majority of its instances. The other class involves repeated mention of the same referent either as having different functions with respect to the same action (such as in John hit himself), or as having the same or different functions with respect to distinct events (such as in John came home and he had dinner). These are excluded as reduplicative constructions by the criterion that form-repetitions not be matched by meaning repetition in the interpretable meaning representation of the utterance. Whereas this present study is concerned with which (non-repetitive) meaning structures have repetitive forms in language and what kinds, the study of these constructions pertains to the question of how the repetitiveness of meaning is preserved, or not preserved, in the corresponding linguistic form. All studies of identity deletion belong here.

by its particular subtypes, as opposed to those that are never conveyed by quantitative differences or never by some particular subtype of them ?

3. Given now that we have determined the particular form patterns and meaning patterns that cross-linguistically characterize reduplicative constructions, what does it depend on whether a particular utterance includes a reduplicative construction? In other words, given that a language has reduplicative constructions, when exactly are these used, and which are the languages that have reduplicative constructions and particular subtypes of them in the first place?

With respect to each of these questions, the purpose is to precisely define both the total range of logically possible answers and also the total range of actually true ones; since it is the particular difference between these two sets of answers that we ultimately want to explain.

In the main part of the paper which now follows, I will take up these three questions in turn, attempt to outline the total range of logical possibilities in each case, and try to make generalizations about the actually occurring subsets of these. In the closing part, I will summarize the explananda that thus will have emerged and will briefly consider avenues of explanations for some of them.

2. Reduplicative Constructions

2.1 Form properties

Although the definition of reduplicative constructions adopted above does exclude a large number of linguistic constructions from this class, it nonetheless admits of considerable form variation within it. The number of reduplicative construction types that is defined is in fact infinite. The range of form variation permitted can be conveniently characterized in terms of four major parameters: the properties of the constituent that is reduplicated; the number of times it is reduplicated; the presence or absence of additional non-repetitive form differentiation; and the temporal relations that the copy or copies assume in relation to each other and the rest of the utterance. The logical possibilities available for each of these four parameters can be informally surveyed as follows.

A. Properties of the reduplicated object   Constituents to be reduplicated may in principle be definable either monomodally or

bimodally. Thus, they may be definable either by their meaning
properties only, or by their sound properties only, or in reference
to both. They may, in other words, be either semantic-syntactic
constituents, such as one or more semantic-syntactic features,
or morphemes, or words, or phrases, or sentences, or discourses;
or they may be phonetic-phonological terms, such as one or more
phonetic-phonological features, or segments, or syllables; or they
may be morphemes of a particular phonetic shape, or sentences of
a particular number of phonetic segments; etc. The quantitative
form differences associated with a particular meaning distinction
may involve repetition of one semantic-syntactic constituent, or
that of more than one semantic-syntactic constituent that may stand
in various grouping relations to each other, and it may involve
repetition of one single phonetic-phonological constituent or that
of more than one string. Reiteration may be either total or partial:
it is total if it involves the repetition of the whole semantic-syntactic
or of the whole phonetic-phonological string whose meaning is correspondingly changed; and it is partial if it involves the reiteration
of only part of the semantic-syntactic or phonetic-phonological constituent whose meaning is accordingly modified. Partial reduplicative constructions fall into further logically possible subtypes,
depending on how the particular subpart to be reduplicated is defined. Thus, given that it is a semantic-syntactic part, it may be
a head, or a non-head, or the first constituent, or the last, or
always an adjective; etc. If it is a phonetic-phonological part, it
may be the first or the second or the third or the middle or the
penultimate or the last part of the string, if it is defined by absolute linear position at all; or it may be distinguished by phonetic
properties such as, for example, it being the vowel(s) of the string,
or the stressed syllable of the string, or the first or only voiceless
labial plosive contained in the string.

B. How many times is the object in question reduplicated There
is nothing in the concept of language tacitly assumed here that would
put a bound on the number of times a constituent could be reduplicated. The possibilities are thus: one repetition, two repetitions,
three repetitions, 60 repetitions, 134 repetitions — up to infinity.

C. Additional non-iterative form differentiation A particular
meaning difference may be signalled either by total or partial repetition only, or by the modification of (i.e. (non-repetitive) addition to, or deletion of, or substitution of) some other part of the
utterance as well.

D. Temporal relations of the copies to each other and to the rest
of the utterance Given any one copy and its temporal relation to

other copies and to the rest of the utterance, all the logically possible temporal relations that any event can bear to any other are
logically available, such as simultaneity, immediate precedence,
non-immediate precedence, overlap, inclusion, and interlocking.

Consideration of actual instances of reduplicative constructions
in various languages suggests that there may indeed be limits on
the actually manifested form variability of reduplicative constructions in natural human languages. In what follows, I will propose
some statements stipulating such constraints that I see as consistent with all facts known to me, and I will exemplify each.

A'. Properties of the reduplicated object   Of the six basic
logically possible types defined by the mode of the constituent and
by the extent of reduplication, two occur in my sample and four
do not. The two that are manifested are the two bimodal types;
none of the four monomodal ones are. What is excluded, therefore, is a reduplicative construction which involves the reduplication of a syntactic constituent regardless of its form (i. e. total or
partial syntactic reduplication), or which involves the reduplication
of a phonetic string regardless of its meaning (i. e. total or partial
phonological reduplication). What is claimed is that in reduplication reference is always made both to the meaning and to the sound
form of the constituent to be reduplicated. It is also true, however,
that bimodal reference is always of a very restricted kind; in particular, the constituent whose meaning is to be altered by the process of reduplication always has to be characterized in terms of
specific semantic-syntactic constants, and possible reference to
phonetic-phonological properties is restricted to lexical identity,
syllable number and/or properties of consonantality and vowelhood. In what follows, I will exemplify the two occurring types
and demonstrate the constraints on bimodal reference just mentioned.

Total bimodal reduplication is exemplifiable from EWE, or LA-
TIN, or MANDARIN.

EWE: asíasíi 'hand by hand' (así 'hand') (Ansre 1963)
LATIN: quisquis 'whoever' (quis 'who?') (Coyaud & Hamou 1971)
MANDARIN: jangjang 'every sheet' (jang 'sheet') (Chao 1968: 202)

What makes the EWE and LATIN examples bimodal is that repetition must involve not only a morpheme of the same meaning but
also one of the same lexical form; if EWE also had another morpheme meaning 'hand' which has a form distinct from así, that,
I infer, could not serve as the reduplicated counterpart of así in
the double sequence; and if LATIN had a hetermorphous synonym

for <u>quis</u>, that similarly could not form a reduplicative construction
with <u>quis</u>.   Reference to phonetic form is present, therefore, but
it is restricted to stipulation of phonological identity of lexical
forms.   The same lexical identity constraint also holds in MAN-
DARIN but there additional and more specific reference is also
made to phonological form: according to Chao (1968: 203), total
reduplication of measure terms is restricted to those measure
terms that satisfy the phonological condition of monosyllabicity.
The form <u>jialuen</u> 'gallon,' for instance, cannot be reduplicated
since it is not monosyllabic; the concept 'every gallon' is expressed as <u>meei-jialuen</u>.   I noted similar syllable number constraints
(always involving a differentiation between mono- versus multi-
syllabic constituents) in ROTUMAN (Churchward 1940: 103), and,
possibly, in WASHO (Winter 1970: 196).

There are some cases where what appears to be a distinction
between total and partial reduplication is actually a distinction between forms of different length whose reduplication, however, is
governed by the same principle.   Thus, in MARSHALLESE (cp.
Bender 1969: 38, 1971: 453), the principle according to which the
last CVC sequence of a stem is reduplicated generates both instances of partial reduplication for bisyllabic words (e.g. <u>takin</u>
'socks,' <u>takinkin</u> 'wear socks;' <u>kagir</u> 'belt,' <u>kagirgir</u> 'wear a belt')
and instances of total reduplication for monosyllabic words (e.g.
<u>wah</u> 'canoe,' <u>wahwah</u> 'go by canoe;' <u>wit</u> 'flower,' <u>witwit</u> 'wear a
flower').

Partial bimodal reduplication involves the repetition of a syntactic constituent or phonetic string which is only part of the constituent whose meaning is accordingly modified; such that the
specification of the process requires reference both to semantic-
syntactic and to phonetic-phonological properties.   One subtype
of this pattern involves reduplicating a constituent that is specified
in terms of specific semantic-syntactic constants and by variable
reference to phonological form necessitated by the above-mentioned
lexical identity condition.   This interesting pattern can be exemplified by the following:

HUNGARIAN:
(verb prefix reduplicated for modification of verb meaning)
<u>elelmegy</u>   "away-away-goes" 'He occasionally goes there.'
(<u>elmegy</u> "away-goes" 'He goes there.')
<u>belebelenéz</u>   "into-into-looks"   'He occasionally looks into it.'
(<u>belenéz</u> "into-looks" 'He looks into it.') (cp. Tauli 1966: 182)

YORUBA:
(adjective reduplicated to unambiguously pluralized noun phrase)
à ̣à burúkú burúkú "custom   bad bad" 'bad customs'
(à ̣à burúkú "custom bad" 'a bad custom / bad customs')
(Bamgbo ̣e 1966:113)

TZELTAL:
(numeral reduplicated for distributive noun phrase meaning)
ʔoš ʔoš pešu "three-three peso" 'pesos, three after three after three'
(ʔoš pešu "three pesos" 'three pesos' (?))
lahlahuneb' pešu "ten-ten-eb' peso" 'pesos, ten after ten after ten'
(Berlin 1963: 213f)

DYIRBAL:
(either constituent of a compound noun phrase reduplicated for
pluralizing the compound noun phrase itself)
midibaḍunbaḍun   "small-very-very" ⎫
midimidibaḍun   "small-small-very" ⎬ 'lots of very small ones'
(midibaḍun "small-very" 'very small one' (?))
yanagabungabun   "man-another-another" ⎫ 'lots of other men/
yanayanagabun   "man-man-another"   ⎬ strangers'
(yanagabun "man-other" 'other man (?))
(Dixon 1972: 242)

Compare also ROTUMAN (Churchward 1940: 103).

Another subtype of partial bimodal reduplication involves reduplicating a phonetic string that is a proper part of the phonetic
string whose meaning is effected by the reduplication, such that
reference is made to the particular meaning and the process is
subject to the lexical identity condition. There are various further
subtypes of this pattern depending on how the phonetic string to be
reduplicated is defined. As mentioned above, my data permit a
very restrictive generalization in this respect. In particular,
whereas the relevant string could in principle be defined by any
phonetic property (segmental or suprasegmental) or in terms of
absolute linear position, or in terms of simply the number of adjacent segments involved; and it could also be left undefined (i.e.
"reduplicate any one or more segments in the total string"), reduplicated phonetic strings I found invariably defined in reference
to consonant-vowel sequences and absolute linear position. In other
words, all such specifications are of the type: "reduplicate the
first C and V of the word" or "reduplicate the middle C" and never
of the type: "reduplicate the first two segments (regardless of

whether they are consonants or vowels" or "reduplicate the second
voiced fricative." I will now exemplify this subtype and its vari-
ties.

1. Initial reduplication

    a. C -: MARSHALLESE:
       ļļiw 'angry' (ļiw 'scold') (Bender 1971: 452; cp. also
       Harrison 1973: 443ff for this type in other MICRONESIAN
       languages)

    b. V -: QUILEUTE:
       á'á't'cit 'chiefs' (á't'cit 'chief')
       é'ela·'xali 'I leave him often' (éla·'xali 'I left him')
                                    (Andrade 1933:187)

       SHILH:
       ggen 'to be sleeping' (gen 'to sleep') (Sapir 1949: 78)

    c. CV -: PAPAGO:
       kuukuna 'husbands' (kuna 'husband')
       paapaga 'holes' (paga 'hole')   (Langacker 1972: 266f)

       QUILEUTE:
       cici·p·hókwat' 'negroes' (ci·phókwat' 'negro' (?))
       qaqa·x 'bones' (qa·x 'bone')   (Andrade 1933:189)

    d. CVC -: TURKISH:
       dopdolu 'quite full' (dolu 'full')
       bembeyaz 'quite white' (beyaz 'white') (Godel 1945: 6)

       AZTEC:
       womwoman 'he is barking at' (woman 'bark at') (Key 1965)

    e. CVCV -: FOX:
       wa:pawa:pamɛ:wa 'he keeps looking at him'
       (wa:pamɛ:wa 'he looks at him')   (Bloomfield 1933: 218)

       DYIRBAL:
       banibaniɲu "come-come-unmarked: tense"
               'come more than appropriate'
       (baniɲu "come-unmarked: tense" 'come')
       miyamiyandaɲu "laugh-laugh-unmarked:tense"
                'laugh more than is appropriate'
       (miyandaɲu "laugh-unmarked:tense" 'laugh')
                           (Dixon 1972: 251)

2. Final reduplication

   a. -C: CHINANTECO:
   <u>hmmm?</u> $^{2-4}$ 'your$_{pl}$ blood' (<u>hm?m</u>^{4} 'your$_s$ blood')
   (Key 1965: 94)

   b. -CV: HOPI:
   <u>?ewíwita</u> 'flickering flames occur' (<u>?ewi</u> 'a flame occurs')
   (Key 1965: 91)

   HAUSA:
   <u>sunanaki</u> 'names' (<u>suna</u> 'name')   (Sapir 1949: 78)

   c. -VC: TZELTAL:
   <u>-nititan</u> 'push it rapidly in a curvy, crooked path'
   (<u>-nit</u> 'push it')   (Berlin 1963)

   d. -CVC: MOKILESE:
   <u>pwirejrej</u> 'be dirty' (<u>pwirej</u> 'dirt/soil') (Harrison 1973: 417)

   MARSHALLESE:
   <u>jiwijwij</u> 'wear shoes' (<u>jiwij</u> 'shoes')   (Bender 1971)

   e. -CVCV: SIRIONO:
   <u>erasirasi</u> 'he continues being sick' (<u>erasi</u> 'he is sick')
   (Key 1965: 91)

3. Internal reduplication

   a. -C-: SYRIAN ARABIC:
   <u>ra??as</u> 'make someone dance' (<u>ra?as</u> 'dance$_v$')
   <u>?arra</u> 'have someone read' (<u>?ara</u> 'read')
   (Cowell 1964: 240ff, 253ff)
   (On internal consonant reduplication in various AFRO-
   ASIATIC languages, cp. Greenberg 1952, 1955.)

   b. -V-: QUILEUTE:
   <u>bí'i'b·a'à·</u> 'blind men' (<u>bi'b·a'à·</u> 'blind man')

   COEUR D'ALENE:
   <u>lu?up</u> 'it became dry' (<u>lup</u> 'dry')
   <u>na?as</u> 'it became wet' (<u>nas</u> 'wet')   (Reichard 1959: 243)

   (Also, possibly, in NUER; cp. Crazzolara 1933: 9.)

c. -CV-: SAMOAN:
alolofa 'they love' (alofa 'he loves') (Pratt 1862)

(Also, possibly, in QUILEUTE (Andrade 1933) and in
AZTEC (Key 1965: 94).)

The most obvious gaps here are: initial VC reduplication,
internal VC, CVC and CVCV reduplication, any reduplication
pattern that involves more than one adjacent consonant or vowel
in the unreduplicated form,[5] and any reduplicated partial string
that involves more than two vowels.

There are also examples of partial reduplication where the
phonetic strings to be reduplicated are discontinuous. Compare
the following examples from MARSHALLESE (Bender 1971: 453):

ka-rriwwew   'distribute by two-s'   (riwew 'two')
ka-jjilliw   'distribute by three-s' (jiliw 'three')
yekkilablab leyen "he-club:distributive man-that" 'He's always
                      at the club.' (kilab 'club/go drink at a club')
kkarjinjin   'kerosene:distributive' (karjin 'kerosene')

The question arises, of course, whether substrings to be redup-
lixated must be defined in terms of sequences of consonants and
vowels. Two alternatives come to mind: substrings may be definable in terms of number of segments regardless of their consonantality and vowelhood; and substrings may be defined in terms
of number of syllables, rather than number of segments. The
number-of-segments hypothesis is easily refutable. It if were
true, this would mean that in a language where the first CV of
consonant-initial stems is reduplicated, in vowel-initial stems the
first VC should be reduplicated. I have seen no language of this
kind; I found it uniformly true, on the other hand, that if the first
CV of consonant-initial stems is reduplicated, then in vowel-initial
stems the initial vowel by itself will be. Compare, for instance,
AZTEC:

se   'one'   sehse   'ones / one by one'
makwil   'five'   mahmakwil 'fives / five by five'
ome   'two'   ohome   'twos / two by two'
eyi   'three' eheyi   'threes / three by three'
                              (Elson and Pickett 1965: 46)

---

[5] Cluster simplification occurs, for instance, in EWE: compare
zɔ 'walk,' zɔzɔ 'walking;' gbla 'exert himself,' gbagbla 'exerting himself' (where gb is one segment); bia 'ask,' babia 'asking' (Ansre 1963).

Similarly, in AGTA the first CVC of consonant-initial stems is reduplicated; but in vowel-initial stems it is not the first VCV that is reduplicated, as we would expect if the rule were defined by the number of segments, but the first VC only:

takki	'leg'	taktakki	'legs'	
uffu	'thigh'	ufuffu	'thighs'	(Healey 1960: 6ff)

Also, in MOKILESE the CVC- of CVCV stems but the CV (and not CVV) of CVV(C) stems is reduplicated (Harrison 1973: 416, 423).

The other alternative, of defining the string to be reduplicated in terms of the number of syllables, arises as a possibility in all instances where the string to be reduplicated involves at least one vowel. In instances where a single C is reduplicated, this alterna- tive does not arise, which already shows that all partial reduplica- tions could not be properly defined in terms of number of syllables anyway. Now, as far as those cases are concerned where the string to be reduplicated involves at least one vowel, I have evidence to indicate that some such strings in some languages cannot be defined as syllables anywhere. Thus, in QUILEUTE, as explicitly pointed out by Andrade (1933:189), the initial CV to be reduplicated is often a proper part of the first syllable. In the above-given examples, for instance, this is the case; since in ci·phókwat' 'negro' ci· is reduplicated, although the first syllable of the word is ci·p; and in qa·x 'bone' qa is reduplicated, although the whole word is one single syllable. Whereas these facts conclusively indicate the non- sufficiency of a syllabic definition of the reduplicated string in QUILEUTE, similar evidence is not available to me to indicate the necessity of such a definition in any language. Thus, in PAPAGO, for instance, all the data given by Langacker involve words that are of the CVCV type in their unreduplicated form; thus, the initial CV which is what is reduplicated can in all cases be sufficiently defined either as the first CV or as the first syllable. Evidence that would indicate the necessity of a syllabic definition would be a language where in VC-, CVCV-, and CVCCV-initial words the V, CV and CVC sequences are reduplicated, respectively; since in this case the syllable would provide the only uniform definition of the three otherwise disparate strings. [6]

---

[6] Key (1965: 91) suggests that in SIRIONO "the final two moras of the stem" are reduplicated and gives the examples erasi 'he is sick' — erasirasi 'he continues being sick;' ečisia 'he cuts' -- ečisiasia 'he continues to cut.' Since in the first example the final CVCV, and in the second, the final CVV have been reduplicated,

I therefore take all facts cited here to be consistent with the hypothesis that the only phonetic properties that partial reduplication rules may refer to are consonantality and vowelhood; and that all partial reduplication rules where the part to be reduplicated is not syntactically defined do in fact make such reference.

B'. How many times is the object in question reduplicated
According to our definition, for a construction to be reduplicative one, it has to include at least two instances of the same form; the question is whether there are examples of this construction type that include more than two instances of the same form. As the examples cited have already shown, there are indeed instances of multiple reduplication in many languages and possibly in all. Examples fall into these three types: a) both one-time and multiple reduplication possible with respect to the same form, with an additional meaning accruement of the same type in each case; b) both one-time and multiple reduplication possible with respect to the same form, the additional meaning change being of different kinds; c) only multiple reduplication possible with respect to a form. I will now illustrate and discuss each of these.

a) There are at least two kinds of meanings that may be reinforced by additional reduplication. One is emphasis: it is perhaps true in all languages that an emphatic modifier (such as very) can be open-endedly reduplicated for additional degrees of emphasis. The other is continuity: both in MOKILESE and in SHIPIBO, increased temporal extent of an action can be suggested by additional reduplication. Compare MOKILESE: roar 'give a shudder,' roarroar 'to be shuddering,' roarroarroar 'to continue to shudder;' soang 'tight,' soangsoang 'being tight,' soangsoangsoang 'still tight' (Harrison 1973: 426); SHIPIBO: ?a 'do,' ?aa 'doing,' ?aa'?aa 'keep on doing' (Key 1965: 91). (In MOKILESE, CVC reduplication is involved, whereas in SHIPIBO, total reduplication; hence three copies in MOKILESE and four in SHIPIBO.) (Compare also ROTUMAN (Churchward 1940: 105).)

(ftnt. 6 cont.)
this indeed appears to be a case of reduplication where the string is defined in terms of syllables rather than consonants and vowels. Given, however, that the e- appears to be a separate lexeme (the third person singular subject marker), it is also possible that this is a case of total, rather than partial, reduplication. Pending further information, I do not thus take SIRIONO to provide conclusive evidence in favor of syllable-based reduplication.

b) An example of stages of multiple reduplication corresponding to distinct, i.e. not only quantitatively differing, meanings come from TWI. As the following examples show, the predicative form of the verb is simple, the adjectival form is once-reduplicated, and the adverbial form includes either three or four copies:

duá ti yè fe	'This tree is fine.'
mfoníní fèfe	'a fine picture'
wógòru { feféfe / fefé(f)efe }	'They play very nicely.' (Christaller 1875: 47)

c) Examples of simple forms that may be multiply but not only once reduplicated are TELUGU śrī 'prosperous' and some verbs of MOKILESE such as doau 'climb.' According to Krishnamurti (p.c.), on medieval TELUGU inscriptions the adjective śrī 'prosperous' occurs triplicated but not duplicated; e.g. in śrī śrī śrī gaṇapalīdēva mahārājulum gāru 'O, three-times-prosperous King Ganapalideva....' In MOKILESE, whereas some verbs express "progressivity of action" by one-time-reduplication and "continuity of action" by triplication, as was seen above, some verbs have this semantic contrast neutralized and are both expressed by the triplicative form; e.g. doau 'climb,' doaudoaudoau 'be/continue climbing,' *doaudoau (Harrison 1973: 427).

At least in some languages multiply reduplicated forms are resisted or, if used, degrees of multiple reduplication are not correlated with distinct meanings. Thus, in KANURI language names are derived ordinarily from tribe names by total reduplication; e.g. Kanəmbú '(tribe name),' kanəmbukanəmbú '(corresponding language name);' but this is not possible if the tribe name already has a reduplicative form; e.g. from the tribe name Kare-kare, the corresponding language name is mánà Karekarevè and not *Karekarekarekaré (Lukas 1937: 8). In MOKILESE the distinction between the progressive and continuative verbal aspect, unambiguously expressible by the distinction between one-time and two-time reduplication, is often neutralized and is expressed either by the duplicated or by the triplicated form, depending on the verb; e.g. doau 'climb,' doaudoaudoau 'be/continue climbing,' *doaudoau; pakad 'to defecate on,' pakpakad 'be/continue defecating on,' *pak-pakpakad (Harrison 1973: 427).

C'. Additional non-iterative form differentiation Our definition of reduplicative constructions allows for reduplication not being the only carrier of a meaning difference between two forms; the question

is whether it ever occurs, indeed, that in addition to a purely
quantitative form change there is also an additional kind, such as
something else added to the reduplicated form or deleted from it,
or some part of it replaced. Whereas I found no example where
substitution would take place, and only one clear example where
something is deleted in the reduplicated form as compared with
the simple form, there are many examples of not-purely-quantita-
tive additions accompanying reduplication. My single clear example
involving deletion comes from MOKILESE where reduplication and
the deletion of a phonetic string from the end of a transitive verb
render them intransitive; compare <u>koso</u> 'cut$_{tr}$,' <u>koskos</u> 'cut$_{intr}$;'
<u>sipis</u> 'tie$_{tr}$,' <u>sipsip</u> 'tie$_{intr}$' (Harrison 1973: 415). Form-addition
occurs both in conjunction with total and in conjunction with partial
reduplication; and the added string may take place between the
"copy" and the "original," or it may occur on the periphery of the
word. The additional string is between the "copy" and the "original,"
for instance, in AZTEC and in AGTA. In AZTEC it is an <u>h</u> (e.g.
<u>se</u> 'one,' <u>sehse</u> 'ones / one by one;' <u>eyi</u> 'three,' <u>eheyi</u> 'threes / three
by three' (Elson and Pickett 1965: 46)), in AGTA it is <u>ala</u> (e.g. <u>wer</u>
'creek,' <u>walawer</u> 'small creek;' <u>kwák</u> 'my thing,' <u>kwalakwák</u> 'my
small thing' (Healey 1960: 6)). An instance of total reduplication
cooccurring with a suffix comes from MANDARIN, and an instance
of total reduplication cooccurring with a prefix comes from SUN-
DANESE. MANDARIN: <u>huang.jang</u> 'flustered,' <u>huang.huang.jang</u>.
<u>jang</u> 'flustered (vivid form)' (Chao 1968: 206); SUNDANESE: <u>udag</u>
'to pursue,' <u>paudagudag</u> 'to chase each other;' <u>iriŋ</u> 'to follow,'
<u>pairiŋiriŋ</u> 'to walk in groups' (Robins 1959: 363). Partial redupli-
cation with an added affix on the same periphery of the stem occurs
in TZELTAL, for instance; the affix is added on the opposite periphery in SUNDANESE. TZELTAL: <u>-nit</u> 'to push it,' <u>-nititan</u> 'to
push it rapidly in a curvy, crooked path;' <u>-net'</u> 'to press it down,'
<u>-net'et'an</u> 'to press it down, twisting rapidly the ball of the hand'
(Berlin 1963: 214); SUNDANESE: <u>kolot</u> 'be old,' <u>kokolotan</u> 'look old,'
<u>budak</u> 'child,' <u>bubudakan</u> 'behave like a child' (Robins 1959: 361).

D'. <u>Temporal relations of the copies to each other and to the
rest of the utterance</u> Of the various pertinent questions, I will only
consider one here which is that of the adjacency relation of copies.
As the examples already cited in this paper show, in instances of
partial reduplication copies are often but not always adjacent to
each other. If they are not adjacent, they may be separated from
each other a) either by part of the stem, b) or by all of the stem,
c) or by an additional string not in the original stem. Part of the
stem intervenes in QUILEUTE, for instance: the first consonant
is reduplicated here and inserted after the first syllable: <u>tsi'ko</u>
'he put it on,' <u>tsítsko</u> 'he put it on (frequentative);' <u>tukô'yo'</u> 'snow,'

tutkô·yoʼ 'snow here and there' (Andrade 1933: 187). The whole stem intervenes in TILLAMOOK, for instance: tq 'break,' q-tə̂q-ən 'they
tried to break it;' t·ɬ 'tell,' s-ɬ-tuɬ-ən 'they went and told him'
(Reichard 1959: 243). A string not belonging to the stem is inter-
posed in AZTEC and in AGTA as examples under C' illustrated. [7]

All the facts explicitly discussed or otherwise drawn upon above
appear to me to be consistent with the following universal hypotheses
about the form properties of reduplicative constructions:

1. There is no reduplication pattern where the constituent to be
   reduplicated may be freely chosen from among the included
   subconstituents.

2. There is no reduplication pattern where the number of repetitions is freely chosen from the set of all numbers.

3. There is no reduplication pattern which would not involve
   reference to lexical identity. [8]

4. There is no reduplication pattern that would involve reference
   to phonological properties other than syllable number, con-
   sonantality-vowelhood, and absolute linear position. [9]

---

[7] An interesting question is whether temporal precedence relations have to be defined for the "copy" in relation to the "original."
For some consideration of this question in THAI, compare Haas
1942; for the criterion of affix synonymy as deciding this question,
see Wilbur 1973: 11.

[8] For a related claim, according to which all rule-applicational
exceptions related to reduplicative construction can be explained
by the requirement of the phonetic identity of the original and the
copies, see Wilbur 1973. Lexical identity is not always required,
as in the above examples; in some instances of reduplication it is
excluded. For such synonym reduplications, see Noss (1964: 59)
on THAI, and Politzer 1961 and Malkiel 1959 in other languages.
My claim is that in no instance of reduplication is it immaterial if
(all of part of) the same lexical item is involved in the repetition
or (all or part of) a lexical item that has the same meaning but a
different form.

[9] It is possible that stress is significant in some languages in
determining which part of the stem be reduplicated. This is particularly likely in instances of internal reduplication, such as in
SAMOAN. I have, however, not investigated this question any further.

2.2 Meaning properties

There is no a priori reason why reduplication, or any other form device of language, should serve as the expression of some meanings rather than as that of others. Nonetheless, as pointed out by a number of linguists, the particularly meanings associated with reduplication strikingly recur across languages. [10]

Before considering what these particular cross-linguistically recurrent meanings are, two general observations are in order. First, the relation between the meaning of a reduplicative construction and its unreduplicated counterpart is almost always that of proper inclusion, with the former properly including the latter. In other words, reduplicative constructions almost always entail everything that their unreduplicated counterparts do and, in addition, also some thing(s) that their unreduplicated counterparts do not. Specifically, I have found no clear example of an unreduplicated constructions' meaning properly including the meaning of the corresponding reduplicated one, or of the two overlapping; although there are some possible examples of the fourth logically possible semantic relation. [11]

---

[10] Cross-linguistic discussions of reduplicative constructions that I am familiar with fall into two classes. Some of them include in their scope only languages of some genetic group or of some areally defined one; e.g. Gonda 1949 (on INDONESIAN languages), Harrison 1973 (on MICRONESIAN languages), Haeberlin 1918 and Reichard 1959 (on SALISH languages), and Godel 1945 (on TURKISH and ARMENIAN); compare also Watson 1966 which discusses PACOH data only, but gives a useful bibliography on reduplication in other, mostly SOUTH-ASIAN, languages as well. Others include languages of varying genetic and areal affiliation; compare, for instance, Bloomfield 1914: 156-157, Sapir 1949: 76-78, Dressler 1968, Key 1965, and Wilbur 1973. For further references to such cross-linguistic discussions, see also Thun 1963. Pott's work on reduplication (August Friedrich Pott 1862, Doppelung (Reduplikation, Gemination) als eines der wichtigsten Bildungsmittel der Sprache, beleuchtet aus Sprachen aller Welttheile, Lemgo und Detmold) whose title promises a large inventory of interesting data has unfortunately not been available to me. Most of these works discuss reduplication data according to the meaning categories expressed; for a work of exclusive concern for the form of these constructions, see Wilbur 1973.

[11] The mutual exclusion of the two meanings was excluded by our definition of reduplicative constructions. Scattered examples of an

The other striking fact is that within the small set of meanings that most reduplications convey in various languages there are some meanings that appear to be opposites. Such are, for instance, augmentation and diminution; and endearment and contempt. In some cases, some reduplicative construction is used to express such opposite concepts even within the same language.

As far as particular meaning properties are concerned, the most outstanding single concept that reduplicative constructions recurrently express in various languages is the concept of increased quantity. There are two basic subtypes of this meaning: quantity of referents and amount of emphasis.

I will first discuss various subtypes of quantity of referents. Referents may be participants of event or events themselves; the former I have found expressed by noun reduplication or by verb reduplication and the latter, by verb reduplication only. In both cases, the set of referents whose plurality is conveyed by reduplication may either be one whose members are understood not to occur at the same place or time, but to be spatially or temporally scattered; or it may be a set where no such specification is understood. I will now consider noun reduplication and verb reduplication in turn.

Simple (unmarked) plurality of the participants of an event as expressed by noun reduplication is exemplifiable by SAMOAN and PAPAGO constructions. SAMOAN: tuafāfine 'brother's sisters' (tuafafine 'brother's sister') (Pratt 1862: 7; he describes this process as "lengthening (properly doubling) a vowel in the word.") PAPAGO: baabana 'coyotes' (bana 'coyote'), tiitini 'mouths' (tini 'mouth') (Langacker 1972: 267). (For AMHARIC, TIGRINA and

---

(ftnt. 11 cont.)
unreduplicated and a corresponding reduplicated construction being synonymous come from SUNDANESE, MANDARIN and SYRIAN ARABIC. For instance, Robins glosses both tamu and tatamu in SUNDANESE as 'guest' (Robins 1959: 354); Chao says of MANDARIN that "the simple verb... heng and its reduplicate heng.heng 'grunts, groans, hums (a tune)' do not differ much even in connotation" (Chao 1968: 204); and according to Cowell, in SYRIAN ARABIC "many augmentatives which are theoretically intensives are in actual usage virtually synonymous with their underlying simple verb: raƐab and raƐƐab 'to scare, startle,' fareḥ and farfaḥ 'to rejoice,' etc." (Cowell 1964: 253). Some instances of synonymy between duplicative and triplicative forms occur in MOKILESE; see Harrison 1973, cp. my Sec. 2.1 under B'.

TIGRE, compare Leslau 1945:166.) Of the more specific plural
meanings, 'every X' and 'all X' are expressed by reduplication in
PACOH; 'every X' in YORUBA, TAGALOG and MANDARIN; and
'very many X' in TZELTAL:

PACOH: damo damo 'everyone' (damo 'whichever one')
             tamo tamo 'from everywhere' (tamo 'from wherever')
             kakom 'all the black' (kom 'black')
             babar 'all two' (bar 'two') (Watson 1966: 83, 99)

YORUBA: ọsọ̀ọ̀sẹ̀ 'every week' (ọ̀sẹ̀ 'week')
             alaalẹ́ 'every enemy' (alẹ́ 'enemy') (Bamgboṣe 1966: 151)

TAGALOG: arawᶜáraw 'every day' (araw 'day') (Blake 1917: 425ff)

MANDARIN: renren 'everybody' (ren 'man') (Chao 1968: 202)

TZELTAL: hiʔhiʔtik 'very much sand' (hiʔ 'sand')
             nanatik 'very many houses' (na 'house')(Berlin 1963:212)

Languages where the reduplicated plural is restricted to plurality
of individuals that are either of different kinds or scattered in location are MALAY and QUILEUTE. In written classical MALAY,
according to Gonda (1949), the reduplicative plural is used "mainly
to express diversity;" e.g. anak means 'child' and anakanak means
'various children.' In QUILEUTE, according to Andrade (1933: 190),
reduplication denotes "the existence or occurrence of conceptually
identical objects or actions in different situations or occasions;"
although he also points out that the younger generation of speakers
uses reduplication to denote ENGLISH-type (unmarked) plurals as
well. Various versions of distributive plurals crop up in a number
of other languages as well, some of which are exemplified here:

TURKISH: čors čors kalel 'to march four by four' (čors 'four')
             (Godel 1945: 12)

SIERRA   sehse 'ones; one by one' (se 'one') (Elson and
AZTEC: Pickett 1965: 46)

TWI: dú dú 'ten each' (dú 'ten') (Christaller 1875: 53)

YORUBA: mẹ́.ta mẹ́.ta 'three each' (mẹ́.ta 'three') (Bamgboṣe
             1966: 151)

MITLA   šse.šseʔ-ni 'each its own place' (šseʔ 'place')
ZAPOTEC: (Briggs 1961: 74)

Reduplication is also used when not <u>all</u> members of a class of objects are referred to, but when <u>any one</u> or <u>some one</u> member of it is. As discussed by Coyaud and Hamou (1971), indefinite pronouns are formed by the reduplication of interrogative pronouns or of some other morpheme in a great many different languages; such as ILA, ELE, LATIN, JAVANESE, MALAY, VIETNAMESE and NGBANDI. Some examples from languages not mentioned in their study:

SUNDANESE: <u>sahasaha</u> 'whoever' (<u>saha</u> 'who?')
                <u>manamana</u> 'wherever' (<u>mana</u> 'where?') (Robins 1959: 355)

KHASI: <u>ka?eyka?ey</u> 'someone' (<u>ka?ey</u> 'who?/what?')
                <u>kumnukumnu</u> 'somehow' (<u>kumnu</u> 'how?') (Rabel 1961: 110ff)

Reduplication of verbs, as aptly pointed out by Andrade in connection with QUILEUTE, may express either repeated or continued occurrence of an event with the same participant(s) performing in it at different times or places; or it may express the repeated occurrence of an event (possibly at different times and places) performed by different participants.   I will first discuss and exemplify repeated or continued occurrence with an event involving the same participants. Some examples of this are the following:

TZELTAL: <u>-pikpik</u> 'touch it lightly repeatedly' (<u>-pik</u> 'touch it lightly')
              <u>-suhsuh</u> 'continue to urge that it be done' (<u>-suh</u> 'urge it done') (Berlin 1963: 214)

THAI: <u>khãw dǝǝn, dǝǝn: paj naan</u> 'He walked and walked for a long time.' (<u>dǝǝn</u> 'walk') (Noss 1964: 69)

QUILEUTE: <u>é'ela·'xali</u> 'I leave him often' (<u>éla·'xali</u> 'I left him')
              <u>o·'o·'xwal</u> 'he carries water often' (<u>o·xwal</u> 'he carries water') (Andrade 1933: 187)

SUNDANESE: <u>guguyon</u> 'to jest repeatedly' (<u>guyon</u> 'to jest')
                <u>gogodǝg</u> 'to keep shaking the head' (<u>godǝg</u> 'to shake the head') (Robins 1959: 354)

TWI: <u>tẽetẽem'</u> 'to cry out (repeatedly)' (<u>tẽem'</u> 'to cry out (once)') (Christaller 1875: 64)

EWE: <u>zɔzɔ</u> 'be walking' (<u>zɔ</u> 'walk')

EWE (cont.):   babía 'be asking' (ba 'ask') (Ansre 1963)

ROTUMAN: leleume 'to come repeatedly, frequently, or
               habitually' (leume 'to come') (Churchward 1940)

(MOKILESE examples were given in Sec. 2.1, compare Harrison
1973: 426f; for examples from KONDA see Krishnamurti 1969: 312;
for examples from many other languages see Dressler 1968: 62-65.)
As the last ROTUMAN example indicates, habituality is sometimes
also understood; cp. AZTEC zazazanilia 'to have the habit of nar-
rating' (zanilia 'to narrate') (Dressler 1968: 74).

Sometimes reduplication expresses the repeated occurrence of
the same event involving the same participants, but with participant
roles reversed:

YAMI: mipalupalu 'strike each other' (palu 'strike')
               (Gonda 1949: 182)

TZELTAL: -mahmah 'fight' (-mah hit it') (Berlin 1963: 214)

PACOH: târhŏm hŏm 'to bathe each other' (hŏm 'to bathe')
               târchom chom 'to know each other' (chom 'to
               know') (Watson 1966: 96)

DYIRBAL: ḍurgayḍurgaybariɲu 'spear each other' (ḍurgay
               'spear$_v$')
               ɲundalɲundalbariɲu 'kiss each other' (ɲundal
               'kiss$_v$' (Dixon 1972: 92f)

Examples of reduplication expressing repeated action with different participant(s) and possibly even at the same time are these:

TWI: wuwu 'die (in numbers)' (wu 'die (of one or
               several persons)'
               bubu 'bend/break a thing in many places / break
               many things (e.g. sticks)' (bu 'bend/break')
               (Christaller 1875: 64)

SAMOAN: mamate 'they die' (mate 'he dies')
               alolofa 'they love' (alofa 'he loves') (Pratt 1862)

QUILEUTE: kwe·'k^{u}tsa 'several people are hungry' (kwe·'tsa'
               'he is hungry') (Andrade 1933: 187)

SOMALI: fenfen 'gnaw at on all sides' (fen 'gnaw at')
                 (Sapir 1949: 77)

TSIMSHIAN: am?am 'several are good' (am 'good') (Sapir
                 1949: 77)
                 əl?alɟix 'speak of several people' (alɟix 'speak')
                 (Bloomfield 1915: 157)

SYRIAN   kassar 'break (into many pieces)' (kasar 'break
ARABIC: (e.g. into two)')
                 ?aṭṭaf 'pick (e.g. many flowers)' (?aṭaf 'pick
                 (e.g. a flower)' (Cowell 1964: 253)

Intuitively speaking, intensity appears related to quantity in that
it involves quantity of energy investment or size of effect. If an
action is performed with greater intensity, this does not mean that
somebody necessarily performs it repeatedly or continuing it over
some length of time, nor does it mean necessarily that the active
and passive participants involved are a multitude; what it means
is that it is performed more thoroughly and/or with greater than
ordinary effect. That intensity is felt to be related to quantity is
indicated by expressions such as Many thanks! or Thanks a million!
in ENGLISH and corresponding ones in other languages; as well as
by the fact that increased intensiveness is often expressed in various languages by reduplication; e.g.

TURKISH: dopdolu 'quite full' (dolu 'full')
                 bembeyaz 'quite white' (beyaz 'white') (Godel 1941:6)

SUNDANESE: hayaŋhayaŋ 'want very much' (hayaŋ 'want')
                 ramerame 'be very jolly' (rame 'jolly') (Robins
                 1959: 355)

AGTA: dádána 'very old' (dána 'old')
                 magbíbilag 'run hard and far' (magbílag 'run')
                 (Healey 1960)

TELUGU: śri śri śri gaṇapalídēva mahārājulum gāru 'O,
                 very prosperous King Ganapalideva!' (śri 'pros-
                 perous') (Krishnamurti, p.c.)

THAI: díidii 'to be extremely good' (dii 'to be good')
                 wăanwăan 'to be extremely sweet') (wăan 'to be
                 sweet') (Haas 1946: 128)

EWE: gégblé 'be very much spoiled' (gblé 'be spoiled')
              (Ansre 1963)

TAGALOG: magkabasagbasag 'get thoroughly broken' (mabasag
              'get broken')
              magkasirasira 'get thoroughly damaged' (masira
              'be damaged') (Schachter and Otanes 1972: 339)

In some cases intensive constructions have the added connotation
of "more than appropriate;" such as in DYIRBAL: miyamiyandaɲu
'laugh more than is appropriate' (miyadaɲu 'laugh$_V$'), balgabalgan
'hit too much' (balgan 'hit') (Dixon 1972: 251).

As already pointed out, side by side with the meaning of increased
quantity and intensity, there is also the meaning of diminution and
attenuation: these, too, are senses conveyed by reduplication in
various languages.[12] Examples are these:

a. for diminution (often associated with endearment):

AGTA: walawer 'small creek' (wer 'creek')
              kwalakwák 'my small thing' (kwák 'my thing')
              (Healey 1960: 6)

NEZ PERCE: temulté·mul 'sleet' (té·mul 'hail')
              xoyamacxóyamac 'small child' (xóyamac 'child')
              (Aoki 1963)

THOMPSON: ṣ̌ō'ṣpaʼ 'little tail' (ṣ̌ō'paʼ 'tail')
              sqa'qxaʼ 'little dog/horse' (sqa'xaʼ 'dog/horse')
              (Haeberlin 1918: 156)

---

[12] The intralingual cooccurrence of reduplication patterns expressing opposing meanings can be exemplified from AGTA and
TZELTAL. In AGTA reduplication may express either intensity
or attenuation: e.g. dána 'old,' dádána 'very old,' but magbílag
'run,' bilabilagan 'run gently' (Healey 1960: 6ff). In TZELTAL
reduplication in color terms may express either increased or reduced intensity of color: e.g. ʔihkʼ 'black,' ʔihkʼbʼohbʼoh 'very
black (as mouth),' ʔihkʼʔihkʼtik 'blackish;' kʼan 'yellow,' kʼanteltel
'very yellow (as bunch of bananas),' kʼankʼantik 'yellowish' (Berlin
1963: 216f). In both instances, however, the particular reduplicative
pattern differs depending on which meaning it expresses.

b. for attenuation:

QUILEUTE: kwaya'.ti' 'he tried a little' (kwáti' 'he tried')
t'łeyéx 'rather stiff' (t'lè'x 'stiff') (Andrade
1933: 188)

SWAHILI: maji-maji 'somewhat wet' (maji 'wet' (?)) (Ashton
1952: 316)

THAI: kàw-kàw 'oldish' (kàw 'old (of things)')
kɛ̀ɛ-kɛ̀ɛ 'elderly' (kɛ̀ɛ 'old (of people)') (Noss 1964:
68)

MANDARIN: tauoh.tauoh(l) 'sits a while' (tauoh 'sit')
pao.pao 'runs a little' (pao 'run') (Chao 1968: 205;
cp. also Thompson 1973: 362)

TAGALOG: mahiyahiya 'be a little ashamed' (mahiya 'ashamed')
magwaliswalis 'sweep a little' (magwalis 'sweep')
(Schachter and Otanes 1972: 340)

The meaning 'similar to X' appears to be close to the meaning
of attenuation; and the meaning 'pretend to X' is again close to
'similar to X':

MALAY: lamitlamit 'cloth canope / palate of the mouth'
(lamit 'sky') (Gonda 1949: 172, 190f)

THAI: ŋən ŋən 'money and that sort of thing' (ŋən 'silver/
money')
mɔ̂ɔ mɛ̂ə 'pots and pans' (mɔ̂ɔ 'pot') (Noss 1964: 52f)

TURKISH: havlú mavlú 'towels and the like' (havlú 'towel'(?))
kitáp mitáp 'books and such' (kitáp 'book') (Swift
1963; cp. also Lewis 1967: 235ff)

PACOH: táq qâmbíq bíq 'pretend to sleep' (bíq 'sleep$_v$')
táq qaqay qay 'act sick' (qaqay 'sick') (Watson 1966:95)

SUNDANESE: wawanian 'to pretend to be brave' (wani 'to dare')
pipintəran 'to feign wisdom' (pintər 'to be wise')
(Robins 1959: 360)

Reduplicative constructions may have other derogatory connota-
tations as well, in addition to implied falsehood just exemplified.

Of some EWE reduplicative constructions, Ansre writes (1962):
"Often, they are alleged sayings, giving notions that need be
corrected and one can infer that they are quotations on which pro-
hibitive or exhortative pronouncement is based." Allegedness may
be implied by reduplication in HUNGARIAN as well; compare:

Speaker A: Holnap megcsinálom.
             "tomorrow I-will-do-it"
             'Tomorrow I will do it.'

Speaker B: Holnap, holnap ... mindig azt mondod!
             "tomorrow tomorrow always that you-say-it"
             'Tomorrow... — you always say that!'

For general derogatory connotation, compare also YIDDISH reduplications of the type book-shmook.

Apart from the meanings of increased quantity, intensity,
diminution and attenuation which are concepts capable of pulling
together many superficially disparate uses of reduplicative constructions, such constructions also serve to differentiate members
of one grammatical category from another. Some of these derivational uses of reduplication do appear to be relatable to one or
another of the above-mentioned broad meaning categories in that
in some cases the difference in meaning between the reduplicated
construction and its unreduplicated counterpart is both a difference
in basic grammatical category and also a difference of one of the
above types; in other cases, however, no such relation is apparent.
Some examples where categorial distinction is also paralleled by
additional meaning differences relatable to the above types are
these:

a. Reduplication correlated with denominal verb derivation and
   distributive meaning:
   PACOH: bâmbar 'to divide by two' (bar 'two')
               pâmpe 'to divide by three' (pe 'three')
                                        (Watson 1966: 99)

b. Reduplication correlated with denominal adjectivalization
   and connotation of fullness of something:
   MOKILESE: dikolkol 'lumpy' (dikol 'lump')
               koalohlo 'full of roots' (koalo 'root')
                                        (Harrison 1973: 424)
   TWI: aboabó 'stony' (abó 'stones')
               nsoensóe 'thorny' (nsóe 'thorns')
                                        (Christaller 1875: 46)

c. Reduplication correlated with denominal or deverbal agent
   nominalization with implied connotation of habitualness:
   TAGALOG: ta:ta:wa 'one who will laugh' (ta:wa 'a laugh')
            qa:qa:wit 'one who will use' (qa:wit 'thing of use')
                                        (Bloomfield 1933: 218, 221f)
   EWE: sisílá 'escaper' (sí 'escape$_V$')
            nyanyralá 'raver' (nyra 'rave$_V$') (Ansre 1963)

d. Reduplication correlated with deverbal action nominalization
   with implied connotation of continuity:
   EWE: fofo 'beating' (fo 'beat$_V$')
            kpɔkplɔ 'leading' (kplɔ 'lead$_V$') (Ansre 1963)

There is, however, an equally large and indeed disparate set of
examples of derivational meanings that cannot be seen related to
any of the non-derivational meaning categories surveyed above.
Thus, for instance, reduplication can serve to derive adverbs from
verbs or adjectives as in THAI (e. g. wɛɛw-waaw 'brilliantly' (wɛɛw
'brilliant'); krasíb-krasâab 'in whispers' (krasíb 'to whisper')
(Noss 1964: 53)), or to derive intransitive verbs from transitive
verbs as in MOKILESE or TWI (MOKILESE: koskos 'cut$_{intr}$' (koso
'cut$_{tr}$'); kidkid 'wrap$_{intr}$' (kidim 'wrap$_{tr}$') (Harrison 1973: 415);
TWI: didi 'eat$_{intr}$' (di 'eat$_{tr}$') (Christaller 1875: 64)), or to derive
transitive verbs from intransitive ones such as in SUNDANESE
(ŋarɤrɤwas 'to frighten' (rɤwas 'to be afraid'); mapanas/mamanas
'to anger' (panas 'to be angry') (Robins 1959: 354)).   There are,
in addition, many non-derivational uses of reduplication which also
do not fit the above broad meaning categories; such as expressing
perfectivity, as in SANSKRIT, GREEK, LATIN and GOTHIC (cp.,
for instance, Karstien 1921 on such reduplication in GERMANIC
languages), or meaning 'come to do something' as in COEUR D'A-
LENE (Reichard 1959: 244); etc.

Given that reduplication is neither the exclusive expression of
any one meaning category in languages, nor are the meanings that
it is an expression of all subsumable under general classes, no
explanatory or predictive generalization about the meanings of
reduplicative constructions can be proposed. All we may note is
that such constructions often express meanings related to increased
quantity, intensity, diminutiveness and attenuation.

2.3 Distribution

So far we have considered subtypes of reduplicative constructions
as defined by their form properties and their meaning properties.
The remaining question to ask is what are the conditions under which

reduplicative constructions occur at all. How, in other words, can the subset of all human utterances be characterized that include reduplicative constructions as opposed to its complement set whose members do not? How can we predict that a sentence will include a reduplicative construction?

Logically possible bases for such predictions are the following. First of all, it is possible in principle that the occurrence of a reduplicative construction or even that of some particular subtype of it is predictable just from the meaning that the sentence conveys. This would be the case if reduplicative constructions or some subtype of them did not have synonyms, but would serve as the sole conveyors of some meanings in all languages that do provide for the expression of that meaning. If, however, reduplicative constructions do turn out to have synonyms, then meaning by itself cannot be used as a criterion for predicting if a sentence will include a reduplicative construction or not. The question that arises, then, is this: given the range of forms that can all equally serve as alternative expressions of those meanings that reduplication can also express, how can we predict that a particular sentence whose meaning includes one of those meanings will use reduplication as its expression or one of the other alternative forms? Possible conditions determining the answer may be of three kinds. First, it may be that all those sentences that utilize reduplication (or some particular subtype of it) for the expression of that meaning are characterized by some structural — meaning-related or form-related — property that is unique to them, and from which the occurrence of reduplication (or a particular subtype of it) can be predicted. Second, it is possible that there is something about the structure of the other sentences of the same language in terms of which the occurrence of reduplication as the conveyor of particular meanings can be predicted. Thirdly, it is possible that there is something about the spatial and temporal distribution of the language in question, or about the particular function of the style or register in question, that is predictive of the occurrence of reduplication (or a particular subtype of it) as the chosen expression of some meaning. In sum: the occurrence of reduplication or some subtype of it in a sentence may in principle be predicted a) from meaning only, b) from meaning and intrasentential structural properties, c) from meaning and intralingual (but not intrasentential) structural properties, d) from meaning and non-structural properties of the language or style in question, e) from any combination of b), c) and d).

As against these logically available bases of prediction, the actual facts appear to me to admit of no generalizations of the types

a), b) and e), but they are consistent with some generalizations of
the types c) and d). First of all, no generalization of the type a)
is possible in that reduplicative constructions or any form-related
subtypes of them are not the sole conveyors of any meaning. All
meanings that can be expressed by reduplication can also be expressed in some other way, either in another language or often
within the very same language as well; and all meanings that can
be expressed by some particular form-related subtype of reduplication can also be expressed by some other particular form-
related subtype of it, either in another language or in the same
one. An example of intralingual synonymy between reduplicative
and non-reduplicative constructions may come from KANURI: as
pointed out above, the name of a tribe's language is formed in some
cases by reduplication and in other cases periphrastically; e.g.
yaravayaravá 'the language of the Yarava tribe;' but máná Boleave
'the language of the Bolea tribe' (Lukas 1937: 8). An example of
interlingual synonymy of reduplicative and non-reduplicative constructions may come from the expression of plurality in SUNDA-
NESE and ENGLISH: the plural of paturunan 'descendant' in
SUNDANESE is paturunanpaturunan (Robins 1959: 367), but the
plural of descendant in ENGLISH is descendants. An example of
the intralingual synonymy of two reduplicative constructions of
different subtypes may come from MALAY, where, according to
Gonda 1949: 171, both puyu-puyu and pĕpuyu mean 'climbing perch'
and both labulabu and lĕlabu mean 'pipkin.' Finally, an example
of interlingual synonymy relations between reduplicative constructions of various subtypes may come from TURKISH and HUNGARIAN.
In TURKISH 'very full' is expressed by partial reduplication: dopdolu (dolu 'full') (Godel 1945: 6), and it is expressed by total reduplication in HUNGARIAN: telisteli (teli 'full'). Such evidence indicates
that the occurrence of reduplication in a sentence or the occurrence
of some particular subtype of it cannot be predicted from the meaning alone that the construction is to convey.

Secondly, search for a condition of type b) also fails: I simply
have not found any distinctive semantic or form-related property
present in just those sentences that include reduplication in various
languages.

I know of two hypotheses of the type c)-hypotheses, that is, in
terms of which reduplication patterns are predicted from structural
properties of other intralingually cooccurring sentences — for which
my limited investigation revealed no counterexamples. Both are
of the subtype predicting the occurrence of one kind of reduplicative
pattern from another kind (rather than predicting the occurrence of
any kind or one kind of reduplication from the existence of some

other non-reduplicative structural properties of the language).
One of them was proposed by Wilbur (1973: 11f; cp. also Moravcsik
1977: Sec. 2.2). She suggests, in effect, that whether word-internal
reduplication is initial, final, or medial may be predictable from
the ordering of synonymous non-reduplicative segmental affixes in
the language: if a prefix has a reduplicative synonym in the language,
it will be initial reduplication; if a suffix has a reduplicative synonym
in the language, it will be final reduplication; and if an infix has a
reduplicative synonym in the language, it will be internal reduplication. Types of languages that this hypothesis excludes from the set
o f possible natural human languages are, for instance, one where
nominal plurality is expressed by a suffix in some nouns and by the
reduplication of initial CV sequence in others; or one where diminution is expressed either by a prefix or by a medial vowel duplication; etc. The other hypothesis serves to predict the existence of
total reduplication in languages by proposing that all languages that
have partial reduplication also have total reduplication. This hypothesis thus asserts that there is no language with partial reduplication only; although there may be both languages that have total
reduplication only, and languages that have both total and partial
reduplication, and also languages that have neither.[13]

Whereas I know of no possible statement in terms of which the
occurrence of reduplication patterns in language could be predicted
from the spatial and/or temporal properties of the language (statements, that is, about the historical origin or downfall of reduplication
patterns), there are many remarks in the literature on reduplication
about the correlation of such patterns and the particular use of the
styles and registers in which they occur. Frequent occurrence of
reduplication is pointed out in pidgins and creoles (Hall 1966: 65), and
in baby talk (i.e. the register used by adults when talking to little

---

[13] Whereas I have indeed found many examples of languages that
have both partial and total reduplication (such as SUNDANESE or
TURKISH) and also some that do have total reduplication but may
not have partial (such as KANURI or MITLA ZAPOTEC), I am
uncertain if there are any languages at all without any kind of reduplication. The meaning category that is most like to be universally expressible by reduplication is continued action, such as in
ENGLISH He walked and walked and walked. Should this or some
other meaning category be universally expressible through total
reduplication, then the proposed typological statement about the
dependence of partial reduplication on total reduplication in a language should be replaced by an unrestricted universal statement
asserting the universal occurrence of total reduplication.

children) (for MANDARIN see Chao 1968: 202, for various languages see Gonda 1949: 174 and especially Ferguson 1966, 1974 and
additional references there). Reduplication also occurs in arti-
ficially constructed "secret" languages such as what HUNGARIAN
children use (e.g. the standard HUNGARIAN sentence Te vagy a
hibás 'You are the culprit' is translated into this language as Teve
vavagy ava hivibávás, the rule being that each vowel should be
reduplicated with an inserted, immediately preceding v and pro-
nounced immediately following its original) or the ones mentioned
by Key (1965). Tentative hypotheses consistent with the facts known
to me would be that all pidgins and creoles and all baby talk registers include some reduplicative patterns.

3. Conclusions

The domain of a structural study of language is delimitable either
by meaning or by form. In other words, we may either hold a particular meaning, such as determination, constant, and ask how it
is expressed in one or more languages; or we may hold a particular
form pattern constant, such as agreement, and ask what meanings
it is correlated with in one or more languages. In this present
study, a particular form property has been chosen as criterial to
the delimitation of the subject matter; in particular, intralinguis-
tically cooccurring pairs of utterances were investigated whose
form includes a meaning-differentiating quantitative form difference.
Of such utterances pairs, we wanted to know, first of all, which
subtypes of those form-related types that fall within the definition
actually occur and which do not; what meanings are expressed by
them and what meanings are not; and what are the conditions that
determine the occurrence of these forms in a sentence. With respect to each of these three questions, an attempt was made to
consider both the logically possible answers and also the actual
facts, the result of which was a small set of generalizations about
what form-related subtypes of reduplicative constructions do exist
and which do not (although they could), and what conditions may be
predictive of the occurrence of reduplicative patterns in an utterance and what conditions do not seem to be (although they could).
Each of these generalizations serves to explain particular facts
about reduplicative constructions. Each, however, is an explanandum itself: we want to know why just those answers are the true
ones to our questions that have so far been found to be true, and
not the others included in the logically possible sets of answers.

In principle, explanations to such generalizations within linguistics could be provided by grammatical rules, rule-applicational

principles, metaconstraints on rules and rule-applicational principles and on their intralingual cooccurrences, and by generalizations about the temporal, spatial and functional distribution of languages and styles. This paper, however, has been an informal study and no true explanations will even be attempted. In the closing paragraphs I would nonetheless like to point out some facts about non-reduplicative constructions that, informally speaking, appear relatable to some of our observations about reduplicative patterns and which may thus eventually be subsumed under the same explanatory generalizations that also explain properties of reduplicative constructions. There are three such remarks that I can make.

First, it was noted that phonological properties determining which part of a string be reduplicated in cases of partial reduplication are restricted to "canonical form"-type properties; e.g. consonantality, vowelhood, and linear precedence among the segments and boundaries. It is striking that in those scattered cases in languages where the temporal ordering of morphemes is (partly) determined by phonological properties (such as in TAGALOG or in CHINESE), the crucial property type is syllable number which appears related to CV sequencing.

Second, a tendency has been noted for languages to use reduplicative patterns -- i.e. quantitative form differentiation -- for the expression of meanings that have something to do with the quantity of referents. This kind of onomatopoeic use of a form device also appears to have parallels outside the domain of reduplicative constructions: temporal precedence of phrases, for instance, is used in some cases to parallel the temporal precedence of referent events (such as in John went home and had dinner, where it is understood that the first-mentioned event occurred first and the last-mentioned event occurred last), and quality of sound is often used to evoke the image of a similar referent sound (such as in animal calls; see also Ultan 1970).

Third, a strong tendency was noted for reduplicative constructions to express a more specific meaning that their unreduplicated counterparts. There is, in other words, in most cases a strong correlation between "increased phonological body" and "increased specificity of meaning." As pointed out to me by Merritt Ruhlen, this correlational tendency is not restricted to reduplicative constructions: (non-reduplicative) affixing or modifier-addition, for instance, are also generally correlated with increased semantic specificity (cp. Greenberg 1966).

I hope that the results of this study, limited and informal as it has been, will contribute to the understanding of the role of quantitative form differences in linguistic expression, and through it to the understanding of the relation of sound and meaning in language.

BIBLIOGRAPHY

Andrade, M.J. 1933. Quileute. New York: Columbia University Press.

Ansre, G. 1962. Reduplication in Ewe. Journal of African Languages 1.3. 128-132.

Aoki, H. 1963. Reduplication in Nez Perce. International Journal of American Linguistics [IJAL] 29.1. 42-44.

Ashton, E.O. 1944. Swahili grammar (including intonation). London, New York: Longmans, Green and Co.

Bamgboṣe, A. 1966. A grammar of Yoruba. Cambridge: Cambridge University Press.

Bender, B.W. 1969. Spoken Marshallese: an intensive language course with grammar, notes, and glossary. Honolulu.

_____. 1971. Micronesian languages. Current trends in linguistics, ed. by T. Sebeok, vol. 8: 426-465.

Blake, F.R. 1917. Reduplication in Tagalog. American Journal of Philology 38.4. 425-431.

Bloomfield, L. 1914. An introduction to the study of language. New York: H. Holt and Co.

_____. 1933. Language. New York, Chicago: Holt, Rinehart and Winston.

Berlin, B. 1963. Some semantic features of reduplication in Tzeltal. IJAL 29.3. 211-218.

Briggs, E. 1961. Mitla Zapotec grammar. Mexico.

Catford, J.C. 1968. The articulatory possibilities of man. Manuel of phonetics, ed. by B. Malmberg, 309-333. Amsterdam: North Holland.

Chao, Y.R. 1968. A grammar of spoken Chinese. Berkeley, Los Angeles: University of California Press.

Christaller, J.G. 1875. A grammar of the Asante and Fante language called Tshi (Chwee, Twi). Basel, Gregg Press Inc.

Churchward, C.M. 1940. Rotuman grammar and dictionary. Australasian Medical Publishing Company, Ltd.

Cowell, M.W. 1964. A reference grammar of Syrian Arabic. Washington D.C.: Georgetown University Press.

Coyaud, M. and K.A. Hamou. 1971. Un universal dans les quantificateurs indéfinis. Al-Lisāniyyāt 2. 5-20.

Crazzolara, Rev. J.P. 1933. Outlines of a Nuer grammar. Wien.

Dixon, R.M.W. 1972. The Dyirbal language of North Queensland. Cambridge: Cambridge University Press.

Dressler, W. 1968. Studien zur verbalen Pluralität. Wien: Hermann Böhlaus Nachf.

Elson, B. and V. Pickett. 1965. An introduction to morphology and syntax. Santa Ana, Calif.: Summer Institute of Linguistics.

Emeneau, M.B. 1969. Onomatopoeia in the Indian linguistic area. Language 45.2, part 1, 274-299.

Ferguson, C.A. 1964. Baby talk in six languages. American Anthropologist 66.6, part 2, 103-114.

_____. 1974. Baby talk as a simplified register. Manuscript.

Godel, R. 1945. Formes et emplois du redoublement en turc et en arménien moderne. Cahiers Ferdinand de Saussure 5. 5-16.

Gonda, J. 1949. The functions of word duplication in Indonesian languages. Lingua 2. 170-197.

Greenberg, J.H. 1952. The Afro-Asiatic (Hamito-Semitic) present. Journal of American Oriental Society 72. 1-9.

Greenberg, J.H. 1955. Internal a-plurals in Afro-Asiatic (Hamito-Semitic). Afrikanische Studien D. Westermann zum 80. Geburtstag gewidmet, 198-204. Berlin: Akademie-Verlag.

Greenberg, J.H. 1966. Language universals. Current trends in linguistics, ed. by T. Sebeok, vol. 3:61-112. The Hague: Mouton.

Haas, M. 1942. Types of reduplication in Thai. Studies in Linguistics 1.4 (New Haven, Conn.).

_____. 1946. Techniques of intensifying in Thai. Word 2.127-130.

Haeberlin, H.K. 1918. Types of reduplication in the Salish dialects. IJAL 1.2. 154-174.

Hall, R.A. 1966. Pidgin and Creole languages. Ithaca, London.

Harrison, S.P. 1973. Reduplication in Micronesian languages. Oceanic Linguistics 12.1-2. 407-454.

Healey, Phyllis M. 1960. An Agta grammar. Manila.

Karstien, C. 1921. Die reduplizierten Perfekta des Nord- und Westgermanischen. Giessen: V. Münchow.

Key, H. 1965. Some semantic functions of reduplication in various languages. Anthropological Linguistics 7.3, part 2, 88-101.

Krishnamurti, B. 1969. Koṇḍa or Kūbi, a Dravidian language.

Langacker, R.W. 1972. Fundamentals of linguistic analysis. New York, Chicago: Harcourt, Brace, Jovanovich, Inc.

Leslau, W. 1945. Grammatical structure of Tigré (North Ethiopic). JAOS 65. 164-203.

Lewis, G.L. 1967. Turkish grammar. Oxford.

Lukas, J. 1937. A study of the Kanuri language: grammar and vocabulary. London, New York: Oxford University Press.

Malkiel, Y. 1959. Studies in irreversible binomials.

Moravcsik, E.A. 1977. On rules of infixing. Indiana Linguistics Club.

_____. (forthcoming) Necessary and possible universals of temporal constituent relations in language.

Noss, R.B. 1964. Thai reference grammar. Washington, D.C.: Foreign Service Institute.

Politzer, R.L. 1961. Synonym repetition in late Latin and Romance languages. Language 37.4, part 1, 484-487.

Pratt, G. 1862. A Samoan dictionary: English and Samoan, and Samoan and English, with a short grammar of the Samoan dialect. London.

Rabel, Lili. 1961. Khasi, a language of Assam. Louisiana State University Studies, Humanities Series 10.

Reichard, G.A. 1959. A comparison of five Salish languages, V. IJAL 25.4. 239-253.

Robins, R.H. 1959. Nominal and verbal derivation in Sundanese. Lingua 8. 337-369.

_____. 1964. General linguistics: an introductory survey. Bloomington, Indiana.

Sapir, E. 1949 (1921). Language: an introduction to the study of speech. New York: Harcourt, Brace, and World, Inc.

Schachter, Paul and F. Otanes. 1972. Tagalog reference grammar. Berkeley and Los Angeles: University of California Press.

Swift, L.B. 1963. A reference grammar of Modern Turkish. Bloomington, Indiana.

Tauli, V. 1966. Structural tendencies in Uralic languages. London, The Hague: Mouton.

Thompson, S.A. 1973. Resultative verb compounds in Mandarin Chinese: a case for lexical rules. Language 49.2. 361-379.

Thun, N. 1963. Reduplicative words in English. Uppsala.

Ultan, R. 1970. Size-sound symbolism. Working Papers in Language Universals 3. S1-S31. Stanford University.

Watson, R.C. 1966. Reduplication in Pacoh. Unpublished M.A. thesis, Hartford Seminary Foundation, Hartford, Connecticut.

Wilbur, R.B. 1973. The phonology of reduplication. Indiana University Linguistic Club.

Winter, W. 1970. Reduplication in Washo: a restatement. IJAL 36.3 190-198.

Lexical Universals
of Body-Part Terminology

ELAINE S. ANDERSEN

ABSTRACT

The lexical structure of human body part terms across languages reveals a limited set of patterns. This domain tends to
be organized into a hierarchical structure with five (or occasionally six) levels, in which visually perceptible properties, especially properties of shape (e.g. round, and long) and of spatial
location (e.g. upper body versus lower body) play a major role.
Developmental data from children further support the premise
that the universal principles of categorization and of nomenclature
that determine this regularity of structure are largely the same
as those operating in many other semantic domains, and derive
from the ability of the human perceptual apparatus to deal with
attributes like shape, size, and spatial orientation.

The preparation of this paper was supported in part by the National Science Foundation Grant BNS75-17126 and in part by an
Andrew Mellon Postdoctoral Fellowship. I am grateful to Joseph
H. Greenberg who provided me with the first examples of possible
organizing principles within the body-part domain and to Eve V.
Clark and Herbert Clark for helpful comments on earlier versions
of this paper.

CONTENTS

1   Introduction

Modern linguistics has devoted relatively little attention to lexical semantics in general and even less to universals of lexical
fields.[1] This neglect is due in part to the structuralist belief that
meaning can not be studied as objectively or as rigorously as syntax and phonology, and in part to what was seen as the arbitrary
"semantic mapping" displayed by languages.[2] Most of the studies
that have been done either have concentrated on the structure of one
semantic domain in one language (e.g. Friedrich 1971; Lehrer 1969) or
have compared the structures of the same domain in two or more languages to reveal variation in categorization (e.g. Conklin 1955).

Among the studies that compared semantic domains in different
languages, most have been carried out by anthropological linguists
interested in the interplay of language and culture, from a relativ-
istic point of view. With this perspective, the general findings
were not at all surprising:

> The results obtained [of investigation of various se-
> mantic fields in the vocabularies of different lan-
> guages] have conclusively demonstrated the value of
> the structural approach to semantics, and have con-
> firmed the pronouncements of such earlier scholars
> as von Humboldt, de Saussure and Sapir to the effect
> that the vocabularies of different languages (in cer-
> tain fields at least) are non-isomorphic: That there
> are semantic distinctions made in one language which
> are not made in another; moreover that particular
> fields may be categorized in a totally different way
> by different languages.
>
> (Lyons 1968:429)

---

[1]A lexical field is a group of words closely related in meaning,
often subsumed under a general term, e.g. color, animals, cook-
ing terms (see Lehrer 1974).

[2]Uriel Weinreich emphasized the consequences of neglect at the
Dobbs Ferry Conference on Language Universals in 1961, when he
suggested that there were basically only two universal semantic
properties of languages on which linguists could agree: one was
that all languages are information-conveying mechanisms of a
unique type; the other was that "the semantic mapping of the
Universe by a language is in general arbitrary and the semantic
map of each language is different from those of all other languages."
(Weinreich 1963:114).

The "certain fields" to which Lyons was alluding included: kinship,
color, flora and fauna, military ranks, and moral and asthetic
evaluations. In the few years since Lyons made this statement,
however, a number of studies, largely in those very fields he cited,
have suggested that his conclusions were premature. Instead, in
semantic domains such as color, folk biology, and spatial relations, investigations have discovered a high degree of orderliness
and predictability across languages which reflects the basic modes
of cognition and perception which human beings share. [3]

In this paper, I will examine another semantic domain, that of
human body parts. [4] Although languages differ slightly in the way
they categorize this domain, there appear to be a number of con-
stancies and a limited set of patterns that characterize this domain
for any given language. The premise of this paper is that the universal principles of categorization and of nomenclature that determine this regularity of structure are largely the same as those
operating in many other semantic domains, and derive from the
facility of the human perceptual apparatus to deal with particular
attributes (e.g. shape, size, spatial orientation).

2   Universals of lexical fields

Until a few years ago, color terminology was traditionally
cited as a prime example of the way in which the same substance
could have a different form imposed on it by different languages;
it was thought of as "a happy hunting-ground for relativist semantics" (Leech 1974 : 234).   Numerous studies were available to
demonstrate that languages differ widely and unpredictably in the
way in which they cut up the continuum of color, indeed that color
distinctions may even be made according to quite different principles (see Lyons 1968). One of the most commonly cited studies
was one by Conklin (1955) of color terms in Hanunóo, a language
of the Philippines. He argued that while English divides the color

---

[3]Other semantic domains which have revealed universal principles of categorization include: kinship (Greenberg 1966), cook-
ing terms (Lehrer 1974), and folk botanical life forms (Brown
1977).

[4]Note that throughout this paper, the focus is limited to external
body parts, as opposed to internal organs, a separate, but related
domain in which there has already been some interesting work
(see, for example, Ultan 1975, 1976; Matisoff, in press).

continuum mainly on the basis of hue (and luminosity and satura-
tion) Hanunóo's four main color terms are associated with light-
ness, darkness, wetness and dryness -- 'proof' that color, in the
Western technical sense, was not a universal concept.

Less than two decades after Conklin's study, pioneering work
by Berlin and Kay (1969) led to a complete re-evaluation of relativism in the field of color terminology. Their investigation of almost
100 different languages revealed an orderliness that makes color
semantics predictable within quite narrow limits. By determining
the "basic color terms" in each language and by then identifying
the common foci (i.e. the best or most typical example) rather
than the boundaries of these colors, Berlin and Kay were able to
show that there exists a universal set of 11 basic color categories,
from which each language takes a subset.[5] Moreover, there is a
hierarchy of importance and development within this set, such that
if a language has a term for X (e.g. red), then it also has terms
for Y and Z (e.g. black and white). Establishment of this hierarchy allows us to limit the 2,048 possible combinations of 11 color
terms to the 33 types which actually occur.

Experimental work by Heider (1971, 1972) on selecting, naming,
and matching colors (by young children and by adult speakers of
23 different languages) has supported Berlin and Kay's finding of
11 universal color foci, and reinforced the idea that the basis for
these universals lies in the greater perceptual saliency of these
colors over all others in the spectrum. There is also growing
evidence that it is the actual physiology of the human visual system
that accounts for much of the regularity of color categories (Bornstein 1975).[6]

Color categories are the most frequently cited example of universals in a semantic field, largely because they were once thought
of as the best illustration of linguistic and cultural relativism.
There are other areas, however, in which investigators have uncovered interesting principles of lexical structure; and in each, as
in the case of color, studies in language acquisition and in child

---

[5]Basic terms differ from secondary terms in that: they are
commonly known; they are morphologically simple; they are not
restricted in application; and their domain of reference is not included in that of any other term.

[6]See, for example, Bornstein's (1975) discussion of studies
with infants, as well as McDaniel (1974) and deValois and Jacobs
(1968) on the Hering "opponent" theory of color vision (Hering 1920).

psychology lend support to the notion that the basis for lexico-
semantic universals lies in the way people universally categorize
perceptual information and organize their conceptual knowledge.
For example, work in folk biology (Berlin, Breedlove, and Raven,
1973) has helped isolate general principles of hierarchical organization and of labeling of natural categories, while work on adjectival opposites, on terms for spatial dimensions and relationships,
and on classifier systems has suggested certain perceptual sali-
encies and universal cognitive biases which determine cross-
language regularities within these fields. (See Clark and Clark
(1977) for a more complete review of these studies than presented
here.)

    Berlin et al. (1973) investigated the way people in a wide variety
of languages organize the field of "folk biology." Their findings
have shown that all people divide this field into two categories, analogous to the English categories PLANTS and ANIMALS. More interestingly, these major categories are always hierarchically organized into taxonomies of five levels of abstraction, such that a (sub)-
category at one level always belongs to a category at the next
higher level, and all categories at any given level are mutually
exclusive.[7] Furthermore, it is argued that among these five levels,
level three (which they term the "generic level") is the most basic:
there are more categories at this level than at others; the categories are at the most useful and "natural" level of abstraction; and
category labels are linguistically simpler than the peripheral words
found lower in the taxonomy (e.g. apple versus Pippin apple).[8]
That the generic level represents a natural way to divide up the
world (i.e. that relevant shared attributes are the most salient
at this level) is supported by Berlin et al.'s findings not only
that people felt generic terms to be primary but also that these
labels were the first ones learned by children in the societies
they studied.

    Lexico-semantic universals in adjectival opposites and terms
for spatial dimensions are somewhat different from those in taxonomic structure. The universals suggested in these domains derive

---

[7]For example, the categories tulip and daisy occur at the same
taxonomic level and are mutually exclusive, but both belong to the
immediately superordinate category flower.

[8]Compare these criteria with those discussed for identifying
basic color terms in footnote 5.

from consistent asymmetries between pairs of related words such
that whenever a language treats members of such a pair unequally,
the same member will always be the more basic (i.e. unmarked)
one, regardless of the particular language. For instance, in the
case of paired adjectival opposites like happy/unhappy (sad) or
good/bad, Greenberg (1966) has demonstrated that in all languages
which do not treat both members equally, there exists a marking
relation in which the positive member of the pair (e.g. happy,
good) is always unmarked. The linguistic criteria he proposed
for deciding which of two categories of thought was the marked one
included morphemic complexity and contextual neutralization. By
the first criterion, if a term b consists of term a plus an additional morpheme, then b is marked in relation to a; by the second
criterion, if one term (a) occurs with a 'general' meaning in
certain syntactic positions (e.g. in questions and in nominaliza-
tions) that the other term (b) does not, then b is marked (i.e.
more complex) than a. Thus, for the categories happy/unhappy
(sad) in English, happy is unmarked by both criteria: it is morphologically simpler than unhappy, and it is the neutral question term. [9]
In the case of good/bad, the first criterion is particularly applicable
in that there are a number of languages which have a term for
good, with its negative counterpart expressed as "ungood," but
few or no languages which have only a term bad, with a counterpart "unbad."

The criterion of contextual neutralization is probably easiest to
see in the spatial terms, for example: high/low, wide/narrow,
long/short, far/near. These words are all morphologically simple,
yet contextual neutralization reveals that in each pair the first term
is unmarked, the second marked. The neutral question forms for
these pairs all involve the first term; that is, in a situation where
a speaker has no prior knowledge or expectation, he asks, "How
high/wide/long/far is X?" To use the "marked" term involves certain presuppositions--e.g. "How short is she?" presupposes 'she'
is short. Moreover, when one of these paired spatial terms furnishes the basis for the name of the dimension itself, it is always
the unmarked member, giving height, width, length, etc. [10]

---

[9] That is, the question "Is she happy?" presupposes nothing
about her emotional state, whereas "Is she sad?" presupposes
she is sad.

[10] In the case of far/near, the superordinate (i.e. distance) is
related to neither term. Note, however, the related terms distal
and distant.

What is the basis for the marking relationships between terms in this domain? Cross-linguistic evidence suggests it is that in all languages (except where such terms are treated equally) those that describe "having extent" are all linguistically unmarked and positive, as compared to those "lacking extent" (Greenberg 1966). Lyons (1968) captures this phenomenon nicely:

> The fact that the distinction between antonyms is neutralized in certain syntactic positions (questions; nominalizations) contributes no doubt to our feeling that one antonym has a 'positive' and the other a negative polarity. We tend to say that small things lack size, rather than large things 'lack smallness.' And in general, the 'unmarked' is used for what is felt as 'more than' . . . the norm.
>
> (Lyons 1968:467)

That the foundation for this distinction lies in the structure of human cognition again finds support in a number of language acquisition studies that show that young children attend more to objects having extent. In comprehension tasks designed to test knowledge of the comparative and superlative forms of a number of dimensional adjective pairs (e.g. longer/shorter, longest/shortest), three-and-a-half-year-olds responded correctly more often when the adjective used referred to the unmarked (i.e. more extended) end of the dimension. Likewise, in production, children have been found to prefer unmarked, positive-pole adjectives to their marked negative-pole counterparts (Donaldson and Wales 1970; Wales and Campbell 1970). (Also, these unmarked adjectives are comprehended faster by adults--see H. Clark 1974.)

   In addition to this extension-favoring asymmetry between the two poles of any spatial dimension, there is also in this semantic field a dominance hierarchy among the different dimensions themselves, such that, for any object, either height (for a vertical orientation, e.g. a tree) or length (for a horizontal orientation, e.g. a bench) will always refer to its most extended dimension, with width and then thickness referring to lesser extensions (Bierwisch 1967). H. Clark (1973) has suggested that the particular dimensions languages pick out are "natural" dimensions in the sense that they are tied to aspects of the "real world," i.e. of nature. Verticality, for example, is the dimension defined by gravity, and its natural plane of reference is the ground. This dimension is also particularly salient in "real world" objects, like the human body, where it is perceptually obvious as the line running from head to toe. Perpendicular to this line in the body is the horizontal front/back plane, with a third line, the sagittal plane, splitting the body into symmetrical right and left sides.

Clark and Clark (1977) suggest that these natural dimensions have natural directions, with evidence that terms representing these directions, though not always linguistically unmarked, are easier to handle conceptually. For example, "upward" and "forward", which cover the optimally perceptible space above ground and in front, are therefore "positive" directions, and the positive terms related to these directions (e.g. in front of, ahead, above) are easier to process (H. Clark 1974). Further evidence of the dominance relationships and the directional asymmetries comes from work on children's early perceptual strategies: young children show an attentional bias for vertical and horizontal orientations of objects or designs, focusing most strongly on the vertical, and they show a preference for the upper part of a vertical orientation over the lower part and for top over bottom (see Ghent 1960, 1961; E. Clark, in preparation).[11]

Classifier systems are one other area that has revealed universal features of categorization which seem to derive from human perception. A classifier is a word or a particle--used in some cases with numeral-noun combinations and in other cases with certain types of verbs--that assigns entities to common categories on the basis of shared characteristics. For example, in languages that use numeral classifiers, the classifier typically names an observable property of the individual objects being counted, along with the class to which they belong, as in "nine round-things stones/ apples/stars" (see Greenberg 1972).

There have been several investigations of the numeral and verbal classifier systems prevalent in American Indian and Southeast Asian languages (see, for example, Hoijer 1951; Talmy 1972; Adams and Conklin 1973). Interestingly, striking resemblances appear between the distinctions marked in such systems and the criteria young children use in setting up early categories as they learn the semantics of their native language (E. Clark 1977).

---

[11]Thus, if children are presented with pictures of figures and random configurations, they show a strong tendency to orient them vertically, and to focus on the upper parts of the figure in preference to the lower parts. For instance, presented with a picture of a line with a circle at one end, they orient the picture so that the line is vertical with the circle at the top, e.g. ? is preferred over | or ──o (Ghent 1961).

The primary distinction made in classifier systems is between
animate and inanimate--a distinction based partly on perceptual
properties, such as movement. In addition, both animate and non-
animate objects are quite often categorized on the basis of shape.[12]
In particular, the shapes "round," "long," and (less frequently)
"flat" are most often pickedout, and are used either alone or with
some secondary feature like "rigidity," "relative size," or "orientation" (i.e. vertical versus horizontal) to classify objects. Thus,
ASSAMESE classifies rope and thread together [long and flexible],
while THAI classifies bead, stone, and seed together [round and
small] (Adams and Conklin 1973).

In the early stages of language acquisition, when children make
mistakes in labeling categories, they most often define a term (e.g.
dog) on the basis of one or more criterial properties (e.g. "four-
leggedness"), thereby often overextending the term to cover objects
(e.g. cats or cows) outside the adult category. The criterial
properties children use for such "overextensions" include shape,
movement (a factor in distinguishing animate/inanimate), size,
and texture. Of these the largest class of overextensions is based
on features of shape, most frequently on roundness, with length
also quite common. The strong resemblance these criteria bear
to the distinctions marked in classifier systems can be seen in the
following examples of (1) classifier categories and (2) children's
overextensions (from E. Clark 1973, 1977):

   1a. INDONESIAN - fruit, pea, eye, ball, stone [round]

    b. JAPANESE   - tree, pole, cut flower, arm, leg,
                     pencil [long and cylindrical]

   2a. FRENCH   - nipple (first referent)→ point of bare
                      elbow, eye in portrait, face in photo-
                      graph [round and small]

    b. ENGLISH   - stick (first referent)→cane, umbrella,
                      ruler, old-fashioned razor, board or
                      wood [long]

---

[12]Though a few classifiers depend on function, they are much
more likely to be language-specific and to reflect particular cultural orientations (Adams and Conklin 1973). Similarly, although
young children occasionally overextend words on the basis of function
(Bowerman 1975), function-based categorization seems in general
to be ignored until much later, when the child is more familiar
with the culture-specific mores of his society (Andersen 1975).

These similarities suggest not only the major role of visual perception, but also the importance of the shape features <u>round</u> and <u>long</u> in the formation of categories.

To summarize, recent studies of the semantics of various lexical fields suggest that, contrary to the warnings of earlier scholars, one may be able to "talk profitably" about semantic structure as the imposition of form upon an underlying (perceptual, physical, or conceptual) substance common to all languages. Though there are always differences from language to language that reflect accidental properties of thought and culture, there are a number of organizing principles that appear to derive from human cognitive-perceptual capacities. These principles can be subsumed into three general propositions that can then be tested in other domains:

(1) Natural categories tend to be organized into hierarchical structures of a certain number of levels (usually five), with (a) all (sub)categories at any given level mutually exclusive, (b) each category at one level always belonging to a superordinate category at the next higher level, and (c) basic terms at a middle, "generic" level (usually level 3).

(2) There is a cognitively based organization of spatial dimensions that is reflected in languages by universal marking relations and dominance hierarchies: (a) extension (and hence terms referring to it) along any dimension is conceptually unmarked and positive, as opposed to lack of extension; (b) certain natural dimensions are perceptually more salient than others and are often reflected in real world objects, like the human body -- especially salient orientations are verticality (the dimension defined by gravity and perceptually obvious in the human body as the line from head to toe), and, less so, horizontality (corresponding to a front-back plane in the body); (c) there are natural directions to these dimensions, such that "upward" (e.g. <u>above</u>, <u>on top</u>) and "forward" (e.g. <u>in front</u>) which are optimally perceptible, are positive, or conceptually unmarked, directions.

(3) In general, visually perceptible properties of objects, especially properties of shape, play a major role in forming categories. More particularly, the shape features <u>round</u> and (secondarily) <u>long</u> are especially salient and are therefore likely to be involved in classifying objects.

3.0 <u>The body-part domain</u>

If any of these suggested universal organizing features of language hold across domains, they would most likely be found in a "natural category," one that is neither composed of artifacts nor highly dependent on sociocultural institutions (see Lehrer 1974: 170). The body-part domain is promising because it is one for which we can assume a common perceptual reality--human bodies are structurally the same, no matter what the culture.

Of the many semantic questions that can be asked of this domain, several were raised over a decade ago by linguists like Weinreich (1963) and Ullman (1963), both of whom lamented the scarcity of data that could support or disconfirm hypotheses about the semantics of body-part vocabulary. The questions they suggested include the following: Are there signs, or designata (such as eye), that are shared by all languages? What "degree of terminologization" is likely to exist for a limited lexical domain; in particular, how many levels of contrast, and what is the incidence of polysemy?[13] Are there recurrent patterns of polysemous disjunction in languages, such that eye and ear, hand and foot, elbow and knee, are called by the same name, or that arm and hand, leg and foot, toe and finger, typically participate in polysemy? And how pervasive are parallel metaphors (like foot of a hill and leg of a table) and metonymic associations (as in tongue for language) which reveal a "common core of human experience" (Ullmann 1963; Weinreich 1963, 1966)?

In the last few years, a number of studies have suggested at least preliminary answers to these questions. Most of them have detailed the semantic structure of body-part vocabulary in various languages: QUECHUA (Stark 1969), TARASCAN (Friedrich 1969, 1970, 1971), NAVAHO (Werner and Begishe 1970), SERBO-CROATIAN (Liston 1972), GNAU (Lewis 1974), FINNISH (Ultan 1975), and HUASTEC (Brown et al. 1976). A few have looked at larger language families like Tibeto-Burman (Matisoff, in press) and Mayan (Brown, n.d.) or have compared aspects of body-part vocabulary for a small variety of languages: GERMAN, ROMANIAN, and SAXON (McClure 1975); FINNISH, FRENCH, GERMAN, ENGLISH, MASAI, and SWAHILI (Ultan 1976), and there is one major study of general principles of classification and nomenclature in human anatomical partonomy based on data from 41 globally distributed languages (Brown 1976).[14,15] The discussion of body-part vocabulary which follows draws heavily

---

[13]'Polysemy' is the name given, since Breal, to use of the same word in two or more distinct meanings. (See Ullman 1963 or Lehrer 1974 for a discussion of the difference between polysemy and homonymy.)

on these sources (particularly Brown 1976), together with data I
collected from speakers of several different languages.[16]

3.1 Universals in the structure of the domain

As in other fields, like folk biology, there is a hierarchical
organization to body-part domains in all languages. However, the
organization is somewhat different from that of other domains and
is best described as a partonomy (consisting of 'part of' relationships) as opposed to the more typical taxonomy (consisting of 'kind
of' relationships). To see this difference, one might consider the
following simplified schemata of the lexical fields of 'flower types'
versus 'body-parts':

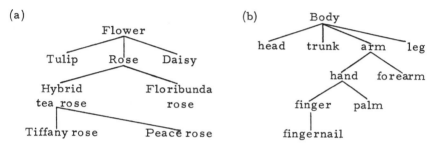

(a) Flower: Tulip, Rose, Daisy; Rose → Hybrid tea rose, Floribunda rose; Hybrid tea rose → Tiffany rose, Peace rose

(b) Body: head, trunk, arm, leg; arm → hand, forearm; hand → finger, palm; finger → fingernail

---

[14]The languages on which the Brown (1976) paper is based in-
clude: twelve American Indian languages (e.g. HUASTEC, NAVAHO,
QUECHUA, TARASCAN); ten European (e.g. ENGLISH, FRENCH,
GERMAN, RUSSIAN, SERBO-CROATIAN, SPANISH); five sub-
Saharan African (IBO, SWAHILI); four Mideastern and Western
Asian (ARABIC, FARSI, URDU); five Southeast Asian (MALAY,
THAI); two Chinese; and two Micronesian (PONAPEAN and
TRUKESE).

[15]Relevant data also appear in an earlier source: C.D.Buck's
Dictionary of Selected Synonyms in the Principal Indo-European
Languages (1949).

[16]I am grateful to the following people who patiently answered
my many questions and provided additional data: Cecil Brown
(HUASTEC and other Mayan languages); Linda Brown (POCOMCHI);
Vera Henzl (CZECH); Avi Omri (HEBREW); Miriam Petruck
(FINNISH); Kenneth Stallcup (MOGHAMO); Mohamed Tairu and
William Leben (HAUSA).

The first classification is a taxonomy: categories at different
levels are associated by 'kind of' relationships, such that a Tiffany
rose is a kind of hybrid tea rose, a hybrid tea rose is a kind of
rose, and a rose is a kind of flower. Although there are associations of this type within the body parts (e.g. arms and legs are
'kinds of' extremities), the domain is best characterized by a
partonomic classification, as illustrated in (b). In this case,
categories at different levels are associated by 'part of' relationships, such that a fingernail is part of a finger, a finger is part of
a hand, and so on up the tree.[17]

Most of the recent work on body parts has examined their
partonomic structure (cf. Brown 1976, McClure 1975, Liston 1972,
Stark 1969). Perhaps the most striking universal of these partonomies is what has been referred to as the 'depth principle' (Brown
et al. 1976). Just as Berlin et al. (1973) found for the structure of
biological folk taxonomies, there appears to be a limit on the
number of hierarchical levels that partonomies of human body-
parts may contain. Thus:

Body-part partonomies rarely exceed five levels and never
exceed six. In the few cases in which the lexical structure of the
domain contains six levels (where the first level is the 'unique be-
ginner'), there are never more than two categories at the fifth
level which dominate categories at the sixth, and these sixth-level
categories are always possessed by the categories FINGER and/or
TOE (i.e. when there is a sixth level, it is usually composed of
fingernail and/or toenail).[18,19] Three examples of body-part
partonomies (omitting details of subdomains) are illustrated in
the tree diagrams on the following pages.

---

[17]One difference between these two types of classification may
be that, unlike the case for taxonomies, the associations within a
partonomy are not always transitive. Thus, while all speakers
consider a SPIDER ORCHID to be a 'kind' of FLOWER, not all consider a FINGERNAIL to be a 'part of ARM' (cf. McClure 1975).

[18]One exception is the example given by Liston (1972) of
SERBO-CROATIAN 'noktiste' (half-moon) which is possessed by
'nokat' (nail).

[19]In the discussion that follows I have used the following notation: an underlined form in lower case -- like eye -- refers to the
lexical item; a form in upper case -- EYE -- indicates the actual
body-part referent.

Figure 1. The Body-Part System in Quechua

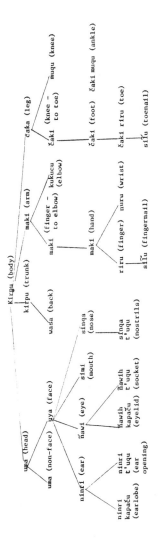

(Adapted from Stark, 1969)

Figure 2. The Body-Part Systems in Huastec

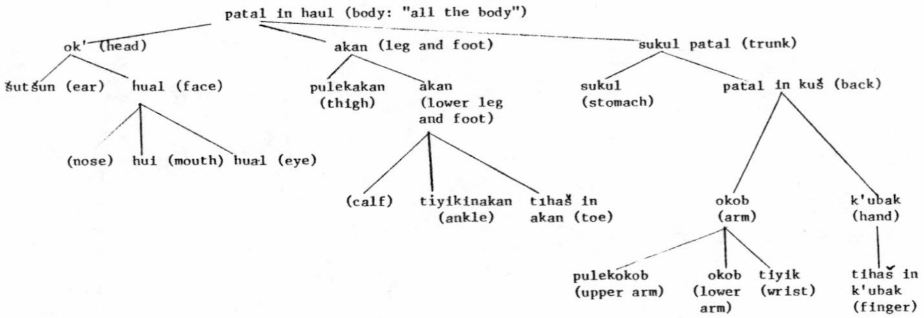

patal in haul (body: "all the body")

akan (leg and foot)

sukul patal (trunk)

ok' (head)

hual (face)

śutśun (ear)

puļekakan (thigh)

akan (lower leg and foot)

sukuļ (stomach)

patal in kuś (back)

(nose)   huļ (mouth)   huaļ (eye)

(calf)   tiyikinakan (ankle)   tihaś in akan (toe)

okob (arm)

k'ubak (hand)

puļekokob (upper arm)

okob (lower arm)

tiyik (wrist)

tihaś in k'ubak (finger)

(adapted from Brown et al., 1976)

Figure 3. The Body-Part System in Serbo-Croatian

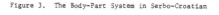
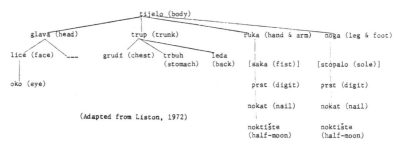

In addition to the depth principle, there are several other
universals which characterize this domain, some of them unrestricted universals, others either implicational or statistical universals.
Some of these pertain to what is named, i.e. categorization principles regarding what body-parts are universally perceived and
given recognition, while others pertain to how perceived parts are
named, i.e. nomenclature principles concerning (i) typical patterns of polysemy or (ii) what is labeled by a basic term, what by
a derived term. While these principles are often related (see
Brown 1976), for the purposes of this paper they will be treated
separately.

3.11 Principles of categorization

While all languages may recognize and label the head, the
trunk, and the upper and lower limbs, they often divide these parts
up somewhat differently. There is not always an exact correspondence across languages for the reference of a given term. For instance, in one language (or group of languages) the term glossed as
leg may refer to the area from the top of the thigh to the ankle, in
another it includes the foot to the point where the toes begin, while
in still another it refers to the area from the thigh to the tip of the
toe (i.e. including the entire foot). Similarly, while in some languages (e.g. ENGLISH) the term for nose refers to the area from
the bridge to the distal point, in others it may also include the
forehead (e.g. TARASCAN). With this caution in mind, universals
of categorization for the domain of human body-parts include the
following:[20]

---

[20]Many of these principles are found also, in somewhat different terms, in Brown (1976).

a) The BODY is labeled in all body-part partonomies.

b) Every language includes a term for HEAD in its lexical field of body-parts, and the term is always immediately possessed by BODY. Other categories which, in addition to HEAD, usually occur at the second level of the partonomy include TRUNK, ARM (and HAND), and LEG (and FOOT).[21]

c) All languages label EYES, NOSE, and MOUTH.

d) The upper limb, ARM (and HAND), is named by a distinct term in all languages.

e) The categories FINGER and TOE are always labeled (by one of four general patterns of nomenclature--see section 3.12).

f) All languages name (FINGER)NAIL and (TOE)NAIL (by one of two patterns--see 3.12 below).

g) A term for LEG (labeled in most languages) implies a separate term for ARM.[22] Thus, while many languages have terms for both LEG and ARM, and some have a term for ARM alone, none have a term LEG alone.

h) A label for FOOT implies a separate term for HAND. The categories HAND and FOOT, which are often but not always labeled (see Figure 3), never share the same label, in contrast to other 'symmetrical' parts of the upper and lower body, like FINGER/TOE (see 3.12 below). When these body parts are not labeled (as in CHIRAH-MBWA, a language of the CAMEROUNS), the limbs are partitioned at the point where the digits meet the hand or foot.

i) Terms for INDIVIDUAL TOES imply terms for INDIVIDU- AL FINGERS. Thus, there are languages which label (1) no indi- vidual digits, (2) some individual fingers but no individual toes, and (3) a subset of both fingers and toes. However, I could find no language that labels some individual toes but no individual fingers.

---

[21]Parentheses indicate that a part may or may not be included across languages in the reference of a term. Thus, language A may have a term which refers to ARM including HAND, while B has a term which refers to ARM ending at the wrist.

[22]At least three languages, HOPI, INUPIK, and TARASCAN, do not label LEG (+FOOT) though they do label subparts (e.g. THIGH, CALF).

Examples of languages that label individual digits are ENGLISH
(and FINNISH) (pattern b), which have the terms thumb (peukalo)
and pinkie (pikkirilli), CZECH (pattern c), which labels both big
toe and thumb with the term palec, and HEBREW (also pattern c),
which has the terms agudal (thumb) and bohen (big toe). (HEBREW,
like CZECH, also has labels for the other fingers, e.g. kmitza
(ring finger), zeret (pinkie).)

Although the universals listed here are probably not the only
universals of categorization in this domain, they are the main ones
for which sufficient relevant data were available.

3.12 Polysemy and basic versus derived terms

English has a more highly differentiated body-part domain
than many other languages in the sense that it has a high proportion
of morphologically simple, univocal terms.[23] In examining this
domain in other languages, however, one is struck by two general
phenomena: (1) certain types of polysemous relationships appear
over and over again in unrelated languages; (2) a number of categories are (almost) universally given the least complex expression,
with other categories often derived from them in fairly predictable
ways.

The categories in the present data that are usually given
morphologically simple expression include the following: HEAD
(always labeled by a basic, unanalyzable term); ARM (the one exception to this is the Finnish kasivarsi, or "hand handle"); LEG, if
labeled; FACE; EYE; MOUTH; and EAR. Other universally labeled
parts which are often but not always allotted basic terms are
FINGER/TOE and FINGERNAIL/TOENAIL.

For the categories FINGER/TOE, four patterns of nomenclature occur: (1) the least common, the English system—found
also in FINNISH and ESKIMO—with different basic terms for each
category (this pattern implies distinct basic terms for HAND and
FOOT); (2) the SERBO-CROATIAN pattern (Figure 3) with one
polysemous basic term (also in CZECH, HEBREW, SPANISH,
ALEUT, MAYAN; (3) the HUASTEC system (Figure 2) with different labels derived from the same root (also in MANDARIN
CHINESE and HOPI); and (4) the QUECHUA pattern (Figure 1) of
one basic unanalyzable term for FINGER, with TOE derived from
it (also in HAUSA, MOGHAMO, MALAY, RUSSIAN, SWAHILI,

---

[23]A univocal term has one meaning.

LATIN, and SHANGHAI dialect CHINESE). Thus, languages frequently refer to toes as "fingers of the foot, " but never to fingers
as "toes of the hand."

For the categories FINGERNAIL/TOENAIL, only two patterns
occur: either the same basic term (analogous to ENGLISH <u>nail</u>) is
applied to both categories (as shown in Figures 1 and 3 for QUECHUA
and SERBO-CROATIAN, respectively), or different terms are derived from a common root, as in ENGLISH, SYRIAN ARABIC (<u>difr</u>
<u>ℓˀid</u> / <u>difr   ℓˀižr</u>), and THAI (<u>lap mur/lap tin</u>).

Basic terms are frequently polysemous and often provide the
source for derived terms referring to other body-parts. In each
instance, the recurrent patterns of nomenclature using these terms
seem to derive from one of two possible sources: the relationships
are based either on structural similarity or on spatial contiguity.

Structural similarity means that there are properties of <u>shape</u>
that are common to the lexically related parts (e.g. both are long
and thin) and/or that the denotata are located at <u>parallel positions</u>
(e.g. at the distal end of both upper and lower limbs). Tables 1 and
2 contain examples of (1) polysemy and (2) derived terms based on
structural similarity.

Table 1:   Some examples of polysemy based on structural similarity

Referents named by same lexical item	Example of lexical item		Examples of other languages
head/knee	- čž -	(Tarascan)*	Several Mayan languages
eye/face	lẽ	(Sango)	Tarascan, Huastec and over 30 other Mayan languages
neck/calf of leg (just under knee)	-ča-	(Tarascan)	
forearm/calf of leg	dantsi	(Hausa)	
finger/toe	etzbaot	(Hebrew)	Romanian, Aleut, Spanish, Kayan, several Slavic languages
fingers/fingers minus thumbs	fanyar	(Saxon)	German, English
fingernail/toenail	farce silu	(Hausa) (Quechua)	French, Spanish, Hebrew, Serbo-Croatian, Czech

*Tarascan body-part morphemes are suffixes which must be added to stems
(see Friedrich 1969).

Table 2: Some examples of derived terms based on structural similarity

Basic term and referent	Derived term and referent	Language (other languages)
nah : head	→ nah ch'ehk : knee (head of lower leg)	Pocomchi (Quechua, Tzotzil, Jacaltec, and a number of other Mayan langs.)
paa : head	→ kynärpää : elbow (cubit head)	Finnish
nah : head	→ nahtuuq : buttocks (head of leg)	Pocomchi
paa : head	→ sormenpää : fingertip (finger head)	Finnish (Pocomchi)
nah : head	→ nah oquis : toe (head of foot)	Pocomchi
nah : head	→ nah teleb' : shoulder (head of arm)	Pocomchi (Finnish)
mɛʔ-ší : eye	→ khɨ-mɛ̂ʔ-ší : ankle ("eye of foot")	Lahu (many East and SE Asian Languages, Malay, Burmese, Indonesian
wach : face	→ wach teleb : forearm (face, i.e. surface of arm)	Pocomchi
wach : face	→ wachtuuq : thigh (face of leg)	Pocomchi
wach : face	→ wach ch'ehk : shin (face of lower leg)	Pocomchi
wach : face	→ rwacha-ch'chk : knee (face of foreleg)	Tzutujil
juʔ : nose	→ juʔqʼobʼis : finger (nose of hand)	Pocomchi
juʔ : nose	→ juʔ oqis : toe (nose of foot)	Pocomchi
wuya : neck	→ wuyarhannu : wrist (neck of arm/hand)	Hausa (Pocomchi)
wuya : neck	→ wuyarƙafa : ankle (neck of leg/foot)	Hausa
zglob : wrist	→ zglob na nozi : ankle ("wrist or joint of leg")	Serbo-Croatian (Huastec)
prst : finger	→ prst na nozi : toe (finger of leg)	Serbo-Croatian (Hausa, Quechua, Moghano, Malay, Russian, Swahili, Chinese, most Romance Languages)
sonci : fingernail	→ tukni-sonci : toenail	Zuni (Finnish)
gwiwa : knee	→ gwiwar hannu : elbow (knee of arm)	Hausa (Moghano)
muqu : knee	→ čaki muqu : ankle (lower leg/foot - knee, or hill)	Quechua
muqu : knee	→ wasa muqu : shoulder blade (1 back-knee or hill)	Quechua
tihas : ("long, thin object")	→ tihas in kʼubak : finger tihas in akan : toe	Huastec (Arabic, Hopi, Mandarin Chinese)

The paired terms illustrated in Table 1 are based mainly on
shape. Pairs like head/knee and eye/face refer to roundish objects; that the latter analogy is based on shape is suggested by
trans-field polysemy, in which these same terms refer also to
fruit, seeds, and 'glowing coal'--all round (Samarin 1967).
Similarly, pairs like finger/toe and neck/calf of leg refer to long,
thin objects.[24] Most of these matchings also reflect a common
conceptualization of the parallel structure between upper and lower
limbs (e.g. fingernail/toenail). Moreover, in each of these pairs
the first referent is the primary meaning, in the sense that it is
the referent in most neutral contexts. For example, when hual,
the HUASTEC term for EYE/FACE is used in compounded forms
designating diseases, the forms usually refer to conditions of the
eye rather than conditions of the face, e.g. ya? ul-hual "eye irri-
tation" (Brown, personal communication). The primacy of the
first referents is also reflected in the pattern of basic and derived
terms shown in Table 2. Here, one category is primary and has a
unitary label, the other is secondary and has the same label, usually with a modifier. Thus, terms for HEAD, EYE, FINGER, and
WRIST (to name a few) are the basis for derived terms referring
to KNEE, ANKLE (an analogy between the eye and the small round
bone on the outside of the ankle), TOE, and ANKLE (by spatial
analogy), respectively. As in Table 1, many examples in Table 2
capture the symmetry between parts of the upper and lower body.
And in each case, the basic term refers to a body-part above the
waist, the derived term to one below it. The one exception is
knee/elbow (e.g. HAUSA), where the term for the 'front' body-
part (KNEE) is basic, and the term for the analogous 'back' part
(ELBOW) is derived. Moreover, in several of these instances,
the basic term is also a generic one which covers both the primary
and secondary categories.[25] In ROMANIAN (and other Romance
languages), for example, the term deget refers to FINGERS and
TOES (i.e. digits), but in neutral contexts or when unmodified it
refers only to the upper digits, FINGERS (McClure 1975). Likewise, WRIST and ANKLE may be included under one generic term
(which may be glossed as joint) that also refers to the upper joint,
WRIST, alone, but to express ANKLE alone an addendum is

---

[24]Actually, Friedrich (1969) suggests the latter polysemy may
derive from the spatial concept of "narrowing."

[25]Note that this type of repetition of the same term at different
levels has often been discussed as a common marking property, as
in man → man/woman (see Greenberg 1966).

necessary. There are analogous examples for head/knee and for fingernail/toenail.

Tables 3 and 4 provide typical examples of polysemy and derived terms based on spatial contiguity. Spatial contiguity is involved when the same or related terms refer to body-parts that are anatomically adjacent to one another. The most widespread polysemous relationships of this type appear to involve ARM/HAND and LEG/FOOT. In each of these pairs, the referents consist of a long, thin object (e.g. ARM) and an independently movable part (e.g. hand) at its distal end (i.e. at the point of greatest extent from the trunk). There are also other pairs involving both ARM and LEG, as well as a number of examples with EYE.

Among the derived terms based on contiguity (Table 4) the linguistic form sometimes makes the spatial relationship quite explicit: e.g. face = "along the eye" (GOTHIC), wrist = "behind the fist" (CZECH). Even here, however, the role of shape is clearly important, as evidenced by the expressions "eye cape" (QUECHUA for eyelid), "ear leaf" (FINNISH for earlobe), "spoon of the arm/leg" (HEBREW for hand/foot), "hand handle" (FINNISH for arm), or even "eyeball" and "eye-egg" (ENGLISH and FINNISH, respectively).

Because those terms that serve as the primary meaning in polysemy or as the source for derived terms are so often also terms for body-parts which are universally perceived and given recognition (see 3.11 above), it appears that there is something especially salient about these body-parts. McClure (1975) suggested that in most examples of polysemy among the three languages she looked at, a given term referred to a 'whole' (e.g. BODY) and its most salient part (e.g. TRUNK). HUASTEC informants give support to this notion when they explain that hual (FACE/EYE, and BODY in 'patal in hual') refers to what is "looked at" when one encounters another human (Brown et al. 1976). But what makes a part "most salient"? In the example from McClure cited above, size might make TRUNK the most visually perceptible part of the BODY. In other cases, such as MOUTH/LIPS, EAR/EXTERNAL EAR, visual perception is clearly involved. The majority of the examples presented in Tables 1-4, however, suggest that perceptual salience of particular shapes (namely, 'round,' 'long and thin') and spatial dimensions (especially the vertical dimension and its positive, upward direction) underlie these lexical relationships.

Table 3: Some examples of polysemy based on spatial contiguity

Referents named by same lexical item /	Examples of lexical item /	Examples of other languages
head/head without face	uma (Quechua)	Serbo-Croatian
eye/face[a]	nari (Tarascan)	Sango Huastec, and over 30 other languages
eye/body	" "	
eye/eyeball	Auge (German)	Romanian, Saxon
nose/forehead	ru (Tarascan)	
mouth/lips	gura (Romanian)	Saxon, German Tarascan
ear/external ear	eyr (Saxon)	German, Romanian
cheek/face	obraz (Romanian)	Czech
body/trunk[b]	goof (Hebrew)	Quechua, Romanian, Saxon, German
body/body without head[c]	tijelo (Serbo-Croatian)	Hausa, English Saxon
arm/hand	ruka (Russian)	German, Polish, Greek, Irish, Saxon, Quechua, Hausa, Czech, Romanian, Lahu, and other Tibeto-Burman languages
arm/forearm	okob (Huastec)	Quechua
arm/upper arm	brat (Romanian)	German
leg/foot	cos (Irish)	Finnish, Czech, Romanian, Saxon, German, Serbo-Croatian, several Tibeto-Burman languages
leg and foot/lower leg and foot	caka (Quechua)	Huastec
side/upper leg	ta (Tarascan)	

[a] Tarascan body-part morphemes are suffixes which must be added to stems (see Friedrich, 1969).

[b] In a number of languages, there is a polysemous term meaning body/skin— This is also the case for Pidgin English spoken in the Camerouns.

[c] In English, for instance, we can say "He has a nice face but an ugly body."

Table 4: Some examples of derived terms based on spatial contiguity

Basic term and referent	Derived term and referent	Language (other languages)
pää : head	päpänahka : scalp (head leather)	Finnish
augō : eye	andaugi : face (along eye)	Gothic (Greek)
hual : eye/face	patal in hual : body (all the eye)	Huastec (Tarascan)
silmä : eye	silmä muna : eyeball (eye egg)	Finnish (English
ñawi : eye	ñawih t'uqu : eye socket	Quechua
ñawi : eye	ñawih kapacu : eyelid ("eye cape")	Quechua (English)
korva : ear	korvan lehti : earlobe (ear leaf)	Finnish (English, Quechua)
ninri : ear	ninri t'uqu : ear opening	Quechua
sinqa : nose	sinqa t'uqu : nose opening	Quechua
yad : arm (+ hand)	kaf-yad : hand (shovel/spoon of arm)	Hebrew
käsi : hand	käsi varsi : arm (hand handle)	Finnish
là⁷ : hand	là⁷-cì : wrist (hand joint)	Lahu
pěst : fist	zá pesti : wrist (behind fist)	Czech
sukul : stomach	sukul patal : trunk (all the stomach)	Huastec
regel : leg (and foot)	kaf regel : foot (shovel/ spoon of leg)	Hebrew

3.2 Body-parts in language acquisition and child development

Although acquisition of body-part terms per se has not been investigated, diary studies and children's early vocabulary lists provide some information about which body-part terms are used. Some of these studies (e.g. Boyd 1914; Moore 1896; Nice 1915) describe the child's vocabulary at a particular age, but provide no order of emergence for distinct terms. Table 5 gives some examples. Other studies also supply information about the order of acquisition for specific terms. Data from some of these are presented in Table 6.

Children in these different studies tended to acquire their body-part vocabulary in parallel ways. For example, they learned terms for parts of the head early, followed by terms for parts of the ex-tremities, and only later by terms for the rest of the body (e.g. chest, stomach). In general, their earliest terms apply to parts of the face; among these, eye (referring to a small, round, moveable part) ap-pears first in many vocabularies, and is always one of the first three body-part words acquired. (Note that some languages have a polyse-mous term for FACE and EYE.) In all cases, eye is learned be-fore its derived terms, eyebrow, eyelash, etc. (analogously, finger

before fingernail). Moreover, most early body-part terms come
from the most useful "middle level of categorization" (Rosch et al.
1976). Terms like eye and ear tend to be learned not only before
more specific terms like eyelash or earlobe, but also before more
general terms like body or head.

The rest of the parallel patterns of acquisition reflect the
same upper-body/lower-body and front/back relationships noted
earlier. Hand, for instance, usually comes in before foot (occasionally at the same time), arm before leg, and knee (+front)
before elbow (-front). In this regard, Melissa Bowerman (personal communication) observed an interesting mistake by one of her
daughters (aged 2;10). The child asked her mother to "hold onto
my ankles" while extending her wrists. When asked a few days
later where her ankles were, the child pointed to her wrists.
Asked where her wrists were, she pointed to her forearms. While
this may at first seem to contradict the hypothesized upper/lower
relationship, I believe it supports the general principles suggested
in this paper (a) by showing a clear analogy based on structural

Table 5: Some early body-part words acquired by age two [a,b]

Boyd	Moore	Nice
arm	back	ear
bosom	body	eye
brow	chin	finger
cheek	eye	foot
chin	ear	hair
ear	feet	hand
eye	finger	head
face	hand	knee
feet	head	mouth
finger	lap	nose
hair	leg	toe
hand	lip	
knee	mouth	
leg	nose	
mouth	nail	
nail	neck	
neck	stomach	
nose	thumb	
skin	toe	
thumb		
toe		

[a] In alphabetical order
[b] Children acquiring English

Table 6: Order of acquisition of body-part terms [a]

Bowerman [c]

Column A
- nose, chin, eye } 16 mos.
- eye
- hand
- ear, toes(e) } 17 mos
- arm, face, hair } 18 mos
- tummy, body, lips, foot
- knee, finger } 19 mos
- mouth, thumb
- neck } 20 mos

Column B
- eye – 15 mos.
- arm – 16 mos.
- ear, hair, mole, mouth, hand, knee } 17b mos
- head, nose, leg, feet, fanny, back, body } 18 mos
- face, neck } 19 mos
- tummy, shoulder, elbow, finger, lip } 21 mos
- thumb, toe, ankle, chin, cheek, eyebrow, skin, trunk } 24 mos

Giant (1915) — Column G
- hand, mouth } 16 mos.
- ear, eye, forehead, hair } 17 mos
- chin, nose } 18 mos
- back, cheek, face, feet, heel, nail, neck } 19 mos
- finger, knee, leg, lip, shoulder, toe } 20 mos
- arm, elbow, finger, stomach, waist, wrist } 21 mos
- fingernail, skin } 23 mos

Leopold (1939)

Column D (English)
- eye, knee } 19 mos.
- ear, nose } 20 mos
- feet, mouth, neck } 22 mos
- hair } 23 mos

Column D (German)
- auge (eye), knie (knee) } 19 mos.
- nase (nose) } 20 mos
- füss (foot), haar (hair) } 22 mos

Nelson (1973)

Column E
- ear, eyes, toes } 15b mos

Column F
- toes } 18 mos

Column G
- eye, nose, hand } 19b mos
- ears, knee } 20b mos

Column H
- eyes } 19 mos
- nose, ear, leg, skin } 22 mos

Column I
- eye, mouth, nose } 17b mos

Column J
- eye } 23 mos
- mouth, nose } 24 mos

Column K
- eyes } 20 mos

Smith (1973) — Column L
- arm, back, cheek, elbow, eye, feet, finger, hand, head, knee, mouth, nose, skin } 26 mos
- neck, eyebrow } 28 mos
- behind, eyelash, face, hair, thumb, tummy } 29 mos
- chin, leg, lip } 30 mos

a All English, except Leopold.
b In order of acquisition that month.
c Column heading refers to author of study; I am grateful to Melissa Bowerman, who provided me with the unpublished data from the first two subjects.

similarity (one that indeed occurs formally in a number of languages), and (b) by suggesting a solution based on spatial contiguity. Moreover, even though the child may have used the adult term for "lower leg joint" first, she thought it meant the corresponding (upper-body) arm joint, and so it was as if she had learned WRIST first.

Salience of the upper body is further evidenced by children's listings of body-parts. Both ENGLISH- and PORTUGUESE-speaking four-year-olds, when asked to name the body-parts of a doll, began with parts of the head and ended with the feet or the toes.[26] They also tended to name basic-level terms (eye, mouth, hand) rather than more general or more specific ones. This same preference shows up in children's early drawings of human figures, a skill that has been considered a useful measure of cognitive development (Harris 1963; Lowenfeld and Brittain 1970). Children's first recognizable drawings are usually of people; the first part drawn is a round head, which first shows eyes, a mouth, and ears (all roundish). In the next stage, two long vertical lines, directly attached to the head, appear as legs. Shorter lines are then added as arms, with roundish hands at the ends; a nose is added to the face; finally a trunk and a neck appear. Both heads and hands are often drawn disproportionately large. Thus, in graphic representation as well as in vocabulary development, there appears to be a ranking of importance from the head and its parts (especially the eyes) to the extremities (all long and thin) to the trunk. It is interesting to note that studies of infant perception have suggested a developmental sequence in which infants at seven to eight weeks fixate on black dots on an oval or a round surface, at two to three months show a preference for realistically portrayed eyes (even when presented with an empty "under-face"), and only later require more detailed portrayal of a face to elicit smiling (Ahrens 1954; Gibson 1969). Whether the eyes attract attention mainly by their movement, their round shape, or their shininess is not entirely clear, but some combination of these properties seems to contribute to special perceptual salience of the eyes.[27]

---

[26]These data come from a pilot study by Lyris Wiedemann (n.d.), with additional data collected by the present investigator from English-speaking children and adults.

[27]Somewhat older children (three years) appear to give special importance to the visibility of their eyes in deciding whether they can be seen by others (John H. Flavell, personal communication.)

3.3 Principles underlying lexical structure and language acquisition

A comparison of the body-part terms across a variety of languages reveals a number of organizing principles similar to those reflected in children's acquisition of body-part terms and also present in other lexical domains. First, the domain tends to be organized into a hierarchical structure with five (or occasionally six) levels, with basic terms at a middle, "generic" level (usually level three). Secondly, visually perceptible properties of the referents, especially those of shape and of spatial location, play a major role in category formation and in lexical relations. Buck (1949) argued that, in Indo-European languages at least, diachronic evidence exists for the importance of these properties:

> So far as we can judge from the words whose etymology is clear, the underlying notion [of body-part terms] is more often related to the position or shape of the part than to its function. The inherited words for EYE, EAR, NOSE, MOUTH, FOOT, are not derived from any of the usual verbs for 'see', 'hear', 'smell', 'speak' (or eat), 'walk', and so far as some cognates of the former are applied to function, this is probably, and in most cases certainly secondary. (Buck 1949: 197)

Thus, for example, words for BACK come from notions like 'bent' or 'hind-part', and words for HEAD are from the idea 'top', 'summit', or through skull from 'bowl', 'cup', etc. In particular, the shape features 'round' and (secondarily) 'long' are especially salient and are therefore likely to be involved in classifying and labeling objects. Ultan (1975, 1976) provides additional support from his investigation of descriptivity in the domain of body-part terms in six languages. Not only are physical forms (most common) and location the main sources of descriptive terms in these languages (see Table 7), but also the particular shape

Table 7: Percentage of body-part terms motivated by
Shape, Location, or Function [a,b]

	German	French	Finnish	Masai	Ewe	Swahili
Shape	62.0	36.4	63.2	54.5	48.7	50.0
Location	20.4	37.8	11.8	33.4	41.0	28.1
Function	17.6	25.8	25.0	12.1	10.3	21.9

[a] Adapted from Ultan, 1976, p. 14

[b] These figures are based on both external and internal body-part terms, with the latter contributing more to the function category

features 'round', as in eye and head, and 'long and thin', as in arm, most often motivate derived, descriptive terms.

Similarly, the natural directions 'upward', or 'above', and 'forward', or 'in front', which are optimally perceptible, appear to be conceptually unmarked directions in categorizing and label- ing body-parts, and serve as the basis for deriving terms whose referents are in the lower or back portions of the body.

3.4 Conclusion

Unlike the sometimes capricious and apparently arbi- trary classification of certain social phenomena, all men appear to be constrained in their conceptualization of the world of plants and animals.

(Berlin 1972: 53)

As in other domains like plants and animals, regularities in the lexical structure of human body-part terms across languages suggest basic modes of cognition that human beings share. In this paper, I have argued that these regularities are based in good part on the perceptual salience of certain shapes and certain spatial dimensions. In unrelated languages, there are recurrent patterns of nomenclature (e.g. of polysemy and of word-derivation) in which the motivating factor appears to be analogy based on shape, espec- ially the shape features round and (secondarily) long. Likewise, in countless cases of lexical relations between terms for symmetrical upper- and lower- body-parts (e.g. finger/toe), there appears to be a marking relationship by which terms referring to parts of the lower-body are marked, those referring to parts of the upper-body unmarked. Developmental data from children support the premise that the universal principles of categorization and of nomenclature that determine this regularity of structure are largely the same as those operating in many other semantic domains and derive from the ability of the human perceptual apparatus to deal with attributes like shape, size, and spatial orientation.

BIBLIOGRAPHY

Adams, K. L. and N. F. Conklin. 1973. Toward a theory of natural classification. In Papers from the Ninth Regional Meeting, Chicago Linguistic Society, 1-10.

Ahrens, R. 1954. Beiträge zur Entwicklung des Physioanomie und Mimikerkennes. Zeitschrift für Experimental und angewandte Psychologie 2. 412-54, 599-633.

Andersen, E. S. 1975. Cups and glasses: Learning that boundaries are vague. Journal of Child Language 2. 79-103.

Berlin, B. 1972. Speculation on the growth of ethnobotanical nomen-clature. Language in Society 1. 51-86.

Berlin, B. and E.A. Berlin. 1975. Aguaruna color categories. American Ethnologist 2. 61-87.

_____, D. Breedlove and P. Raven. 1973. General principles of classification and nomenclature in folk biology. American Anthropologist 75. 214-42.

_____ and P. Kay. 1969. Basic color terms: Their universality and evolution. Berkeley: University of California Press.

Bierwisch, M. 1967. Some semantic universals of German adjectivals. Foundations of Language 3. 1-36.

Bohn, W.E. 1914. First steps in verbal expression. Pedagogical Seminary 21. 578-95.

Bornstein, M. 1975. The influence of visual perception on culture. American Anthropologist 77. 774-98.

Bowerman, M. 1975. The acquisition of word meaning. Third Inter-national Child Language Symposium, London, September 1975.

Boyd, W. 1914. The development of a child's vocabulary. Pedagogical Seminary 21. 95-124.

Brown, C. n.d. Folk anatomy and language change.

Brown, C.H. 1976. General principles of human anatomical partonomy and speculations on the growth of partonomic nomenclature. American Ethnologist 3. 400-24.

_____, J. Kolar, B. Torrey, T. Truong-Quang, and P. Volkman. 1976. Some general principles of biological and non-biological folk classification. American Ethnologist 3. 73-85.

Buck, C.D. 1949. A dictionary of selected synonyms in the principal Indo-European languages: A contribution to the history of ideas. Chicago: University of Chicago Press.

Clark, E.V. 1973. What's in a word? On the child's acquisition of semantics in his first language. In T.E. Moore (ed.) Cognitive development and the acquisition of language. New York: Academic Press. 65-110.

Clark, E.V. 1977. Universal categories: On the semantics of classifiers and children's early word meanings. In A. Juilland (ed.), Linguistic studies offered to Joseph Greenberg on the oc-casion of his sixtieth birthday (Vol. 1). Saratoga, California: Anma Libri. 449-62.

Clark, E.V. Forthcoming. Where's the top? On the acquisition of orientational terms. Stanford University. In preparation.

Clark, H.H. 1973. Space, time, semantics, and the child. In T.E. Moore (ed.), Cognitive development and the acquisition of language. New York: Academic Press. 28-63.

_____. 1974. Semantics and comprehension. In T.A. Sebeok (ed.), Current trends in linguistics. Vol. 12, Linguistics and adjacent arts and sciences. The Hague: Mouton. 1291-1498.

_____ and E.V. Clark. 1977. Psychology and language: An introduction to psycholinguistics. New York: Harcourt Brace Jovanovich.

Conklin, H.C. 1955. Hanunóo color categories. Southwestern Journal of Anthropology 11:339-44.

deValois, R. and G. Jacobs. 1968. Primate color vision. Science 162:533-40.

Donaldson, M. and R. Wales. 1970. On the acquisition of some relational terms. In J.R. Hayes (ed.), Cognition and the development of language. New York: John Wiley. 235-68.

Fillmore, C.J. 1969. (Review of componential analysis of general vocabulary by E.H. Bendix.) General Linguistics 9. 41-65.

Friedrich, P. 1969a. Metaphor-like relations between referential subsets. Lingua 24. 1-10.

_____. 1969b. On the meaning of the Tarascan suffixes of space. IJAL 35. 1-49.

_____. 1970. Shape in grammar. Language 46. 379-407.

_____. 1971. The Tarascan suffixes of locative space: Meaning and morphotactics. Bloomington: Indiana Univ. Press.

Ghent, L. 1960. Recognition by children of realistic figures in various orientations. Canadian J. of Psychology 14. 249-54.

_____. 1961. Form and its orientation: The child's eye view. Am. J. of Psychology 74. 177-90.

Gibson, E. 1969. Principles of perceptual learning and development. New York: Appleton-Century-Crofts.

Goodenough, W.H. 1956. Componential analysis and the study of meaning. Language 32. 195-216.

Grant, J.R. 1915. A child's vocabulary and its growth. Pedagogical Seminary 22. 183-203.

Greenberg, J.H. 1966. Language universals. The Hague: Mouton.

_____. 1972. Numeral classifiers and substantival number: Problems in the genesis of a linguistic type. WPLU 9. 1-39.

Harris, D. 1963. Children's drawings as a measure of intellectual maturity. New York: Harcourt Brace and World.

Heider, E.R. 1972. Universals in color naming and memory. J. of Experimental Psychology 93:10-20.

_____. 1971. "Focal" color areas and the development of color names. Developmental Psychology 4:447-55.

Hering, E. 1964. Outlines of a theory of the light sense (1920). Cambridge, Massachusetts: Harvard University Press.

Hoijer, H. 1951. Cultural implications of some Navaho linguistic categories. Language 27:110-20.

Landar, H. and J.B. Casagrande. 1962. Navaho anatomical reference. Ethnology 1:370-3.

Leech, G.H. 1974. Semantics. Harmondsworth, England: Penguin.

Lehrer, A. 1969. Semantic cuisine. J. of Linguistics 5:39-55.

_____. 1974. Semantic fields and lexical structure. Amsterdam: North Holland.

Leopold, W.F. 1939. Speech development of a bilingual child (Vol. 1). Evanston, Illinois: Northwestern University Press.

Lewis, G. 1974. Gnau anatomy and vocabulary for illnesses. Oceania 45:50-78.

Liston, J.L. 1972. The semantic structure of body-part terms in Serbo-Croatian: The part-whole hierarchy. Anthropological Linguistics 14:323-38.

Lowenfeld, V. and W. Brittain. 1970. Creative and mental growth (5th ed.) New York: Macmillan.

Lyons, J. 1968. Introduction to theoretical linguistics. London: Cambridge University Press.

Matisoff, J. Variational semantics in Tibeto-Burman: The "organic" approach to linguistic comparison. Wolfenden Society Monograph No. 1. Philadelphia: ISHI Press. (In press.)

McClure, E.F. 1975. Ethno-anatomy: The structure of the domain. Anthropological Linguistics 17:78-88.

McDaniel, C.K. 1974. Basic color terms: Their neurophysiological bases. Paper presented at Annual Meeting of the American Anthropological Association, Mexico City, November 1974.

Moore, Kathleen C. 1895. The mental development of a child. Psychological Review, Monograph Supplements, vol. 1.

Nelson, K. 1973. Structure and strategy in learning to talk. Monographs of the Society for Research in Child Development 38 (Serial No. 149).

Nice, M.M. 1915. The development of a child's vocabulary in relation to environment. Pedagogical Seminary 22:35-64.

Rosch, E., C.Mervis, W.Gray, D.Johnson and P.Boyes-Braem. 1976. Basic objects in natural categories. Cognitive Psychology 8:382-439.

Samarin, W. 1967. A grammar of Sango. The Hague: Mouton.

Smith, N.V. 1973. Acquisition of phonology: A case study. Cambridge: University Press.

Stark, L. 1969. The lexical structure of Quechua body parts. Anthropological Linguistics 11:1-15.

Talmy, L. 1972. Semantic structures in English and Atsugewi. Unpublished Ph.D. dissertation, University of California, Berkeley.

Ullmann, S. 1963. Semantic universals. In J. Greenberg (ed.), Universals of language. Cambridge, Massachusetts: M.I.T. Press. 172-207.

Ultan, Russell. 1975. Descriptivity grading of Finnish body-part terms. Arbeiten des Kolner Universalien-Projekts 16.

_____. 1976. Descriptivity in the domain of body-part terms. Arbeiten des Kolner Universalien-Projekts 21.

Wales, R.J. and R.Campbell. 1970. On the development of comparison and the comparison of development. In G.B. Flores d'Arcais and W.J.M. Levelt (eds.), Advances in psycholinguistics. Amsterdam: North Holland. 373-96.

Weinreich, U. 1963. On the semantic structure of language. In J. Greenberg (ed.), Universals of language. Cambridge, Massachusetts: M.I.T. Press. 114-171.

_____. 1966. Explorations in semantic theory. In T. Sebeok (ed.), Current trends in language, III. The Hague: Mouton.

Werner, O. and K.Y Begishe. 1970. A lexemic typology of Navajo anatomical terms, I: The foot. IJAL 36:247-65.

On the Expression
of Spatio-Temporal Relations
in Language

ELIZABETH CLOSS TRAUGOTT

ABSTRACT

In this paper the semantic features of spatial expressions of
tense, sequencing, and aspect are explored, and implicational
hierarchies of features are established for each of the three categories. Tense, sequencing, and aspect are shown to select asymmetric features of locational relationship and plane, but not of
dimensionality or shape. The possible absence of an imaginary
time-line in languages and the patterning of asymmetric terms
confirm the importance of reference to body-space and the canonical encounter rather than to the unidirectionality of physical time
in accounting for the universal semantics of temporal relations in
language.

This work was supported in part by an American Council of
Learned Societies Fellowship for 1975-6. An initial study of certain aspects of spatio-temporal expressions for tense and sequencing appeared in Traugott 1975. I am grateful to Bernard Comrie
and Paul Friedrich for comments on that paper, and to the large
number of colleagues and students who have contributed examples,
bibliographical references, and valuable suggestions.

CONTENTS

1. Introduction

It has been suggested by many linguists that at least some sub-parts of the temporal system of language[1] are locative in underlying structure. Anderson 1972, 1973, Jessen 1975 and Bennett 1975 have demonstrated that the whole temporal system, that is, tense, sequencing, aspect, and the time adverbials which form part of these categories or establish further, secondary reference points, must be generated as locatives in a semantic base. In this paper I assume the correctness of this argument. The question to be explored is: 'Given that temporal relations are locative, which semantic features of location are associated with tense, sequencing and aspect?'[2]

In this study 'tense' is defined as the semantactic category that establishes the relationship which holds between the time of the situation or event talked about and the time of utterance, 'sequencing'

---

[1]When we discuss time we need to distinguish at least four kinds: 1) physical time, the time that is unidirectional, a thermodynamic principle of entropy, 2) psychic time, the time that we perceive, 3) calendrical time -- measurement according to seconds, minutes, hours, years, light-years and so forth, and 4) linguistic time which locates events and situations talked about to reference-points (for similar distinctions, see Bull 1960). It is only linguistic time that concerns us here.

[2]While the form of the question depends on the assumption that temporals are locatives, the basic content does not. Even in a theory that made no claims about the underlying identity of locatives and temporals, a weaker question must be asked: 'Given that spatial terms are used for temporal relations, apparently in all languages, what constraints are there on the kind of space we select to express them?' However, the claim that temporals are locative in underlying structure does have the far-reaching consequence of showing that spatial expressions for time are not metaphorical (at least, not those of the sort discussed here; there are metaphors of time, such as 'going round a corner in time,' but they are distinguishable from basic spatio-temporal expressions in that they all add specific spaces, dimensions, or shapes to the fundamental space of linguistic time).

It should be noted that although the analysis is made throughout in terms of semantic features, it could equally well be made in terms of semantic predicates. No strict formalization is attempted here.

as ordering of events or situations talked about, and 'aspect' as
the way of viewing the situation or event, for example, as continuative, habitual, iterative, completive, perfective and so forth.[3]
In no language are the distinctions absolute in surface structure.
In some languages one of the categories may have to be overtly
present in main clauses; for example, in ENGLISH the progressive (be +ing) is always accompanied by tense (cf. He is/was running). Sometimes elaborate multidimensional networks may be
developed, as in the case of 'pluperfects' and similar complex
structures that involve all three categories. Such interconnections
(as well as a tendency to base analysis on surface forms only, or
even on the system of LATIN), have led to a proliferation of views
on the temporal systems of languages. For some comparative
studies of approaches and terminologies, see Holt 1943, Dietrich
1973, Friedrich 1974, Jessen 1975. Furthermore, the temporal system is deeply interconnected with other categories of the language,
most notably future tense with modality (Ultan 1972), sequencing
with numeration, aspect with quantification (Verkuyl 1972; Friedrich
1974) and numerous other categories. Anderson 1973: 15-27 and
Welmers 1973: Chapter XI, for example, discuss the dependency
between progressive aspect, locative and possessive constructions.
'Perfect' tense-aspect (defined as presenting 'an event as occurring
at or since some (unspecified) point in the past and as having some
"present relevance" '), is shown in Anderson 1973: 27-36 to be in-
terdependent with indefiniteness, transitivity (hence also passive),
possession, dative of interest, ablative, and adjectives of state;
to these should be added ergativity (Anderson 1972b: 54) and inferential modality (Comrie 1976: 108-10). Nevertheless, the differences
in the types of spatial configurations involved in tense, sequencing,
and aspect, and the distinct functions they have in the grammar
suggest clear distinctions between the three in underlying structure.

It is the purpose of the present study to characterize the basic
semantic spatial features that remain constant across languages
and across various types of grammaticalization and lexicalization.
Therefore the temporal categories are defined not morphologically
but semantactically. They may appear overtly in very different
ways in different languages or even in the same language. They
may be realized as grammatical formatives like inflections (e.g.
GERMAN past -te), derivative affixes (e.g. GERMAN perfective-
terminative ver- as in verblühen 'fade' [='bloom to an end']), particles (e.g. ENGLISH burn up 'completely burn,' drive on 'continue

---

[3] See Comrie 1976 for similar definitions of tense and aspect.

to drive,' work away 'continue to work'), auxiliary verbs (e.g. I have drunk, I am going to drink), or fully lexicalized adverbs (e.g. I have already drunk, I am in the process of finishing) and so forth. Finally, they may be expressed covertly, that is, they may be part of the lexical meaning of the verb and have no independent morphological realization, as in the case of the stative perfective verbs like know, remember, possess (as opposed to a verb like run which does not involve completed realized state).

As the examples in the preceding paragraph demonstrate, spatial expressions for temporal relations are most readily found in periphrastic constructions and in derivative formatives. It has frequently been pointed out that synchronically an exact correlation between spatial and temporal terms is infrequent, if not unknown (cf. among others Pottier 1962: 126-7; Wierzbicka 1973: 628; Bennett 1975: 94-99; Jessen 1975: 427; Comrie 1976: 98-106). For example, up in burn up, finish up and so forth in no way presupposes the kind of vertical plane that prepositional or adverbial locative up do. One possibility is to argue that the use of spatial terms to express temporal relations is purely a diachronic phenomenon -- the 'overextension' of spatial to temporal terms in some kind of metaphoric process – but at no synchronic point in a language is the relation sufficient to justify the claim that there is underlying identity (cf. Pottier and Wierzbicka). Such an approach fails to account for a variety of factors. For one, it provides no motivation for the 'overextension.' Most importantly, it ignores the fact that the basic function of temporal categories is locative (cf. Bennett, Jessen, Comrie). Tense relates or locates situations and events with respect to the time of utterance, sequencing orders them with respect to each other, and aspect is a way of viewing situations and events as wholes, or as journeys, in other words, as objects with spatial characteristics. Child language studies suggest that these relations are not just metatheoretical, but psychologically real, since several researchers have noted that young children understand temporal when-questions as where-questions (cf. E. Clark 1971). The position taken here is that a theory of language must account not only for such acquisitional facts but also for the tendency for tenses, sequencers and aspects to be constantly revitalized in language acquisition, language change and language contact from a highly constrained set of features. In other words, it must be a dynamic theory, accounting for potentials for semantic -syntactic-morphological relations, including potentials for spatiotemporal relations (cf. Traugott 1976).[4]   Such a theory would

---

[4] For an initial formalization of dynamic theory, but with reference

account for why a term like up can be selected as a completive in
natural languages by introducing aspects as a subtype of locative
in underlying structure, along with a hierarchy of associated features. At the same time it would allow for the distribution of spatial up to differ from that of temporal up on the grounds that temporal
relations are more specialized ('marked') than spatial ones and
therefore distributionally different.[5]

2.   The Spatial Features of Tense, Sequencing, and Aspect

2.1.   Tense
'Tense relates the time of the situation referred to to some
other time, usually the moment of speaking' (Comrie 1976:1-2).[6]
Since the moment of speaking shifts reference, so that now is past
the moment it has been referred to, and so that tomorrow becomes
today and today becomes yesterday, tense is a deictic structure
or 'shifter' (cf. among others Benveniste 1965; Lyons 1968; Huddleston 1969; Wunderlich 1970; Jakobson 1971; Kuryłowicz 1972).

As a deictic, tense is basically a Proximal-Distal relation,
formalizable as [+Proximal]. This is reflected not only in its
lexicalization by adverbials like now and then, which are sometimes indistinguishable from locative deictics, cf. OLD ENGLISH
þa 'there, where, then, when,' but also in its grammaticalized
forms. For example, the na-anterior of KATHLAMET is derived
from pan-CHINOOKAN na-factive 'there-then,' as is probably the
na-factive/past of TILLAMOOK (Silverstein 1974: S68-9, S82-83).

(ftnt. 4 cont.)
only to phonology, see Bailey 1973.
    Such a theory would of course also show how temporal relations
form networks with non-spatial categories, for example, future
with modalities.

[5] The problem of how languages get non-natural ('crazy') rules
synchronically as the result of telescoping of natural processes of
change has concerned linguists ever since the question was raised
by Bach and Harms (1972) in the context of phonological theory. The
relation between temporal and spatial up in ENGLISH is of a similar
kind synchronically and, like phonological crazy rules, must be accounted for language-specifically rather than universally.

[6]Other axes of orientation than time of utterance are possible.
This is especially true in written fiction, where time of writing
may be irrelevant for tense-relations, only the characters' time
or the readers' time (cf. Weinrich 1964).

Caldwell hypothesizes that the CANARESE preterite d and present utu both derive from the demonstrative *-d (Caldwell 1956: 381, 391, 402). Then may be simply not-now, with subcategorizations according to degree of closeness to speaker or secondary reference point. Thus HIGHLAND TOK PISIN has a particle nau that indicates both immediate past ('just now,' action started in the immediate past), and 'immediate future' (Wurm 1971: 41, 48);[7] EWE etso is a term for both 'yesterday' and 'tomorrow' (Blok 1955-6: 388).

In some languages [+Proximal] may be the only organization of tense, without any concept of time-line. For example, KIKSHT shows not only an original 'anterior' -na- 'there-then' distal (related to TILLAMOOK and KATHLAMET na-), but also further subclassification of tenses as [+ Proximal]. Proximal and Distal in this language combine with aspect (completed versus now-continuing) and, within the category of completed action, with the deictics today and this seasonal round each with their own [+ Proximal] (within-beyond) distinctions, to provide eleven of twelve possible overt terms for six oppositions. These eleven terms cannot be understood in terms of a time-line, only of a terminal nearest the time of utterance (Hymes 1975: 325). In other languages focus is not exclusively on the term nearest the present; in addition Ego is the (terminal) center of orientation from the past, and the starting point of orientation to the future along the imaginery path of a time-line. [8]

Orientation to a time-line involves division of then into past and future. These two terms are typically asymmetrical in their realizations. In ENGLISH, for example, we have inflections for past and non-past (e.g. walks-walked), but an auxiliary for the 'future' (will). On the other hand, in FRENCH there is a future inflection as well as a present inflection. Only in the written language is there a matching past, the 'passé simple;' in the spoken

---

[7] These are distinguished by position. The 'just now' meaning is restricted to position after the verb, the 'immediate future' meaning to pre-subject position. According to Gillian Sankoff (private communication), post-verbal nau is currently being used as a punctual (i.e. as an aspectual), and as a marker of narrative relevance rather than as a tense-marker.

[8] In the study of European languages we are so accustomed to speak of time-lines that it may appear incorrect to speak of addition rather than alternative choices. However, as ENGLISH clearly shows, the two are not mutually exclusive. We use now-then and also past-non-past, the first not requiring a time-line, the second requiring one.

language there is effectively only an auxiliary, the 'passé composé'
(je viendrai, je viens, je suis venu). The ternary past-present-
future system of LATIN is in fact rather rare and certainly not
original in INDO-EUROPEAN (even in LATIN an asymmetry shows
up in the subjunctive — indicative distinguishes past, present and
future completives and incompletives inflectionally, but the subjunctive distinguishes only past and non-past). We therefore cannot consider a ternary tense system as universal, though we can
establish now-not now (proximal and distal to speaker), and further
a past and future [+Prior], of which the future is the 'marked' or
more specialized term, frequently only being expressed adverbially
(as in tomorrow, soon). MODERN YORUBA and IGBO, and possibly PROTO-INDO-EUROPEAN, are among languages which appear to have no grammaticalized tense markers (Comrie 1976: 82-83),
although they do distinguish [± Prior] adverbially.

The spatial features of tense systems that include a time-line
seem to be universally as follows: participants in events designated [+Prior] are oriented, whether statically or dynamically,
from the there of other time to the here of now; that is, one comes
from the past, which is in the Source, or ablative, relation. Participants in events designated [-Prior] are oriented from the here
of now to the there of not-now; that is, one goes toward the future,
which functions as Goal, or allative. It should be noted in passing
that while the spatial orientations involving a time-line under discussion are clearly tenses in that they involve deixis (cf. FRENCH
venir de 'immediate past' and aller 'immediate future'), they are
closely interrelated with other categories of language. Specifically,
the ablatives are often completive while the allatives are frequently
irrealis or intentional (in either case modal) or resultative (cf.
Anderson 1973: 28, 36-37, 85; Comrie 1976: 60-61, 64-65).[9] See
discussion of ablatives and allatives as terminatives in Section
2.3.2.

For examples of terms involving the ablative case relation for
(recent) past in SCOTTISH GAELIC, BASQUE, and TIBETAN see
Anderson 1973: 28-29, and of the allative case for future, especially
immediate future, in EGYPTIAN, CHIRU (KUKI-CHIN group), IRISH,
HEBREW and ARABIC see Anderson 1973: 36. The ablative-allative
relations are particularly commonly expressed by motion verbs

---

[9] The forms under discussion are frequently called 'retrospec-
tives' and 'prospective' aspect. To assign them to aspect is clearly
incorrect since they are primarily deictic and only secondarily
(and not obligatorily) aspectual.

equivalent to come and go. If a language uses deictic come-go
verbs for tense, both members of the pair do not necessarily
appear. A symmetrical case such as FRENCH venir de - aller
is in fact much rarer than an asymmetric one such as ENGLISH
where only the go-future occurs.[10] In such asymmetric systems
it is the future, not the past which selects the deictic verb. Examples of go-futures, whether symmetric with come-past or not, are
ENGLISH go, FRENCH aller, IGBO gá (with statives only; Welmers
1973: 354), CORA me, ra, ke, xu (Preuss 1932: 60). Givón 1973:
918 also cites SPANISH, PALESTINIAN ARABIC, HEBREW, KI-
SHAMBA, and KRIO.

Although go-futures predominate, some languages use come-
futures. Among INDO-EUROPEAN languages, SWEDISH provides
the clearest example. It may be the source of FINNISH and KAMA-
SIN SAMOYED come-futures (Tauli 1966: 81). Several African
languages have come-futures, e.g. SWAHILI ja (Ashton 1947: 273),
AKAN b + mid vowel, from bá, EFIK -dí- 'contrastive future,'
LUGANDA jjá 'indefinite future' (Welmers 1973: 353-355).[11]

---

[10]It is important to note that come and go are not symmetrical as
spatial terms, for in the case of come the goal is specified as a
deictic center, whereas go involves neither a determined goal nor
a determined source, but rather orientation away from a deictic
center (cf. Fillmore 1972). Such an asymmetry is consistent with
other spatial pairs used for temporal expressions, such as front-
back, up-down.
    Guillaume (1941) suggested that the suppletive formants in the
FRENCH verb aller 'go' derive from the fundamental semantics of
go. They throw an interesting perspective on the indeterminateness
of orientation associated with this verb. According to Guillaume,
the future, from LATIN ire 'to go,' expresses non-determined goal.
The singular present, from LATIN vadere 'move toward a determined place,' presents action as limited by the immediate time of
utterance (in this case the end of the past; since time of utterance
is determined by the act of speech an indeterminate meaning is not
possible for the present first singular). The present plural, past,
infinitive, subjunctive and so forth, are derived from LATIN
ambulare 'walk,' and indicate a broad range of movement, with
neither source nor goal fully determined. A similar example is
provided by ENGLISH go the past of which derives from OLD ENG-
LISH wendan 'to turn in a new direction.'

[11]Welmers 1973: 415 says that SWAHILI uses kwenda 'to go' +
infinitive to form recent past. However, Madan 1903 cites enda
'go' as future (beside ja), while Ashton analyses it as a continuative
(1947: 274). Furthermore, the regular negative past is ja. So it is
not clear that SWAHILI has a come-go pair signalling tense.

Passing comments in various grammars suggest that the come-future originates in ingressive, inchoative and even resultative expressions (i.e. 'start to be,' 'get to be,' 'come to be'), cf. Ebneter 1973: 273 on SWEDISH and RHAETO-ROMANCE, or in sequencing, cf. Ashton's examples of the ja-future in SWAHILI, most of which involve consecutive clauses, and Welmers' translation of this form as 'then, later' (Welmers 1973: 415). Such futures can, then, be hypothesized to be derived, not part of the basic tense-hierarchy.

Source ablative and Goal allative tense relations are directly determined by [+Proximal], and conceptually require a time-line or imaginery path, but involve no particular spatial planes. The latter are, however, found in such idiomatic and metaphorical expressions as: we look forward to the years ahead, we look back on the past, all that is past lies behind us. These expressions make direct use of the perceptual plane running through the body separating front from back. Everything in front of this plane is perceptually visible, everything behind it is not. What is visible can be considered positive, what is invisible can be negative (cf. the positive terms ahead, forward, and the negative term back) (H. Clark 1973: 211). Selection of terms from this perceptual plane would seem to derive from the idea of going along a path. In as far as the path may be unknown it is irrealis. It is at this point that 'future' and irrealis coincide (note that irrealis does not require a time-line, since things can be unknown but not assigned to a path).

These features of tense may be characterized informally as in figure 1   (T stands for 'imaginery time-line'):

[-Proximal] (then) [+Proximal] (now) [-Proximal] (then)
T——T
[+Prior] (past)   [-Prior] (future)
Source   Goal
come ——➤   go ——➤
[-Front] (behind, back)   [+Front] (forward, ahead)

Figure 1

Somewhat more formally, this represents an implicational hierarchy of the type:[12]

---

[12] The hierarchy makes no mention of the time-line since the latter is a presupposition of [+Prior] for temporals.

$\pm$Proximal $\geq$ $\pm$Prior $\geq$ $\pm$Orientation $\geq$ $\pm$ Dynamic $\geq$ $\pm$ Front
Constraints on this hierarchy are that only [-Proximal] can be
[$\pm$Prior], and only [+Orientation] (Source, Goal) can be [$\pm$Dynamic];
furthermore, only [+Prior] can be [-Front], only [-Prior] can be
[+Front]. General rules for assigning the correct orientation toward deictic centers will account for come and go and similar
terms carrying the feature [+Orientation] (cf. Wunderlich 1970;
Fillmore 1971, 1972 for further details of what such rules should
account for).

2.2 Sequencing

Sequencing, as opposed to tense, is the system whereby events
and situations E_1, E_2...E_n are ordered with respect to each other.
They may be ordered as being in succession (E_1 before E_2), as
simultaneous (E_1 and at the same time E_2) or overlapping (e.g.
during E_1, E_2). While the time-reference of tense shifts with the
'now' of the speaker, the relative relation of two events does not
(Jakobson 1971).

2.2.1 Sequencing of the type E_1 before E_2.

The ordering of events in succession is manifested in various
ways in languages, from simple iconic narrative (the first event is
mentioned first, followed by the second, and so forth, without overt
markers of any sort), to aspectual organization of the type finish X,
he Y,[13] to combinations of tense and aspect as in the 'secondary
tenses' such as pluperfect and future-perfect, to overt co-ordinators
and subordinators such as first, second, or before-after. In this
section only the co-ordinator/subordinator types will be discussed.

Like tense, sequencing may be considered without respect to a
time-line (c.f. first, second, or next [a spatial term derived from
OLD ENGLISH neah 'near' + superlative]). As such it is basically
a system of the type E_1 + other + other, i.e. [$\pm$Initial], sometimes
with deictic accretions (next involves closeness, then distance).
Many of these deictic accretions are not primarily speaker-deictic
but, rather, discourse-deictic, that is, they establish narrative

---

[13]Such aspectual organization is particularly well illustrated in
child language acquisition (cf. Ferreiro 1971) and in the development
of contact languages, cf. TOK PISIN (Wurm 1971:72); acquisitionally
they develop earlier than before-after constructions which suggests
an implicational relationship between the categories of aspect and
sequencing of the type: aspectual organization of sequence $\geq$ overt
sequencing in terms of coordinators and subordinators.

relevance and belong to the topicalization system (cf. Fillmore 1971 on discourse- versus speaker-deixis).

If the sequence is conceived as related to a time-line, E_1 is earlier than E_2 and E_2 is later than E_1. The question arises whether earlier and later should be specified as [+Prior], that is, whether they can be assigned the same semantic feature as was used in the tense system. Since essentially the same space is used for sequencing as for tense (but with an entirely different distribution, as we shall see), there appears to be some justification for such an analysis. The distributional differences depend on the fact that in the case of tense [+Prior] is combined with the feature [-Proximal] and is related directly to the speaker (and is therefore deictic), while in the case of sequencing it is combined with [-Initial] and related directly to another event. Given such an analysis we can show that while tense does indeed involve ordering, at least in those languages where time-lines are used, as has been argued for instance by Reichenbach 1967: Chapter VII; Bruce 1972; Bogusławski 1975, ordering is conceptually quite different from the ordering of sequencing (i.e. it involves deictic relations whereas true sequencing does not), and at the same time we can show that tense and true sequencing share certain properties ([+Prior] and orientation on a time-line).

If sequencing is realized in a language by the feature [+ Prior], then there may in addition be a feature of orientation on a plane. If so, E_1 is in front of or before (i.e. in the fore of) E_2, and E_2 is behind or after (i.e. in the aft of) E_1. That E_1 selects the positive term front and E_2 the negative term back can be explained in terms of the concept of the canonical encounter, also known as 'facing' (Fillmore 1971; H. Clark 1973; Kimball 1974). It was suggested in discussion of tense that [+Front] is assigned on the basis of the basic body-space and perceptual field as we walk along a path. As we walk along this path there may be an encounter (we face the future); in sequencing there necessarily is. The normal, 'canonical,' type is the face-to-face encounter with Speaker as the deictic center, cf. The type-writer is in front of me (rather than I am in front of the typewriter). From this viewpoint additional type-writers in a row are normally behind the one in front of me. Similarly, there is a canonical encounter with events such that E_1 is in front E_2, and E_2 behind E_1. However, there is a difference from assignment of [+Front] to tense in that the assignment of [+Front] to events in sequence, once established in terms of the encounter, remains constant, wherever the speaker is in the sequence of events, because sequence is not deictic in its basic structure (but see

below for deictic accretions). In other words, E_1 is disassociated
from the speaker and remains in front, whether the event is in the
future or the past.

[+Front] may themselves be further subcategorized as [±Dynamic].
In ENGLISH before and after are neutral to the static-dynamic opposition. However, there are also terms like preceding and following which are solely dynamic. Such dynamic terms appear to be
highly marked (cf. the borrowing from LATIN of preceding to express the combination [+Prior, +Front, +Dynamic]). Examples of
terms realizing [±Prior, ±Front, ±Dynamic] in sequencing include
ENGLISH before, after, and forward, back, as in put a meeting
forward/back;[14] OLD FRENCH ainz 'before' from LATIN ante
'in front;' FRENCH avant 'before' from LATIN ab ante 'from the
front,' et puis 'and then' from LATIN post 'behind' (Imbs 1956: 419,
354); CHINESE yiichyan 'before' (chyan= 'in front'), yiihow 'after'
(how = 'behind') (Chao 1968: 119); SRANAN a fesi 'before, at the
face,' baka 'after, at the back' (Voorhoeve 1962: 51); KAFIR kamva
'later' from umva 'back,' ukukova 'to sit on one's backside, to
cower,' with meaning extended to 'immediately afterwards' (Bourquin 1912-3: 286, 1913-4: 135).

As these examples suggest, not all languages use front-back
pairings for E_1 and E_2, e.g. GERMAN which uses a front-back
pair for tense (hinter 'behind, past,' vor 'in front, future'), but
only front for subordinators of sequencing (E_1 is vor 'in front' but
E_2 is nach)[15] (Marcq 1973). The pairing does, however, occur
(with a deictic attached) in the adverbial system; vorher 'earlier,'
hinterher 'afterwards.' Similarly, in FRENCH only the front term
is present in the subordinating system (avant),[16] whereas in the

---

[14] There is dialectal variation here. Those speakers for whom
putting/moving a meeting back a week means scheduling it for a
later date follow the system outlined here; speakers for whom the
same expression means scheduling the meeting for an earlier date
are treating the original date as a deictic center, on analogy with
the tense system.

[15] Note, however, that nach is spatial. In non-temporal expressions it means 'toward.' It is related to nah 'near,' cf. ENGLISH
next discussed above.

[16] Après is not used spatially, except in extensions like C'est
après la maison 'It's after the house,' i. e. "You will find it after
you have passed the house." It derives from LATIN ad presse 'toward pressingly,' hence 'immediately,' and is only by extension
'behind' (cf. press on behind someone).

adverbial one both are present: en avant 'at the beginning, before-
hand,' puis 'afterward.' Sufficient evidence is not available, but
it is possible that in those languages which have developed non-iconic
strategies for sequencing through topicalization and various types
of subordination, the positive spatial relation in front predominates.
This is suggested by studies of child language acquisition of ENG-
LISH where before in both the iconic order A before B and in the
non-iconic order before B A is acquired before after (E. Clark 1971,
1973). In languages like pidgins and early creoles, however, where
iconicity is the predominant strategy for all narrative, whether by
adults or children, it appears that the behind term is acquired first
and that it predominates even when a front term exists, because
first mention is always understood as first occurrence, and sequencing is relevant only to show closeness of relationship. Thus
although TOK PISIN has in its lexicon long bipo 'at before' and
behain, the former is rarely used, whereas the latter occurs regularly in narrative and is also extended to tense (see below) (Sankoff,
private communication).

It has sometimes been claimed that association of front with earlier (also wrongly called 'past') and of back with later (also wrongly
called 'future') implies moving-time, as opposed to association of
front with future and back with past, which implies moving-ego. For
example, in an otherwise extremely insightful article, Benveniste
claims that we position events 'as points seen as behind or ahead
in relation to the present. (Behind or ahead since man moves to
meet time or time moves to meet man, according to our image of
the process.)' (Benveniste 1965: 8). As we have seen, tense does
not necessarily involve moving-ego, and sequencing does not necessarily involve moving-event. In any case, they belong to different
systems: the most general features of the hierarchy are different
([$\pm$Proximal] versus [$\pm$ Initial]), and the hierarchic relations between [+Orientation] (Source-Goal), [$\pm$ Dynamic] and [$\pm$Front] are
different. The different feature combinations and relations hypothesized as underlying tense and sequencing automatically explain
how it is that, despite sharing some of the same features, they can
never be mirror images of each other.

The relations discussed so far may be schematized as:

$$
T\overline{\begin{array}{ll} [+\text{Initial}] \ (E_1, \ \underline{\text{first}}) & [-\text{Initial}] \ (E_2, \ \underline{\text{second}}) \\ \hline [+\text{Prior}] \ (\underline{\text{earlier}}) & [-\text{Prior}] \ (\underline{\text{later}}) \\ [+\text{Front}] \ (\underline{\text{before}}) & [-\text{Front}] \ (\underline{\text{after}}) \end{array}}T
$$

$\blacktriangleleft$---preceding $\blacktriangleleft$---following

Figure 2

The implicational hierarchy is:

± Initial ≥ ± Prior ≥ ± Front ≥ ± Dynamic

with the constraint that [+Prior] is [+Initial], and [+Front] is [+Prior]; similarly that [-Prior] is [-Initial], and [-Front] is [-Prior] (that is, that either all features are + or all are -).

In languages with [+Dynamic] sequencing, the interrelation of tense and sequencing can give rise to come-go structures. For example, when the speaker perceives him- or her-self in direct relation to both time-line and to E_1 and E_2 we find deictic terms being used. Here speaker-deixis is involved. The come-go terms are distributed in ways that suggest the reverse of the tense system since later events come and earlier events have gone. Thus in the coming months means 'in the months moving from the there of other time to the here of now' and in the years gone by means 'in the years that have been moving from the here of now to the there of other time.' Schematically this is, with other details left out:

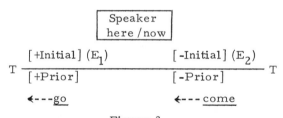

Figure 3

If we impose this schema on the tense schema, we can see how constructions of the type I am going to do it come Friday are structured (speaker is moving forward to the future; Friday, being later than the time of utterance, is moving toward the speaker).

Other possibilities can be found for the use of deictic terms in sequencing. These are discourse-deictic. Discourse strategies allow events to be made into deictic centers, irrespective of the speaker, but always in consistent relation to each other. Hence in 'neutral' discourse we can find now (E_1)... then (E_2)...then (E_3)... It is even possible for E_2 to go (presumably not from E_1 but simply from some unspecified point to another that is not the canonical center), as in EWE hé 'and then, go away, distance oneself' (Westermann 1907: 98); SWAHILI consecutive tense ka from the verb ka 'go' (Meinhof 1906: 72); KAFIR ukusuka 'stand up and go, then immediately afterward,' related to BANTU vuka 'go away' (Bourquin

1913-4: 143).[17] In 'excited narrative' and discourse strategies such as 'historical present' we also find $\underline{now}$ (E_1) ... $\underline{now}$ (E_2) ... $\underline{now}$ (E_3) ..., in other words events can be treated as pairs, the second of which is reanalysed as the initiating point and point of interest:

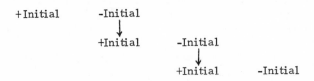

Such specialized discourse strategies may be generalized and give rise in neutral discourse to $\underline{come}$ sequencers. E_2 then $\underline{comes}$ to the norm of E_1; cf. CRIOULO OF GUINE $\underline{biŋ}$ 'come, then' (Wilson 1962: 25); SWAHILI auxiliary $\underline{ja}$ 'then, later' (sometimes called 'future') (Welmers 1973: 415) from the main verb $\underline{ja}$ 'come;' KAFIR $\underline{ukuza}$ 'then later,' also related to $\underline{ja}$ (Bourquin 1913-4: 144).[18] The former type, where E_2 is $\underline{other}$ than E_1, i.e. $\underline{then}$, is the more usual of the two.

In some languages, in addition to the front-back space of sequencing, there is a vertical up-down space. We have hypothesized that front-back derives from the canonical encounter. It is neutral to both horizontal and vertical planes, as well as to dimensionality. If E_1 selects the canonical term $\underline{front}$ in a language, then it can also select the canonical vertical term $\underline{up}$, $\underline{over}$ (note that $\underline{up}$ is canonical to our vertical posture when we walk, just as $\underline{front}$ is). In the languages studied so far, the clearest $\underline{up-down}$ pairs for sequencing appear where the situation is as in Figure 3, i.e. when speaker is involved, cf. CHINESE E_1 $\underline{shang}$ 'above, last (Saturday),' E_2 $\underline{shiah}$ 'below, next (Saturday)' (Chao 1968: 548-9) and ENGLISH expressions like $\underline{good, that's over}$ (i.e. 'past'), $\underline{we'll move the}$

---

[17] Bourquin identifies $\underline{ukusuka}$ with 'immediately afterward,' $\underline{ukuza}$ with 'neutral sequence' (immediacy is irrelevant). Immediacy in a sequence does not necessarily imply immediacy to the speaker in discourse, and therefore the KAFIR examples do not contradict the hypothesis that $\underline{come}$ involves 'discourse immediacy.'

[18] See footnote 8 for an example of the $\underline{now}$-deictic used as an indicator of narrative relevance and immediacy in TOK PISIN. This phenomenon is particularly common in oral varieties of language.

meeting up a week (not paired with down);[19] GERMAN es geht alles
vorüber 'everything passes,' i.e. "it all goes in front over" (Marcq
1973: 31). However, not all vertical terms imply relation of speaker
to event, cf. LATIN subinde 'immediately after' (i.e. "under from
there") (Ernout-Meillet 1939); MIDDLE PIEDMONTESE soubr'an
'before/the end of the year' (i.e. "above") from LATIN super 'above'
(Wartburg 1948).[20] This suggests that the vertical terms belong to
the basic sequencing hierarchy, not to derivative systems, and that
they imply the presence of front-back terms. Further study will
indicate whether ±Up implies [±Dynamic], or whether the reverse
is true. Deictic come-go, now-then are not basic to sequencing
and are therefore not relevant to the hierarchy. As indicated, they
are derived from speaker- and discourse-deixis by universal rules
that weight the latter over sequencing.

Certain terms for sequencers appear in certain subcategories
of both tense and aspect, presumably as extensions from sequencing. Since tense is basically deictic, it follows that the deictic discourse sequencers come and go should neutralize naturally to tense
(cf. SWAHILI ja). Unusual and marked as they are in the sequencing
system, they can be expected to be unstable. Where go expresses
the and then relation in future time it coincides with future go;
where come expresses the and then relation in future time it con-

---

[19]Up pairs with back, so neutralizing a distinction according to
planes in a manner typical of asymmetrical pairs: the marked
member shows fewer distinctions than the unmarked (cf. Greenberg 1966). For speakers to whom move up a meeting means
'schedule it later,' the original date is the deictic center, cf.
footnote 14.

[20]In INDO-EUROPEAN languages in general there are anomalies
related to the fact that the original term meant 'below, (up) from
below,' giving rise to antonyms like AVESTAN uperō 'higher,'
SANSKRIT úparaḥ 'lower, neighboring' (Ernout-Meillet 1939: sub).
Another problem is that in the quantification system the 'lower
number' is the 'earlier' in the sequence, the 'higher number' the
'later;' hence he lived to be over a hundred involves 'more than a
hundred' and only by implication 'after a hundred.' Sequencing
and quantification coincide in speed up (more speed means earlier
arrival) and slow down (less speed means later arrival) but con-
flict in slow up (up is temporal only).

trasts with future go but coincides with inception, which is one of
the sources of future, and in some languages may contribute to the
development of come-futures (see 2.1 above). The specialized
case of idioms like in the days gone by, in the days to come, where
go expresses E_1 and come E_2 (Figure 3) appears not give rise to
go-pasts.

The commonest extensions involve the behind term. This may
be reinterpreted on the one hand as a term for degree of proximity
or distance in the deictic tense system, or on the other as an aspectual. An example of the first case is the extension in contemporary TOK PISIN of bihain from 'later' to indication of remote
future, when combined with the future marker bai, cf. Bihain
b'mipla lainim 'later we're going to learn' (= "later future we
learn it"), but also Ating behain behain bai, tok ples bai i nogat ia
'I think after a long time, Tok Ples (native language) will not exist
here any more' (="I think later later future, Tok Ples future not-
exist here") (data from Gillian Sankoff).[21] Here the feature of
'otherness' that we have seen give rise to go- sequencers is clearly
the feature that has been extended. If speaker identifies him- or
herself with E_2, however, then behind may give rise to an immediate past ('have just') as in GAELIC and HEBREW (Bull 1960: 26;
Anderson 1973: 28; Comrie 1976:106). In this configuration the
speaker is behind (immediately after) the event mentioned.

In other languages behind and terms for motion, especially
motion in pursuit, give rise not to deictics but to the continuative
aspect, cf. ENGLISH go on Xing; PORTUGUESE, SPANISH, CATA-
LAN seguir (Dietrich 1973:141); FRENCH (18th century) être après
de (Brunot 1966. 6: 1486); HAITIAN CREOLE ap- from FRENCH
après, defined by Sylvain as 'une action non arrivée à son terme,'
whether progressive or future (Sylvain 1936: 88, cited in Taylor
1963: 805). Alternatively, the front term, especially terms for
motion ahead of E_2 may also give rise to a continuative, as do
LATIN prae- and pro-prefixes (Barbelenet 1913: 338). Such extensions of sequencers are natural since certain types of continued
action can be thought of as repeated (sequenced) action, for example singing songs all evening long. Whether the front or the back
term is selected depends on discourse strategies.

---

[21]Behain bai 'distant future' is in opposition to klostu bai 'immediate future.'

2.2.2   Other types of sequencing.

The materials gathered so far suggest that simultaneity is primarily expressed by co-ordination (and can be either and then or
at the same time in many languages). Overlap of E_1 and E_2 is
expressed aspectually (e.g. While she was singing he left the room).
Such subordinators as there are, are rarely spatial (during is related to LATIN durus 'hard,' hence qualitative rather than spatial,[22]
and while derives from OLD ENGLISH hwil 'time'). Significantly
missing are terms for side (side by side is spatial only; aside from
is 'out of order,' not 'simultaneously'). The only language in which
side terms have been found in temporal use is CHINESE, and here
left and right do not occur separately, only together; furthermore,
they do not express simultaneity, only approximate time: tzuoo-
yow 'thereabouts' (Chao 1968: 551). The reason for this lack of side
terms presumably is that left and right, although they develop asymmetrical relationships in many languages and have come to be associated with sinister and negative entities on the one hand and justice
on the other, are perceptually symmetrical. The body-space that
assigns front-back, up-down to time provides a pair of spaces only
one of which is canonical; left-right do not conform to this kind of
pairing and are therefore outside the central spatio-temporal system.

2.3 Aspect

While tense and sequencing are defined relatively consistently in
different grammars, the nature of aspect is less widely agreed on.
Here we take the position that 'aspects are different ways of viewing the internal temporal constituency of a situation,' for example
as unanalyzable wholes, or as wholes with phases, particularly
beginning, middle and end (Comrie 1976: 3, based on Holt 1943: 6).

It is not yet clear whether there is just one basic aspectual opposition in the languages of the world or whether there are various
possibilities. Friedrich (1974) has suggested that there may be one
basic type: durative versus non-durative, or at the most two types:
the latter and completive versus non-completive. Comrie suggests
that the primary opposition is between imperfective and perfective
(analysed situations versus unanalysed ones), with several subcategories. Yet another position is taken by Jessen, who argues for
different kinds of aspectual relations that interrelate, rather than
subcategorization. Basing her definition on Anderson 1973, she

---

[22] Note, however, the extension of hard to space in hard by.

argues that aspect in general 'is the linguistic reflex of the existential status or structure of the situation characterized by the
basic proposition' (Jessen 1975: 236). She then goes on to differentiate aspect proper (e.g. perfective, progressive), which is
concerned with whether the situation is 'alive, dead or to be born,'
from 'aktionsarten' (e.g. ingressive, egressive, terminative,
continuative), which are concerned with the progression of the situation through its life (354).[23] Further studies of spatio-temporal
relations from a variety of points of view including language acquisition and language change especially in contact situations will clarify which of these (or other) positions should be taken.

Since progressive and perfective (particularly of the terminative
type) are the two aspects most widely and least ambiguously discussed in the literature, spatial expressions for only these two
aspects will be discussed here. It will be suggested that from this
admittedly scanty evidence Jessen's distinction between aspect
proper and aktionsart is a valuable one.

2.3.1 Progressive

Progressive aspect, a subcategory of continuative, itself a subcategory of imperfective in Comrie's analysis, involves the 'combination of continuousness with nonstativity' (Comrie 1976: 12). There
is overwhelming evidence from a large number of languages that
the underlying spatial feature of progressives is of the type be at
or be in. This feature may be extended to other types of imperfective, most usually habitual, but also to imperfectives in general.
Therefore, it must be considered basic to progressive rather than
to the more general imperfective type (ibid.: 103).[24]

---

[23] A further class of 'proposition types' is established for states,
achievements, and similar largely lexicalized aspectuals. These
will not concern us here.

It is important to note that the terms aspect and aktionsart, although borrowed from long-standing GERMAN and SLAVIC linguistic
vocabulary, have been redefined. The terms no longer refer to
largely grammaticalized versus lexicalized features, that is, to
morphological differences. Instead, they have been given a consistent semantic perspective by the overall definition of aspect as
a reflex of the existential status of situations.

[24] Many progressives also express contingent, temporary activity
or state. This category, whether progressive or not, also typically
selects be at/be in (Anderson 1973: 52).

There are two major types of grammaticalized expressions for the progressive:

i) 'Cases' (whether inflections, prepositions, postpositions, particles, or 'locative auxiliaries' [Friedrich 1975: 34]) that in general answer the LATIN ubi? 'where?' and in particular have the feature of contiguity (at) or withinness (in), as in FRENCH en train de; SCOTTISH GAELIC ag 'at' + verbal noun, WELSH yn 'in' + verbal noun (Comrie 1976: 99-100); FINNISH inessive case (Hakulinen 1961: 332); EASTERN ARAMAIC b- 'in, at, with' + infinitive + copula, e.g. b + pərāqā + īli (biprāqili) (Rundgren 1963: 73); SWAHILI na 'in nearness of, with' (Welmers 1973: 328) and also IGBO na (ibid.: 312); EWE -m 'inside' added to the infinitive (Westermann 1907: 66), lè 'locative' (ibid.; Welmers 1973: 309).[25] Several other examples from YORUBA and KPELLE are given in Welmers 1973: 313-315, and of MANDING languages in Spears 1972. See also Anderson 1973: 15-19 for further examples in BASQUE, EGYPTIAN, MARGI, KAMILAROI, UZBEK, TURKISH, MANIPURĪ and CHEREMIS, and Comrie 1976: 99-102 for further examples in DUTCH, ICELANDIC, GEORGIAN, and MANDARIN CHINESE.

ii) Locative/existential/possessive copulas, as SPANISH estar (as opposed to descriptive ser); JAPANESE ari / ori / iru (Lewin 1959: 164);[26] CORA -ve, -ka 'be at, be present' (Preuss 1932: 43, 67).

Two additional sources for progressive surface forms are widely found, one with features related to i) and ii) above, the other involving directionals. It is not clear whether all these forms are primarily progressive or whether some are generally continuative:

iii) Verbs with the feature 'be in existence, be located at' in combination with more specific features, especially for remaining, standing, sitting or lying; cf. SPANISH estar[27] and ITALIAN stare which are cognate with LATIN stare

---

[25] In West African languages 'cases' and 'verbs' are often difficult to distinguish. According to Welmers the verbal/prepositional status of lè is particularly unclear.

[26] Defined as 'imperfect,' but see the implicational scale above.

[27] SPANISH estar is listed here as well as in the preceding paragraph on the grounds that synchronically it functions as 'locative-contingent' be, while it originated in a stand verb.

'stand' and which are all progressive and continuative (Comrie
1976: 102); MIDDLE SPANISH seer from LATIN sedere (Keniston
1936:170);[28] EASTERN ARAMAIC stative ki is said to derive from
durative *qā 'stand,' e.g. ki pāriq 'is finished' from *qā'im pāriq
'he stands ending' (Rundgren 1963: 82); MODERN AMHARIC täqäm-
mätä 'be seated, limited duration' (Kapelink 1969:122); TUNICA
ʔu'na 'sit,' ʔu'ra 'lie' (Haas 1940: 49, 112); YATYƐ ahyè 'squat,lie'
(Stahlke 1970: 65); CHI-BEMBA -lāa-/-léé-, hypothesized to derive
from lāál 'sleep' (Givón 1972:130); MODERN AMHARIC qʷäyyä
'wait, stay, limited duration,' norä 'live, inhabit, unlimited duration' (Kapelink 1969: 122, 127); HINDI-URDU rəhna, PUNJABI rəýna
'live, stay, remain' (Comrie 1976: 102); MANDARIN CHINESE zhù-
zai 'live at, progressive' (ibid.); TOK PISIN i-stap 'stay, continue,
be at rest' from ENGLISH stop (Wurm 1971: 39).

In some languages, come and go progressives and especially
continuatives occur, for example ENGLISH go on Xing (continuative
rather than progressive) and its equally continuative derivative i-go
(as opposed to progressive i-stap) in TOK PISIN (Wurm 1971: 45);
SPANISH progressive venir (Keniston 1936:170); OLD FRENCH,
cf. Chanson de Roland En France irat Charlemagne guerant 'Charlemagne was fighting in France' (= "In France went C. fighting") (Brunot
1966.1: 242); MODERN AMHARIC hedä 'go, progressive increase in
action or state' (Kapelink 1969: 130). In the grammars investigated
it is not clear whether these are truly continuative and progressive.
Rather, they appear to maintain features of their sources: inchoative
aspect and sequencing. A further, non-oriented verb of movement
such as SPANISH andar (Keniston 1936:170) may also occur, presumably a neutralized form of come or go, which conforms more
adequately to the non-oriented space of progressive.[29] In all three
cases, come, go, move, the motion verbs may be considered derived from discourse strategies.

2.3.2 Terminative
Terminative/resultative aspect is realized by two main sets of
terms:

---

[28] This verb was progressive/durative in MIDDLE SPANISH; it
evolved into the descriptive ser while estar remained locative/
contingent/progressive.

[29] The term 'progressive' is misleading, since it suggests change
of state.

i) Source terms answering LATIN unde? 'whence?'; ENGLISH out as in work out;[30] GOTHIC prefix fra- 'away,' GERMAN ver- (from fra-), er- (from GERMANIC *uz- 'out'), aus- 'out,' as in verblühen 'bloom to an end, fade,' erklettern 'climb (to the top/ goal),' ausarbeiten 'work out' (Priebsch-Collinson 1958: 253, 257); LATIN aspectual prefixes ex- and de- (Barbelenet 1913: 288); GREEK prefix ἀπό 'from' (Friedrich 1974: S39); FINNISH ablative (Hakulinen 1961: 333); MARTINICAN (FRENCH) CREOLE sôti 'leave' (Taylor 1963: 807). Here may be included the verb finish which occurs in a large number of languages, and which is ablative in underlying structure (Anderson 1973: 59), as in SPANISH acabar de (Dietrich 1973:4); JAPANESE completive shimatta 'finished' (Lewin 1959:169); TOK PISIN pinis (Wurm 1971: 39); BANTU me- from kumala 'finish' (Meinhof 1906: 73); EWE vo 'be finished' (Westermann 1907: 98); SWAHILI isha (as auxiliary and also undergoing change to an infix sha) (Givón 1972:132); Anderson 1973: 35 cites further examples from the KUKI-CHIN group and GILBERTESE; Bull (1960: 26) states that finish terms occur for completive in TURKISH, MAGYAR, ARABIC, AMHARIC, MALAY, PUNJABI, HINDI, URDU and BURMESE. All the verbal forms (sôti, finish) have a tendency to indicate immediate past as well as completion. Whether aspect or recent past is the basic term in all cases is not clear. Anderson 1973: 85 proposes an implicational scale 'ablative retrospective -> perfect -> point past' (equivalent in our terminology to recent past -> past action with present relevance -> general past). 'Completive' does not enter directly into this scale. For reasons which will be discussed below, it appears best to hypothesize that there are two separate sources: terminative aktionsart and tense. Since both are associated with the feature ablative it is possible that either category may be extended to the other. On the other hand, since events in the recent past are normally interpreted as completed, whereas completion does not presuppose recentness, it may be that the implicational scale is:

$$\text{recent past} \begin{cases} \geq \text{past with present relevance} \geq \text{general past} \\ \geq \text{terminative} \end{cases}$$

This hypothesis awaits further investigation.

ii) Goal terms answering LATIN quō? 'wither?'; LATIN ad prefix (Barbelenet 1913: 353); FINNISH illative and allative (Hakulinen 1961: 332); SWAHILI prepositional infix -i- (Ashton 1947: 220); EWE

---

[30]For discussion of this and other aspectual uses of particles in ENGLISH see Bolinger 1971: chapter VIII.

sé 'finally succeed, completive' from an allative preposition derived from the verb 'to reach' (Westermann 1907: 98).

In addition, in some languages there are:

iii) Path terms, answering LATIN quā? 'via what route?': ENG-
LISH particle through as in see it through (i.e. 'to completion');
LATIN inter- as in interficere 'kill' (inter 'through' + facere 'do'),
interire, perire 'die' (inter/per 'through' + ire 'go') (Juret 1950: 2);
GERMAN ver- (cognate with per-) as in verdienen 'serve to the
end → deserve' (Priebsch-Collinson 1958: 253).

The data suggest an implicational scale among true terminatives
of the type:

Terminative aspect ≥ Source term ≥ Goal term ≥ Path term

The array of forms discussed has implications for choosing between analyses of aspect. Comrie treats 'terminative' aspect as a
specialized subcategory of perfective. Perfectivity is defined as
the aspect which 'indicates the view of a situation as a single whole,
without distinction of the various separate phases that make up that
situation' (Comrie 1976: 16). Comrie points out that while perfectives are always complete, they are not necessarily completed or
resultative (i.e. successfully completed). He allows, however,
that emphasis can be put on the initial (ingressive) or final (completive, terminative) stage of the situation (18, 21). If perfectivity is
indeed primarily a perspective on situations as wholes ('blobs' rather
than 'points'), then the spatial features associated with this subcategory of perfective are anomalous. Jessen's treatment of terminatives as aktionsarten rather than 'pure aspects' (which include
perfective) therefore appears to be more explanatory. I hypothesize
that where languages have perfectives ('wholes' in Comrie's sense)
that are expressed by any of the types of expression listed above,
an extension from terminative to perfective has taken place. Furthermore, the spatial features for terminatives strongly support
Miller's analysis of RUSSIAN 'perfectives' as involving an underlying semantactic structure of the type:

X went into, was in and came out of a state

(1971: 231), in other words as involving change of state, and specifically a journey from a Source (ablative) to a Goal (allative). However, these 'perfectives' must strictly speaking be 'terminatives.'[31]

---

[31] That RUSSIAN, BULGARIAN and other SLAVIC languages rich

A fourth set of terms is found for terminatives in several languages, having to do with the vertical plane. Whereas the vertical
plane is polarized for sequencing (earlier = up, later = down), no
such polarization is to be found in completives; instead, the distinction is either largely neutralized (cf. drink up, drink down;
although drinking down presupposes some dislike of the liquid in
question, there is no aspectual difference here) or the negative
term down retains its locative features more fully than the positive
up term as in burn down vs. burn up (consider, for example, the
difference between burning paper down and burning paper up: in the
former case the paper must be understood to be in stacks, hanging,
or in some other vertical position). Other examples in ENGLISH
include be over, kill off. Similar vertical terms occur in GERMAN,
e.g. auf- in aufessen 'eat up' (Priebsch-Collinson 1958: 257). That
verticality is not solely an INDO-EUROPEAN phenomenon is shown
by TUNICA ha- 'up, down, completive' (Haas 1940: 115).

Like the vertical terms for sequencing, aspectual up-down appear
to derive ultimately from the concept of canonical space. In particular, Bolinger 1971: 98 suggests that up is the direction in which
most physical acts of completion take place, for example, when a
glass is filled the level moves closer to the eye of the viewer, hence
fill up.

The evidence is insufficient to establish the relation of vertical
terms to the semantic hierarchy. We may, however, postulate
that vertical terms presuppose at least Source terms and possibly
also Goal terms.

3. Conclusion

The primary features of space are: i) location (relation, static
or dynamic, to a point or points of reference, e.g. here-there,
from-to), ii) plane or dimension, e.g. front-back, up-down, at-in,
and iii) shape, e.g. round, square, curved (Friedrich 1971: 12).
Of these three, tense, aspect and sequencing select exclusively
location and plane (there is no evidence that the in of progressive
requires three-dimensionality; boundedness within a plane is sufficient). In no language investigated so far has shape been relevant.

(ftnt. 31 cont.)
in prefixal perfectives are not discussed in detail in this paper stems
from the fact that the prefixes have a spatial origin so generalized
that universal constraints do not emerge clearly.

Where pairs of terms are used, they are selected from asymmetric spatial relationships like come-go, front-back, up-down, not from symmetric ones like left-right. The absence of time-lines in some languages and the selection of canonical terms in the different sub-categories of space/time suggest that such asymmetries cannot be explained by the concept of the 'unidirectionality of time,' which is basic to the philosophy and physics of time,[32] but rather by reference to body-space and the canonical encounter (cf. especially Cassirer 1972; Friedrich 1971; H. Clark 1973). Discussions of the temporal systems of language that are based on the concept of unidirectionality and the 'logic of time' confuse physical time with linguistic time and inevitably run into insoluble difficulties.

BIBLIOGRAPHY

Anderson, John M. 1972a. Remarks on the hierarchy of quasi-predications. Revue roumaine de linguistique 17.23-44, 121-140, 193-202, 319-335.

_____. 1972b. The grammar of case. New York: Cambridge University Press.

_____. 1973. An essay concerning aspect: some considerations of a general character arising from the Abbé Darrigol's analysis of the Basque verb. (Janua Linguarum Series Minor, CLXVII.) The Hague: Mouton.

Ashton, E.D. 1947. Swahili grammar. London: Longmans, Green. 2nd ed.

Bach, Emmon and Robert T. Harms. 1972. How do languages get crazy rules? Linguistic change and generative theory, ed. by Robert P. Stockwell and Ronald K.S. Macaulay, 1-21. Bloomington: Indiana University Press.

---

[32] When the Queen in Lewis Carroll's Alice through the looking glass characterizes the world of 'living backwards,' it is the logic of sequence that is reversed (crime before punishment is reversed to punishment before crime), but the purely temporal relations remain the same, for sequence qua sequence (as opposed to logical connection) simply concatenates, and events can be assigned [±Prior] arbitrarily.

Bailey, Charles-James N. 1973. Variation in linguistic theory.
Arlington, Va.: Center for Applied Linguistics.

Barbelenet, D. 1913. De l'aspect verbal en Latin ancien et parti-
culièrement dans Térence. Paris: Champion.

Bennett, David C. 1975. Spatial and temporal uses of English
prepositions: an essay in stratificational semantics. London:
Longman Group.

Benveniste, Emile. 1965. Language and human experience.
Diogenes 51.1-12.

Blok, H.P. 1955-6. Localism and deixis in Bantu linguistics.
Lingua 5.382-419.

Bogułwski, Andrzej. 1975. On the status of temporal expressions.
Charakterystyka Temporalna Wypowiedzenia, 7-60. Polska Aka-
demia Nauk, Institut Języka Polskiego.

Bolinger, Dwight. 1971. The phrasal verb in English. Cambridge,
Mass.: Harvard University Press.

Bourquin, Walter. 1912-3, 1913-4. Adverb und adverbiale Umschreib-
ung im Kafir. Zeitschrift für Kolonialsprachen 3. 230-243, 279-
326; 4. 68-74, 118-155, 231-248.

Bruce, Bertram C. 1972. A model for temporal references and
its application in a question-answering program. Artificial
Intelligence 3. 1-25.

Brunot, Ferdinand. 1966. Histoire de la langue française des
origines à nos jours. Paris: Colin. 2nd ed., 13 volumes.

Bull, William E. 1960. Time, tense, and the verb; a study in
theoretical and applied linguistics, with particular attention
to Spanish. (University of California Publications in Linguistics,
19.) Berkeley and Los Angeles: University of California Press.

Caldwell, Robert. 1956. A comparative grammar of the Dravidian
or South-Indian family of languages. Madras, reprint of 3rd ed.,
1913.

Cassirer, Ernst. 1972. La philosophie des formes symboliques.
Trans. by Ole Hansen-Love and Jean Lacoste. Paris: Editions
Minuit.

Chao, Yuen Ren. 1968. A grammar of Spoken Chinese. Berkeley and Los Angeles: University of California Press.

Clark, Eve V. 1971. On the acquisition of the meaning of before and after. Journal of Verbal Learning and Verbal Behavior 10. 266-275.

_____. 1973. How children describe time and order. Studies of child language development, ed. by Charles A. Ferguson and Dan I. Slobin, 585-606. New York: Holt, Rinehart and Winston.

Clark, Herbert. 1973. Space, time, semantics and the child. Cognitive development and the acquisition of language, ed. by T. E. Moore, 28-63. New York: Academic press.

Comrie, Bernard. 1976. Aspect. London: Cambridge University Press.

Dietrich, Wolf. 1973. Der periphrastische Verbalaspekt in den romanischen Sprachen. Untersuchungen zum heutigen romanischen Verbalsystem und zum Problem der Herkunft des periphrastischen Verbalaspekts. Tübingen: Max Niemeyer.

Ebneter, Theodor. 1973. Das Bündnerromanische Futur. Syntax der mit 'vegnir' und 'habere' gebildeten Futurtypen in Gegenwart und Vergangenheit. (Romanica Helvetica, 84.) Bern: Francke.

Ernout, A. and A. Meillet. 1939. Dictionnaire étymologique de la langue Latine: histoire des mots. Paris: Klincksieck.

Ferreiro, Emilia. 1971. Les relations temporelles dans le langage de l'enfant. Genève: Droz.

Fillmore, Charles J. 1971. Lectures on deixis. University of California, Santa Cruz, Summer Program in Linguistics. Mimeo.

_____. 1972. How to know whether you are coming or going. Linguistik 1971, ed. by Karl Hylgaard-Jensen, 369-379. Frankfurt: Athenäum.

Friedrich, Paul. 1971. The Tarascan suffixes of locative space: meaning and morphotactics. (Indiana University Publications, Language Science Monographs, 9.) Bloomington: Indiana University Press.

Friedrich, Paul. 1974. On aspect theory and Homeric aspect. IJAL 40.4, Part 2; Memoir 28.

_____. 1975. Proto-Indo-European syntax. Journal of Indo-European Studies, Monograph 1.

Givón, Talmy. 1972. Studies in ChiBemba and Bantu grammar. Studies in African Linguistics 3, Supplement 3.

_____. 1973. The time-axis phenomenon. Lg. 49. 890-925.

Greenberg, Joseph H. 1966. Language universals. (Janua Linguarum Series Minor, LIX.) The Hague: Mouton.

Guillaume, Gustav. 1941. De la répartition des trois radicaux d' 'aller'. Le français moderne 9. 171-181.

Haas, Mary. 1940. Tunica. New York: J.J. Augustin.

Hakulinen, Laura. 1961. The structure and development of the Finnish language. Trans. by John Atkinson. (Indiana University Publications, Uralic and Altaic Series, 3.) Bloomington: Indiana University Press.

Holt, Jens. 1943. Études d'aspect. Acta Jutlandica 15.2.

Huddleston, Rodney. 1969. Some observations on tense and deixis in English. Lg. 45. 777-806.

Hymes, Dell. 1975. From space to time in Kiksht. IJAL 41. 313-329.

Imbs, Paul. 1956. Les propositions temporelles en ancien français; la détermination du moment. Publications de la faculté des lettres de l'université de Strasbourg.

Jakobson, Roman. 1971. Shifters, verbal categories, and the Russian verb. Selected Writings 2. 130-147. The Hague: Mouton. (first published 1957).

Jessen, Marilyn E. 1975. A semantic study of spatial and temporal expressions in English. Unpublished Ph.D. dissertation, Edinburgh University.

Juret, A. 1950. Formation des idées étudiées au moyen de l'étymologie; groupe semantique de la 'limite.' Revue de linguistique romane 17.1-27.

Kapelink, Olga. 1969. Auxiliaires descriptifs en Amharique. Proceedings of the International Conference on Semitic Studies, Jerusalem 19-23 July 1965, 116-131. Jerusalem: Publication of the Israel Academy of Sciences and Humanities.

Keniston, Hayward. 1936. Verbal aspect in Spanish. Hispania 19.163-176.

Kimball, John. 1974. The grammar of facing. Mimeo. (Available from the Indiana Linguistics Club.)

Kuryłowicz, Jerzy. 1972. The role of deictic elements in linguistic evolution. Semiotics 5.174-183.

Lewin, Bruno. 1959. Abriss der japanischen Grammatik auf der Grundlage der klassischen Schriftsprache. Wiesbaden: Harrassowitz.

Lyons, John. 1968. Introduction to theoretical linguistics. New York: Cambridge University Press.

Madan, A.C. 1903. Swahili-English dictionary. London: Oxford University Press.

Marcq, Philippe. 1973. Localisation sur l'axe du temps à l'aide de prépositions; étude partielle. Cahiers d'allemand; revue de linguistique et de pédagogie 5.26-34.

Meinhof, Carl. 1906. Grundzüge einer vergleichenden Grammatik der Bantusprachen. Berlin: Reimer.

Miller, J. 1971. Towards a generative semantic account of aspect in Russian. JL.8. 217-236.

Pottier, Bernard. 1962. Systématique des éléments de relation; étude de morphosyntaxe structurale romane. Paris: Klincksieck.

Preuss, K. Th. 1932. Grammatik der Cora-Sprache. IJAL 7. 1-84.

Priebsch, R. and W.E. Collinson. 1958. The German language. London: Faber and Faber, 4th ed.

Reichenbach, Hans. 1967. Elements of symbolic logic. London: MacMillan.

Rundgren, Frithiof. 1963. Erneuerung des Verbalaspekts im Semitischen; funktion-diachronische Studien zur semitischen Verblehre. Uppsala: Almqvist and Wiksells.

Silverstein, Michael. 1974. Dialectal developments in Chinookan tense-aspect systems: an areal-historical analysis. IJAL 40,4, Part 2, Memoir 29.

Spears, Richard A. 1972. A typology of locative structures in Manding languages. Conference on Manding languages, School of Oriental and African Studies, London. Mimeo.

Stahlke, Herbert. 1970. Serial verbs. Studies in African linguistics 1. 60-99.

Sylvain, Suzanne. 1936. Le créole haïtian: morphologie et syntaxe. Wetteren, Belgium, and Porte-au-Prince, Haiti.

Tauli, Valter. 1966. Structural tendencies in Uralic languages. (Indiana University Publications; Uralic and Altaic Series, 17.) The Hague: Mouton.

Taylor, Douglas. 1963. The origin of West Indian Creole languages: evidence from grammatical categories. American nthropologist 65. 800-814.

Traugott, Elizabeth C. 1975. Spatial expressions of tense and temporal sequencing; a contribution to the study of semantic fields. Semiotica 15. 207-230.

_____. 1976. Natural semantax: its role in the study of second language acquisition. Cinquième colleque de linguistique appliquée, Neuchâtel 20-22 May. Forthcoming in the proceedings.

Ultan, Russell. 1972. The nature of future tenses. Working Papers on Language Universals 8. 55-100.

Verkuyl, H.J. 1972. On the compositional nature of the aspects. (Foundations of Language Supplementary Series, 15.) Dordrecht, Reidel.

Voorhoeve, Jan. 1962. Sranan syntax. Amsterdam: North-Holland.

Wartburg, Walther von. 1948-. Französisches etymologisches Wörterbuch. Tübingen: J.C.B. Mohr.

Weinrich, Harald. 1964. Tempus. Stuttgart: Kohlhammer.

Welmers, William E. 1973. African language structures. Berkeley: University of California Press.

Westermann, Diedrich. 1907. Grammatik der Ewe-Sprache. Berlin: Reimer.

Wierzbicka, Anna. 1973. In search of a semantic model of time and space. Generative grammar in Europe, ed. by F. Kiefer and R. Ruwet, 616-628. (Foundations of Language Supplementary Series, 13.) Dordrecht: Reidel.

Wilson, W.A.A. 1962. The crioulo of Guiné. Johannesburg: Witwatersrand University Press.

Wunderlich, Dieter. 1970. Tempus und Zeitreferenz im Deutschen. (Linguistische Reihe, 5.) Munich: Max Hueber.

Wurm, S.A. 1971. New Guinea Highlands Pidgin: course materials. Pacific Linguistics, Series D, no. 3.

Idiomaticity
as a Language Universal

ADAM MAKKAI

ABSTRACT

Diversification and neutralization are viewed as universals of
natural languages, as a result of which there arise morphotactic
and lexotactic 'ambiguities.' Such ambiguity, when on the lexemic
level, is viewed as a lexemic idiom, and as a sememic idiom when
on the clause or sentence level. The linguistic mechanism for idiom
formation in all known languages is the Multiple Reinvestability Principle (MRP), and the psycho-semantic mechanism is quite likely to
be the Thass-Thienemann/Fabricius Kovacs-Kronasser phenomenon
of repressed taboo meanings being obsessively repeated in adjacent
senses ("synsemantica"), and the development of meaning from the
concrete towards the abstract, and hence 'mental.'

CONTENTS

1. Purpose and Scope

The purpose of the present paper is to offer a theoretical discussion of idiomaticity as an empirical language universal. It is
not intended as a catalog of the multi-word lexical items of Standard
Average European (SAE) or Exotic Languages (ELs); that would
involve one in an immense project of 'Ecological Lexicography.'[1]
The scope of the present paper will, therefore, be necessarily
limited to an illustration of the fundamental relationships of neutralization and diversification, as the two main factors universally
responsible for the historical emergence and synchronic existence
of idioms in all of the world's known natural languages.

---

[1] Ecological lexicography (cf. Makkai 1973, 1974a, 1974b) arranges
items in a lexicon according to semantic nests or synonym groups
à la Roget's Thesaurus, but with some important modifications:
whereas Roget does not give the collocational range of some of his
synonyms, nor any indication where the item is used (e.g. exclusively British, universal English, exclusively Southern US, exclusively Western Australia), an ecological dictionary of ENGLISH
(EDE) would systematically give all the National Area Indications
and Major Dialect Area Indications as well as the speakers' sociological status (SSS). At the same time these semantic nests would
be listed in the frequency of their occurrences, but accompanied by
an alphabetical master-look up and an a-tergo look up (a reverse
dictionary). Multiword expressions (e.g. to fly off the handle
'become angry') could be looked up under EMOTIONAL STATES,
ANGRY as semantic nests, but also under fly, handle, off, and
the, the expression's constituent lexons. (A lexon is a constituent
of a lexeme which, further on, is realized as a morpheme. This
is a crucial distinction to make, because frequently the constituent
morpheme clearly maintains its formal relationship with the morpheme class it belongs to while having no semantic connection with
it. Consider understand and withstand which have nothing in common synchronically with the lexeme stand and which, nevertheless,
form their pasts, -stood: understood, withstood. This phenomenon
recurs with such frequency in inflecting languages that it is negli-
gent not to account for it. Stand in understand, then, is a constituent
lexon whose morphemic realization coincides with that of the lexeme
stand, as one "rule" will account for their respective past tenses.
For a fuller discussion cf. Makkai 1972, Lockwood 1972, but also
Lamb 1966.) In an EDE multiply reinvested morphemes are listed
but once — i.e. stand-stood is listed only once regardless of what
longer lexemes it recurs in. As such it is, of course, also connected to the lexeme stand whose meaning is 'to be erect on one's

2. Where Do Idioms Come from?

There is reason to believe that during the course of the evolution
of natural languages there came a time when the relatively limited
set of vocal utterances characteristic of Neanderthal speech (cf.
Wescott 1969:197) became insufficient for the cataloging of the human environment. If we, for illustration's sake, imagine that an

---

(ftnt. 1 cont.)
feet.' The morpheme stand has its own spoken and written frequency indicators cross-listed with the National Area Indicators
and the Major Dialect Area Indicators, and the SSS in each instances;
but it is also cross-listed with EMOTIONAL STATES just as fly off
the handle is because of one of its meanings 'tolerate,' as in I can't
stand this pain any longer. The EDE, in short, tries to model a
mature native speaker's knowledge of his language from the point
of view of lexis (from this point of view it would be a competence
dictionary), but it also tries to arrange this knowledge in a form
which is immediately accessible upon the right situational context
(whereby it is also a model for performance). When a person is
asked to describe his wrist watch, he does not search for words
alphabetically in his memory, but goes to the words big hand, small
hand, one, two, three, twelve, date window, etc. immediately, as
the human brain -- unlike mechanical digital computers -- has instan-
taneous pattern recognition capability. Obviously no printed dictionary could possibly do justice to the speed and versatility of the human
brain, thus the EDE would not be a printed book. The EDE, as it
is envisaged today, would be a high-speed computer retrieval system with video and audio playback capability, somewhat like the
PLATO system now widely in use on US campuses. The user receives a 120 pp. instruction booklet on how to ask questions from
the computer which can be typed in at a terminal. Example:
INPUT ENTRY: get away with; INSTRUCTION: define and give
range. ANSWER: 'perpetrate illicit act without repercussions;'
RANGE: Universal English; frequency: upper 90%.
INPUT ENTRY: inspect; INSTRUCTION: give synonyms and range.
ANSWER: round up (US exclusive); RANGE: cattle breeding, ex.:
the farmer rounded up his herd. Australia: muster; the farmer
mustered his herd.
INPUT ENTRY: give US senses of muster, give British senses of
muster. ANSWER: muster: US: she mustered all her courage;
'conjure up, gather.' British: the Queen mustered the Royal Guard.
Etc. The entry round up would, of course, be cross-listed with
round and up as morphemes as well as with the semantic nest
CATTLE BREEDING and ANIMAL HUSBANDRY.

average intelligent 20-year old Neanderthal human adult had roughly
500 concepts in his consciousness and roughly 500 distinct utterances
to vocalize them by, the resulting 1:1 relationship between his concepts and his available vocalizations can be diagrammed as follows:

Mg_1 Mg_2 Mg_3 Mg_4 Mg_5 $\longrightarrow$ etc.

Ss_1 Ss_2 Ss_3 Ss_4 Ss_5 $\longrightarrow$ etc.

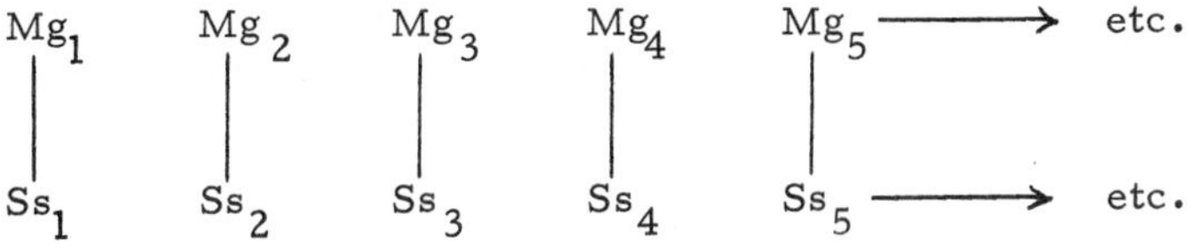

(Mg = 'meaning;' Ss = 'sound symbol')

Figure 1

Since it is common knowledge that there are no homogeneous
speech communities and since we know that not even children are
entirely systematic in their pre-adult language idiosyncratic arche-
speech (Halliday 1975), it goes without saying that the state of affairs
diagrammed in Fig. 1 is a reductionistic oversimplification which
probably never existed in reality. It is, nevertheless, a possible
model of idiom-free speech where each distinct concept corresponds
to one and only one signal. (Some modern computer languages are
built, in fact, on this principle.) Algeo (1970) calls this type of
communication 'Martian' because of its unambiguous, 'logical' nature. That the type of communication described here does exist
elsewhere in nature is becoming more and more evident from zoo-
semiotics, especially in the lower species. The logical opposite of
this non-primate, "Martian," computer-style communication would
be, again, the imaginary "system," in which every concept could
be expressed by any sound, and vice versa: and Ss could be the
carrier of any Mg. If carried to an extreme, such a set-up would
amount to no communication system at all, as it would clearly end
in chaos. Since poets and creative writers like to use conventional
words for the designation of novel concepts, Algeo (1970: 216-7) has
coined the term 'Venusian' for this type of communication. It can
be diagrammed as follows:

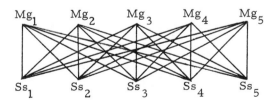

Figure 2

Thus, if a poet likens a girl to a flower, he is using 'Venusian' communication. A girl is a girl is a girl, just as a rose is a rose is a rose, as Gertrude Stein saw fit to remind us in order to cut through the stylistic morass that an overindulgence in Venusianism can often create in <u>belles lettres</u>.

Now modern human languages on the hither-side of Cro-Magnon, that is languages whose speakers have undergone the 'unprecedented mushrooming out of the human neo-cortex' as described in Koestler (1967) are neither purely 'Martian' nor purely 'Venusian,' but show a singularly 'Tellurian,' i.e. Earth-language admixture of both. The result is the universal property of natural languages to have a) direct realization, b) neutralization, and c) diversification side by side. The situation is diagrammed in Fig. 3 below:

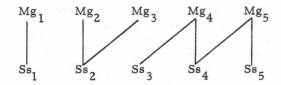

Figure 3. Tellurian, or Earth Language, replete with direct realization ('Martian') and interlocking diversification and neutralization ('Venusian').

2.1 <u>Direct realization</u>

Direct realization is what computer programmers aim for. Ambiguity is avoided and the decoding process is not blocked or derailed. In the sentence

1. The Emperor of Japan has an old wife.

the lexemes realize the concepts (or sememes) via direct realization, in the straightforward way:

the	definite article
Emperor	a kind of potentate
of	possessive marker
Japan	a Far Eastern country
has	present 3rd sing. of the verb <u>have</u> 'to possess;' hence possesses
a(n)	indefinite article
old	adjective, 'aged,' 'not young'
wife	female spouse

We thus understand that 1. means, paraphrased, 'The potentate of the Far Eastern country (known as) Japan possesses a wedded female spouse who is not young.' However, if we encounter the expressions Emperor of Japan and old wife in 2, our decoding process gets temporarily blocked and derailed:

2. My naughty cat ate my Emperor of Japan and my old wife.

If this sentence were to be decoded in the 'Martian' fashion, using the definitions given in the little glossary above, we would come up with a mis-decoding that would disinform us as to the following: 'My ill-behaved domesticated feline pet consumed the potentate of the Far Eastern country known as Japan and the no longer young wedded female spouse (both of which) I possess.' And this paraphrase would make no sense. Coded in the deep memory of each fluent speaker of ENGLISH is the incompatibility of cat, eat: human being, as cats usually do not eat humans, especially if the cat is not a leopard, a lion, or a Bengal tiger. It thus follows that Emperor of Japan and old wife must be things that a cat can eat; additionally, we must also account for the fact that I can own an oriental potentate, which ordinarily is, of course, impossible. The reason why we have been unsuccessful in understanding 2. is that we went about it via direct realization which led us to Glossary A. As familiar aquarium fishes, Emperor of Japan and old wife are fair game for cats, of course.

2.2 Neutralization

In order to be able to understand 2. (as well as thousands upon thousands of expressions like it), we must come to grips with the fact that homo sapiens' Tellurian abounds in neutralization. The concept of neutralization has been well understood in linguistics with regard to phonological matters ever since the days of the Prague school and Troubetzkoy's influential Grundzüge der Phonologie (1939), but the fact that it exists on other levels of linguistic structure as well was not so readily recognized, despite the extreme importance of the phenomenon. In the transformational-generative theory of syntax, examples such as the shooting of the hunters, visiting professors can be boring, etc. have all been introduced because of the fact that neutralization occurs on the morphological and the sentence levels as well, but without explicit recognition being given to neutralization.

If neutralization on all levels had been recognized as a structural possibility in natural languages, grammarians would have been able to account for what came to be known as "ambiguity"

on all levels in static fashion, purely within synchronic description.
Just as phonological neutralization can be accounted for in terms
of morphophonemes, i.e. the units on the next highest morphological stratum, so morphological neutralization can be accounted for
in terms of lexemes (the units on the next highest level of lexology),
and lexological neutralization (i.e. "ambiguous sentences with
identical surface structures") can be accounted for in terms of
meaning, formalized on the linguistic-semantic level of the semol-
ogy. In short, neutralizations on any given level can be dealt with
by examining the units and relations (whose neutralization the investigated phenomenon is) always on the next higher level. The
advantages of "disambiguating ambiguities" by treating them as
neutralizations behind which — on the next higher stratum — there
stand clearly identifiable elements and relations is that the gram-
marian so doing does not have to resort to a series of ordered
rewrite rules or transformations. Not using rewrite rules and
transformations, on the other hand, leads to the distinct advantage
that one is not forced to relegate certain linguistic observations
to "competence" while leaving others to a less important area
referred to as "performance." Not being forced to separate competence and performance in this way, in turn, offers the advantage
of greater psychological realism in one's linguistic description.
Transformationalists have rightly called our attention to ambiguities in syntax, where earlier structuralist treatments tended to
bypass the issues, or were simply ill-equipped to deal with them.
This was clearly a step in the right direction, and we are now
more aware of linguistic structure than we were before 1957. Yet
the recognition that neutralization is not just a Pragueian phonological phenomenon but a morphological and lexo-syntactic one as
well, could have saved modern linguistics the relatively excessive
price of having to posit various degrees of abstractness in psychologically unjustifiable deep structures with a series of ordered
intermediate derivations.

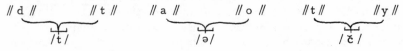

[di: hant̪, di: hend̪ə]   [krasívəyə dámə](fem.)   [ðætl gečə]
die Hand, die Hände   красивая дама   that will get you

[das kint̪, di: kind̪ə]   [krasívəyə pjeró](neut.)   [wɔt hičə]
das Kind, die Kinder   красивое перо   what hit you?

(Sounds between double slants indicate morphophonemes;
sounds between single slants stand for realized phonemes.)

Figure 4. Phonological neutralization

Fig. 4 above shows some phonological neutralizations. (For a more detailed treatment of this phenomenon from a highly formalized point of view, cf. Sullivan 1975).

But neutralization also occur on the morphological level:

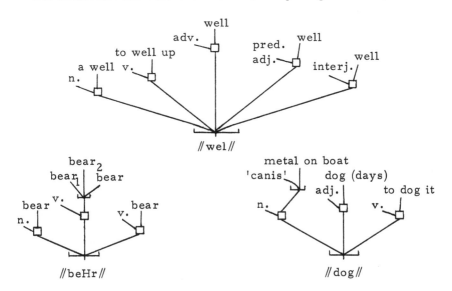

Figure 5. Morphological neutralization

Fig. 5 indicates, in simplified relational network format, what every fluent speaker of ENGLISH knows about the morphemic signs //wel//, //beHr// and //dog//, understood here as syllables primarily, which can be the expressions not just of different meanings but of different syntactic functions ('parts of speech') as well. Thus,//wel// occurs as a noun as in the farmer dug a deep well; it occurs as a verb as in tears welled up in his eyes when he found no water; as an adverb, as in the sentence he used to dig poorly but now he digs well; as an adjective as in he was very ill but now he is well again; and as an interjection as in well, I guess that's all for this syllable. The morphemic sign //beHr// occurs as a noun meaning 'ursus;' as a verb there are at least three uses of it, as in she bears children; then as in she bears children but she can't bear the pain, so she has herself sedated; (another verbal sense of bear is rare in American ENGLISH: the bearers are rebelling and refuse to bear our gear); and as in she bared her soul in public. As to which sense of bear belongs to which morpheme class can easily be tested by the past tense formations; whereas we can say she bared her soul, we do not say *she bore her soul; and whereas we say she bore many

a child in her lifetime, we do not say *she bared many a child in
her lifetime. The syllable // dog // (with phonemic / ɔ / in most
American dialects) is mostly known as a noun meaning 'canis familiaris domesticus,' but it has a good many other nominal senses
as well, such as: ' brass T on sailing boats to which ropes are
tied;' 'affected dignity' as in Max always puts on the dog with us,
etc. An attributive use of dog is seen in I can't stand the late July
dog days any more; and verbal senses, less familiar, also exist,
especially in urban slang, as in you're really dogging it these days,
aren't you?

Morphological neutralization of this sort has been traditionally
known as homonymy along with its similar, but non-identical relative, polysemy. (For an excellent discussion of these terms and
what they imply for the lexicographer, see Zgusta 1971 and my
review of it in Kratylos 1977.)

Modern linguistics has been reluctant to see beyond phonological
and morphological neutralization, although taking the next logical
step would have been easy. After phonological and morphological
neutralization, we encounter syntagmatic or lexotactic neutralization
in every known natural language. A typical example from ENGLISH
follows below.

2.2.1 The morpheme // dog //

As a single noun, it is commonly known in at least seven senses
(other less frequent ones are ignored here). These are: S/dirty
deal/ (the closing was a dog); S/difficult job/ (my math exam was
a dog); S/despicable human being/ (Max calls Hermione a dog);
S/the human foot/ (my dogs are barking = 'I am tired'); S/affected
dignity or pomp/ (don't put on the dog with me!) and, finally, of
course, S/canis familiaris domesticus/ (what kind of dog is that
shaggy one?). The morpheme dog functions in these instances as
a single noun, unmodified, and not modifying anything. Considerable as a case of traditional homonymy-polysemy, we might call
these the 'single investments' of the morpheme dog in seven different senses. If the meaning of the 'morpheme' dog could be 'divided'
by 7 in any meaningful way (arithmetically it is, of course, feasible)
we would get the figure 0.1428577, or expressed as percentages,
14.28577% of the meaning of the morpheme dog has been scattered
over 7 sememes. This mathematical exercise serves a useful purpose which will become evident in a moment. But first let us take
a look at the better known compound investments of the morpheme
dog. It occurs with high frequency in at least the following expressions:

1. doghouse$_1$ 'abode for the canis familiaris domesticus'
                   (derivable compositionally)
2. doghouse$_2$ 'disfavor, fallen from grace,' as in: Max is in
                   the doghouse with Hermione.
3. doghouse$_3$ 'protuberance for instruments on a rocket,
                   aerospace jargon,' as in: The solar sensors
                   were packaged up in the doghouse on the Thor-11.
4. dog leg$_1$ 'the leg of a dog' (derivable compositionally)
5. dog leg$_2$ 'a sharp angle in a human leg like that of a dog'
                   -- not an idiom.
6. dog leg$_3$ 'fairway including sharp left and right turns,'
                   (golfers' usage) as in: Watch out for that dog
                   leg behind the bushes after the third tee.
7. dog leg$_4$ 'directional turn made in a launch trajectory in
                   order to achieve a better orbit inclination,'
                   (aerospace usage) as in: The engineers at the
                   Cape programmed a dog leg into the trajectory
                   of the Titan IV.
8. dog star$_1$ 'the star Sirius'
9. dog star$_2$ 'the star canis maior'
10. dog rose   'rosa canina, a wild rose'
11. dogwood   'a blossoming tree or shrub of the species Cornus'
12. dog days   'the hottest days of July and August, the canicula'
13. hot dog$_1$ 'cooked or grilled frankfurter in a bun'
14. hot dog$_2$!   'exclamation of animated approval'
15. dogged   'stubborn, unyielding'

$1:15 = 0.0666666$, or 6.66666%; thus, one could say that the meaning of the morpheme dog is divided by 15 and yields 6.66666% of 'dog' in each of the compounds listed. For a total scatter of the 'divisibility' of the meaning of the morpheme dog, we can add up the seven ghost-investments and the 15 multiple, or real investments, and divide $1:7+15 = 1:22$; the result is 0.0454545, or 4.54545%.

Since obviously neither 0.14% nor 14%, 6.6% nor 4.5% of a 'dog' means anything at all, we have here hard mathematical evidence (even though only inverse evidence) to the fact that:

a. morphemes are not necessarily 'meaningful,' but are potential meaning carriers; and that
b. consequently morphemes, lexemes, and sememes belong on separate strata, since
c. the identical morpheme dog can be materially verified to be present in 7 single investments, and in 15 compound investments, minimally, giving the morpheme a $1:22 = 4.5454\%$ multiple reinvestment ratio (MRR).

The MRR of verbal, adjectival, adverbial etc. morpheme in
ENGLISH can be similarly calculated. To return to our examples
in Fig. 5, the MRRs are: $^M/\!\!/$wel$/\!\!/$1 : 5 = 0.2 = 20\%$; $^M/\!\!/$beHr$/\!\!/$1 : 6 =
0.1666666, or 16.66666\%.

One way to characterize these morphemes, then, is to say that
some have a higher MRR than others; taking the three examples of
dog, well, and bear, one could rank them as follows:

  dog = 4.5454\% of retained meaning; the morpheme is highly
         idiom-prone.
  bear = 16.66666\% of retained meaning; the morpheme is less
         idiom-prone.
  well = 20\% of retained meaning; this morpheme is the least
         idiom-prone of the three compared.

Notice, incidentally, how this kind of ranking by percentages
does not take into account proverbial idioms and collocations in
which the words dog, well and bear might show up. Taking those
into consideration also, the percentages would go significantly
down, i.e. the MRR of each form would go up. From the foregoing observations concerning neutralization, we might set up the
following pseudo-rule:

  The higher the MRR of a morpheme, i.e. the lower its percentage of retained meaning over the number of compound
  lexemes and sememes of which it is a realization, the greater
  the semantic depletion of that morpheme.

But this is a pseudo-rule. The reason is obvious: meaning is not
a mathematically divisible, quantifiable concept. Furthermore,
the retention of the 'original meaning' of dog 'canis familiaris' is
entirely different in the forms doghouse as in Max is in the doghouse
with Hermione, and in dogwood, 'a kind of blossoming shrub or tree
of the genus Cornus.' The original meaning retains its metaphorical
translucence in the former and has none in the latter. (To be out of
favor is easily likened to having to live in an actual doghouse, whereas
the shrubs of the species Cornus have nothing associative or metaphorical about them tying them to dogs.) Thus, if meaning-retention
is to be measured in idioms, it is not to be done numerically, but
by comparing the idiomatic meaning of the form to its literal meaning and then trying to establish a principle of gradation. For a set
of initial proposals dealing with this knotty problem, see Makkai 1975.

Why bother, then, with the MRR and the numerical percentages
it yields? For the practical purposes of ecological lexicography

(cf. Makkai 1972: part II and 1975) which systematically allows the
user of a lexicon to go from any expression carrier to any content,
and vice versa. Imagining for the sake of argument that the 22
examples cited exhaust ENGLISH dog (which is false), we would,
by the MRR gained mathematically, be able to calculate the size
of the computational storage necessary to account for all of the
occurrences of dog. The following rule is a real one, as opposed
to the above pseudo-rule:

> The higher the MRR of a morpheme (i.e. the lower its occur-
> rence-percentage over all of its linked meanings), the more
> units in computational memory storage the morpheme will
> require.

In human terms, this simply means that the more senses there are
to a form, the more memorization a child or a foreign learner has
to do to master the full range of that form. In terms of practical
lexicography, it means that the longer the definition section and
the number of the cross-references to that entry will be.

2.2.2 A definition of the idiom from the point of view of ecological lexicography

An idiom is an entry in an Ecological Dictionary (ED) of a natural
language such that the number of cross-references is minimally
twice the number of its constituent free morphemes (or words) (i.e.
once for every lexeme as expression carrier and once for each
lexeme as one of the possible realizations of a certain semantic
nest, i.e. a synonym group) plus any of its own idiomatic meanings
which remain not deducible from the meanings of the constituent
forms. (Compare this discussion with the more detailed statements
concerning ecological lexicography in footnote 1.)

Thus, put up is multiply idiomatic, since it has, besides the
literal sense (as in put up those books on the shelf, won't you?),
the following nonpredictable senses:

put up$_1$ 'preserve,' as in: Mother puts up peaches for
                    the winter.
put up$_2$ 'stage,perform,' as in: The students put up a tremen-
                    dous show. / The inmates put up a protest rally.
put (someone) up$_3$ 'give lodging,' as in: Let's put John up for a
                    night. / Let's put up the Smiths for a night.

With the additional words with, to, someone and something, put
up yields further unpredictable senses:

put up with$_4$ 'tolerate,' as in: We can't put up
                                             with this weather.
put someone up to something$_5$ 'persuade to do,' as in: You put
                                             me up to this!
put something up to someone$_6$ 'leave to someone's discretion,'
                                             as in: I put it up to you.
                                                    (cf. Makkai 1972: 250)

But in order fully to appreciate what this means, we must now look at the linguistic phenomenon which is the logical reverse of neutralization: diversification.

2.3 Diversification

Whereas in neutralization we have several meanings being co-realized by the same expression, in diversification we have the reverse: closely related meanings are (not identical ones!) realized by a multitude of expressions. Alfred D. Sheffield's 1959 edition of Soule's Dictionary of English Synonyms lists the following 'synonyms' for the semantic nest or macrosememe 'stupid':

1. senseless, witless, dull, brainless, weak-headed, addle-pated, muddle-headed, beef-witted, fat-headed, shallow-brained, lack-witted, short-witted, dull-witted, blunt-witted, shallow-pated, clod-pated, thick-skulled, wooden-headed, dunder-headed, bull-headed, slow, doltish, stolid, obtuse, thick, foolish, sluggish, insensate, muddy-headed, sottish, and dumb.
2. unentertaining, prosaic, pointless, prosy, vacant, inept, fatuous, inane, asinine, crass, flat, heavy, insipid, tame, vapid, bald, uninteresting, humdrum, dull, tiresome, tedious, idiotic, and imbecile.
3. stupefied, drowsy, torpid, heavy, comatose, lethargic, and morbidly sleepy.

The 1964 edition of Roget's Thesaurus in Dictionary Form edited by Norman Lewis has quite a few additional adjectives for 'stupid,' such as:

unintelligent, insipient, incapacious, birdbrained, boneheaded, brainless, mindless, chuckleheaded, empty-headed, empty-minded, empty-pated, empty-skulled, loggerheaded, lunk-headed, rattlebrained, rattleheaded, rattlepated, rattleskulled, muddleheaded, sapheaded, simple-headed, simple-minded, simple-witted, blockish,...duncical, duncish, duncelike, gawky, loutish, senile, and anile;

continued under the bold-face entry dim-witted with seven lines of
further synonyms and with an additional three lines under the bold
face entry inane and five lines' worth under the bold face entry
feeble-minded. The noun stupidity (an obvious semantic relative
of the adjective stupid) boasts a collection of 30 lines with speci-
mens such as misintelligence, dullardism, dotage, second child-
hood, moroncy, hebetude, etc.

But then perhaps the case of the sememe-nest 'stupid' is a
special case. After all, it is unpleasant and ridiculous: enough
incentive to want to avoid it as a topic (the 'taboo repression effect'
of Thass-Thienemann 1968 and 1969) whose unconscious correlate,
'obsessive repetition in diverse shapes,' may be the psychological
reason for the extraordinarily heavy load in the storage in terms
of various and sundry surface tokens.

Yet, on further inspection, it turns out that 'stupid' is by no
means alone in this regard. The macrosememe 'to die' is just as
rich in surface tokens: to kick the bucket, to dance on air, to bite
the dust, to return to Abraham's bosom and to cash in one's chips
are some of the better known idiomatic realizations. Whether a
surface token realizing a sememe-nest will be an idiom (i.e. a
multiword unit which, if taken literally, can disinform the unpre-
pared ill-decoder) or just another word (whether monomorphemic
or polymorphemic, but semantically translucently constructed) is
entirely unpredictable and depends on the anthropological and sociological history of the speech community under investigation. Thus,
the five forms cited above in connection with 'die' are all idioms,
whereas many of the synonyms for 'stupid' (e.g. doltish, crass,
inane, etc.) are not, whether or not one chooses to analyze doltish
as dolt +ish and inane as in +ane, or as unanalyzable units. (What
is *dolt and *ane?) Literalizations of the five idioms relating to
'die' are all possible:

The Chicago fire started when a cow kicked the bucket with a
candle on it which fell into the hay.
After my first drink in the new 747, I felt that the jet was
dancing on air.
The hungry men had no time to clean their apples and bit the
dust on them with their first mouthful.
The kitten fell asleep on his chest; when Abe snored, it started
up and leaped off; then, in a little while, it stretched, yawned,
and returned to Abraham's bosom.
He decided not to push his luck any further and, gathering his
winnings, he hurried to the window and cashed in his chips.

Needless to say, a proper context has to be constructed around each of these idioms in order to achieve the literalization.

3. Some Putative Universals Concerning Idioms

a. All natural languages are subject to the Multiple Reinvesta-bility Principle (MRP) of their minimal meaningful elements in novel senses, regardless of genetic and typological affilia-tion.

b. The result of the MRP, an evolutionary force in natural languages is i) neutralization and ii) diversification on the synchronic level, findable in all natural languages regardless of type or family.

c. The MRP, having resulted in neutralization and diversifica-tion, allows, on the one-word level, for homonymy, synonymy, and on the multiword or phrase level, for idiomaticity.

d. Homonymy, synonymy and idiomaticity, jointly, allow for the simultaneous availability of i) literal meaning, ii) idio-matic meaning, iii) literalized idiomatic meaning, iv) various forms of punning.

e. The MRP as an evolutionary force in natural language rests on the phoricity of human perception and, consequently, on the phoricity of human speech. The main types of phoricity are: exophora (situational reference) and endophora (textual reference); if endophora is chosen, we have a subsequent choice between anaphora (reference to what was said before) and cataphora (reference to what will be said later). (This classification follows closely Halliday and Hasan 1967.) The unique nature of the metaphor is that it links situational reference (exophora) to textual reference (endophora) by virtue of recombining already existing linguistic elements in order to describe, assimilate, approximate, or just stand in for a new situation, some of which were already in mem-ory storage, but some of which were missing.

3.1 The Gardners' chimpanzee, Washoe, as a metaphoric idiom generator

Washoe, after she already knew well over 300 signs of the Amer-ican SIGN LANGUAGE, including the signs for water and for bird, was shown a duck in a pond. The trainer, Roger, who explains the

event in the 65 minute 1976 NOVA television presentation from
which this example is taken, was trying to teach Washoe the sign
for 'duck,' but she spontaneously signed 'water bird' on her own
and has stuck to that lexemic idiom for 'duck' ever since. Other
chimps have picked it up and <u>duck</u> has become 'water bird' in the
chimpanzee's sign language.

The point to be made here is that the lexeme ^{L}/water bird/ (not
spoken, but signed, of course!) is a multiword realization of the
sememe ^{S}/duck/, where an exophoric, referential-visual inspection of the entity 'duck' convinced the chimpanzee that what she saw
answered the description of what she stored in her memory as 'bird'
in conjunction to what she also stored in memory as 'water.' This
exophoric-situational reference (i.e. the visual identification of
two knowns in an unknown, new context) was now brought into the
sign language (i.e. <u>metaphéretai</u> 'is brought over,' <u>translatus est</u>
from <u>transfero</u>, -<u>ferre</u>) whose already familiar elements ('lexemes'),
<u>water</u> and <u>bird</u>, were now recombined (that is, multiply reinvested)
in order to designate a bird on water. If an incident such as Washoe's
designating <u>duck</u> as 'water bird' occurs only once and is instantly
forgotten, the metaphor is ephemeral and unique; it will not be remembered and socialized. (Socialization and remembering go hand
in hand; the order is arbitrary. Neither can exist without the other
(cf. Halliday 1975).) Washoe apparently remembered it and hence
succeeded in lexicalizing it; furthermore, she transmitted it to the
other chimps, and apparently even to her human trainer, Roger,
who found this so remarkable and pleasingly original that he himself started to use the sign for 'water bird' meaning 'duck.'

3.2 <u>Washoe</u> — <u>Neanderthal</u> -- <u>Cro Magnon</u> -- <u>*IE</u> -- <u>Old English</u>--
<u>Shakespeare</u> — <u>NASA and the space industry</u>

If we rethink our steps regarding neutralization, diversification
and direct realization in view of the evidence that even a chimpanzee can be an original creator of idioms, it stands to reason to
suspect that human speech was never idiom-free at any stage of
its development. Hockett's universal 2.13 in Hockett 1961-65 (in
Greenberg 1963-66) reads: "Duality of Patterning. Every language
has both a cenematic subsystem and a plerematic subsystem."
Hockett writes:

By virtue of duality of patterning, an enormous number of minimum semantically functional elements (pleremes, morphemes)
can be and are mapped into arrangements of a conveniently small
number of minimum meaningless but message-differentiating

elements (cenemes, phonological components). No animal
system known to the writer shows a significant duality.
   Some contemporary investigators strongly suspect that a
human language involves not just two, but at least three major
subsystems: for example 'phonemic,' 'morphemic,' and 'sememic.'

In a footnote Hockett mentions the then (1961) not yet published proposals of Lamb and Trager on the subject.

   Fifteen years later, in 1977, it is also accepted by many, that
human languages may be universally stratified in a quadripartite
manner:

>   SEMOLOGY
>   LEXOLOGY
>   MORPHOLOGY
>   PHONOLOGY

with these four strata, or structural layers constituting the grammar
of a language. Lamb 1966, Lockwood 1972, Makkai 1972, Makkai
and Lockwood 1973 give a readily accessible account of this view of
the matter. The kind of evidence that would successfully refute the
claim of the universality of such quadripartite stratification would
have to be the discovery of a number of natural languages well analyzed and described that would obviously lack at least two of the
central strata, e.g. the lexology and the morphology, yet carrying
out the business of human communication successfully as a mere
two-way mapping between sense and sound. Such a language could
have a fully developed dictionary of notions (i.e. a "semicon" in
the sense of Lamb 1966), but to each entry in the semicon there
would have to correspond one specific set of sound sequence, bearing no structural resemblance to any other sound sequence. The
basic building blocks of the sound system could be, to take a familiar example, the short and long beeps of the Morse code whose 24
combinations would have to be greatly expanded by arithmetical
permutation and variation to generate a specific signal matching
each entry in the semicon. Such a language would have the 'duality
of patterning' while it could be called justifiably bi-stratal rather
than quadristratal. Such a language, in other words, would not
have availed itself during the course of its evolution of the MRP
discussed earlier.

   If we assume that structural stratification is a universal, it will
automatically follow that idiomaticity has been an integral part of

every natural language once human languages became distinct
from animal communication systems. In her natural animal state
Washoe would probably not have come up with <u>water bird</u> for 'duck,'
but given the human training of the signs for 'water' and 'bird,' she
made the connection on her own. Thus, human languages from
Neanderthal through Cro Magnon must have had some idioms in
them. *IE, a highly developed and grammatically complex bundle
of dialects, must certainly have contained idioms, since Homeric
GREEK, LATIN and SANSKRIT all have them. I will cite as evidence but a small number of morphologically complex LATIN verbs,
all of which have an abstract sense built on some concrete, primary senses, in accordance with the Fabricius-Kovács/Kronasser
phenomenon according to which semantic change moves in a statistically significant number of cases, well studied in LATIN, SLAVIC,
etc., from the concrete towards the abstract. It helps in our understanding of idiomaticity if we dub concrete as 'literal' and abstract
as 'idiomatic,' bearing in mind, of course, that this is merely in
order to draw a historical parallel in terms of semantic change.
What is often 'abstract' in a Latinate one-word entry today (e.g.
<u>comprehend</u> literally from 'grasp, seize with the hand') is merely
heavily specified in an idiom. For example, <u>hot potato</u> (literally
'a potato that is hot') shows up idiomatically as 'embarrassing
issue.' Here we have both a change toward unpredictability and
specificity as well as abstractness, but in the case of <u>white ele-
phant</u> 'unwanted property hard to manage or sell,' the development
is less toward the abstract and more toward the unpredictable.

> <u>compraehendere</u>: 'to comprehend, understand,' from <u>together</u>,
> <u>before</u>, and <u>seize</u>; cf. Mod. Eng. <u>grasp</u>, and Mod. Germ.
> <u>Begriff</u>, from <u>greifen</u>, cog. Mod. Eng. <u>grab</u>.

> <u>resistere</u>: 'to resist,' from <u>re-</u> 'against, back' and <u>sisto</u>,
> <u>sistere</u> 'to stand;' cf. Mod. Eng. <u>withstand</u>. (The physical
> image is a man leaning against a barn door that others are
> trying to push in from the outside.)

> <u>metaphora</u> (Gk.): from <u>meta</u> 'across' and <u>pherein</u> 'carry,' lit.
> 'a carrying over, a carry-over.' (There is no physical
> carrying in metaphors.)

> <u>transferro-ferre,tuli, latus</u> gives rise to <u>translate</u>: 'to carry
> over,' but in another sense, here 'from one language to the
> other;' (otherwise <u>metaphor</u> and <u>translation</u> should mean
> the same thing)

consisto-ere: 'to consist,' from together and stand. (A mixture
  that consists of ingredient a and b does not literally 'stand
  together.')

referro-ferre: 'refer,' from re 'back' and ferre 'carry.' (When
  we refer to something we do not carry anything back physi-
  cally; it is a mental activity.)

The examples are well known and could be multiplied ad nauseam.
The important point here is that nowadays nobody considers
ENGLISH forms such as metaphor, transfer, translate, resist,
consist and comprehend as idioms, as the temptation to translate
them literally does not arise for average speakers; it only haunts
the linguist and the scholar of classics. Accordingly, in my
Idiom Structure in English (1972) I have called such forms "post-
idioms."

They are monolexemic entries in the lexicon on ENGLISH today,
as is the learned and highly specialized term investiture as in
Prince Charles' investiture as the Prince of Wales took place in
1969. The idiomatization process can be well illustrated with an
imaginary example. Suppose that speakers of ENGLISH become
tired of such Latinate forms and express them in short, monosyllabic Anglo-Saxon based words. Investiture could then show up
as the dréss-up. If the term (with loud stress on dress as usual
in such phrasal verb nouns) becomes socially accepted for the
special occasion of the investiture and at the same time not used
for other occasions when people dress up (such as gala receptions),
dress-up would become a bona fide multiword idiom referring to
a social institution.

Forms such as give up, get up, to that end, put to flight, to
smile at, for the rest, what is the matter? extremely frequent
today were already used by Shakespeare (examples from Henry the
VIIIth and Othello); many idioms of his day died out, e.g. chronicle
small beer (Othello) meant 'to keep petty accounts,' to heave the
gorge (Othello) meant 'be nauseated,' gross in sense (Othello) meant
'perfectly clear.' Examples abound; the 1942 Houghton Mifflin
edition of the Collected Works (W.A. Neilson, ed.) has a glossary
on the bottom of each of the volume's 1407 pp. of text, and roughly
a fifth of all of these glosses are multiword idioms, now extinct.
In a significant majority of them the Fabricius-Kovács/Kronasser
principle is at work, words in their literal concrete sense chain
up to stand for something mental and nonconcrete.

With this principle firmly entrenched in the language, post World War II twentieth century NASA coinages follow exactly the same principle. The Space ENGLISH meaning of doghouse has been discussed earlier in connection with the morpheme //dog//. Fire in the hole does not mean 'Feuer im Loch,' 'feu dans le trou,' but is the space idiom referring to a complex maneuver in mid-flight:

Lunar Module maneuver during lunar-surf ace liftoff, descent, or inflight abort in which the ascent engine (AE) fires while the ascent and descent stages are mated but not bound together. Lunar orbit rendezvous (LOR) follows. (Makkai 1973a: 23)

A barrier reef refers to a hazardous area and not the familiar ocean phenomenon; a barber pole is a black and white diagonally striped indicator found in both the Command Module and the Lunar Module; it shows, by turning, that a system is operating. Needless to say, modern Space ENGLISH has an overwhelming number of GREEK and LATIN-based technical terms; nevertheless, it is characteristic of idiomaticity in general that well known, ordinary words are once again recombined to describe a technical innovation, an abstract concept.

4. Examples of Multiple Re-investment

In the remainder of this paper I will try to show, from a variety of languages, how the MRP operates, and what universal causes there might be thought of in causing it.

In general, one can observe that the more frequent a word is in literal use, the more often it will be found in combinations which then take on a specialized, nonpredictable meaning. This hypothesis has been mathematically computed by Pierson's r of correlation, and found to be due to chance in a 1:100 proportion in Makkai 1972, regarding the literal and idiomatic occurrences of common verbs such as go, get, take, come, etc., and common prepositional-adverbial formants such as up, down, in, out, etc.

But this is not restricted to ENGLISH. Below I present 136 phrases and expressions in which a single morpheme is reinvested, always with a different shade of meaning. I have relied on Végh and Rubin (1966) and have supplied a number of my own examples elicited from native speakers of FRENCH. Coup 'blow' is one of the most heavily reinvested FRENCH morphemes. It occurs in at least the following expressions:

1. coup monté   'preconceived plot, fellony or mischief'
2. coup d'autorité   'an act of _fiat_, of arbitrary power'
3. coup   de bec   'ironic or sarcastic remark'
         de langue
         de dent
         de patte
         de griffe
4. coup de boutoir   'unexpected verbal repartee'
5. coup de chapeau   'a greeting, a lifting of the hat'
6. coup de chien   'a surreptitious attack' (a Jap-test)
7. coup du père François   'a shot in the back'
8. coup de dés   'a risky affair'
9. coup d'encensoir   'base flattery'
10. coup d'essai   'a first trial at something'
11. coup de fer_1 'the ironing of clothes, trousers'
12. coup de fer_2 'a permanent in lady's hair, or generally
                                    the grooming of hair'
13. coup de feu_1 'a shot'
14. coup de feu_2 'great diligence in work, feverish work'
15. coup de feu_3 'rush hour traffic, traffic jam'
16. coup de $filet_1$ 'the casting of a net in fishing'
17. coup de $filet_2$ 'an unexpected gain in business or gambling'
18. coup de $foudre_1$ 'a strike of lightening'
19. coup de $foudre_2$ 'unexpected, strong effect'
20. coup de $foudre_3$ 'love at first sight'
21. coup de $foudre_4$ 'unexpected fatality, tragedy'
22. coup de $fusil_1$ 'a gun shot'
23. coup de $fusil_2$ 'a huge bill in a restaurant or a hotel'
24. en coup de fusil (adv.)   'of an oblong, narrow shape'
25. coup de $main_1$ 'a catching of criminals in the act'
26. coup de $main_2$ 'a daring, risky undertaking'
27. donner un coup de
    main à quelqu'un   'to give someone a helping hand'
28. coup de maître   'a masterpiece, a masterly touch'
29. coup de $massue_1$ 'a severe blow'
30. coup de $massue_2$ 'astonishing news'
31. coup de $massue_3$ 'unexpectedly heavy bill in a restaurant or hotel'
32. coup du milieu   'a small glass of apple brandy or other
                                    short drink taken neat during the course
                                    of a meal'
33. coup du $partie_1$ 'game ball'
34. coup du $partie_2$ 'decisive event or decision'
35. coup de pied de Vénus   'the claps, venereal disease'
36. sans coup férir (adv.)   'without a blow of a sword, without any
                                    resistance or trouble'

37. avoir le coup dans
    quelque chose   'to be an insider in some business'
38. avoir un coup de vieux   'suddently to grow old'
39. commettre les cents
    coups; faire les (cents)   'to commit mischief, to act up, to
    cents-dix-neuf coups   mess around, act promiscuously'
40. être aux cent coups   'to be extremely worried about sth.'
41. mettre q. aux cent coup   'to cause someone to dispair'
42. donner un coup de téléphone 'to give someone a phone call'
43. donner un coup de pied
    jusqu'à Versailles   'to go on a small excursion'
44. ne pas se donner des
    coup de pied   'to be satisfied with oneself'
45. donner un coup de reins   'to make a great effort'
46. entrer/venir en coup de
    vent   'to come in a great hurry (like a storm)'
47. passer en coup de vent   'to make a one minute appearance
                               somewhere and leave immediately'
48. c'est un coup d'épée
    dans l'eau   'it is futile, it is in vain'
49. être dans le coup   'to be with it, to know where it's at'
50. n'être pas sujet au coup 'to be able to dispose of one's time
    de cloche/marteau   as one wishes'
51. faire son coup   'to succeed in one's plans'
52. faire le coup   'to do it, to be the one who commits sth.'
53. faire d'une pierre deux
    coups   'to kill two birds with one stone'
54. juger des coups   'to remain an uninvolved spectator'
55. manquer son coup   'not to succeed in a venture, to give up'
56. en mettre un coup   'to make a great effort in order to
                               achieve something'
57. monter le coup à q.   'to set a trap for someone'
58. poter coup   'to have the desired of expected effect'
59. en prendre un bon coup   'to pay dearly for something committed'
60. en prendre un sacré bon
    coup   'to draw a severe spanking or beating'
61. rompre un coup   'to stave off a blow, as in boxing'
62. rompre le coup   'to see to it that someone else's under-
                               taking fails'
63. tenir le coup   'to endure, to be able to withstand
                               hardships'
64. ça vaut le coup   'it's worth the pain/cost/trouble etc.'
65. en venir aux coups   'to start fighting over an issue'
66. encore un coup   'once more, "hit me again"(to bartender)'
67. à ce coup   'this time, for now'
68. à coups de...   'with the help of, by means of sth.'

69. à coup perdu	'blindly, at random, without forethought'
70. à coups redoublés	'with one's full might, with all one's strength'
71. à coup sûr	'certainly, for sure'
72. à tous les coups	'at every step, always, all the time'
73. après coup	'after the fact, after the event, too late'
74. du coup	'immediately, right away'
75. pour le coup	'this time, this instance, for this occasion'
76. sous le coup de qch.	'under the weight, dint, impact of sth.'
77. sur le coup	'right away, immediately'
78. d'un coup de baguette	'at the waving of a magic wand'
79. donner un coup de balai	'rapidly to dismiss, fire the employees, rapidly to settle a messy affair'
80. avoir reçu un coup de bambou	'dizzy, giddy, intoxicated, silly, mad, to have lost one's marbles'
81. boire un coup	'to have a drink'
82. donner un coup de caveçon	'to give someone a humiliating punishment'
83. recevoir un coup de caveçon	'to become offended, to turn one's nose up'
84. donner le coup de cloche	'to warn someone'
85. coller un coup à q.	'to give someone a good smack'
86. coup de collier	'a great effort'
87. donner un coup de collier	'a great effort'
88. il n'en perd pas un coup de dent	'he couldn't care less' ('he doesn't lose any sleep over something')
89. encaisser des coups	'to get badly beaten up'
90. casser le nez à coups d'encensoir	'clumsily to praise someone to their face'
91. donner un coup d'épaule à q.	'to give someone a leg up, to help out'
92. essuyer le coup de fusil$_1$	'to smell gunpowder, to realize a fight is impending'
93. coup d'Etat$_1$	'a fast and successful political/military take-over'
94. coup d'Etat$_2$	'a daring step'
95. boir le coup d'étrier	'to have one for the road, to drink farewell'
96. c'est un sale coup pour la fanfare!	'trouble ahead; something is rotten in the State of Denmark'
97. donner le coup de fion	'to put the last touches on something'
98. avoir un bon coup de fourchette	'to be a man of good appetite'
99. coup fourré$_1$	'a double-cut, the "one-two"'
100. coup fourré$_2$	'a ruse, a trap, attacking so. in the back'
101. en foutre un coup$_1$	'to work like a dog, to work extremely hard'
102. en foutre un coup$_2$	'to belt somebody very hard'

103. frapper un coup   'to start something dangerous'
104. frapper un grand coup$_1$ 'to accomplish something grandiose'
105. frapper un grand coup$_2$ 'to strike and demolish someone,
                                          to wipe out someone'
106. frapper les grands coups$_1$ 'to use the strongest possible measures'
107. frapper les grands coups$_2$ 'to accomplish something extraordinary'
108. frapper son coup   'to make the mark, to achieve the
                                          desired effect'
109. donner/pousser un coup
     de geule   'to shout, to sing very loudly'
110. avoir un coup de hache
     (à la tête)   'to have lost one's marbles'
111. coup de Jarnac   'a lowly attack, stabbing one's
                                          with lowly words'
112. se coller un coup de jus   'to have a stiff drink and get drunk'
113. il est là pour un coup   'he's a good-looking lad'
114. marquer le coup   'to indicate that a remark has been
                                          registered, that a hurt won't be for-
                                          gotten, that an allusion has been
                                          understood, etc.'
115. marquer de coups   'to give someone a good beating'
116. marquer un coup   'to gain a point, to make an advance'
117. avoir un coup de marteau   'to be silly, stupid'
118. un monteur de coups   'a swindler'
119. tirer son coup de   'to fire one's biggest shot in a debate,
     pistolet   to make the winning argument'
120. tirer des coups de
     pistolet dans la rue   'to behave as an exhibitionist'
121. un coup de piston   'special favors, protection'
122. faire le coup de poing   'to start a fist fight'
123. donner le coup de pouce$_1$ 'to help, support, to administer the
                                          last touch'
124. donner le coup de pouce$_2$ 'to kill, to strangle'
125. donner le coup de pouce
     à une balance   'to cheat behind the counter'
126. coup de soleil$_1$ 'sunburn'
127. coup de soleil$_2$ 'drunkenness'
128. coup de soleil$_3$ 'infatuation, falling in love'
129. jeter un coup de sonde   'to feel one's way around in the dark'
130. coup de tête$_1$ 'a provocative, challenging gesture'
131. coup de tête$_2$ '(soccer) a bouncing of the ball with
                                          the head'
132. agir sur un coup de tête   'to act out of emotional rather than
                                          reasoned considerations'
133. coup de théâtre   'an unexpected turn of events (both on
                                          stage and in real life)'

134. ce sera le coup de torchon   'the whole personnel will be fired'
135. se flanquer un coup de torchon 'to start up a fight'
136. un coup de Trafalgar   'a catastrophe, a disaster'

Wescott (1962) calls such heavily reinvested morphemes 'culture
words' or 'ethnologs.' He writes:

> ...the point is that these words occur in a disproportionately
> large number of constructions with what seem, at least to an
> outsider, an astonishing variety of meanings.

He cites ENGLISH get as one such ethnolog. In Makkai 1972
it is statistically calculated to be one of the most idiom-prone verbs
in the ENGLISH language. Wescott also cites the verb gbé from
BINI, a Nigerian language, whose basic meaning 'to beat' (cf. the
above-quoted FRENCH coup 'a blow, a strike') also occurs in the
meanings 'to strike,' 'to break,' 'to kill,' 'to perform,' 'to dance,'
'to pick or pluck,' 'to catch or trap,' 'to dawn,' 'to rot or to be finished,' 'to do something intensely, repeatedly or to excess.' Ethnologs, then, are probably also universal, as one cannot escape the
strking similarity between these meanings of BINI gbé and FRENCH
coup. The most likely explanation is the putative psychological
universal of Thass-Thienemann (1968, 1969) which states, in essence,
that if a word, at some time in its history, had a strong sexual connotation, it underwent taboo repression in the original sexual sense,
with subsequent obsessive repetition on the surface in related senses.
These latter can be collectively called the surface synsemantica of
the original, suppressed meaning.

Intuitively, both FRENCH coup 'blow, strike,' and BINI gbé
would qualify as sexual taboo words, as there is a universal tendency in languages to refer to the sex act as striking, blowing, or
piercing. Thus, in HUNGARIAN, the taboo word baszni 'to fuck'
derives from OLD OSMANLI TURKISH bas- whose basic meaning
was 'to press.' FINNO-UGRIC etymologies have been proposed
but are discounted by the authorities (Benkő, Kiss, Papp 1967: vol.
I, 256) and it is suggested that the TURKIC loanword had a euphe-
mistic ring to it. In OLD TURKISH itself, however, the term makes
perfect sense as a member of the strike-blow-press-impregnate
semantic nest, bearing witness to the Thass-Thienemann hypothesis.

It is another language universal that such 'obsessively repeated'
taboo words tend to lose their original meaning during the course
of use. Allen Walker Read (1976) cites the example this fuckin' fuck
won't fuck heard from a British soldier during WW II, meaning
'this damned contraption won't work;' in this example the morpheme

// fək // shows up as noun, adjective and verb, all in the same short sentence. Examples abound from the unrelated HUNGARIAN military jargon baszdmán ide azt a kibaszott baszást mert nem baszik se jobbra se' balra "fuck then already over here that fucked-out fucking because it doesn't fuck neither left nor right" — meaning something like 'hand me that no-good object because it won't budge neither left nor right' -- personal observation, 1974.

If unpleasantness is a psychological pre-requisite for 'obsessive repetition' in adjacent senses, the unpleasant object can be a repulsive animal, like the rat. Accordingly, FRENCH has rat petit, not 'little rat' but 'ballet student;' rat de bibliothèque, not 'library rat' but 'bookworm' (this being a case of translating an idiom with another, unidiomatically 'excessively studious person who reads too much'); rat d'église, not 'church rat' but 'church janitor,' or 'pious person;' the expression rat d'hôtel does not mean a rodent infesting a hotel, but a 'hotel thief;' rat de prison does not refer to rats living in ill-kept jails, but to a 'lawyer.' In comparisons and set similes we have gueux comme un rat d'église, familiar from ENGLISH in 'poor as a church-mouse;' il lui passe quelque rat par la tête does not mean that a 'rat is going through his head' (as if he were a corpse), but 'he gets a stupid idea.' Il lui prend un rat means 'he gets fixed ideas,' and prendre un rat means at least three different things: 1) 'to go bad, stop functioning, go dead on somebody,' 2) 'suddenly to forget one's words on stage,' and 3) 'to end without a result.'

Death as an unpleasant subject repressed and avoided in its simple form is also responsible for a wide array of idioms in a series of unrelated languages. In ENGLISH slang criminals bite (the) dust; the HUNGARIAN hoodlum fübe harapott, i.e. 'bit the grass.' Presumably both dust and grass are unpleasant for humans to bite into. A hanged criminal is said to dance on air, the Hungarian dead, if made fun of, element Földvárra deszkát árulni, a pun on the village Földvár, literally 'earth castle,' meaning 'went to earth-castle to sell planks' (i.e. is lying in a wooden coffin underground), or alulról szagolja az ibolyát, i.e. 'smells the violets from underneath.' To cash in one's chips 'die' conjures the image of the quitting gambler; its unrelated HUNGARIAN counterpart says bemondta az unalmast 'he declared "I am bored",' 'he is quitting,' 'he died.'

Thievery, or theft is similarly responsible for a large number of idioms in scores of unrelated languages. Better known examples from ENGLISH and HUNGARIAN (to stick to these two as two unrelated types) include to make off with, to rip off (multiword idioms),

to liberate (a one word euphemism), and to pilfer (an apalliative);
HUNGARIAN here offers meglovasítani 'to turn into a horse' (which
can run away), olajra léptetni 'to cause to step on oil' (and slip away),
along many one-word forms, some of them borrowed from ROMANY,
SLAVIC, YIDDISH and GERMAN.

The collocational attractions of ENGLISH steal are all unpredictable for a nonnative speaker and he has to learn them as if they
were monolexemic units which, of course, they are not. (A steal,
even alone, besides an act of thievery, can be an unusually lucky
deal, as in you only paid $600 for that car? That was a steal! and
in golf it means a long shot which accidentally lands the ball in the
whole.) Small wonder, therefore, that new inventions may be stolen;
that a nonpaying passenger steals a ride; that a clever act of getting
ahead of a competition can be referred to as stealing a march on
someone; that a furtive kiss is referred to as to steal a kiss, and
that a surreptitious or furtive glance is referred to as to steal a
glance; to outshine another actor or actress on stage (or in life)
is referred to as stealing the show. Notice that none of the items
enumerated are objects that can be literally stolen, i.e. 'unlawfully
expropriated.' If someone cautiously and secretely approaches
something, he is said to steal his way up to something. The over-
riding principle, again, seems to be obsessive repetition in related
or adjacent senses. The principle can be represented as follows:

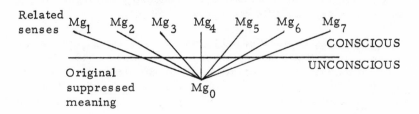

Figure 6

(Cf. Fig. 5, neutralization. The 'suppressed taboo meaning'
is not a neutralization of the consciously-obsessively repeated
synsemantica, but rather in the reverse: the synsemantica
are a quasi-upward diversification of the original, suppressed
meaning. That, certainly, is the chronological implication
of the Thass-Thienemann hypothesis as the main driving force
behind a) synonym creation, and b) idiom creation.)

The object of metaphoric comparison is frequently a familiar
animal or a part of the body, even in clause-length proverbial

idioms: RUSSIAN <u>vjidjen kak na ladonji</u> says 'visible as if in one's palm,' where the corresponding ENGLISH idiom would compare the clarity of a matter to <u>daylight</u> (clear as daylight). <u>Odna lastočka vesny nje djelajet</u> 'one swallow doesn't make spring,' i.e. 'it is not enough to have one witness to an entire seasonal sequence.' This is echoed by HUNGARIAN <u>egy fecske nem hoz nyarat</u> 'one swallow doesn't bring summer.' <u>Koška iz doma, myškam volja</u> 'cat out of house, fun for mice' has a transparency of meaning echoed in the unrelated HUNGARIAN <u>ha nincs otthon a macska, cin-cognak az egerek</u> 'when the cat is not at home, the mice have a concert.' ENGLISH <u>to let sleeping dogs lie</u>, i.e. 'not to arouse trouble while there is none' is expressed in RUSSIAN as <u>razbudjitj spjaščego ljva</u> 'to awaken the sleeping lion;' and the visibility of guilt-feeling is expressed by saying 'the cat knows she ate the meat,' in RUSSIAN <u>znajet koška, što mjaso s'ela</u>. If an untoward or clumsy person accidentally succeeds in doing something well, the Russians liken him to a blind chicken that by accident found a seed to eat while poking around in the yard: <u>i sljepaja kurica naxodjit zěrnyško</u> 'even the blind chicken finds a grain.' The saying is echoed by the HUNGARIAN <u>vak tyúk is talál szemet</u> meaning literally the same. The ENGLISH admonition <u>don't count your chickens before they're hatched</u> traceable to Aesop's fables throughout Western Europe, shows up in other European languages regarding the <u>bear</u>: thus, in FRENCH we have <u>ne vendez pas la peau de l'ours avant de l'avoir tué</u> 'don't sell the bear's hide before killing him,' echoed verbatim by the ITALIAN <u>no vendere la pelle di orso prima di averlo preso</u>. The Hungarian warns about not to drink a toast to the bear's hide in advance, saying <u>ne igyál előre a medve bőrére</u>, and the Russian mentions the fact that the hunt isn't over yet: <u>mjedvjedj ešče v lovje, a ty mjedvjedja prodaješ</u> 'the bear is still in the hunt but thou sellest the bear.' The virtue of patience is compared to the energy of water slowly eroding the bank both in RUSSIAN and in HUNGARIAN: <u>tixaja voda berega podymaet</u> 'quiet water washes the bank,' and <u>lassú viz partot mos</u>.

The recurrent universal throughout these examples is easy to observe: every-day objects, familiar to everyone, are invoked as familiar images, starting from concrete experiences and concrete meanings. The idiomatic meanings, in general, tend to be morals, also expressible in learned language or abstract vocabulary. The <u>palm of the hand</u> relates to <u>obviousness</u>; <u>swallow</u> relates to <u>new start</u>, <u>new beginning</u>; <u>cat</u> and <u>mice</u> relates to <u>ruler</u> and <u>ruled</u>, <u>boss</u> and <u>underlings</u>; <u>sleeping dogs</u> and <u>lying lions</u> relate to <u>dormant danger</u>; the <u>cat that ate the meat</u> relates to a <u>person who knows he committed an offense</u>. The <u>blind chicken</u> denotes the <u>untoward</u>

person; counting chickens relates to celebrating the outcome of an
undertaking or counting the profits of an investment; the bear's
hide and the bear proper both relate to accomplishment, material
goods gained and the like. The quiet water refers to perseverance,
patience and energy; the river bank to the opposition, the force that
contains and resists the quiet pressure of the individual trying to
get his own way.

In his essay "À propos d'une loi sémantique" Ferenc Fabricius-
Kovács (1961) properly suggests that the idea suggested by Heinz
Kronasser in his Handbuch der Semasiologie (1952) is in fact a powerful universal statable thus: meaning will always change from the
concrete toward the abstract. Fabricius-Kovács has devoted numerous essays to SLAVIC prefix + verb constructions showing the
same principle, one inexplicitly suggested and subscribed to by
most semanticists ever since Bréal 1886. The following examples
from the Indian subcontinent all bear witness to the same phenomenon which I propose to call the 'Fabricius-Kovács-Kronasser
Phenomenon of universal semantic development.' Thus, in DRA-
VIDIAN, represented here by TELUGU and TAMIL, we find examples
such as:[2]

TELUGU:
    N   V
1. kadupu nanta
    "stomach burns"
    'jealousy'

    N   V   N
2. appu chesi pappukudu
    "loan take feast"
    'to take a loan to give a feast;' idiomatically: 'exceeding
    one's limits unnecessarily. '

    N   Prep   N
3. pundu meedha ka:ram
    "wound   on   chili-powder"
    'chili powder on [raw] wound;' i.e. 'to hurt someone further
    when they're already suffering.'

---

[2] I am indebted to Mrs. Shashikala Boddhula, M.A., University
of Illinois at Chicago Circle for the examples from the Indian Subcontinent. Any errors in interpreting these are strictly my own.

    N   V   N
4. adavi ka:china vennala
"forest shine moonlight"
'moonlight in the forest;' i.e. 'Good gestures are wasted on
an undeserving person' (just as it does the forest no good
for the moon to be shining upon it).

    N   N
5. bu:diḍhalo panniru
"ashes-in rosewater"
'rosewater in ashes;' i.e. '[you are] wasting goodness on
the underserving' (cf. ENGLISH (Western Biblical) <u>don't</u>
<u>cast your pearls before swine.</u>)

TAMIL :
    N   N   N   V   Adv
1. kurangu kaiyil   poonma:lai kodutharpoul
"monkey hands flower-garland   give-like"
'like giving a garland to a monkey;' i.e. 'Giving valuables
into the hands of a destructive person' (cf. TAMIL (5.) and
ENGLISH <u>don't cast your pearls</u>...)

    N   Prep   V   N   N Prep
2. kazhudhaiku   theriyuma karpoora vasunai?
"donkey-for   know   fragrance camphor-of"
'Does the donkey know the fragrance of camphor?' i.e.
'Can a fool appreciate valuable things?' (cf. TELUGU (1.),
TAMIL (5.) and ENGLISH <u>don't cast your pearls</u>...)

   Num N   N Prep Num   N   V
3. oru paanai sothuku   oru   soru   padam
"one pot rice-for   one grain-of-rice testing"
'By testing one cooked grain of rice you can tell whether
the entire potful is cooked; ' i.e. 'By a single deed of a
person you can tell the nature of that person.'

   N   Poss   N   Adj   N
4. kakaiku-thun kunju   pon   kunju
"crow-its   little-one (∅ copula) golden little-one"
'The crow's little one is its golden bird;' i.e. 'Everyone
appreciates their own [offspring or other possession] however ugly it may be.'

   Num   V + Neg   Num   V + Interrog.
5. eindhil valayaḍḍadu eimbadil valayuma?
"five   bend-not   fifty   bend-whither? "

(5. cont.)
'If you can't adjust at the age of five, can you at the age
of fifty?' i.e. 'It is better to start training at an early age.'

The unrelated INDO-EUROPEAN HINDI offers the following
examples:

    Num Num Num
1. nau dho jyarah
   "nine two eleven"
   'Nine and two equals eleven;' i.e. 'to run away, to leave
   unnoticed.'

The expression translates into an idiomatic verb phrase resembling
FRENCH partir en anglais. It is unique in its internal syntactic
transformation from three numerals adding up to a verbal phrase.

    N   N   V
2. lal   peela hona
   "red yellow become"
   'to turn red and yellow;' 'to become very angry.'

    V   Neg   V   N   Adj
3. naach na   jaane,   aangan   teda
   "dance not know-how, courtyard crooked"
   'One who doesn't know how to dance says it's the courtyard
   that's crooked;' i.e. 'not finding the true fault with oneself
   but blaming it on exterior circumstances.'

    N   V-Prep   V
4. dum dubakar, bhagna
   "tail pull-in,   run"
   'to pull in one's tail and run;' i.e. 'not to face up to reality
   or challenges.'

    Adj   N   N
5. kaala akshar bhains
   "black print   buffalo"
   'Black print is equal to a buffalo;' i.e. 'It's all Greek to
   me, I cannot understand any of what you said.'

    N   Prep N   V
6. aankh se   aankh milana
   "eye   to   eye look-into"
   'One eye looks into the other;' i.e. 'Tell me like it is,
   come clean!'

In 6. above we see a declarative phrase used as an intimate imperative.

```
      N       V
7. gale    padna
```
"neck fall"
'The neck falls;' i.e. 'to pressure someone to do something despite their will.'

BINI, a WEST AFRICAN language of Nigeria, offers interesting examples constructed basically on the same principle:[3]

àbééjá	'the right (hand) side,' from òbǫ́ 'hand, arm' and érhá 'father;' thus the 'father-side' is the right side.
ègbáàmę̀	'river bank,' from ègbé 'body' and àmę̀ 'water,' where ègbé connotes what is solid as opposed to liquid, 'body-water' adding up to 'river bank.'
íkpáànró	'eye-balls, brow-ridges or biased verdict.' (This progression in itself is a classic of the Fabricius-Kovács Kronasser principle.) From i- (noun prefix) + kpaa 'to lift' + àrò 'eye' or 'face.' The lifting of the eye refers idiomatically to biased verdict.
gbàà rò ghèé	'to take care of,' from gbé 'to strike' + àrò 'eye;' hence 'to look at,' 'look after.' Cf. ENGLISH to keep an eye on in the idiomatic sense 'watch, supervise,' etc.
údègbóótǫ̀	'strong (palm) wine,' from u- (noun prefix) + de 'to fall' + gbé 'to strike' + òtǫ̀ 'earth, ground;' hence lit. 'fall-hit-earth;' hence id. 'knock-out drink,' a drink so strong that one falls down and hits the dirt. According to Wescott (personal communication) this can also be interpreted as a sentential noun (cf. ENG. forget-me-not) meaning literally 'you must fall down and complete the act of striking the ground,' since de has the imperative

---

[3] These examples from BINI I owe to Roger W. Wescott. The accent system is the simplified 'missionary spelling.' Prof. Wescott is in no way responsible for any possible misinterpretation of these data.

údègbóótọ̀ (cont.)

> tone and <u>gbe</u> has the perfective tone with the <u>u</u>- then interpretable as the second person singular pronominal prefix. Be this as it may, the expression is a classical example of concrete-to-specific idiomatization.

àgùùkíísîmwíígìe

> 'Venus, the morning or evening star,' from <u>a</u>-(noun prefix) + <u>gi</u>/<u>gu</u> 'to be associated with' + <u>ùkî</u> 'moon' + <u>simwi</u> 'to be kin to, to usurp' + <u>ògìe</u> 'chief' (chieftaincy); thus lit. 'the one who rivals the moon in hegemony (over the night sky).'

ámááhéékpòlìîkpóòlèéghóò

> 'very early morning,' from <u>a</u>- 'fourth person sing. pron. prefix (meaning "one" as opposed to "he" or "she") + <u>ma</u> 'has not done' (a negative perfective co-verb) + <u>he</u> 'has already/yet done' (a completive co-verb) + <u>kpolo</u> 'to sweep' + <u>ìkpóòlò</u> 'the act of sweeping' + <u>èghóò</u> 'rubbish;' i.e. 'the time when one has not yet swept away one's refuse.' A striking example of concrete to general change.

THAI,[4] from South East Asia (in the notation that follows mid tone is unmarked, ` indicates low tone, ^ stands for falling tone, ´ indicates the high tone, and ˇ indicates the rising tone) offers some interesting examples all following essentially the same principle:

1. kîŋ - t'ɔɔŋ bai-jòg
   "twig-gold leaf-jade"
   'a twig of gold and a leaf of jade'/'a gold twig and a jade leaf;' idiomatically: 'a compatible pair' (especially a compatible married couple who are each as good as the other. Notice that without familiarity with the culture the comparison eludes the observer).

---

[4] I owe these THAI examples to Miss Chitrabbha Kritakara, M.A., University of Illinois at Chicago Circle. She is in no way responsible for any possible misinterpretation of her data.

2. k'ài nai hĭn
"egg in rock"
'an egg in (on) the rocks;' idiomatically: 'a delicate or vul-
nerable person who needs to be very well cherished and
protected' (who is like an egg on a rock, i.e. easy to break).

3. k'lŷyn krat'ób fàŋ
"surf hit   shore"
'a surf hits the shore;' idiomatically: 'a once widely known
and talked-of subject which is finally and totally forgotten
after a period of time (as the surf, after impact, dies on the
beach).

4. tii ŋuu k'àaŋ hăaŋ
"hit snake part tail"
'hit a snake on its tail;' idiomatically: 'an imprudent or im
practical action which is useless, risky and harmful' (as
the act of hitting a snake on the tail, since when a snake is
caught or hit on the tail, it is still forceful and can swiftly
wound its enemy).

5. t'am naa bon lăŋ k'on
"do field on back man/people"
'plant crops on people's backs;' idiomatically: 'benefit from
or take advantage of other people in a selfish manner; to
profit from the investment of others.'

6. t'íŋ p'âi bai sùdt'áaj
"put-down card leaf last"
'put down the last card;' idiomatically: 'to make the best and
final effort' (since if you have lost from the beginning in a
card game, the last card may still save you).

7. náam t'ûam pàag
"water flood mouth"
'the mouth is full of water;' idiomatically: 'unable to speak,
forced to be silent' (as if his/her mouth were full of water).

8. p'àakfiriw hɔ̀ɔ t'ɔɔŋ
" rag   wrap gold"
'gold wrapped in a rag;' idiomatically: 'a person who is
actually wealthy but seems or pretends to be poor' (as a
piece of gold can be wrapped up in a cheap looking rag).

9. péd   tàd péd
"diamond cut diamond"

9. 'a diamond cuts another diamond;' idiomatically: 'two
    people who are of equal wit or talent; one cannot easily
    judge which one of them is better' (since diamond is the
    hardest substance; when two diamonds cut against each
    other, it is unpredictable which, if any, will break).

10. jóg   t'oŋ k'ǎaw
    "hoist flag white"
    'hoist a white flat;' idiomatically: 'to surrender'
    (This is echoed in numerous unrelated languages as the
    universal symbol of surrendering, but not too often said;
    cf. ENGLISH to give up, to give in, to bury the hatchet,
    to bury the axe, etc.)

11. jɔ̌ɔm mɛɛw k'ǎaj
    "dye cat   sell"
    'dye a cat and sell it;' idiomatically: 'dishonest commercial;
    to conceal bad or inferior merchandise under some disguise
    or pretense and offer it to others.'

12. rya lôm mỹa cɔ̌ɔd
    "boat sink when park"
    'a boat turns over just as it reaches the bank;' idiomatically:
    'difficulty arises just as one is about to succeed or as work
    is about to be completed.'

13. wâa klɔɔn sòd
    "cite verse fresh"
    'cite a fresh verse;' idiomatically: 'to speak without prep-
    aration, to make a spontaneous speech.'

14. wád   rɔɔj-t'âaw
    "measure$_v$ foot-track"
    'measure a foot-track;' idiomatically: 'try to equate or
    surpass a superior' (a child tries to compare the imprint
    his foot leaves with that of his father).

15. sâaŋ wímaan bon aakàad
    "build castle on air"
    'build a castle in the air;' idiomatically: 'to imagine impos-
    sible events or things' (cf. ENGLISH: stop building castles
    in the air!)

16. jìg   léb cèb nýa
    "pinch fingernail hurt flesh"
    'pinch a fingernail but hurt the flesh;' idiomatically: 'aim
    at one thing but affect another which is too close to it.'

17. sĭa   nɔ́ɔj   sĭa jâag, sĭa mâag sĭa ŋâaj
    "lose a-little lose hard lose much lose easy"
    'it is hard to lose a little, but it is easy to lose much;'
    idiomatically: 'One has to lose much more than one expected
    because one wouldn't accept even a little loss' (i.e. big losses
    are usually caused by extreme greed).

18. kamp'ɛɛn mii hŭu pratuu mii taa
    "wall   have ear   door have eye"
    'the wall has ears, the door has eyes;' idiomatically: 'The
    less one talks, the better; one has to be careful if one does
    not want to take the risk of giving one's secrets away; as
    there might be hidden or unsuspected-of listeners.' (Cf.
    ENGLISH: little pitchers have big ears; HUNGARIAN: füle
    van a falnak; LATIN: mus est in muro, etc.)

19. ŋom   k'ĕm nai mahâasamùd
    "seek needle in ocean"
    'seek a needle in the ocean;' idiomatically: 'to do an ex-
    tremely difficult or impossible task.' (Cf. ENGLISH: to
    look for a needle in a haystack.)

20. càb   plaa sɔ́ɔŋ myy
    "grasp fish two hand"
    'to hold two fish in one hand;' idiomatically: 'to lose every-
    thing because of greed or indecisiveness; to refuse to choose
    one feasible thing out of two alternatives' (one fish is hard
    enough to hold as it is slippery; two can become impossible).

HUNGARIAN,[5] the FINNO-UGRIC language with most speakers
(ca. 15 million in total) yields a morphologically complex set of
lexical idioms via agglutination. I will present below a limited set,
that of the verbal prefix idioms of HUNGARIAN. A verbal prefix
(VbP) is a word-initial affix whose meaning may build to the stem
of the verb literally, or unpredictably, much as the perfectivizing
verbal prefixes do in RUSSIAN. The HUNGARIAN and RUSSIAN
systems differ, of course, insofar as in RUSSIAN the 'perfective
aspect,' reminiscent of the GREEK aorist, partakes in a fully
fledged INDO-EUROPEAN type verb conjugation system, whereas
in HUNGARIAN the 'futurity' of the prefixed forms is an independent

---

[5] These examples are my own, as HUNGARIAN is my native language. A smaller but comparable portion of this material has been
published in Makkai 1972. Standard HUNGARIAN orthography is
used.

development. Thus RUSSIAN vjidjitj 'see,' if inflected in the present tense with the perfectivizing prefix u, uvjižu, uvjidjiš, uvjidjit,
etc. becomes 'I will see,' 'thou wilt see,' 'he-she-it will see,' etc.,
is typologically similar to the parallel HUNGARIAN phenomenon
látom, látod, látja, 'I see it, thou seest it, he/she/it sees it' versus
meg (the VbP in question) +the verb, meglátom, meglátod, meglátja,
'I, thou, he/she/it will see it,' but the two stem from different historical sources and the typological similarity may have been strengthened by the strong areal affinity between SLAVIC and FINNO-UGRIC.
The major HUNGARIAN VbPs are:

be	'into'
fel	'up'
le	'down'
ki	'out'
el	'away'
meg	(originally 'behind,' from migé, dialect mög, now the perfectivizer)
át	across, through
rá	onto, to the top of
oda	hither, thereunto, thataway
szét	asunder (GERMAN zer-)
össze	together, into one
vissza	back (GERMAN zurück)
széjjel	apart, asunder

(There are others as well, but less frequent and thus not important for this discussion.)

If we take the common verbs lát 'see,' néz 'look,' ver 'strike' —
leaving this sample very short indeed, we can 'generate' morphologically 13 x 3 = 39 possible forms, some of which, however, do not
occur; and many of which have unpredictable meanings. Thus:

Belát literally means 'to be able to see in a place,' as in Pista
magas, belát as ablakon 'Steve is tall, he (can) see in the window.' Inflected transitively, however, belát (valamit) means
'to see the point, to agree to someone else's point,' as in Pista
belátja, hogy igazam van 'Steve agrees that I am right.'

Fellát can occur only literally in the sense 'to see up, to see as
high as,' as in Pista fellát a hegyre 'Steve (can) see to the top
of the mountain.'

Lelát, again, can only be literal, meaning 'to see down from,'
as in Pista lelát a kilátóról a városra 'Steve (can) see down to
the city from the look-out tower.'

Kilát, too, is only literal, 'to see out;' Pista magas, kilát a veremből, 'Steve is tall, he can see out of the ditch.'

Ellát, however, is an idiom; its primary meaning is 'to provide someone with something,' as in elláttuk minden jóval 'we provided him/her with everything good;' the nominalization ellátás means 'provisions.' (Cf. video 'see' as the underlying etymon of pro-vision, from pro-video, lit. 'to see for;' further cf. MOD. ENG. to see to it that....) This is a clear-cut example of the Fabricius-Kovács/Kronasser phenomenon; 'sight' is brought into (metapheretai) into the abstract world. Ellát, literally, also occurs, as in ellátni odáig? 'can one see that far?' Here the transitive-intransitive conjugational dichotomy of HUNGARIAN can be seen as a tip-off whether the form will be idiomatic or not; the intransitive of the pair tends to be the literal and the transitive the idiomatic; as to what the meaning of the transitive pair is, one must learn.

Meglát, with meg, the 'pure' perfectivizer, means 'to catch sight of, suddenly to see,' reminiscent — though totally unrelated to — the GREEK aorist. In the past, megláttam Pistát 'I suddenly caught sight of Steve,' the meaning is predictable once one knows the meaning of the combination, in the present tense (like in RUSSIAN) a promissory future is implied: meglátom means 'I'll see (and think about it).'

Átlát has two literal meanings; intransitively used as in átlátni innen a tó tulsó felére? 'can one see across to the other side of the lake?' transitively (though not with the expected accusative but with the superessive -on-en-ön) 'to see through, to psych out,' as in átláttam Pistán 'I saw through Steve (i.e. his schemes and plots).'

Rálát is possible but rare; the meaning would be 'to see onto,' as in jól rálátni a házunk tetejére a dombról 'one can easily see (onto) the roof of our house from the hilltop;' this form yields no idioms.

Odalát is only possible literally, 'to see there, to see as far as;' szét, össze, vissza and széjjel yield only visszalát 'to see back,' meant literally; the others do not occur in standard speech and would take a most inventive poet to make any sense of.

The verb néz 'look' yields a logical 'look into' with be: Pista benéz az ablakon 'Steve looks in (through) the window.'

Néz with fel is possible both literally and idiomatically: felnéz-
ett a holdra 'he looked up to the moon' is literal; but Pista felnéz
az apjára is quite like the ENGLISH 'Steve looks up to his dad, '
i.e. 'respects him.' (Looking and respect, from re-specto,
must again be intimately tied up both with the Fabricius-Kovács/
Kronasser and the Thass-Thienemann phenomenon: the concrete-
to-abstract development can be seen in the 'eye' > 'admiration'
development; the taboo repression of the eyeball-to-eyeball
quasi-physical contact between man and man, father and son,
perhaps being due to 'homosexual panic;' at any rate we witness
the development of a psychological force, 'respect,' stemming
from one man's ability to look into the eye of the other, re-
spectare (LAT.) means to 'look back.' It is the particular development of ENGLISH, having both Latinate and Anglo-Saxon
etyma, that explains the simultaneous availability of both look
up to and respect, as close synonyms.)

That this is not just mere speculation but real insight into an
underlying system of semantic development is proven by the
opposite: lenézni. Literally it means to 'look down,' as in
Pista lenézett a fáról 'Steve (having climbed it) looked down
from the tree;' idiomatically (inflected in the transitive mode)
it means 'to look down on someone, to scorn,' as in Pista le-
nézi az apját 'Steve looks down on his father, Steve scorns his
dad.' Here again, the unrelated IE-GERMANIC ENGLISH and
the FU HUNGARIAN use the same physical sense, sight, to
express 'scorn, contempt.' No primary Latinate form exists;
we do have, however, disrespect, i.e. respect with a privative
prefix, dis-.

Kinéz 'to look out' occurs literally: Pista kinézett az ablakon
'Steve looked out the window;' inflected transitively it idioma-
tizes and means 'to cast mean glances at someone so as to make
him uncomfortable and leave;' Pista kinézte a vendégeket a
szobából 'Steve eyeballed the guests out of the room.' (This is
not to be confused with saw them out; to see someone out; 'usher
out' is a polite gesture in ENGLISH, implying solicitude, accom-
paniment, etc. HUNGARIAN does not use 'see' here; he saw
the guests out is rendered Pista kikisérte a vendégeket 'Steve
accompanied them out.')

Elnézni is very rare literally and can be justified only in some
such sentence as elnézett a végtelen messzeségbe 'he stared
into infinity;' the standard meaning is an idiomatic one: 'to
forgive, to overlook.' Notice again the concrete-abstract

development: not to look at something (i.e. to over-look it) implies not noticing it, i.e. pretending not to notice it; hence forgiveness. E.g. Pista elnézte Jancsi hibáit 'Steve overlooked Johnny's shortcomings.'

Megnézni means 'to take a (good) look at, to get a load of, to look and have seen': Megnézzük a Rembrandt kiállítást? 'Shall we go (look and see) the R. exhibition?'

Átnézni can mean two things, strangely they are both idioms: Jancsi átnézett a szomszédba does not mean 'Johnny "looked over" to the neighbors,' but rather he 'paid them a short visit;' Jancsi átnézte a könyvelést meaning 'J. perused, cursorily glanced at the book-keeping.' (Cf. ENG. look in on someone 'pay someone a short visit,' or look up someone 'visit,' also look up (words in a dictionary)=GER. nachschlagen, HUNG. felütni a szótárt lit. 'to strike up the dictionary (at a certain place).')

Ránézni is only literal and means 'to look onto;' Pista ránézett a lányra és elpirult 'Steve looked (at/onto) the girl and blushed.'

Odanézni means literally 'to look over there yonder,' most frequently used in the imperative nézz oda! or odanézz!; This literal sense, however, assumed a secondary idiomatic sense 'watch out,' just as ENG. look out! did. (Looking means seeing, i.e. the perceiving of danger; once again we move from the concrete toward the abstract.)

Össze, vissza and széjjel (szét) can only work in a science fiction movie where the casting of a glance has telekinesic power and hence one can 'look something asunder,' i.e. make it disintegrate by looking at it; nevertheless senses exist, as in Pista és Jancsi szétnéztek a mezőn 'Steve and Johnny looked around in the field,' where szétnézni is an intransitive idiom meaning 'to look around (in search of something);' összenézni, again, can only be intransitive and means 'to exchange a secret glance of solidarity;' Jancsi és Juliska összenéztek 'Jack and Jill exchanged (a furtive) glance;' visszanézni (in science fiction) could work in a sentence such as a Marslakó visszanézte uta- zását, ami most megjelent a földlakók képernyőjén 'the Martian mentally reproduced (by looking back on it) the history of his journey which now materialized on the television screen of the Tellurians;' with some effort this would also work for látni and has, in fact, been used by poetess Eszter Tóth múltját ki látja, ki látja vissza? 'who (can) see his past back?' Széjjelnézni

occurs intransitively and means 'to sweep the landscape from
left to right and back in search of something;' any transitive
sense would be extremely forced; with <u>széjjellátni</u> quite impossible '*to see asunder.'

The action verb <u>ver</u> 'strike' promises at first glance easier
literal combinations but turns out, on closer inspection, to be just
as idiomatic as <u>lát</u> 'see' and <u>néz</u> 'look':

<u>Bever</u> 'strikes in' is said intransitively of snow or rain driven
at an angle by strong winds; <u>bever as eső</u>, <u>bever a hó</u> 'the rain/
snow blows/strikes in (sideways)' (as when walking under a
supposedly top-covered underpass whose sides are open, or
through a leaky window); this is intransitive. Transitively, we
have: <u>Pista beverte a fejét</u> 'Steve banged (or bashed in) his
head;' with the dative case <u>beverni valakinek</u> it means a) 'to
give someone the one-two punch,' or b) in current sex-slang
'to make pregnant' (cf. to <u>knock up</u> a girl). (<u>Knock</u>, <u>strike</u>, <u>blow</u>,
FR. <u>coup</u>, BINI <u>gbé</u>, etc.: the Fabricius-Kronasser-Thienemann
effect.)

In modern slang <u>ráverni valamire</u> (apalliative for <u>rábaszni vala-
mire</u>) means 'to muck up something' (which in turn is an apalliative for 'to fuck up').

<u>Odaverni</u> is literal and means 'to deliver a strike to a certain
place;' <u>Pista jól odavert a sivalkodó gyereknek</u> 'Steve gave a
good smack to the screeching child.'

<u>Szétverni</u>, transitively, yields the predictable meaning 'to strike
something asunder,' cf. GER. <u>zerschlagen</u>; <u>Pista szétverte a
dióhéjakat a kalapáccsal</u> 'Steve struck the nutshells to tiny pieces
with his hammer;' intransitively, it means to 'restore order
(among riotous kids) by first striking one and then another,' as
in <u>Pista szétvert a zajos gyerekek között</u> 'Steve read the riot act
to the noisy kids' [i.e. hit them at random].

<u>Összeverni</u> means not 'to strike together' (as in a blacksmith
uniting two hot pieces of metal by striking) but 'to beat up very
badly;' <u>Pistát rémesen összeverték a rendőrségen</u> 'Steve was
terribly beat up by the police;' additionally it also means 'shab-
bily to improvise': <u>lazán összevert ócska kis szerkezet volt</u>
'it was a loosely hitched-together cheap little gadget' (recent
Budapest slang). <u>Visszaver</u> is literal: 'he strikes back;'
<u>széjjelver</u> works much like <u>szétver</u> (above).

The important fact to note here is that not even some of the best dictionaries, such as the seven volume HUNGARIAN-HUNGARIAN defining dictionary (Bárczi and Országh et al, 1959) and the Eckhardt FRENCH-HUNGARIAN/HUNGARIAN-FRENCH, or the Országh HUNGARIAN-ENGLISH/ENGLISH-HUNGARIAN dictionary, gives these meanings systematically. The reason is not any lack of scholarship on the part of these lexicographers. It is rather the fact that they have not explored the possibilities of lexicalization via idiomatic morphotactics, where the idiomatic nature of an other-wise straightforward morphotactics is revealed by the arbitrariness of some of the possible assignable meaning. Consider the ENGLISH pseudo-lexeme *transbibe, morphotactically quite well formed from trans 'across, through' and bibe from L. bibo, bibere 'drink.' The raw meaning 'drink across' suggests some sort of absorption of liquid across some barrier. I once tested a class of graduate students on the possibilities that arise. It is a bit like amateur psycho-analysis: every respondent will inject a good deal of his personal background and thinking into the new meaning. Thus, a technologi-cally oriented male student defined *transbibe as a possible technical term useable in connection with one airborne plane refuelling in mid flight by drawing fuel from another. A more socially and romantically inclined female speech and theater major defined it as 'sharing a swig of brandy while kissing with someone under the legal age to drink in the open.' Superficially it looks like a kind of 'generative' activity on the lexical level; truly, however, it goes much deeper and is in fact an act of creative language use. I am firmly convinced that mature native speakers of all natural languages possess such innovating abilities and do frequently use them as well. Which innovation is à propos of what relevant social event and gets therefore socially accepted is, essentially, a paralinguistic, anthro-pological-sociological question which we, as linguists, must begin organically to integrate with our other modes of language description.

5. Theoretical Conclusions

The types of multiple reinvestment, taken from genetically and typologically unrelated languages, move essentially on two levels: the lexemic and the sememic. A lexemic idiom is one which is syntactically identifiable as a form class in the lexotactics (the 'surface structure' in TG parlance), i.e. a part of speech, e.g. noun, verb, adjective, etc. A sememic idiom is one whose decod-ing yields two different (even though perhaps metaphorically linked) sememic traces or networks ('deep structures' in earlier TG par-lance, or 'semantic derivations' in more recent generative seman-ticist parlance). A few brief examples from ENGLISH will suffice:

Hot dog, the White House, white elephant, hot potato, red herring,
etc. are nouns, i.e. their lexotactic function is nominal; they
are subjects or objects in sentences, or nominal modifiers of other
nouns; frequently indirect objects, etc. Back and forth, hither
and yon, to and fro, hammer and tongs ('violently'), are adverbials;
few and far between, ready, willing and able are adjectives. This
identifiability of lexical idioms as to their lexotactic place is discussed fully in Makkai 1972; also see the tagmemic classification
of idioms in sentences by Healey in the appendix of the same.

An intermediate type between the lexemic and the sememic idiom
is the expanded verbal idiom, dubbed a tournure (borrowing from
Sauvageot) in Makkai 1972; these are the kick the bucket, bury the
hatchet, fly off the handle type. They inflect as single verbs (kicked
the bucket, buried the hatchet, flew off the handle) but are limited
in their morphologies (cf. *his kicking of the bucket, but their bury-
ing (of) the hatchet, her flying off the handle), and moreover, are
unpredictable as to their freedoms and limitations. They are between lexemic and sememic idioms, because they can be viewed
as clauses whose literal decoding leads to a sememic trace, different from the socially institutionalized one in certain contexts:
the falcon flew off the handle versus Aunt Hermione flew off the
handle. (Here the semantic feature HUMAN spells the difference
whether it is a bird flying off, or a person losing his/her temper.)

What parts of speech (i.e. surface form classes) will idiomatize
and which will not depends, of course, on the grammar of each
individual language. What concerns us from the point of view of
universals is simply the fact that a considerable amount of lexical
material is bound to be complex (i.e. the result of the multiple
reinvestment principle) and that a significant portion of these complex forms fit in with the noncomplex (or if complex, predictable)
lexemes of the language. This, I believe, is a true language universal, since it can even be found in CHINESE, the classical example
of a monosyllabic isolating language. I cite but one example, ma
shang (from Hockett 1958) 'quickly' which derives from 'horse'
plus 'back,' reminding us, of course, that the fastest way of trans-
portation in ancient China was on horseback. This, then, is a
metaphorically translucent bimorphemic lexemic idiom, syntactically adverbial-adjectival.

The second type of idiom, the sememic type, is characterized
universally by its clause-length. It does not coincide with any
individual form class (noun, verb, adjective, etc.), but is a small
independent piece of text with more than one way to interpret it.

Don't count your chickens before they're hatched, discussed above, will serve as an arch-example.

There is a universal principle at work which unites lexemic and sememic idiomaticity: it is, on the one hand, the Fabricius/Kronasser phenomenon of semantic change from the concrete toward the abstract and, on the other hand, the related but still distinct Thienemann phenomenon of psychological taboo repression with resultant obsessive repetition in adjacent semantic senses. These two principles together seem to be responsible for providing the cognitive and the unconscious force and motivation for the linguistic mechanism of multiple reinvestment in which these two forces are realized in languages on the overt level. To put it the other way around: natural languages on our planet do not seem to be free of the multiple reinvestment of their morpheme stock, just as they are, of course, never free from the multiple reinvestment of their phoneme stock. Lexemes -- or longer, polymorphemic dictionary entries of one word length -- are also subject to multiple reinvestment bringing about the realizations of a variety of denotatively different, yet connotatively similar or related meanings.

It is thus a universal feature of idioms that they come on a scale of metaphorical gradation from completely metaphorically translucent forms to entirely opaque ones (cf. Makkai 1975). Thus go up, as in you'll go up from associate to full next year 'get promoted' in the physical sense. Similar is the case of go down, as in the Titanic went down with hundreds of people left on board in the sense 'sink.' Go in for 'pursue as a hobby' is less translucent: she goes in for stamp collecting is much closer to she goes in for her mail every morning and hence, more misunderstandable. Hot potato 'embarrassing issue' is no longer visually translucent, but can be easily understood (something hot is easily dropped), but with white elephant 'unwanted property difficult to sell or manage,' we reach rather dense idiomatic opacity.

It is the challenging task of the linguist engaged in the study of language universals to find the principles that underlie idiom formation in a variety of languages and to state both those features which are indeed universal and those which are idiosyncratic from one culture to the next.

BIBLIOGRAPHY

Algeo, John. 1970. English: an introduction to language. New York: Harcourt, Brace and World.

Bárczi, Géza and László Ország (eds. general). 1959. A magyar nyelv értelmező szótára ('The defining dictionary of the Hungarian language'). Budapest: Akadémiai kiadó, 7 vols.

Benkő, L., L. Kiss and L. Papp. 1967-- . A magyar nyelv történeti etimológiai szótára. Budapest.

Bréal, Michel. 1897. Sémantique. Paris. (English translation by Mrs. Henry Cust, 1964, Dover publications, New York.)

Eckhardt, Sándor. 1953. Francia-magyar szótár. Budapest.

Halliday, Michael A.K. 1975. Learning how to mean. London: Edward Arnold.

_____ and Ruqaiya Hasan. 1976. Cohesion in English. London: Longmans.

Greenberg, Joseph H. 1966. Universals of language. Cambridge, Mass.: M.I.T. Press (2nd ed.).

Hockett, Charles F. 1958. A course in modern linguistics. New York.

Hockett, Charles F. 1969. The problem of universals in language. In Greenberg 1966:1-30.

Koestler, Arthur. 1967. The ghost in the machine. New York: MacMillan.

Kovács (Fabricius) Ferenc. 1961. À propos d'une loi sémantique. Acta Linguistica Hungarica XI. 3-4. 405-411.

Kronasser, Heinz. 1952. Handbuch der Semasiologie. Heidelberg: Carl Winter Universitätsverlag.

Lamb, Sydney M. 1966. Outline of stratificational grammar. Washington, D.C.: Georgetown University Press.

Lewis, Norman. 1964. The new Roget's Thesaurus of the English language in dictionary form. New York.

Lockwood, David G. 1972. Introduction to stratificational linguistics. New York: Harcourt, Brace, Jovanovich.

Makkai, Adam. 1972. Idiom structure in English. The Hague: Mouton.

_____. 1973a. A pragmo-ecological view of linguistic structure and language universals. Language Sciences 27. 9-22.

_____. 1973b. A dictionary of Space English. Chicago: Consolidated Book Publishers (English Language Institute of America).

_____. 1974a. Grammatica pragmo-ecologica (PEG): per una nuova sintesi della linguistica e dell' antropologia. SILTA III. 1-2. 7-55. (Italian translation of Pragmo-ecological grammar (PEG): toward a new synthesis of linguistics and anthropology. Paper given at the ninth ICAES in Chicago, Ill. English text in press, Mouton, The Hague.

_____. 1975. The metaphorical origins of idiomaticity. Georgetown Working Papers in Linguistics 11. 10-59. Four essays on the metaphor, ed. by Robert J. Di Pietro.

_____. 1977. Review of Zgusta 1971. Kratylos vol. XX, 1975 (1977), 13-19.

Neilson, William Allan (ed.) 1942. The complete plays and poems of William Shakespeare. Cambridge, Mass.: Houghton Mifflin at Riverside Press.

Országh, László. 1969-70. Hungarian-English and English-Hungarian dictionary. Budapest.

Sheffield, Alfred D. (ed.) 1959. Soule's dictionary of English synonyms. New York: Bonanza Books.

Thass-Thienemann, Theodore. 1968. Symbolic behavior. New York: Washington Square Press.

_____. 1969. The subconscious language. New York: Washington Square Press.

Sullivan, William J. 1975. Alternation, transformation, realization and stratification revisited. The first LACUS Forum, 472-522. Columbia, S.C.: Hornbeam Press.

Read, Allen Walker. 1976. The changing context of an insult word. Paper delivered at the Interdisiplinary Conference on Languages and Linguistics, University of Louisville, Louisville, Ky.

Troubetzkoy, Nikolai S. 1939. Grundzüge der Phonologie. Prague,
TCLP 7. (Reprinted in 1958 by Vandenboeck and Ruprecht,
Göttingen; French trans. Principes de phonologie (J. Cantinean),
Paris, 1949, Libraire Klincksieck.

Végh, Béla and Péter Rubin. 1966. Gallicizmusok ('Gallicisms,'
French idioms). Budapest: Terra.

Wescott, Roger W. 1962. Linguistics as a tool in African studies.
Annals of the New York Academy of Sciences, New York.

_____. 1969. The divine animal. New York: Funk and Wagnalls.

Zgusta, Ladislav. 1971. Manual of phonology. Praha: Academia.

Index of Languages

Index of Authors Cited